# Mostly Harmless Econometrics

# Mostly Harmless Econometrics

## An Empiricist's Companion

Joshua D. Angrist

and

Jörn-Steffen Pischke

PRINCETON UNIVERSITY PRESS ■ PRINCETON AND OXFORD

Copyright © 2009 by Princeton University Press

Published by Princeton University Press, 41 William Street,
Princeton, New Jersey 08540
In the United Kingdom: Princeton University Press,
6 Oxford Street, Woodstock, Oxfordshire OX20 1TW

Library of Congress Cataloging-in-Publication Data

Angrist, Joshua David.
Mostly harmless econometrics : an empiricist's companion /
Joshua D. Angrist, Jörn–Steffen Pischke.
p.   cm.
Includes bibliographical references and index.
ISBN 978-0-691-12034-8 (hardcover : alk. paper) —
ISBN 978-0-691-12035-5 (pbk. : alk. paper)   1. Econometrics.
2. Regression analysis.   I. Pischke, Jörn–Steffen.   II. Title.
HB139.A54  2008
330.01'5195—dc22                                    2008036265

British Library Cataloging-in-Publication Data is available

This book has been composed in Sabon
with Hel. Neue Cond. family display

Illustrations by Karen Norberg

Printed on acid-free paper. ∞

press.princeton.edu

Printed in the United States of America

5  7  9  10  8  6

# CONTENTS

# FIGURES

# TABLES

# PREFACE

The universe of econometrics is constantly expanding. Econometric methods and practice have advanced greatly as a result, but the modern menu of econometric methods can seem confusing, even to an experienced number cruncher. Luckily, not everything on the menu is equally valuable or important. Some of the more exotic items are needlessly complex and may even be harmful. On the plus side, the core methods of applied econometrics remain largely unchanged, while the interpretation of basic tools has become more nuanced and sophisticated. Our *Companion* is an empiricist's guide to the econometric essentials ... *Mostly Harmless Econometrics*.

The most important items in an applied econometrician's toolkit are:

1. Regression models designed to control for variables that may mask the causal effects of interest;
2. Instrumental variables methods for the analysis of real and natural experiments;
3. Differences-in-differences-type strategies that use repeated observations to control for unobserved omitted factors.

The productive use of these basic techniques requires a solid conceptual foundation and a good understanding of the machinery of statistical inference. Both aspects of applied econometrics are covered here.

Our view of what's important has been shaped by our experience as empirical researchers, and especially by our work teaching and advising economics Ph.D. students. This book was written with these students in mind. At the same time, we hope the book will find an audience among other groups of researchers who have an urgent need for practical answers regarding choice of technique and the interpretation of research findings. The concerns of applied econometrics are not fundamentally different from those of other social sciences or epidemiology. Anyone interested in using data to shape public policy or to promote public health must digest and use statistical results. Anyone interested in drawing useful inferences from data on people can be said to be an applied econometrician.

Many textbooks provide a guide to research methods, and there is some overlap between this book and others in wide use. But our *Companion* differs from econometrics texts in a number of important ways. First, we believe that empirical research is most valuable when it uses data to answer specific causal questions, *as if* in a randomized clinical trial. This view shapes our approach to most research questions. In the absence of a real experiment, we look for well-controlled comparisons and/or natural quasi-experiments. Of course, some quasi-experimental research designs are more convincing than others, but the econometric methods used in these studies are almost always fairly simple. Consequently, our book is shorter and more focused than textbook treatments of econometric methods. We emphasize the conceptual issues and simple statistical techniques that turn up in the applied research we read and do, and illustrate these ideas and techniques with many empirical examples.

A second distinction we claim is a certain lack of gravitas. Most econometrics texts appear to take econometric models very seriously. Typically these books pay a lot of attention to the putative failures of classical modeling assumptions, such as linearity and homoskedasticity. Warnings are sometimes issued. We take a more forgiving and less literal-minded approach. A principle that guides our discussion is that the estimators in common use almost always have a simple interpretation that is not heavily model dependent. If the estimates you get are not the estimates you want, the fault lies in the econometrician and not the econometrics! A leading example is linear regression, which provides useful information about the conditional mean function regardless of the shape of this function. Likewise, instrumental variables methods estimate an average causal effect for a well-defined population even if the instrument does not affect everyone. The conceptual robustness of basic econometric tools is grasped intuitively by many applied researchers, but the theory behind this robustness does not feature in most texts. Our *Companion* also differs from most econometrics texts in that, on the inference side, we are not much concerned with asymptotic efficiency. Rather, our discussion of inference is devoted mostly to the finite-sample bugaboos that should bother practitioners.

The main prerequisite for understanding the material here is basic training in probability and statistics. We especially hope that readers are comfortable with the elementary tools of statistical inference, such as $t$-statistics and standard errors. Familiarity with fundamental probability concepts such as mathematical expectation is also helpful, but extraordinary mathematical sophistication is not required. Although important proofs are presented, the technical arguments are not very long or complicated. Unlike many upper-level econometrics texts, we go easy on the linear algebra. For this reason and others, our *Companion* should be an easier read than competing books. Finally, in the spirit of Douglas Adams's lighthearted serial (*The Hitchhiker's Guide to the Galaxy* and *Mostly Harmless*, among others) from which we draw continued inspiration, our *Companion* may have occasional inaccuracies, but it is quite a bit cheaper than the many versions of the *Encyclopedia Galactica Econometrica* that dominate today's market. Grateful thanks to Princeton University Press for agreeing to distribute our *Companion* on these terms.

# ACKNOWLEDGMENTS

We had the benefit of comments from many friends and colleagues as this project progressed. Thanks are due to Alberto Abadie, Patrick Arni, David Autor, Amitabh Chandra, Monica Chen, Victor Chernozhukov, John DiNardo, Peter Dolton, Joe Doyle, Jerry Hausman, Andrea Ichino, Guido Imbens, Adriana Kugler, Rafael Lalive, Alan Manning, Whitney Newey, Derek Neal, Barbara Petrongolo, James Robinson, Gary Solon, Tavneet Suri, Jeff Wooldridge, and Jean-Philippe Wullrich, who reacted to the manuscript at various stages. They are not to blame for our presumptuousness or remaining mistakes. Thanks also go to our students at LSE and MIT, who saw the material first and helped us decide what's important. We would especially like to acknowledge the skilled and tireless research assistance of Bruno Ferman, Brigham Frandsen, Cynthia Kinnan, and Chris Smith. We're deeply indebted to our infinitely patient illustrator, Karen Norberg, who created the images at the beginning of each chapter and provided valuable feedback on matters large and small. We're also grateful for the enthusiasm and guidance of Tim Sullivan and Seth Ditchik, our editors at Princeton University Press, and for the careful work of our copy editor, Marjorie Pannell, and production editor, Leslie Grundfest. Last, but certainly not least, we thank our wives for their love and support. They know better than anyone what it means to be an empiricist's companion.

# ORGANIZATION OF THIS BOOK

W e begin with two introductory chapters. The first describes the type of research agenda for which the material in subsequent chapters is most likely to be useful. The second discusses the sense in which randomized trials of the sort used in medical research provide an ideal benchmark for the questions we find most interesting. After this introduction, the three chapters of part II present core material on regression, instrumental variables, and differences-in-differences. These chapters emphasize both the universal properties of estimators (e.g., regression always approximates the conditional mean function) and the assumptions necessary for a causal interpretation of results (the conditional independence assumption; instruments as good as randomly assigned; parallel worlds). We then turn to important extensions in part III. Chapter 6 covers regression discontinuity designs, which can be seen as either a variation on regression-control strategies or a type of instrumental variables strategy. In chapter 7, we discuss the use of quantile regression for estimating effects on distributions. The last chapter covers important inference problems that are missed by the textbook asymptotic approach. Some chapters include more technical or specialized sections that can be skimmed or skipped without missing out on the main ideas; these sections are indicated with a star. A glossary of acronyms and abbreviations and an index to empirical examples can be found at the back of the book.

Part I

# Preliminaries

Chapter 1

# Questions about *Questions*

"I checked it very thoroughly," said the computer, "and that quite definitely is the answer. I think the problem, to be quite honest with you, is that you've never actually known what the question is."

Douglas Adams, *The Hitchhiker's Guide to the Galaxy*

This chapter briefly discusses the basis for a successful research project. Like the biblical story of Exodus, a research agenda can be organized around four questions. We call these frequently asked questions (FAQs), because they should be. The FAQs ask about the relationship of interest, the ideal experiment, the identification strategy, and the mode of inference.

In the beginning, we should ask, *What is the causal relationship of interest?* Although purely descriptive research has an important role to play, we believe that the most interesting research in social science is about questions of cause and effect, such as the effect of class size on children's test scores, discussed in chapters 2 and 6. A causal relationship is useful for making predictions about the consequences of changing circumstances or policies; it tells us what would happen in alternative (or "counterfactual") worlds. For example, as part of a research agenda investigating human productive capacity—what labor economists call human capital—we have both investigated the causal effect of schooling on wages (Card, 1999, surveys research in this area). The causal effect of schooling on wages is the increment to wages an individual would receive if he or she got more schooling. A range of studies suggest the causal effect of a college degree is about 40 percent higher wages on average, quite a payoff. The causal

1

effect of schooling on wages is useful for predicting the earnings consequences of, say, changing the costs of attending college, or strengthening compulsory attendance laws. This relation is also of theoretical interest since it can be derived from an economic model.

As labor economists, we're most likely to study causal effects in samples of workers, but the unit of observation in causal research need not be an individual human being. Causal questions can be asked about firms or, for that matter, countries. Take, for example, Acemoglu, Johnson, and Robinson's (2001) research on the effect of colonial institutions on economic growth. This study is concerned with whether countries that inherited more democratic institutions from their colonial rulers later enjoyed higher economic growth as a consequence. The answer to this question has implications for our understanding of history and for the consequences of contemporary development policy. Today, we might wonder whether newly forming democratic institutions are important for economic development in Iraq and Afghanistan. The case for democracy is far from clear-cut; at the moment, China is enjoying robust economic growth without the benefit of complete political freedom, while much of Latin America has democratized without a big growth payoff.

The second research FAQ is concerned with _the experiment that could ideally be used to capture the causal effect of interest._ In the case of schooling and wages, for example, we can imagine offering potential dropouts a reward for finishing school, and then studying the consequences. In fact, Angrist and Lavy (2008) have run just such an experiment. Although their study looked at short-term effects such as college enrollment, a longer-term follow-up might well look at wages. In the case of political institutions, we might like to go back in time and randomly assign different government structures in former colonies on their independence day (an experiment that is more likely to be made into a movie than to get funded by the National Science Foundation).

Ideal experiments are most often hypothetical. Still, hypothetical experiments are worth contemplating because they help us pick fruitful research topics. We'll support this claim by asking you to picture yourself as a researcher with no budget constraint and no Human Subjects Committee policing your inquiry for social correctness: something like a well-funded Stanley Milgram, the psychologist who did pathbreaking work on the response to authority in the 1960s using highly controversial experimental designs that would likely cost him his job today.

Seeking to understand the response to authority, Milgram (1963) showed he could convince experimental subjects to administer painful electric shocks to pitifully protesting victims (the shocks were fake and the victims were actors). This turned out to be controversial as well as clever: some psychologists claimed that the subjects who administered shocks were psychologically harmed by the experiment. Still, Milgram's study illustrates the point that there are many experiments we can think about, even if some are better left on the drawing board.[1] If you can't devise an experiment that answers your question in a world where anything goes, then the odds of generating useful results with a modest budget and nonexperimental survey data seem pretty slim. The description of an ideal experiment also helps you formulate causal questions precisely. The mechanics of an ideal experiment highlight the forces you'd like to manipulate and the factors you'd like to hold constant.

Research questions that cannot be answered by any experiment are FUQs: fundamentally unidentified questions. What exactly does a FUQ look like? At first blush, questions about the causal effect of race or gender seem good candidates because these things are hard to manipulate in isolation ("imagine your chromosomes were switched at birth"). On the other hand, the issue economists care most about in the realm of race and sex, labor market discrimination, turns on whether someone treats you differently because they *believe* you to be black or white, male or female. The notion of a counterfactual world where men are perceived as women or vice versa has a long history and does not require Douglas Adams-style outlandishness to entertain (Rosalind disguised

---

[1]Milgram was later played by the actor William Shatner in a TV special, an honor that no economist has yet received, though Angrist is still hopeful.

as Ganymede fools everyone in Shakespeare's *As You Like It*). The idea of changing race is similarly near-fetched: in *The Human Stain*, Philip Roth imagines the world of Coleman Silk, a black literature professor who passes as white in professional life. Labor economists imagine this sort of thing all the time. Sometimes we even construct such scenarios for the advancement of science, as in audit studies involving fake job applicants and résumés.[2]

A little imagination goes a long way when it comes to research design, but imagination cannot solve every problem. Suppose that we are interested in whether children do better in school by virtue of having started school a little older. Maybe the 7-year-old brain is better prepared for learning than the 6-year-old brain. This question has a policy angle coming from the fact that, in an effort to boost test scores, some school districts are now imposing older start ages (Deming and Dynarski, 2008). To assess the effects of delayed school entry on learning, we could randomly select some kids to start first grade at age 7, while others start at age 6, as is still typical. We are interested in whether those held back learn more in school, as evidenced by their elementary school test scores. To be concrete, let's look at test scores in first grade.

The problem with this question—the effects of start age on first grade test scores—is that the group that started school at age 7 is . . . older. And older kids tend to do better on tests, a pure maturation effect. Now, it might seem we can fix this by holding age constant instead of grade. Suppose we wait to test those who started at age 6 until second grade and test those who started at age 7 in first grade, so that everybody is tested at age 7. But the first group has spent more time in school, a fact that raises achievement if school is worth anything. There is no way to disentangle the effect of start age on learning from maturation and time-in-school effects as long as kids are still in school. The problem here is that for students, start age

---

[2] A recent example is Bertrand and Mullainathan (2004), who compared employers' reponses to résumés with blacker-sounding and whiter-sounding first names, such as Lakisha and Emily (though Fryer and Levitt, 2004, note that names may carry information about socioeconomic status as well as race.)

equals current age minus time in school. <u>This deterministic link disappears in a sample of adults,</u> so we can investigate pure start-age effects on adult outcomes, such as earnings or highest grade completed (as in Black, Devereux, and Salvanes, 2008). But the effect of start age on elementary school test scores is impossible to interpret even in a randomized trial, and therefore, in a word, FUQed.

The third and fourth research FAQs are concerned with the nuts-and-bolts elements that produce a specific study. Question number 3 asks, <u>*What is your identification strategy?*</u> Angrist and Krueger (1999) used the term *identification strategy* to describe the manner in which a researcher uses observational data (i.e., data not generated by a randomized trial) to approximate a real experiment. Returning to the schooling example, Angrist and Krueger (1991) used the interaction between compulsory attendance laws in American states and students' season of birth as a natural experiment to estimate the causal effects of finishing high school on wages (season of birth affects the degree to which high school students are constrained by laws allowing them to drop out after their 16th birthday). Chapters 3–6 are primarily concerned with conceptual frameworks for identification strategies.

Although a focus on credible identification strategies is emblematic of modern empirical work, the juxtaposition of ideal and natural experiments has a long history in econometrics. Here is our econometrics forefather, Trygve Haavelmo (1944, p. 14), appealing for more explicit discussion of both kinds of experimental designs:

> A design of experiments (a prescription of what the physicists call a "crucial experiment") is an essential appendix to any quantitative theory. And we usually have some such experiment in mind when we construct the theories, although— unfortunately—most economists do not describe their design of experiments explicitly. If they did, they would see that the experiments they have in mind may be grouped into two different classes, namely, (1) experiments that *we should like to make* to see if certain real economic phenomena—when artificially isolated from "other influences"—would verify certain

hypotheses, and (2) the stream of experiments that Nature is steadily turning out from her own enormous laboratory, and which we merely watch as passive observers. In both cases the aim of the theory is the same, to become master of the happenings of real life.

The fourth research FAQ borrows language from Rubin (1991): _What is your mode of statistical inference?_ The answer to this question describes the population to be studied, the sample to be used, and the <u>assumptions made when constructing standard errors.</u> Sometimes inference is straightforward, as when you use census microdata samples to study the American population. Often inference is more complex, however, especially with data that are clustered or grouped. The last chapter covers practical problems that arise once you've answered question number 4. Although inference issues are rarely very exciting, and often quite technical, the ultimate success of even a well-conceived and conceptually exciting project turns on the details of statistical inference. This sometimes dispiriting fact inspired the following econometrics haiku, penned by Keisuke Hirano after completing his thesis:

> _T-stat looks too good_
> _Try clustered standard errors—_
> _Significance gone_

As should be clear from the above discussion, the four research FAQs are part of a process of project development. The following chapters are concerned mostly with the econometric questions that come up after you've answered the research FAQs—in other words, issues that arise once your research agenda has been set. Before turning to the nuts and bolts of empirical work, however, we begin with a more detailed explanation of why randomized trials give us our benchmark.

Chapter 2

# The Experimental Ideal

It is an important and popular fact that things are not always
what they seem. For instance, on the planet Earth, man had
always assumed that he was more intelligent than dolphins
because he had achieved so much—the wheel, New York,
wars and so on—while all the dolphins had ever done was
muck about in the water having a good time. But conversely,
the dolphins had always believed that they were far more
intelligent than man—for precisely the same reasons. In fact
there was only one species on the planet more intelligent than
dolphins, and they spent a lot of their time in behavioral
research laboratories running round inside wheels and
conducting frighteningly elegant and subtle experiments on
man. The fact that once again man completely misinterpreted
this relationship was entirely according to these creatures'
plans.

Douglas Adams, *The Hitchhiker's Guide to the Galaxy*

The most credible and influential research designs use random assignment. A case in point is the Perry preschool
project, a 1962 randomized experiment designed to
assess the effects of an early intervention program involving 123 black preschoolers in Ypsilanti, Michigan. The Perry
treatment group was randomly assigned to an intensive intervention that included preschool education and home visits. It's
hard to exaggerate the impact of the small but well-designed
Perry experiment, which generated follow-up data through
1993 on the participants at age 27. Dozens of academic studies cite or use the Perry findings (see, e.g., Barnett, 1992). Most
important, the Perry project provided the intellectual basis for
the massive Head Start preschool program, begun in 1964,

which ultimately served (and continues to serve) millions of American children.[1]

## 2.1   The Selection Problem

We take a brief time-out for a more formal discussion of the role experiments play in uncovering causal effects. Suppose you are interested in a causal if-then question. To be concrete, let us consider a simple example: Do hospitals make people healthier? For our purposes, this question is allegorical, but it is surprisingly close to the sort of causal question health economists care about. To make this question more realistic, let's imagine we're studying a poor elderly population that uses hospital emergency rooms for primary care. Some of these patients are admitted to the hospital. This sort of care is expensive, crowds hospital facilities, and is, perhaps, not very effective (see, e.g., Grumbach, Keane, and Bindman, 1993). In fact, exposure to other sick patients by those who are themselves vulnerable might have a net negative impact on their health.

Since those admitted to the hospital get many valuable services, the answer to the hospital effectiveness question still seems likely to be yes. But will the data back this up? The natural approach for an empirically minded person is to compare the health status of those who have been to the hospital with the health of those who have not. The National Health Interview Survey (NHIS) contains the information needed to make this comparison. Specifically, it includes a question, "During the past 12 months, was the respondent a patient in a hospital overnight?" which we can use to identify recent hospital visitors. The NHIS also asks, "Would you say your health in general is excellent, very good, good, fair, poor?"

---

[1] The Perry data continue to get attention, particularly as policy interest has returned to early education. A recent reanalysis by Michael Anderson (2008) confirmed many of the findings from the original Perry study, though Anderson also shows that the overall positive effects of the Perry project are driven entirely by the impact on girls. The Perry intervention seems to have done nothing for boys.

The following table displays the mean health status (assigning a 1 to poor health and a 5 to excellent health) among those who have been hospitalized and those who have not (tabulated from the 2005 NHIS):

| Group | Sample Size | Mean Health Status | Std. Error |
|---|---|---|---|
| Hospital | 7,774 | 3.21 | 0.014 |
| No hospital | 90,049 | 3.93 | 0.003 |

The difference in means is 0.72, a large and highly significant contrast in favor of the nonhospitalized, with a $t$-statistic of 58.9.

Taken at face value, this result suggests that going to the hospital makes people sicker. It's not impossible this is the right answer since hospitals are full of other sick people who might infect us and dangerous machines and chemicals that might hurt us. Still, it's easy to see why this comparison should not be taken at face value: people who go to the hospital are probably less healthy to begin with. Moreover, even after hospitalization people who have sought medical care are not as healthy, on average, as those who were never hospitalized in the first place, though they may well be better off than they otherwise would have been.

To describe this problem more precisely, we can think about hospital treatment as described by a binary random variable, $D_i = \{0, 1\}$. The outcome of interest, a measure of health status, is denoted by $Y_i$. The question is whether $Y_i$ is *affected* by hospital care. To address this question, we assume we can imagine what might have happened to someone who went to the hospital if that person had not gone, and vice versa. Hence, for any individual there are two potential health variables:

$$Potential\ outcome = \begin{cases} Y_{1i} & \text{if } D_i = 1 \\ Y_{0i} & \text{if } D_i = 0 \end{cases}.$$

In other words, $Y_{0i}$ is the health status of an individual had he not gone to the hospital, irrespective of whether he actually went, while $Y_{1i}$ is the individual's health status if he goes. We would like to know the difference between $Y_{1i}$ and $Y_{0i}$, which can be said to be the causal effect of going to the hospital for

*[handwritten annotation:]* on average & given everything else in the world relevant to the process is the same as when the data were collected

individual $i$. This is what we would measure if we could go back in time and change a person's treatment status.[2]

The observed outcome, $Y_i$, can be written in terms of potential outcomes as

$$Y_i = \begin{cases} Y_{1i} & \text{if } D_i = 1 \\ Y_{0i} & \text{if } D_i = 0 \end{cases}$$
$$= Y_{0i} + (Y_{1i} - Y_{0i})D_i. \qquad (2.1.1)$$

This notation is useful because $Y_{1i} - Y_{0i}$ is the causal effect of hospitalization for an individual. In general, there is likely to be a distribution of both $Y_{1i}$ and $Y_{0i}$ in the population, so the treatment effect can be different for different people. But because we never see both potential outcomes for any one person, we must learn about the effects of hospitalization by comparing the average health of those who were and were not hospitalized.

A naive comparison of averages by hospitalization status tells us something about potential outcomes, though not necessarily what we want to know. The comparison of average health conditional on hospitalization status is formally linked to the average causal effect by the equation:

$$\underbrace{E[Y_i|D_i = 1] - E[Y_i|D_i = 0]}_{\text{Observed difference in average health}} = \underbrace{E[Y_{1i}|D_i = 1] - E[Y_{0i}|D_i = 1]}_{\text{Average treatment effect on the treated}}$$
$$+ \underbrace{E[Y_{0i}|D_i = 1] - E[Y_{0i}|D_i = 0]}_{\text{Selection bias}}.$$

The term

$$E[Y_{1i}|D_i = 1] - E[Y_{0i}|D_i = 1] = E[Y_{1i} - Y_{0i}|D_i = 1]$$

is the *average causal effect of hospitalization on those who were hospitalized*. This term captures the averages difference between the health of the hospitalized, $E[Y_{1i}|D_i = 1]$, and what would have happened to them had they not been hospitalized,

---

[2]The potential outcomes idea is a fundamental building block in modern research on causal effects. Important references developing this idea are Rubin (1974, 1977) and Holland (1986), who refers to a causal framework involving potential outcomes as the Rubin causal model.

$E[Y_{0i}|D_i = 1]$. The observed difference in health status, however, adds to this causal effect a term called *selection bias*. This term is the difference in average $Y_{0i}$ between those who were and those who were not hospitalized. Because the sick are more likely than the healthy to seek treatment, those who were hospitalized have worse values of $Y_{0i}$, making selection bias negative in this example. The selection bias may be so large (in absolute value) that it completely masks a positive treatment effect. <u>The goal of most empirical economic research is to overcome selection bias,</u> and therefore to say something about the causal effect of a variable like $D_i$.[3]

## 2.2   Random Assignment Solves the Selection Problem

Random assignment of $D_i$ solves the selection problem because random assignment makes $D_i$ independent of potential outcomes. To see this, note that

$$E[Y_i|D_i = 1] - E[Y_i|D_i = 0] = E[Y_{1i}|D_i = 1] - E[Y_{0i}|D_i = 0]$$
$$= E[Y_{1i}|D_i = 1] - E[Y_{0i}|D_i = 1],$$

where the independence of $Y_{0i}$ and $D_i$ allows us to swap $E[Y_{0i}|D_i = 1]$ for $E[Y_{0i}|D_i = 0]$ in the second line. In fact, given random assignment, this simplifies further to

$$E[Y_{1i}|D_i = 1] - E[Y_{0i}|D_i = 1] = E[Y_{1i} - Y_{0i}|D_i = 1]$$
$$= E[Y_{1i} - Y_{0i}].$$

The effect of randomly assigned hospitalization on the hospitalized is the same as the effect of hospitalization on a randomly chosen patient. The main thing, however, is that random assignment of $D_i$ eliminates selection bias. This does not mean that randomized trials are problem-free, but in principle they solve the most important problem that arises in empirical research.

---

[3]This section marks our first use of the conditional expectation operator (e.g., $E[Y_i|D_i = 1]$ and $E[Y_i|D_i = 0]$). We use this to denote the population (or infinitely large sample) average of one random variable with the value of another held fixed. A more formal and detailed definition appears in Chapter 3.

How relevant is our hospitalization allegory? Experiments often reveal things that are not what they seem on the basis of naive comparisons alone. A recent example from medicine is the evaluation of hormone replacement therapy (HRT). This is a medical intervention that was recommended for middle-aged women to reduce menopause symptoms. Evidence from the Nurses Health Study, a large and influential nonexperimental survey of nurses, showed better health among HRT users. In contrast, the results of a recently completed randomized trial showed few benefits of HRT. Worse, the randomized trial revealed serious side effects that were not apparent in the nonexperimental data (see, e.g., Women's Health Initiative [WHI], Hsia et al., 2006).

An iconic example from our own field of labor economics is the evaluation of government-subsidized training programs. These are programs that provide a combination of classroom instruction and on-the-job training for groups of disadvantaged workers such as the long-term unemployed, drug addicts, and ex-offenders. The idea is to increase employment and earnings. Paradoxically, studies based on nonexperimental comparisons of participants and nonparticipants often show that after training, the trainees earn less than plausible comparison groups (see, e.g., Ashenfelter, 1978; Ashenfelter and Card, 1985; Lalonde 1995). Here, too, selection bias is a natural concern, since subsidized training programs are meant to serve men and women with low earnings potential. Not surprisingly, therefore, simple comparisons of program participants with nonparticipants often show lower earnings for the participants. In contrast, evidence from randomized evaluations of training programs generate mostly positive effects (see, e.g., Lalonde, 1986; Orr et al., 1996).

Randomized trials are not yet as common in social science as in medicine, but they are becoming more prevalent. One area where the importance of random assignment is growing rapidly is education research (Angrist, 2004). The 2002 Education Sciences Reform Act passed by the U.S. Congress mandates the use of rigorous experimental or quasi-experimental research designs for all federally funded education studies. We can therefore expect to see many more randomized trials in education research in the years to come. A pioneering randomized study from the field of education is the Tennessee STAR experiment, designed to estimate the effects of smaller classes in primary school.

Labor economists and others have a long tradition of trying to establish causal links between features of the classroom environment and children's learning, an area of investigation that we call "education production." This terminology reflects the fact that we think of features of the school environment as inputs that cost money, while the output that schools produce is student learning. A key question in research on education production is which inputs produce the most learning given their costs. One of the most expensive inputs is class size, since smaller classes can only be achieved by hiring more teachers. It is therefore important to know whether the expense of smaller classes has a payoff in terms of higher student achievement. The STAR experiment was meant to answer this question.

Many studies of education production using nonexperimental data suggest there is little or no link between class size and student learning. So perhaps school systems can save money by hiring fewer teachers, with no consequent reduction in achievement. The observed relation between class size and student achievement should not be taken at face value, however, since weaker students are often deliberately grouped into smaller classes. A randomized trial overcomes this problem by ensuring that we are comparing apples to apples, that is, that the students assigned to classes of different sizes are otherwise comparable. Results from the Tennessee STAR experiment point to a strong and lasting payoff to smaller classes (see Finn and Achilles, 1990, for the original study, and Krueger, 1999, for an econometric analysis of the STAR data).

The STAR experiment was unusually ambitious and influential, and therefore worth describing in some detail. It cost about $12 million and was implemented for a cohort of kindergartners in 1985–86. The study ran for four years, until the original cohort of kindergartners was in third grade, and involved about 11,600 children. The average class size in regular Tennessee classes in 1985–86 was about 22.3. The experiment assigned students to one of three treatments: small classes with 13–17 children, regular classes with 22–25 children and a part-time teacher's aide (the usual arrangement), or regular classes with a full-time teacher's aide. Schools with at least three classes in each grade could choose to participate in the experiment.

The first question to ask about a randomized experiment is whether the randomization successfully balanced subjects' characteristics across the different treatment groups. To assess this, it's common to compare pretreatment outcomes or other covariates across groups. Unfortunately, the STAR data fail to include any pretreatment test scores, though it is possible to look at characteristics of children such as race and age. Table 2.2.1, reproduced from Krueger (1999), compares the means of these variables. The student characteristics in the table are a free lunch variable, student race, and student age. Free lunch status is a good measure of family income, since only poor children qualify for a free school lunch. Differences in these characteristics across the three class types are small, and none is significantly different from zero, as indicated by the $p$-values in the last column. This suggests the random assignment worked as intended.

Table 2.2.1 also presents information on average class size, the attrition rate, and test scores, measured here on a percentile scale. The attrition rate (proportion of students lost to follow-up) was lower in small kindergarten classrooms. This is potentially a problem, at least in principle.[4] Class sizes are significantly lower in the assigned-to-be-small classrooms, which means that the experiment succeeded in creating the desired variation. If many of the parents of children assigned to regular classes had successfully lobbied teachers and principals to get their children assigned to small classes, the gap in class size across groups would be much smaller.

Because randomization eliminates selection bias, the difference in outcomes across treatment groups captures the average

---

[4]Krueger (1999) devotes considerable attention to the attrition problem. Differences in attrition rates across groups may result in a sample of students in higher grades that is not randomly distributed across class types. The kindergarten results, which were unaffected by attrition, are therefore the most reliable.

TABLE 2.2.1
Comparison of treatment and control characteristics in the Tennessee
STAR experiment

| Variable | Class Size | | | P-value for equality across groups |
| --- | --- | --- | --- | --- |
| | Small | Regular | Regular/Aide | |
| Free lunch | .47 | .48 | .50 | .09 |
| White/Asian | .68 | .67 | .66 | .26 |
| Age in 1985 | 5.44 | 5.43 | 5.42 | .32 |
| Attrition rate | .49 | .52 | .53 | .02 |
| Class size in kindergarten | 15.10 | 22.40 | 22.80 | .00 |
| Percentile score in kindergarten | 54.70 | 48.90 | 50.00 | .00 |

*Notes*: Adapted from Krueger (1999), table I. The table shows means of variables by treatment status for the sample of students who entered STAR in kindergarten. The *P*-value in the last column is for the *F*-test of equality of variable means across all three groups. The free lunch variable is the fraction receiving a free lunch. The percentile score is the average percentile score on three Stanford Achievement Tests. The attrition rate is the proportion lost to follow-up before completing third grade.

causal effect of class size (relative to regular classes with a part-time aide). In practice, the difference in means between treatment and control groups can be obtained from a regression of test scores on dummies for each treatment group, a point we expand on below. Regression estimates of treatment-control differences for kindergartners, reported in table 2.2.2 (derived from Krueger, 1999, table V), show a small-class effect of about five percentile points (other rows in the table show coefficients on control variables in the regressions). The effect size is about $.2\sigma$, where $\sigma$ is the standard deviation of the percentile score in kindergarten. The small-class effect is significantly different from zero, while the regular/aide effect is small and insignificant.

The STAR study, an exemplary randomized trial in the annals of social science, also highlights the logistical difficulty, long duration, and potentially high cost of randomized trials.

TABLE 2.2.2
Experimental estimates of the effect of class size on test scores

| Explanatory Variable | (1) | (2) | (3) | (4) |
|---|---|---|---|---|
| Small class | 4.82 | 5.37 | 5.36 | 5.37 |
| | (2.19) | (1.26) | (1.21) | (1.19) |
| Regular/aide class | .12 | .29 | .53 | .31 |
| | (2.23) | (1.13) | (1.09) | (1.07) |
| White/Asian | — | — | 8.35 | 8.44 |
| | | | (1.35) | (1.36) |
| Girl | — | — | 4.48 | 4.39 |
| | | | (.63) | (.63) |
| Free lunch | — | — | −13.15 | −13.07 |
| | | | (.77) | (.77) |
| White teacher | — | — | — | −.57 |
| | | | | (2.10) |
| Teacher experience | — | — | — | .26 |
| | | | | (.10) |
| Teacher Master's degree | — | — | — | −0.51 |
| | | | | (1.06) |
| School fixed effects | No | Yes | Yes | Yes |
| $R^2$ | .01 | .25 | .31 | .31 |

Notes: Adapted from Krueger (1999), table V. The dependent variable is the Stanford Achievement Test percentile score. Robust standard errors allowing for correlated residuals within classes are shown in parentheses. The sample size is 5,681.

In many cases, such trials are impractical.[5] In other cases, we would like an answer sooner rather than later. Much of

[5]Randomized trials are never perfect, and STAR is no exception. Pupils who repeated or skipped a grade left the experiment. Students who entered an experimental school one grade later were added to the experiment and randomly assigned to one of the classes. One unfortunate aspect of the experiment is that students in the regular and regular/aide classes were reassigned after the kindergarten year, possibly because of protests by the parents with children in the regular classrooms. There was also some switching of children after the kindergarten year. But Krueger's (1999) analysis suggests that none of these implementation problems affected the main conclusions of the study.

the research we do, therefore, attempts to exploit cheaper and more readily available <u>sources of variation.</u> We hope to find natural or quasi-experiments that mimic a randomized trial by changing the variable of interest while other factors are kept balanced. Can we always find a convincing natural experiment? Of course not. Nevertheless, we take the position that <u>a notional randomized trial is our benchmark.</u> Not all researchers share this view, but many do. We heard it first from our teacher and thesis advisor, Orley Ashenfelter, a pioneering proponent of experiments and quasi-experimental research designs in social science. Here is Ashenfelter (1991) assessing the credibility of the observational studies linking schooling and income:

> How convincing is the evidence linking education and income? Here is my answer: Pretty convincing. If I had to bet on what an ideal experiment would indicate, I bet that it would show that better educated workers earn more.

The quasi-experimental study of class size by Angrist and Lavy (1999) illustrates the manner in which nonexperimental data can be analyzed in an experimental spirit. The Angrist and Lavy study relied on the fact that in Israel, class size is capped at 40. Therefore, a child in a fifth grade cohort of 40 students ends up in a class of 40 while a child in a fifth grade cohort of 41 students ends up in a class only half as large because the cohort is split. Since students in cohorts of size 40 and 41 are likely to be similar on other dimensions, such as ability and family background, we can think of the difference between 40 and 41 students enrolled as being "as good as randomly assigned."

The Angrist-Lavy study compared students in grades with enrollments above and below bureaucratic class size cutoffs to construct well-controlled estimates of the effects of a sharp change in class size without the benefit of a real experiment. As in the Tennessee STAR study, the Angrist and Lavy (1999) results pointed to a strong link between class size and achievement. This was in marked contrast to naive analyses, also reported by Angrist and Lavy, based on simple comparisons between those enrolled in larger and smaller classes. These comparisons showed students in smaller classes doing worse on standardized tests. The hospital allegory of selection bias would therefore seem to apply to the class size question as well.[6]

## 2.3   Regression Analysis of Experiments

Regression is a useful tool for the study of causal questions, including the analysis of data from experiments. Suppose (for now) that the treatment effect is the same for everyone, say $Y_{1i} - Y_{0i} = \rho$, a constant. With constant treatment effects, we can rewrite (2.1.1) in the form

$$
\begin{array}{ccccccc}
Y_i = & \alpha & + & \rho & D_i & + & \eta_i, \\
 & \| & & \| & & & \| \\
 & E(Y_{0i}) & & (Y_{1i} - Y_{0i}) & & & Y_{0i} - E(Y_{0i}),
\end{array}
$$

$$(2.3.1)$$

where $\eta_i$ is the random part of $Y_{0i}$. Evaluating the conditional expectation of this equation with treatment status switched off and on gives

$$E[Y_i | D_i = 1] = \alpha + \rho + E[\eta_i | D_i = 1]$$
$$E[Y_i | D_i = 0] = \alpha + E[\eta_i | D_i = 0],$$

so that

$$E[Y_i | D_i = 1] - E[Y_i | D_i = 0] = \underbrace{\rho}_{\text{Treatment effect}}$$
$$+ \underbrace{E[\eta_i | D_i = 1] - E[\eta_i | D_i = 0]}_{\text{Selection bias}}.$$

Thus, selection bias amounts to correlation between the regression error term, $\eta_i$, and the regressor, $D_i$. Since

$$E[\eta_i | D_i = 1] - E[\eta_i | D_i = 0] = E[Y_{0i} | D_i = 1] - E[Y_{0i} | D_i = 0],$$

this correlation reflects the difference in (no-treatment) potential outcomes between those who get treated and those who

------

[6]The Angrist-Lavy (1999) results turn up again in chapter 6, as an illustration of the quasi-experimental regression-discontinuity research design.

don't. In the hospital allegory, those who were treated had poorer health outcomes in the no-treatment state, while in the Angrist and Lavy (1999) study, students in smaller classes tended to have intrinsically lower test scores.

In the STAR experiment, where $D_i$ is randomly assigned, the selection bias term disappears, and a regression of $Y_i$ on $D_i$ estimates the causal effect of interest, $\rho$. Table 2.2.2 shows different regression specifications, some of which include covariates other than the random assignment indicator, $D_i$. Covariates play two roles in regression analyses of experimental data. First, the STAR experimental design used conditional random assignment. In particular, assignment to classes of different sizes was random within schools but not across schools. Students attending schools of different types (say, urban versus rural) were a bit more or less likely to be assigned to a small class. The comparison in column 1 of table 2.2.2, which makes no adjustment for this, might therefore be contaminated by differences in achievement in schools of different types. To adjust for this, some of Krueger's regression models include school fixed effects, that is, a separate intercept for each school in the STAR data. In practice, the consequences of adjusting for school fixed effects is rather minor, but we wouldn't know this without taking a look. We have more to say about regression models with fixed effects in chapter 5.

The other controls in Krueger's table describe student characteristics such as race, age, and free lunch status. We saw before that these individual characteristics are balanced across class types, that is, they are not systematically related to the class size assignment of the student. If these controls, call them $X_i$, are uncorrelated with the treatment $D_i$, then they will not affect the estimate of $\rho$. In other words, estimates of $\rho$ in the long regression,

$$Y_i = \alpha + \rho D_i + X_i'\gamma + \eta_i, \qquad (2.3.2)$$

will be close to estimates of $\rho$ in the short regression, (2.3.1). This is a point we expand on in chapter 3.

Inclusion of the variables $X_i$, although not necessary in this case, may generate more precise estimates of the causal effect of interest. Notice that the standard error of the estimated treatment effects in column 3 is smaller than the corresponding standard error in column 2. Although the control variables, $X_i$, are uncorrelated with $D_i$, they have substantial explanatory power for $Y_i$. Including these control variables therefore reduces the residual variance, which in turn lowers the standard error of the regression estimates. Similarly, the standard errors of the estimates of $\rho$ are reduced by the inclusion of school fixed effects because these too explain an important part of the variance in student performance. The last column adds teacher characteristics. Because teachers were randomly assigned to classes, and teacher characteristics have little to do with student achievement in these data, both the estimated effect of small classes and its standard error are unchanged by the addition of teacher variables.

Regression plays an exceptionally important role in empirical economic research. As we've seen in this chapter, regression is well-suited to the analysis of experimental data. In some cases, regression can also be used to approximate experiments in the absence of random assignment. But before we get into the important question of when a regression is likely to have a causal interpretation, it is useful to review a number of fundamental regression facts and properties. These facts and properties are reliably true for any regression, regardless of the motivation for running it.

*[handwritten margin note: So trying to get a higher $R^2$ can improve S.E.'s on your primary effect $\beta_1$]*

Part II

# The Core

Chapter 3

# Making Regression Make Sense

"Let us think the unthinkable, let us do the undoable.
Let us prepare to grapple with the ineffable itself,
and see if we may not eff it after all."
Douglas Adams, *Dirk Gently's Holistic Detective Agency*

Angrist recounts:

I ran my first regression in the summer of 1979 between my freshman and sophomore years as a student at Oberlin College. I was working as a research assistant for Allan Meltzer and Scott Richard, faculty members at Carnegie-Mellon University, near my house in Pittsburgh. I was still mostly interested in a career in special education, and had planned to go back to work as an orderly in a state mental hospital, my previous summer job. But Econ 101 had got me thinking, and I could also see that at the same wage rate, a research assistant's hours and working conditions were better than those of a hospital orderly. My research assistant duties included data collection and regression analysis, though I did not understand regression or even statistics at the time.

The paper I was working on that summer (Meltzer and Richard, 1983) is an attempt to link the size of governments in democracies, measured as government expenditure over GDP, to income inequality. Most income distributions have a long right tail, which means that average income tends to be way above the median. When inequality grows, more voters find themselves with below-average incomes. Annoyed by this, those with incomes between the median and the average may join those with incomes below the median in voting for fiscal policies that take from the rich and give to the poor. The size of government consequently increases.

I absorbed the basic theory behind the Meltzer and Richard project, though I didn't find it all that plausible, since voter turnout is low for the poor. I also remember arguing with my bosses over whether government expenditure on education should be classified as a public good (something that benefits everyone in society as well as those directly affected) or a private good publicly supplied, and therefore a form of redistribution like welfare. You might say this project marked the beginning of my interest in the social returns to education, a topic I went back to with more enthusiasm and understanding in Acemoglu and Angrist (2000).

Today, I understand the Meltzer and Richard study as an attempt to use regression to uncover and quantify an interesting causal relation. At the time, however, I was purely a regression mechanic. Sometimes I found the RA work depressing. Days would go by when I didn't talk to anybody but my bosses and the occasional Carnegie-Mellon Ph.D. student, most of whom spoke little English anyway. The best part of the job was lunch with Allan Meltzer, a distinguished scholar and a patient and good-natured supervisor, who was happy to chat while we ate the contents of our brown bags (this did not take long, as Allan ate little and I ate fast). Once I asked Allan whether he found it satisfying to spend his days perusing regression output, which then came on reams of double-wide green-bar paper. Meltzer laughed and said there was nothing he would rather be doing.

Now we too spend our days happily perusing regression output, in the manner of our teachers and advisers in college and graduate school. This chapter explains why.

## 3.1    Regression Fundamentals

The end of the previous chapter introduced regression models as a computational device for the estimation of treatment-control differences in an experiment, with and without covariates. Because the regressor of interest in the class size study discussed in section 2.3 was randomly assigned, the resulting estimates have a causal interpretation. In most studies, however, regression is used with observational data. Without the benefit of random assignment, regression estimates may or may not have a causal interpretation. We return to the central question of what makes a regression causal later in this chapter.

Setting aside the relatively abstract causality problem for the moment, we start with the mechanical properties of regression estimates. These are universal features of the population regression vector and its sample analog that have nothing to do with a researcher's interpretation of his output. These properties include the intimate connection between the population regression function and the conditional expectation function and the sampling distribution of regression estimates.

### 3.1.1 Economic Relationships and the Conditional Expectation Function

Empirical economic research in our field of labor economics is typically concerned with the statistical analysis of individual economic circumstances, and especially differences between people that might account for differences in their economic fortunes. Differences in economic fortune are notoriously hard to explain; they are, in a word, random. As applied econometricians, however, we believe we can summarize and interpret randomness in a useful way. An example of "systematic randomness" mentioned in the introduction is the connection between education and earnings. On average, people with more schooling earn more than people with less schooling. The connection between schooling and earnings has considerable predictive power, in spite of the enormous variation in individual circumstances that sometimes clouds this fact. Of course, the fact that more educated people tend to earn more than less educated people does not mean that schooling *causes* earnings to increase. The question of whether the earnings-schooling relationship is causal is of enormous importance, and we come back to it many times. Even without resolving the difficult question of causality, however, it's clear that education predicts earnings in a narrow statistical sense. This predictive power is compellingly summarized by the conditional expectation function (CEF).

The CEF for a dependent variable $Y_i$, given a $K \times 1$ vector of covariates $X_i$ (with elements $x_{ki}$), is the expectation, or population average, of $Y_i$, with $X_i$ held fixed. The population average can be thought of as the mean in an infinitely large sample, or the average in a completely enumerated finite population. The CEF is written $E[Y_i|X_i]$ and is a function of $X_i$. Because $X_i$ is random, the CEF is random, though sometimes we work with a particular value of the CEF, say $E[Y_i|X_i = 42]$, assuming 42 is a possible value for $X_i$. In chapter 2, we briefly considered the CEF $E[Y_i|D_i]$, where $D_i$ is a zero-one variable. This CEF takes on two values, $E[Y_i|D_i = 1]$ and $E[Y_i|D_i = 0]$. Although this special case is important, we are most often interested in CEFs that are functions of many variables, conveniently subsumed in the vector $X_i$. For a specific value of $X_i$, say $X_i = x$, we write $E[Y_i|X_i = x]$. For continuous $Y_i$ with conditional density $f_y(t|X_i = x)$ at $Y_i = t$, the CEF is

$$E[Y_i|X_i = x] = \int t f_y(t|X_i = x)dt.$$

If $Y_i$ is discrete, $E[Y_i|X_i = x]$ equals the sum $\sum_t tP(Y_i = t|X_i = x)$, where $P(Y_i = t|X_i = x)$ is the conditional probability mass function for $Y_i$ given $X_i = x$.

<u>Expectation is a population concept.</u> In practice, data usually come in the form of samples and rarely consist of an entire population. We therefore use samples to make inferences about the population. For example, the sample CEF is used to learn about the population CEF. This is necessary and important, but we postpone a discussion of the formal inference step taking us from sample to population until section 3.1.3. Our "population-first" approach to econometrics is motivated by the fact that we must define the objects of interest before we can use data to study them.[1]

---

[1] Examples of pedagogical writing using the "population-first" approach to econometrics include Chamberlain (1984), Goldberger (1991), and Manski (1991).

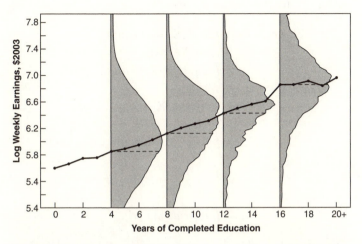

**Figure 3.1.1** Raw data and the CEF of average log weekly wages given schooling. The sample includes white men aged 40–49 in the 1980 IPUMS 5 percent file.

Figure 3.1.1 plots the CEF of log weekly wages given schooling for a sample of middle-aged white men from the 1980 census. The distribution of earnings is also plotted for a few key values: 4, 8, 12, and 16 years of schooling. The CEF in the figure captures the fact that, notwithstanding the enormous variation individual circumstances, people with more schooling generally earn more. The average earnings gain associated with a year of schooling is typically about 10 percent.

An important complement to the CEF is the law of iterated expectations. This law says that an unconditional expectation can be written as the unconditional average of the CEF. In other words,

$$E[Y_i] = E\{E[Y_i|X_i]\}, \qquad (3.1.1)$$

where the outer expectation uses the distribution of $X_i$. Here is a proof of the law of iterated expectations for continuously distributed $(X_i, Y_i)$ with joint density $f_{xy}(u, t)$, where $f_y(t|X_i = u)$ is the conditional distribution of $Y_i$ given $X_i = u$ and $g_y(t)$

and $g_x(u)$ are the marginal densities:

$$
\begin{aligned}
E\{E[\text{Y}_i|\text{X}_i]\} &= \int E[\text{Y}_i|\text{X}_i = u]g_x(u)du \\
&= \int \left[ \int tf_y(t|\text{X}_i = u)dt \right] g_x(u)du \\
&= \int \int tf_y(t|\text{X}_i = u)g_x(u)du\,dt \\
&= \int t \left[ \int f_y(t|\text{X}_i = u)g_x(u)du \right] dt \\
&= \int t \left[ \int f_{xy}(u,t)du \right] dt \\
&= \int tg_y(t)dt = E[\text{Y}_i].
\end{aligned}
$$

The integrals in this derivation run over the possible values of $\text{X}_i$ and $\text{Y}_i$ (indexed by $u$ and $t$). We've laid out these steps because the CEF and its properties are central to the rest of this chapter.[2]

The power of the <u>law of iterated expectations</u> comes from the way it <u>breaks a random variable into two pieces, the CEF and a residual with special properties.</u>

**Theorem 3.1.1** *The CEF Decomposition Property.*

$$
\text{Y}_i = E[\text{Y}_i|\text{X}_i] + \varepsilon_i,
$$

*where (i) $\varepsilon_i$ is mean independent of $\text{X}_i$, that is, $E[\varepsilon_i|\text{X}_i] = 0$, and therefore (ii) $\varepsilon_i$ is uncorrelated with any function of $\text{X}_i$.*

**Proof.** (i) $E[\varepsilon_i|\text{X}_i] = E[\text{Y}_i - E[\text{Y}_i|\text{X}_i]|\text{X}_i] = E[\text{Y}_i|\text{X}_i] - E[\text{Y}_i|\text{X}_i] = 0$. (ii) Let $h(\text{X}_i)$ be any function of $\text{X}_i$. By the law of iterated expectations, $E[h(\text{X}_i)\varepsilon_i] = E\{h(\text{X}_i)E[\varepsilon_i|\text{X}_i]\}$, and by mean independence, $E[\varepsilon_i|\text{X}_i] = 0$.

---

[2] A simple example illustrates how the law of iterated expectations works: Average earnings in a population of men and women is the average for men times the proportion male in the population plus the average for women times the proportion female in the population.

This theorem says that any random variable $Y_i$ can be decomposed into a piece that is "explained by $X_i$"—that is, the CEF—and a piece left over that is orthogonal to (i.e., uncorrelated with) any function of $X_i$.

The CEF is a good summary of the relationship between $Y_i$ and $X_i$, for a number of reasons. First, we are used to thinking of averages as providing a representative value for a random variable. More formally, the CEF is the best predictor of $Y_i$ given $X_i$ in the sense that it solves a minimum mean squared error (MMSE) prediction problem. This CEF prediction property is a consequence of the CEF decomposition property:

**Theorem 3.1.2** *The CEF Prediction Property.*
*Let $m(X_i)$ be any function of $X_i$. The CEF solves*

$$E[Y_i|X_i] = \underset{m(X_i)}{\arg\min}\ E[(Y_i - m(X_i))^2],$$

*so it is the MMSE predictor of $Y_i$ given $X_i$.*

**Proof.** Write

$$(Y_i - m(X_i))^2 = ((Y_i - E[Y_i|X_i]) + (E[Y_i|X_i] - m(X_i)))^2$$
$$= (Y_i - E[Y_i|X_i])^2 + 2(E[Y_i|X_i] - m(X_i))$$
$$\times (Y_i - E[Y_i|X_i]) + (E[Y_i|X_i] - m(X_i))^2.$$

The first term doesn't matter because it doesn't involve $m(X_i)$. The second term can be written $h(X_i)\varepsilon_i$, where $h(X_i) \equiv 2(E[Y_i|X_i] - m(X_i))$, and therefore has expectation zero by the CEF decomposition property. The last term is minimized at zero when $m(X_i)$ is the CEF.

A final property of the CEF, closely related to both the decomposition and prediction properties, is the analysis of variance (ANOVA) theorem:

**Theorem 3.1.3** *The ANOVA Theorem.*

$$V(Y_i) = V(E[Y_i|X_i]) + E[V(Y_i|X_i)],$$

*where $V(\cdot)$ denotes variance and $V(Y_i|X_i)$ is the conditional variance of $Y_i$ given $X_i$.*

**Proof.** The CEF decomposition property implies the variance of $Y_i$ is the variance of the CEF plus the variance of the residual, $\varepsilon_i \equiv Y_i - E[Y_i|X_i]$, since $\varepsilon_i$ and $E[Y_i|X_i]$ are uncorrelated. The variance of $\varepsilon_i$ is

$$E[\varepsilon_i^2] = E[E[\varepsilon_i^2|X_i]] = E[V[Y_i|X_i]],$$

where $E[\varepsilon_i^2|X_i] = V[Y_i|X_i]$ because $\varepsilon_i \equiv Y_i - E[Y_i|X_i]$.

The two CEF properties and the ANOVA theorem may have a familiar ring. You might be used to seeing an ANOVA table in your regression output, for example. ANOVA is also important in research on inequality, where labor economists decompose changes in the income distribution into parts that can be accounted for by changes in worker characteristics and changes in what's left over after accounting for these factors (see, e.g., Autor, Katz, and Kearney, 2005). What may be unfamiliar is the fact that the CEF properties and ANOVA variance decomposition work in the population as well as in samples, and do not turn on the assumption of a linear CEF. In fact, the validity of linear regression as an empirical tool does not turn on linearity either.

### 3.1.2   Linear Regression and the CEF

So what's the regression you want to run? In our world, this question or one like it is heard almost every day. Regression estimates provide a valuable baseline for almost all empirical research because regression is tightly linked to the CEF, and the CEF provides a natural summary of empirical relationships. The link between regression functions—that is, the best-fitting line generated by minimizing expected squared errors—and the CEF can be explained in at least three ways. To lay out these explanations precisely, it helps to be precise about the regression function we have in mind. This section is concerned with the vector of population regression coefficients, defined as the solution to a population least squares problem. At this point we are not worried about causality. Rather, we let the $\kappa \times 1$ regression coefficient vector $\beta$ be defined by solving

$$\beta = \arg\min_{b} E[(Y_i - X_i'b)^2]. \qquad (3.1.2)$$

Using the first-order condition,

$$E[X_i(Y_i - X_i'b)] = 0,$$

the solution can be written $\beta = E[X_iX_i']^{-1}E[X_iY_i]$. Note that by construction, $E[X_i(Y_i - X_i'\beta)] = 0$. In other words, the population residual, which we define as $Y_i - X_i'\beta = e_i$, is uncorrelated with the regressors, $X_i$. It bears emphasizing that this <u>error term does not have a life of its own. It owes its existence and meaning to $\beta$.</u> We return to this important point in the discussion of causal regression in section 3.2.

In the simple bivariate case where the regression vector includes only the single regressor, $x_i$, and a constant, the slope coefficient is $\beta_1 = \frac{Cov(Y_i, x_i)}{V(x_i)}$, and the intercept is $\alpha = E[Y_i] - \beta_1 E[X_i]$. In the multivariate case, with more than one non-constant regressor, the slope coefficient for the $k$th regressor is given below:

REGRESSION ANATOMY

$$\beta_k = \frac{Cov(Y_i, \tilde{x}_{ki})}{V(\tilde{x}_{ki})}, \qquad (3.1.3)$$

where $\tilde{x}_{ki}$ is the residual from a regression of $x_{ki}$ on all the other covariates.

In other words, $E[X_iX_i']^{-1}E[X_iY_i]$ is the $\kappa \times 1$ vector with $k$th element $\frac{Cov(Y_i, \tilde{x}_{ki})}{V(\tilde{x}_{ki})}$. This important formula is said to describe the anatomy of a multivariate regression coefficient because it reveals much more than the matrix formula $\beta = E[X_iX_i']^{-1}E[X_iY_i]$. It shows us that each coefficient in a multivariate regression is the <u>bivariate slope coefficient for the corresponding regressor after partialing out all the other covariates.</u>

To verify the regression anatomy formula, substitute

$$Y_i = \alpha + \beta_1 x_{1i} + \cdots + \beta_k x_{ki} + \cdots + \beta_K x_{Ki} + e_i$$

in the numerator of (3.1.3). Since $\tilde{x}_{ki}$ is a linear combination of the regressors, it is uncorrelated with $e_i$. Also, since $\tilde{x}_{ki}$ is a residual from a regression on all the other covariates in the model, it must be uncorrelated with these covariates. Finally, for the same reason, the covariance of $\tilde{x}_{ki}$ with $x_{ki}$ is just the variance of $\tilde{x}_{ki}$. We therefore have $Cov(Y_i, \tilde{x}_{ki}) = \beta_k V(\tilde{x}_{ki})$.[3]

The regression anatomy formula is probably familiar to you from a regression or statistics course, perhaps with one twist: the regression coefficients defined in this section are not estimators; rather, they are nonstochastic features of the joint distribution of dependent and independent variables. This joint distribution is what you would observe if you had a complete enumeration of the population of interest (or knew the stochastic process generating the data). You probably don't have such information. Still, it's good empirical practice to think about what population parameters mean before worrying about how to estimate them.

Below we discuss three reasons why the vector of population regression coefficients might be of interest. These reasons can be summarized by saying that you should be interested in regression parameters if you are interested in the CEF.

---

[3]The regression anatomy formula is usually attributed to Frisch and Waugh (1933). You can also do regression anatomy this way:

$$\beta_k = \frac{Cov(\tilde{Y}_{ki}, \tilde{x}_{ki})}{V(\tilde{x}_{ki})},$$

where $\tilde{Y}_{ki}$ is the residual from a regression of $Y_i$ on every covariate except $x_{ki}$. This works because the fitted values removed from $\tilde{Y}_{ki}$ are uncorrelated with $\tilde{x}_{ki}$. Often it's useful to plot $\tilde{Y}_{ki}$ against $\tilde{x}_{ki}$; the slope of the least squares fit in this scatterplot is the multivariate $\beta_k$, even though the plot is two-dimensional. Note, however, that it's not enough to partial the other covariates out of $Y_i$ only. That is,

$$\frac{Cov(\tilde{Y}_{ki}, x_{ki})}{V(x_{ki})} = \left[ \frac{Cov(\tilde{Y}_{ki}, \tilde{x}_{ki})}{V(\tilde{x}_{ki})} \right] \left[ \frac{V(\tilde{x}_{ki})}{V(x_{ki})} \right] \neq \beta_k,$$

unless $x_{ki}$ is uncorrelated with the other covariates.

**Theorem 3.1.4** *The Linear CEF Theorem (Regression Justification I).*

*Suppose the CEF is linear. Then the population regression function is it.*

**Proof.** Suppose $E[Y_i|X_i] = X_i'\beta^*$ for a $K \times 1$ vector of coefficients, $\beta^*$. Recall that $E[X_i(Y_i - E[Y_i|X_i])] = 0$ by the CEF decomposition property. Substitute using $E[Y_i|X_i] = X_i'\beta^*$ to find that $\beta^* = E[X_iX_i']^{-1}E[X_iY_i] = \beta$.

The linear CEF theorem raises the question of what makes a CEF linear. The classic scenario is joint normality, that is, the vector $(Y_i, X_i')'$ has a multivariate normal distribution. This is the scenario considered by Galton (1886), father of regression, who was interested in the intergenerational link between normally distributed traits such as height and intelligence. The normal case is clearly of limited empirical relevance since regressors and dependent variables are often discrete, while normal distributions are continuous. Another linearity scenario arises when regression models are saturated. As reviewed in section 3.1.4, a saturated regression model has a separate parameter for every possible combination of values that the set of regressors can take on. For example a saturated regression model with two dummy covariates includes both covariates (with coefficients known as the main effects) and their product (known as an interaction term). Such models are inherently linear, a point we also discuss in section 3.1.4.

The following two reasons for focusing on regression are relevant when the linear CEF theorem does not apply.

**Theorem 3.1.5** *The Best Linear Predictor Theorem (Regression Justification II).*

*The function $X_i'\beta$ is the best linear predictor of $Y_i$ given $X_i$ in a MMSE sense.*

**Proof.** $\beta = E[X_iX_i']^{-1}E[X_iY_i]$ solves the population least squares problem, (3.1.2).

In other words, just as the CEF, $E[Y_i|X_i]$, is the best (i.e., MMSE) predictor of $Y_i$ given $X_i$ in the class of *all* functions of

$X_i$, the population regression function is the best we can do in the class of *linear* functions.

**Theorem 3.1.6** *The Regression CEF Theorem (Regression Justification III).*
   *The function* $X_i'\beta$ *provides the MMSE linear approximation to* $E[Y_i|X_i]$, *that is,*

$$\beta = \arg\min_b E\{(E[Y_i|X_i] - X_i'b)^2\}. \qquad (3.1.4)$$

**Proof.** Start by observing that $\beta$ solves (3.1.2). Write

$$
\begin{aligned}
(Y_i - X_i'b)^2 &= \{(Y_i - E[Y_i|X_i]) + (E[Y_i|X_i] - X_i'b)\}^2 \\
&= (Y_i - E[Y_i|X_i])^2 + (E[Y_i|X_i] - X_i'b)^2 \\
&\quad + 2(Y_i - E[Y_i|X_i])(E[Y_i|X_i] - X_i'b).
\end{aligned}
$$

The first term doesn't involve $b$ and the last term has expectation zero by the CEF decomposition property (ii). The CEF approximation problem, (3.1.4), is therefore the same as the population least squares problem, (3.1.2).

These two theorems give us two more ways to view regression. Regression provides the best linear predictor for the dependent variable in the same way that the CEF is the best unrestricted predictor of the dependent variable. On the other hand, if we prefer to think about approximating $E[Y_i|X_i]$, as opposed to predicting $Y_i$, the regression CEF theorem tells us that even if the CEF is nonlinear, regression provides the best linear approximation to it.

The regression CEF theorem is our favorite way to motivate regression. The statement that regression approximates the CEF lines up with our view of empirical work as an effort to describe the essential features of statistical relationships without necessarily trying to pin them down exactly. The linear CEF theorem is for special cases only. The best linear predictor theorem is satisfyingly general, but seems to encourage an overly clinical view of empirical research. We're not really interested in predicting *individual* $Y_i$; it's the *distribution* of $Y_i$ that we care about.

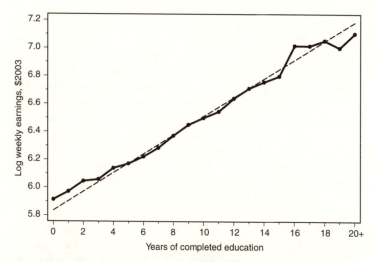

**Figure 3.1.2** Regression threads the CEF of average weekly wages given schooling (dots = CEF; dashes = regression line).

Figure 3.1.2 illustrates the CEF approximation property for the same schooling CEF plotted in figure 3.1.1. The regression line fits the somewhat bumpy and nonlinear CEF as if we were estimating a model for $E[Y_i|X_i]$ instead of a model for $Y_i$. In fact, that is exactly what's going on. An implication of the regression CEF theorem is that regression coefficients can be obtained by using $E[Y_i|X_i]$ as a dependent variable instead of $Y_i$ itself. To see this, suppose that $X_i$ is a discrete random variable with probability mass function $g_x(u)$. Then

$$E\{(E[Y_i|X_i] - X_i'b)^2\} = \sum_u (E[Y_i|X_i = u] - u'b)^2 g_x(u).$$

This means that $\beta$ can be constructed from the weighted least squares (WLS) regression of $E[Y_i|X_i = u]$ on $u$, where $u$ runs over the values taken on by $X_i$. The weights are given by the distribution of $X_i$, that is, $g_x(u)$. An even simpler way to see this is to iterate expectations in the formula for $\beta$:

$$\beta = E[X_iX_i']^{-1}E[X_iY_i] = E[X_iX_i']^{-1}E[X_iE(Y_i|X_i)]. \quad (3.1.5)$$

The CEF or grouped data version of the regression formula is of practical use when working on a project that precludes the analysis of microdata. For example, Angrist (1998) used grouped data to study the effect of voluntary military service on earnings later in life. One of the estimation strategies used in this project regresses civilian earnings on a dummy for veteran status, along with personal characteristics and the variables used by the military to screen soldiers. The earnings data come from the U.S. Social Security system, but Social Security earnings records cannot be released to the public. Instead of individual earnings, Angrist worked with average earnings conditional on race, sex, test scores, education, and veteran status.

To illustrate the grouped data approach to regression, we estimated the schooling coefficient in a wage equation using 21 conditional means, the sample CEF of earnings given schooling. As the Stata output reproduced in Figure 3.1.3 shows, a grouped data regression, weighted by the number of individuals at each schooling level in the sample, produces coefficients identical to those generated using the underlying microdata sample with hundreds of thousands of observations. Note, however, that the standard errors from the grouped regression do not measure the asymptotic sampling variance of the slope estimate in repeated micro-data samples; for that you need an estimate of the variance of $Y_i - X_i'\beta$. This variance depends on the microdata, in particular the second moments of $W_i \equiv [Y_i \ X_i']'$, a point we elaborate on in the next section.

### 3.1.3    Asymptotic OLS Inference

In practice, we don't usually know what the CEF or the population regression vector is. We therefore draw statistical inferences about these quantities using samples. Statistical inference is what much of traditional econometrics is about. Although this material is covered in any econometrics text, we don't want to skip the inference step completely. A review of basic asymptotic theory allows us to highlight the important fact that the process of statistical inference is distinct from the

*A - Individual-level data*

```
. regress earnings school, robust

      Source |       SS       df       MS              Number of obs =  409435
-------------+------------------------------           F(  1,409433) =49118.25
       Model | 22631.4793        1 22631.4793          Prob > F      =  0.0000
    Residual | 188648.31    409433 .460755019          R-squared     =  0.1071
-------------+------------------------------           Adj R-squared =  0.1071
       Total | 211279.789   409434  .51602893           Root MSE      = .67879

-------------+----------------------------------------------------------------
             |               Robust                    Old Fashioned
    earnings |      Coef.   Std. Err.      t             Std. Err.            t
-------------+----------------------------------------------------------------
      school |   .0674387   .0003447   195.63            .0003043       221.63
       const.|   5.835761   .0045507  1282.39            .0040043      1457.38
------------------------------------------------------------------------------
```

*B - Means by years of schooling*

```
. regress average_earnings school [aweight=count], robust
(sum of wgt is    4.0944e+05)

      Source |       SS       df       MS              Number of obs =      21
-------------+------------------------------           F(  1,     19) =  540.31
       Model | 1.16077332        1 1.16077332          Prob > F      =  0.0000
    Residual | .040818796       19 .002148358          R-squared     =  0.9660
-------------+------------------------------           Adj R-squared =  0.9642
       Total | 1.20159212       20 .060079606          Root MSE      = .04635

-------------+----------------------------------------------------------------
     average |               Robust                    Old Fashioned
   _earnings |      Coef.   Std. Err.      t             Std. Err.            t
-------------+----------------------------------------------------------------
      school |   .0674387   .0040352    16.71            .0029013        23.24
       const.|   5.835761   .0399452   146.09            .0381792       152.85
------------------------------------------------------------------------------
```

**Figure 3.1.3** Microdata and grouped data estimates of the returns to schooling, from Stata regression output. *Source*: 1980 Census—IPUMS, 5 percent sample. The sample includes white men, age 40–49. Robust standard errors are heteroskedasticity consistent. Panel A uses individual-level microdata. Panel B uses earnings averaged by years of schooling.

question of how a particular set of regression estimates should be interpreted. Whatever a regression coefficient may mean, it has a sampling distribution that is easy to describe and use for statistical inference.[4]

---

[4] The discussion of asymptotic OLS inference in this section is largely a condensation of material in Chamberlain (1984). Important pitfalls and problems with asymptotic theory are covered in the last chapter.

We are interested in the distribution of the sample analog of

$$\beta = E[X_i X_i']^{-1} E[X_i Y_i]$$

in repeated samples. Suppose the vector $W_i \equiv [Y_i \ X_i']'$ is independently and identically distributed in a sample of size $N$. A natural estimator of the first population moment, $E[W_i]$, is the sum, $\frac{1}{N} \sum_{i=1}^{N} W_i$. By the law of large numbers, this vector of sample moments gets arbitrarily close to the corresponding vector of population moments as the sample size grows. We might similarly consider higher-order moments of the elements of $W_i$, for example the matrix of second moments, $E[W_i W_i']$, with sample analog $\frac{1}{N} \sum_{i=1}^{N} W_i W_i'$. Following this principle, the method of moments estimator of $\beta$ replaces each expectation by a sum. This logic leads to the ordinary least squares (OLS) estimator

$$\hat{\beta} = \left[ \sum_i X_i X_i' \right]^{-1} \sum_i X_i Y_i.$$

Although we derived $\hat{\beta}$ as a method of moments estimator, it is called the OLS estimator of $\beta$ because it solves the sample analog of the least squares problem described at the beginning of section 3.1.2.[5]

The asymptotic sampling distribution of $\hat{\beta}$ depends solely on the definition of the estimand (i.e., the nature of the thing we're trying to estimate, $\beta$) and the assumption that the data constitute a random sample. Before deriving this distribution, it helps to summarize the general asymptotic distribution theory that covers our needs. This basic theory can be stated mostly in words. For the purposes of these statements, we assume the reader is familiar with the core terms and concepts of statistical theory—moments, mathematical expectation, probability

---

[5]Econometricians like to use matrices because the notation is so compact. Sometimes (not very often) we do too. Suppose $X$ is the matrix whose rows are given by $X_i'$ and $y$ is the vector with elements $Y_i$, for $i = 1, \ldots, N$. The sample moment matrix $\frac{1}{N} \sum X_i X_i'$ is $X'X/N$ and the sample moment vector $\frac{1}{N} \sum X_i y_i$ is $X'y/N$. Then we can write $\hat{\beta} = (X'X)^{-1}X'y$, a widely used matrix formula.

limits, and asymptotic distributions. For definitions of these terms and a formal mathematical statement of the theoretical propositions given below, see Knight (2000).

THE LAW OF LARGE NUMBERS    Sample moments converge in probability to the corresponding population moments. In other words, the probability that the sample mean is close to the population mean can be made as high as you like by taking a large enough sample.

THE CENTRAL LIMIT THEOREM    Sample moments are asymptotically normally distributed (after subtracting the corresponding population moment and multiplying by the square root of the sample size). The asymptotic covariance matrix is given by the variance of the underlying random variable. In other words, in large enough samples, appropriately normalized sample moments are approximately normally distributed.

SLUTSKY'S THEOREM

1. Consider the sum of two random variables, one of which converges in distribution (in other words, has an asymptotic distribution) and the other converges in probability to a constant: the asymptotic distribution of this sum is unaffected by replacing the one that converges to a constant by this constant. Formally, let $a_N$ be a statistic with an asymptotic distribution and let $b_N$ be a statistic with probability limit $b$. Then $a_N + b_N$ and $a_N + b$ have the same asymptotic distribution.

2. Consider the product of two random variables, one of which converges in distribution and the other converges in probability to a constant: the asymptotic distribution of this product is unaffected by replacing the one that converges to a constant by this constant. Formally, let $a_N$ be a statistic with an asymptotic distribution and let $b_N$ be a statistic with probability limit $b$. Then $a_N b_N$ and $a_N b$ have the same asymptotic distribution.

THE CONTINUOUS MAPPING THEOREM    Probability limits pass through continuous functions. For example, the probability limit of any continuous function of a sample moment is the function evaluated at the corresponding population moment. Formally, the probability limit of $h(b_N)$ is $h(b)$, where *plim* $b_N = b$ and $h(\cdot)$ is continuous at $b$.

THE DELTA METHOD    Consider a vector-valued random variable that is asymptotically normally distributed. Continuously differentiable scalar functions of this random variable are also asymptotically normally distributed, with covariance matrix given by a quadratic form with the covariance matrix of the random variable on the inside and the gradient of the function evaluated at the probability limit of the random variable on the outside.[6] Formally, the asymptotic distribution of $h(b_N)$ is normal with covariance matrix $\nabla h(b)'\Omega\nabla h(b)$, where *plim* $b_N = b$, $h(\cdot)$ is continuously differentiable at $b$ with gradient $\nabla h(b)$, and $b_N$ has asymptotic covariance matrix $\Omega$.[7]

We can use these results to derive the asymptotic distribution of $\hat{\beta}$ in two ways. A conceptually straightforward but somewhat inelegant approach is to use the delta method: $\hat{\beta}$ is a function of sample moments, and is therefore asymptotically normally distributed. It remains only to find the covariance matrix of the asymptotic distribution from the gradient of this function. (Note that consistency of $\hat{\beta}$ comes immediately from the continuous mapping theorem).[8] An easier and more instructive derivation uses the Slutsky and central limit theorems. Note first that we can write

$$Y_i = X_i'\beta + [Y_i - X_i'\beta] \equiv X_i'\beta + e_i, \qquad (3.1.6)$$

where the residual $e_i$ is defined as the difference between the dependent variable and the population regression function, as

---

[6] A quadratic form is a matrix-weighted sum of squares. Suppose $v$ is an $N \times 1$ vector and $M$ is an $N \times N$ matrix. A quadratic form in $v$ is $v'Mv$. If $M$ is an $N \times N$ diagonal matrix with diagonal elements $m_i$, then $v'Mv = \sum_i m_i v_i^2$.

[7] For a derivation of the delta method formula using the Slutsky and continuous mapping theorems, see Knight (2000, pp. 120–121). We say "the asymptotic distribution of $h(b_N)$," but we really mean the asymptotic distribution of $\sqrt{N}(h(b_N) - h(b))$.

[8] An estimator is said to be *consistent* when it converges in probability to the target parameter.

before. In other words, $E[X_i e_i] = 0$ is a consequence of $\beta = E[X_i X_i']^{-1} E[X_i Y_i]$ and $e_i = Y_i - X_i'\beta$, and not an assumption about an underlying economic relation.[9]

Substituting the identity (3.1.6) for $Y_i$ in the formula for $\hat{\beta}$, we have

$$\hat{\beta} = \beta + \left[\sum X_i X_i'\right]^{-1} \sum X_i e_i.$$

The asymptotic distribution of $\hat{\beta}$ is the asymptotic distribution of $\sqrt{N}(\hat{\beta} - \beta) = N[\sum X_i X_i']^{-1} \frac{1}{\sqrt{N}} \sum X_i e_i$. By the Slutsky theorem, this has the same asymptotic distribution as $E[X_i X_i']^{-1} \frac{1}{\sqrt{N}} \sum X_i e_i$. Since $E[X_i e_i] = 0$, $\frac{1}{\sqrt{N}} \sum X_i e_i$ is a root-$N$ normalized and centered sample moment. By the central limit theorem, this is asymptotically normally distributed with mean zero and covariance matrix $E[X_i X_i' e_i^2]$, since this matrix of fourth moments is the covariance matrix of $X_i e_i$. Therefore, $\hat{\beta}$ has an asymptotic normal distribution with probability limit $\beta$ and covariance matrix

$$E[X_i X_i']^{-1} E[X_i X_i' e_i^2] E[X_i X_i']^{-1}. \qquad (3.1.7)$$

The theoretical standard errors used to construct $t$-statistics are the square roots of the diagonal elements of (3.1.7). In practice these standard errors are estimated by substituting sums for expectations and using the estimated residuals, $\hat{e}_i = Y_i - X_i'\hat{\beta}$ to form the empirical fourth moment matrix, $\sum[X_i X_i' \hat{e}_i^2]/N$.

Asymptotic standard errors computed in this way are known as heteroskedasticity-consistent standard errors, White (1980a) standard errors, or Eicker-White standard errors, in recognition of Eicker's (1967) derivation. They are also known as "robust" standard errors (e.g., in Stata). These standard errors are said to be robust because, in large enough samples, they provide accurate hypothesis tests and confidence intervals given minimal assumptions about the data and model. In particular, our derivation of the limiting distribution makes

---

[9]Residuals defined in this way are not necessarily mean independent of $X_i$; for mean independence, we need a linear CEF.

no assumptions other than those needed to ensure that basic statistical results like the central limit theorem go through. Robust standard errors are not, however, the standard errors that you get by default from packaged software. Default standard errors are derived under a homoskedasticity assumption, specifically, that $E[e_i^2|X_i] = \sigma^2$, a constant. Given this assumption, we have

$$E[X_i X_i' e_i^2] = E(X_i X_i' E[e_i^2|X_i]) = \sigma^2 E[X_i X_i'],$$

by iterating expectations. The asymptotic covariance matrix of $\hat{\beta}$ then simplifies to

$$
\begin{aligned}
E[X_i X_i']^{-1} & E[X_i X_i' e_i^2] E[X_i X_i']^{-1} \\
&= E[X_i X_i']^{-1} \sigma^2 E[X_i X_i'] E[X_i X_i]^{-1} \\
&= \sigma^2 E[X_i X_i']^{-1}.
\end{aligned} \tag{3.1.8}
$$

The diagonal elements of (3.1.8) are what SAS or Stata report unless you request otherwise.

Our view of regression as an approximation to the CEF makes heteroskedasticity seem natural. If the CEF is nonlinear and you use a linear model to approximate it, then the quality of fit between the regression line and the CEF will vary with $X_i$. Hence, the residuals will be larger, on average, at values of $X_i$ where the fit is poorer. Even if you are prepared to assume that the conditional variance of $Y_i$ given $X_i$ is constant, the fact that the CEF is nonlinear means that $E[(Y_i - X_i'\beta)^2|X_i]$ will vary with $X_i$. To see this, note that

$$
\begin{aligned}
E[(Y_i - X_i'\beta)^2 | X_i] \\
&= E\{[(Y_i - E[Y_i|X_i]) + (E[Y_i|X_i] - X_i'\beta)]^2 | X_i\} \\
&= V[Y_i|X_i] + (E[Y_i|X_i] - X_i'\beta)^2. \tag{3.1.9}
\end{aligned}
$$

Therefore, even if $V[Y_i|X_i]$ is constant, the residual variance increases with the square of the gap between the regression line and the CEF, a fact noted in White (1980b).[10]

---

[10] The cross-product term resulting from an expansion of the squared term in the middle of (3.1.9) is zero because $Y_i - E[Y_i|X_i]$ is mean independent of $X_i$.

In the same spirit, it's also worth noting that while a linear CEF makes homoskedasticity possible, this is not a sufficient condition for homoskedasticity. Our favorite example in this context is the linear probability model (LPM). A linear probability model is any regression where the dependent variable is zero-one, that is, a dummy variable such as an indicator for labor force participation. Suppose the regression model is saturated, so the CEF given regressors is linear. Because the CEF is linear, the residual variance is also the conditional variance, $V[Y_i|X_i]$. But the dependent variable is a Bernoulli trial with conditional variance $P[Y_i = 1|X_i](1 - P[Y_i = 1|X_i])$. We conclude that LPM residuals are necessarily heteroskedastic unless the only regressor is a constant.

These points of principle notwithstanding, as an empirical matter, heteroskedasticity may matter little. In the microdata schooling regression depicted in figure 3.1.3, the robust standard error is .0003447, while the old-fashioned standard error is .0003043, not much smaller. The standard errors from the grouped data regression, which are necessarily heteroskedastic if group sizes differ, change somewhat more; compare the .004 robust standard to the .0029 conventional standard error. Based on our experience, these differences are typical. If heteroskedasticity matters a lot, say, more than a 30 percent increase or any marked decrease in standard errors, you should worry about possible programming errors or other problems. For example, robust standard errors below conventional may be a sign of finite-sample bias in the robust calculation.

Finally, a brief note on the textbook approach to inference that you might have seen elsewhere. Traditional econometric inference begins with stronger assumptions than those we have invoked in this section. The traditional set-up, sometimes called a classical normal regression model, postulates: fixed (non-stochastic) regressors, a linear CEF, normally distributed errors, and homoskedasticity (see, e.g., Goldberger, 1991). These stronger assumptions give us two things: (1) unbiasedness of the OLS estimator, (2) a formula for the sampling variance of the OLS estimator that is valid in small as well as large samples. Unbiasedness of the OLS estimators means that $E[\hat{\beta}] = \beta$, a property that holds in a sample of any size and is stronger than consistency, which means only that we can expect $\hat{\beta}$ to be close to $\beta$ in large samples. It's easy to see when and why we get unbiasedness. In general,

$$E[\hat{\beta}] = \beta + E\left\{\left[\sum X_i X_i'\right]^{-1} \sum X_i e_i\right\}.$$

If the regressors are nonrandom (fixed in repeated samples) the expectation passes through and we have unbiasedness because $E[e_i] = 0$. Otherwise, with random regressors, we can iterate expectations and get unbiasedness if $E[e_i|X_i] = 0$. This is true when the CEF is linear, but not in our more general "agnostic regression" framework.

The variance formula obtained under classical assumptions is the same as the large-sample formula under homoskedasticity but—provided the strong classical assumptions are valid—this formula holds in a sample of any size. We've chosen to start with the asymptotic approach to inference because modern empirical work typically leans heavily on the large-sample theory that lies behind robust variance formulas. The payoff is valid inference under weak assumptions, in particular, a framework that makes sense for our less-than-literal approach to regression models. On the other hand, the large-sample approach is not without its dangers, a point we return to in the discussion of inference in chapter 8 and in the discussion of instrumental variables in chapter 4.

### 3.1.4   Saturated Models, Main Effects, and Other Regression Talk

We often discuss regression models using terms like *saturated* and *main effects*. These terms originate in an experimentalist tradition that uses regression to model the effects of discrete treatment-type variables. This language is now used more widely in many fields, however, including applied econometrics. For readers unfamiliar with these terms, this section provides a brief review.

Saturated regression models are regression models with discrete explanatory variables, where the model includes a separate parameter for all possible values taken on by the explanatory variables. For example, when working with a single explanatory variable indicating whether a worker is a college graduate, the model is saturated by including a single dummy for college graduates and a constant. We can also saturate when the regressor takes on many values. Suppose, for example, that $s_i = 0, 1, 2, \ldots, \tau$. A saturated regression model for $s_i$ is

$$Y_i = \alpha + \beta_1 d_{1i} + \beta_2 d_{2i} + \cdots + \beta_\tau d_{\tau i} + \varepsilon_i,$$

where $d_{ji} = 1[s_i = j]$ is a dummy variable indicating schooling level $j$, and $\beta_j$ is said to be the $j$th-level schooling *effect*.[11] Note that

$$\beta_j = E[Y_i | s_i = j] - E[Y_i | s_i = 0],$$

while $\alpha = E[Y_i | s_i = 0]$. In practice, you can pick any value of $s_i$ for the reference group; a regression model is saturated as long as it has one parameter for every possible $j$ in $E[Y_i | s_i = j]$. Saturated regression models fit the CEF perfectly because the CEF is a linear function of the dummy regressors used to saturate. This is an important special case of the linear CEF theorem.

If there are two explanatory variables—say, one dummy indicating college graduates and one dummy indicating sex—the model is saturated by including these two dummies, their product, and a constant. The coefficients on the dummies are known as main effects, while the product is called an *interaction term*. This is not the only saturated parameterization; any set of indicators (dummies) that can be used to identify each value taken on by all covariates produces a saturated model. For example, an alternative saturated model includes dummies for male college graduates, male nongraduates, female college graduates, and female nongraduates, but no intercept.

Here's some notation to make this more concrete. Let $x_{1i}$ indicate college graduates and $x_{2i}$ indicate women. The CEF

---

[11] We use the notation $1[s_i = j]$ to denote the indicator function, in this case a function that creates a dummy variable switched on when $s_i = j$.

given $x_{1i}$ and $x_{2i}$ takes on four values:

$$E[Y_i | x_{1i} = 0, x_{2i} = 0],$$
$$E[Y_i | x_{1i} = 1, x_{2i} = 0],$$
$$E[Y_i | x_{1i} = 0, x_{2i} = 1],$$
$$E[Y_i | x_{1i} = 1, x_{2i} = 1].$$

We can label these using the following scheme:

$$E[Y_i | x_{1i} = 0, x_{2i} = 0] = \alpha$$
$$E[Y_i | x_{1i} = 1, x_{2i} = 0] = \alpha + \beta_1$$
$$E[Y_i | x_{1i} = 0, x_{2i} = 1] = \alpha + \gamma$$
$$E[Y_i | x_{1i} = 1, x_{2i} = 1] = \alpha + \beta_1 + \gamma + \delta_1.$$

Since there are four Greek letters and the CEF takes on four values, this parameterization does not restrict the CEF. It can be written in terms of Greek letters as

$$E[Y_i | x_{1i}, x_{2i}] = \alpha + \beta_1 x_{1i} + \gamma x_{2i} + \delta_1 (x_{1i} x_{2i}),$$

a parameterization with two main effects and one interaction term.[12] The saturated regression equation becomes

$$Y_i = \alpha + \beta_1 x_{1i} + \gamma x_{2i} + \delta_1 (x_{1i} x_{2i}) + \varepsilon_i.$$

We can combine the multivalued schooling variable with sex to produce a saturated model that has $\tau$ main effects for schooling, one main effect for sex, and $\tau$ sex-schooling interactions:

$$Y_i = \alpha + \sum_{j=1}^{\tau} \beta_j d_{ji} + \gamma x_{2i} + \sum_{j=1}^{\tau} \delta_j (d_{ji} x_{2i}) + \varepsilon_i. \quad (3.1.10)$$

The coefficients on the interaction terms, $\delta_j$, tell us how each of the schooling effects differ by sex. The CEF in this case

[12]With a third dummy variable in the model, say $x_{3i}$, a saturated model includes three main effects, three second-order interaction terms $\{x_{1i}x_{2i}, x_{1i}x_{3i}, x_{2i}x_{3i}\}$, and one third-order term, $x_{1i}x_{2i}x_{3i}$.

takes on $2(\tau + 1)$ values, while the regression has this many parameters.

Note that there is a hierarchy of increasingly restrictive modeling strategies with saturated models at the top. It's natural to start with a saturated model because this fits the CEF. On the other hand, saturated models generate a lot of interaction terms, many of which may be uninteresting or estimated imprecisely. You might therefore sensibly choose to omit some or all of these terms. Equation (3.1.10) without interaction terms approximates the CEF using a purely additive model for schooling and sex. This is a good approximation if the returns to college are similar for men and women. In any case, schooling coefficients in the additive specification give a (weighted) average return across both sexes, as discussed in section 3.3.1. On the other hand, it would be strange to estimate a model that included interaction terms but omitted the corresponding main effects. In the case of schooling, this is something like

$$Y_i = \alpha + \gamma x_{2i} + \sum_{j=1}^{\tau} \delta_j (d_{ji} x_{2i}) + \varepsilon_i. \tag{3.1.11}$$

This model allows schooling to shift wages only for women, something very far from the truth. Consequently, the results of estimating (3.1.11) are likely to be hard to interpret.

Finally, it's important to recognize that a saturated model fits the CEF perfectly regardless of the distribution of $Y_i$. For example, this is true for linear probability models and other limited dependent variable models (e.g., non-negative $Y_i$), a point we return to at the end of this chapter.

## 3.2  Regression and Causality

Section 3.1.2 shows how regression gives the best (MMSE) linear approximation to the CEF. This understanding, however, does not help us with the deeper question of when regression has a causal interpretation. When can we think of a regression coefficient as approximating the causal effect that might be revealed in an experiment?

### 3.2.1    *The Conditional Independence Assumption*

A regression is causal when the CEF it approximates is causal. This doesn't answer the question, of course. It just passes the buck up one level, since, as we've seen, a regression inherits its legitimacy from a CEF. Causality means different things to different people, but researchers working in many disciplines have found it useful to think of causal relationships in terms of the potential outcomes notation used in chapter 2 to describe what would happen to a given individual in a hypothetical comparison of alternative hospitalization scenarios. Differences in these potential outcomes were said to be the causal effect of hospitalization. The CEF is causal when it describes differences in average potential outcomes for a fixed reference population.

It's easiest to expand on the somewhat murky notion of a causal CEF in the context of a particular question, so let's stick with the schooling example. The causal connection between schooling and earnings can be defined as the functional relationship that describes what a given individual would earn if he or she obtained different levels of education. In particular, we might think of schooling decisions as being made in a series of episodes where the decision maker can realistically go one way or another, even if certain choices are more likely than others. For example, in the middle of junior year, restless and unhappy, Angrist glumly considered his options: dropping out of high school and hopefully getting a job, staying in school but taking easy classes that would lead to a quick and dirty high school diploma, or plowing on in an academic track that would lead to college. Although the consequences of such choices are usually unknown in advance, the idea of alternative paths leading to alternative outcomes for a given individual seems uncontroversial. Philosophers have argued over whether this personal notion of potential outcomes is precise enough to be scientifically useful, but individual decision makers seem to have no trouble thinking about their lives and choices in this manner (as in Robert Frost's celebrated "The Road Not Taken": the traveler-narrator sees himself looking back on a moment of choice. He believes that the decision to follow the road less traveled "has made all the difference," though he also recognizes that counterfactual outcomes are unknowable).

In empirical work, the causal relationship between schooling and earnings tells us what people would earn, on average, if we could either change their schooling in a perfectly controlled environment or change their schooling randomly so that those with different levels of schooling would be otherwise comparable. As we discussed in chapter 2, experiments ensure that the causal variable of interest is independent of potential outcomes so that the groups being compared are truly comparable. Here, we would like to generalize this notion to causal variables that take on more than two values, and to more complicated situations where we must hold a variety of control variables fixed for causal inferences to be valid. This leads to the *conditional independence assumption* (CIA), a core assumption that provides the (sometimes implicit) justification for the causal interpretation of regression estimates. This assumption is also called selection on observables because the covariates to be held fixed are assumed to be known and observed (e.g., in Goldberger, 1972; Barnow, Cain, and Goldberger, 1981). The big question, therefore, is what these control variables are, or should be. We'll say more about that shortly. For now, we just do the econometric thing and call the covariates $X_i$. As far as the schooling problem goes, it seems natural to imagine that $X_i$ is a vector that includes measures of ability and family background.

For starters, think of schooling as a binary decision, such as whether Angrist goes to college. Denote this by a dummy variable, $c_i$. The causal relationship between college attendance and a future outcome such as earnings can be described using the same potential outcomes notation we used to describe experiments in chapter 2. To address this question, we imagine two potential earnings variables:

$$Potential\ outcome = \begin{cases} Y_{1i} & \text{if } c_i = 1 \\ Y_{0i} & \text{if } c_i = 0 \end{cases}.$$

In this case, $Y_{0i}$ is $i$'s earnings without college, while $Y_{1i}$ is $i$'s earnings if he goes. We would like to know the difference between $Y_{1i}$ and $Y_{0i}$, which is the causal effect of college attendance on individual $i$. This is what we would measure if we could go back in time and nudge $i$ onto the road not taken. The observed outcome, $Y_i$, can be written in terms of potential outcomes as

$$Y_i = Y_{0i} + (Y_{1i} - Y_{0i})C_i.$$

We get to see one of $Y_{1i}$ or $Y_{0i}$, but never both. We therefore hope to measure the average of $Y_{1i} - Y_{0i}$, or the average for some group, such as those who went to college. This is $E[Y_{1i} - Y_{0i}|C_i = 1]$.

In general, comparisons of those who do and don't go to college are likely to be a poor measure of the causal effect of college attendance. Following the logic in chapter 2, we have

$$\underbrace{E[Y_i|C_i = 1] - E[Y_i|C_i = 0]}_{\text{Observed difference in earnings}} = \underbrace{E[Y_{1i} - Y_{0i}|C_i = 1]}_{\text{Average treatment effect on the treated}}$$
$$+ \underbrace{E[Y_{0i}|C_i = 1] - E[Y_{0i}|C_i = 0]}_{\text{Selection bias}}.$$

$$(3.2.1)$$

It seems likely that those who go to college would have earned more anyway. If so, selection bias is positive and the naive comparison, $E[Y_i|C_i = 1] - E[Y_i|C_i = 0]$, exaggerates the benefits of college attendance.

The CIA asserts that conditional on observed characteristics, $X_i$, selection bias disappears. Formally, this means

$$\{Y_{0i}, Y_{1i}\} \perp\!\!\!\perp C_i | X_i, \qquad (3.2.2)$$

where the symbol "$\perp\!\!\!\perp$" denotes the independence relation and random variables to the right of the vertical bar are the conditioning set. Given the CIA, conditional-on-$X_i$ comparisons of average earnings across schooling levels have a causal interpretation. In other words,

$$E[Y_i|X_i, C_i = 1] - E[Y_i|X_i, C_i = 0] = E[Y_{1i} - Y_{0i}|X_i].$$

Now, we'd like to expand the conditional independence assumption to causal relations that involve variables that can take on more than two values, such as years of schooling, $s_i$.

The causal relationship between schooling and earnings is likely to be different for each person. We therefore use the individual-specific functional notation,

$$Y_{si} \equiv f_i(s),$$

to denote the potential earnings that person $i$ would receive after obtaining $s$ years of education. If $s$ takes on only two values, 12 and 16, then we are back to the college/no college example:

$$Y_{0i} = f_i(12); Y_{1i} = f_i(16).$$

More generally, the function $f_i(s)$ tells us what $i$ would earn for *any* value of schooling, $s$. In other words, $f_i(s)$ answers causal "what if" questions. In the context of theoretical models of the relationship between human capital and earnings, the form of $f_i(s)$ may be determined by aspects of individual behavior, by market forces, or both.

The CIA in this more general setup becomes

$$Y_{si} \perp\!\!\!\perp s_i | X_i, \text{ for all } s. \tag{CIA}$$

In many randomized experiments, the CIA crops up because $s_i$ *is* randomly assigned conditional on $X_i$ (in the Tennessee STAR experiment, for example, small classes were randomly assigned within schools). In an observational study, the CIA means that $s_i$ can be said to be "as good as randomly assigned," conditional on $X_i$.

Conditional on $X_i$, the *average causal effect* of a one-year increase in schooling is $E[f_i(s) - f_i(s-1)|X_i]$, while the average causal effect of a four-year increase in schooling is $E[f_i(s) - E[f_i(s-4)]|X_i]$. The data reveal only $Y_i = f_i(s_i)$, that is, $f_i(s)$ for $s = s_i$. But given the CIA, conditional-on-$X_i$ comparisons of average earnings across schooling levels have a causal interpretation. In other words,

$$E[Y_i|X_i, s_i = s] - E[Y_i|X_i, s_i = s - 1]$$
$$= E[f_i(s) - f_i(s-1)|X_i]$$

for any value of $s$. For example, we can compare the earnings of those with 12 and 11 years of schooling to learn about the average causal effect of high school graduation:

$$E[Y_i|X_i, s_i = 12] - E[Y_i|X_i, s_i = 11]$$
$$= E[f_i(12)|X_i, s_i = 12] - E[f_i(11)|X_i, s_i = 11].$$

This comparison has a causal interpretation because, given the CIA,

$$E[f_i(12)|X_i, s_i = 12] - E[f_i(11)|X_i, s_i = 11]$$
$$= E[f_i(12) - f_i(11)|X_i, s_i = 12].$$

Here, selection bias comes from differences in the potential dropout earnings of high school graduates and nongraduates. Given the CIA, however, high school graduation is independent of potential earnings conditional on $X_i$, so the selection bias vanishes. Note also that in this case, the causal effect of graduating from high school on high school graduates is equal to the average high school graduation effect at $X_i$:

$$E[f_i(12) - f_i(11)|X_i, s_i = 12] = E[f_i(12) - f_i(11)|X_i].$$

This is important, but less important than the elimination of selection bias.

So far, we have constructed separate causal effects for each value taken on by the conditioning variables. This leads to as many causal effects as there are values of $X_i$, an embarrassment of riches. Empiricists almost always find it useful to boil a set of estimates down to a single summary measure, such as the unconditional or overall average causal effect. By the law of iterated expectations, the unconditional average causal effect of high school graduation is

$$E\{E[Y_i|X_i, s_i = 12] - E[Y_i|X_i, s_i = 11]\} \qquad (3.2.3)$$
$$= E\{E[f_i(12) - f_i(11)|X_i]\}$$
$$= E[f_i(12) - f_i(11)]. \qquad (3.2.4)$$

In the same spirit, we might be interested in the average causal effect of high school graduation on high school graduates:

$$E\{E[Y_i|X_i, s_i = 12] - E[Y_i|X_i, s_i = 11]|s_i = 12\} \qquad (3.2.5)$$
$$= E\{E[f_i(12) - f_i(11)|X_i]|s_i = 12\}$$
$$= E[f_i(12) - f_i(11)|s_i = 12]. \qquad (3.2.6)$$

This parameter tells us how much high school graduates gained by virtue of having graduated. Likewise, for the effects of college graduation there is a distinction between $E[f_i(16) - f_i(12)|s_i = 16]$, the average causal effect on college graduates, and $E[f_i(16) - f_i(12)]$, the unconditional average effect.

The unconditional average effect, (3.2.3), can be computed by averaging all the $X$-specific effects weighted by the marginal distribution of $X_i$, while the average effect on high school or college graduates averages the $X$-specific effects weighted by the distribution of $X_i$ in these groups. In both cases, the empirical counterpart is a matching estimator: we make comparisons across schooling groups for individuals with the same covariate values, compute the difference in their average earnings, and then average these differences in some way.

In practice, there are many details to worry about when implementing a matching strategy. We fill in some of the technical details on the mechanics of matching in section 3.3.1. Here we note that a drawback of the matching approach is that it is not automatic; rather, it requires two steps, matching and averaging. Estimating the standard errors of the resulting estimates may not be straightforward, either. A third consideration is that the two-way contrast at the heart of this subsection (high school or college completers versus dropouts) does not do full justice to the problem at hand. Since $s_i$ takes on many values, there are separate average causal effects for each possible increment in $s_i$, which also must be summarized in some way.[13] These considerations lead us back to regression.

Regression provides an easy-to-use empirical strategy that automatically turns the CIA into causal effects. Two routes can be traced from the CIA to regression. One assumes that $f_i(s)$ is both linear in $s$ and the same for everyone except for an additive error term, in which case linear regression is a

---

[13]For example, we might construct the average effect over $s$ using the distribution of $s_i$. In other words, we estimate $E[f_i(s) - f_i(s-1)]$ for each $s$ by matching, and then compute the average difference

$$\sum E[f_i(s) - f_i(s-1)]P(s),$$

where $P(s)$ is the probability mass function for $s_i$. This is a discrete approximation to the average derivative, $E[f_i'(s_i)]$.

natural tool to estimate the features of $f_i(s)$. A more general but somewhat longer route recognizes that $f_i(s)$ almost certainly differs for different people, and moreover need not be linear in $s$. Even so, allowing for random variation in $f_i(s)$ across people and for nonlinearity for a given person, regression can be thought of as a strategy for the estimation of a weighted average of the individual-specific difference, $f_i(s) - f_i(s - 1)$. In fact, regression can be seen as a particular sort of matching estimator, capturing an average causal effect, much as (3.2.3) or (3.2.5) does.

At this point, we want to focus on the conditions required for regression to have a causal interpretation and not on the details of the regression-matching analog. We therefore start with the first route, a linear constant effects causal model. Suppose that

$$f_i(s) = \alpha + \rho s + \eta_i. \qquad (3.2.7)$$

In addition to being linear, this equation says that the functional relationship of interest is the same for everyone. Again, $s$ is written without an $i$ subscript, because equation (3.2.7) tells us what person $i$ would earn for any value of $s$, and not just the realized value, $s_i$. In this case, however, the only individual-specific and random part of $f_i(s)$ is a mean-zero error component, $\eta_i$, which captures unobserved factors that determine potential earnings.

Substituting the observed value $s_i$ for $s$ in equation (3.2.7), we have

$$Y_i = \alpha + \rho s_i + \eta_i. \qquad (3.2.8)$$

Equation (3.2.8) looks like a bivariate regression model, except that equation (3.2.7) explicitly associates the coefficients in (3.2.8) with a causal relationship. Importantly, because equation (3.2.7) is a causal model, $s_i$ may be correlated with potential outcomes, $f_i(s)$, or, in this case, the residual term in (3.2.8), $\eta_i$.

Suppose now that the CIA holds given a vector of observed covariates, $X_i$. In addition to the functional form assumption for potential outcomes embodied in (3.2.8), we decompose the random part of potential earnings, $\eta_i$, into a linear function of observable characteristics, $X_i$, and an error term, $v_i$:

$$\eta_i = X_i'\gamma + v_i,$$

where $\gamma$ is a vector of population regression coefficients that is assumed to satisfy $E[\eta_i|X_i] = X_i'\gamma$. Since $\gamma$ is defined by the regression of $\eta_i$ on $X_i$, the residual $v_i$ and $X_i$ are uncorrelated by construction. Moreover, by virtue of the CIA, we have

$$E[f_i(s)|X_i, s_i] = E[f_i(s)|X_i] = \alpha + \rho s + E[\eta_i|X]$$
$$= \alpha + \rho s + X_i'\gamma.$$

The residual in the linear causal model

$$Y_i = \alpha + \rho s_i + X_i'\gamma + v_i \qquad (3.2.9)$$

is therefore uncorrelated with the regressors, $s_i$ and $X_i$, and the regression coefficient $\rho$ is the causal effect of interest.

It bears emphasizing once again that the key assumption here is that the observable characteristics, $X_i$, are the only reason why $\eta_i$ and $s_i$ (equivalently, $f_i(s)$ and $s_i$) are correlated. This is the selection-on-observables assumption for regression models discussed over a quarter century ago by Barnow, Cain, and Goldberger (1981). It remains the basis of most empirical work in economics.

### 3.2.2    The Omitted Variables Bias Formula

In addition to the variable of interest, $s_i$, we have now introduced a set of control variables, $X_i$, into our regression. The omitted variables bias (OVB) formula describes the relationship between regression estimates in models with different sets of control variables. This important formula is often motivated by the notion that a longer regression—one with controls, such as (3.2.9)—has a causal interpretation, while a shorter regression does not. The coefficients on the variables included in the shorter regression are therefore said to be biased. In fact, the OVB formula is a mechanical link between coefficient vectors that applies to short and long regressions whether or not the longer regression is causal. Nevertheless, we follow convention and refer to the difference between the included coefficients in a long regression and a short regression as being determined by the OVB formula.

To make this discussion concrete, suppose the relevant set of control variables in the schooling regression can be boiled down to a combination of family background, intelligence, and motivation. Let these specific factors be denoted by a vector, $A_i$, which we refer to by the shorthand term "ability." The regression of wages on schooling, $s_i$, controlling for ability can be written as

$$Y_i = \alpha + \rho s_i + A_i'\gamma + e_i, \tag{3.2.10}$$

where $\alpha$, $\rho$, and $\gamma$ are population regression coefficients and $e_i$ is a regression residual that is uncorrelated with all regressors by definition. If the CIA applies given $A_i$, then $\rho$ can be equated with the coefficient in the linear causal model, (3.2.7), while the residual $e_i$ is the random part of potential earnings that is left over after controlling for $A_i$.

In practice, ability is hard to measure. For example, the American Current Population Survey (CPS), a large data set widely used in applied microeconomics (and the source of U.S. government data on unemployment rates), tells us nothing about adult respondents' family background, intelligence, or motivation. What are the consequences of leaving ability out of regression (3.2.10)? The resulting "short regression" coefficient is related to the "long regression" coefficient in equation (3.2.10) as follows:

OMITTED VARIABLES BIAS FORMULA

$$\frac{Cov(Y_i, s_i)}{V(s_i)} = \rho + \gamma'\delta_{As}, \tag{3.2.11}$$

where $\delta_{As}$ is the vector of coefficients from regressions of the elements of $A_i$ on $s_i$. To paraphrase, the OVB formula says:

> Short equals long plus the effect of omitted times the regression of omitted on included.

This formula is easy to derive: plug the long regression into the short regression formula, $\frac{Cov(Y_i, s_i)}{V(s_i)}$. Not surprisingly, the OVB formula is closely related to the regression anatomy formula, (3.1.3), from section 3.1.2. Both the OVB formula and the regression anatomy formula tell us that short and long regression coefficients are the same whenever the omitted and included variables are uncorrelated.[14]

We can use the OVB formula to get a sense of the likely consequences of omitting ability for schooling coefficients. Ability variables have positive effects on wages, and these variables are also likely to be positively correlated with schooling. The short regression coefficient may therefore be "too big" relative to what we want. On the other hand, as a matter of economic theory, the direction of the correlation between schooling and ability is not entirely clear. Some omitted variables may be negatively correlated with schooling, in which case the short regression coefficient may be too small.[15]

Table 3.2.1 illustrates these points using data from the NLSY. The first three entries in the table show that the schooling coefficient decreases from .132 to .114 when family background variables—in this case, parents' education—as well as a few basic demographic characteristics (age, race, census region of residence) are included as controls. Further control for individual ability, as proxied by the Armed Forces Qualification Test (AFQT) score, reduces the schooling coefficient to .087 (the AFQT is used by the military to select soldiers). The OVB formula tells us that these reductions are a result of the fact that the additional controls are positively correlated with both wages and schooling.[16]

---

[14] Here is the multivariate generalization of OVB: Let $\beta_1^s$ denote the coefficient vector on a $\kappa_1 \times 1$ vector of variables, $X_{1i}$ in a (short) regression that has no other variables, and let $\beta_1^l$ denote the coefficient vector on these variables in a (long) regression that includes a $\kappa_2 \times 1$ vector of additional variables, $X_{2i}$, with coefficient vector $\beta_2^l$. Then $\beta_1^s = \beta_1^l + E[X_{1i}X_{1i}']^{-1}E[X_{1i}X_{2i}']\beta_2^l$.

[15] As highly educated people, we like to think that ability and schooling are positively correlated. This is not a foregone conclusion, however: Mick Jagger dropped out of the London School of Economics and Bill Gates dropped out of Harvard, perhaps because the opportunity cost of schooling for these high-ability guys was high (of course, they may also be a couple of very lucky college dropouts).

[16] A large empirical literature investigates the consequences of omitting ability variables from schooling equations. Key early references include Griliches and Mason (1972), Taubman (1976), Griliches (1977), and Chamberlain (1978).

TABLE 3.2.1
Estimates of the returns to education for men in the NLSY

|  | (1) | (2) | (3) | (4) | (5) |
|---|---|---|---|---|---|
|  |  |  | Col. (2) and |  | Col. (4), with |
|  |  | Age | Additional | Col. (3) and | Occupation |
| Controls: | None | Dummies | Controls* | AFQT Score | Dummies |
|  | .132 | .131 | .114 | .087 | .066 |
|  | (.007) | (.007) | (.007) | (.009) | (.010) |

Notes: Data are from the National Longitudinal Survey of Youth (1979 cohort, 2002 survey). The table reports the coefficient on years of schooling in a regression of log wages on years of schooling and the indicated controls. Standard errors are shown in parentheses. The sample is restricted to men and weighted by NLSY sampling weights. The sample size is 2,434.

*Additional controls are mother's and father's years of schooling, and dummy variables for race and census region.

Although simple, the OVB formula is one of the most important things to know about regression. The importance of the OVB formula stems from the fact that if you claim an absence of omitted variables bias, then typically you're also saying that the regression you've got is the one you want. And the regression you want usually has a causal interpretation. In other words, you're prepared to lean on the CIA for a causal interpretation of the long regression estimates.

At this point, it's worth considering when the CIA is most likely to give a plausible basis for empirical work. The best-case scenario is random assignment of $s_i$, conditional on $X_i$, in some sort of (possibly natural) experiment. An example is the study of a mandatory retraining program for unemployed workers by Black et al. (2003). The authors of this study were interested in whether the retraining program succeeded in raising earnings later on. They exploited the fact that eligibility for the training program they studied was determined on the basis of personal characteristics and past unemployment and job histories. Workers were divided into groups on the basis of these characteristics. While some of these groups of workers were ineligible for training, workers in other groups were required to take training if they did not take a job. When some of the mandatory training groups contained more workers than training slots, training opportunities were distributed by lottery. Hence, training requirements were randomly assigned conditional on the covariates used to assign workers to groups. A regression on a dummy for training plus the personal characteristics, past unemployment variables, and job history variables used to classify workers seems very likely to provide reliable estimates of the causal effect of training.[17]

In the schooling context, there is usually no lottery that directly determines whether someone will go to college or finish high school.[18] Still, we might imagine subjecting individuals of similar ability and from similar family backgrounds to an experiment that encourages school attendance. The Education Maintenance Allowance, which pays British high school students in certain areas to attend school, is one such policy experiment (Dearden et al. 2003).

A second scenario that favors the CIA leans on detailed institutional knowledge regarding the process that determines $s_i$. An example is the Angrist (1998) study of the effect of voluntary military service on the later earnings of soldiers. This research asks whether men who volunteered for service in the U.S. armed forces were economically better off in the long run. Since voluntary military service is not randomly assigned, we can never know for sure. Angrist therefore used matching and regression techniques to control for observed differences between veterans and nonveterans who applied to the all-volunteer forces between 1979 and 1982. The motivation for a control strategy in this case is the fact that the military screens soldier applicants primarily on the basis of observable covariates like age, schooling, and test scores.

The CIA in Angrist (1998) amounts to the claim that after conditioning on all these observed characteristics, veterans and nonveterans are comparable. This assumption seems worth entertaining since, conditional on $X_i$, variation in veteran status in the Angrist (1998) study comes solely from the fact

---

[17]This program appears to raise earnings, primarily because workers offered training went back to work more quickly.

[18]Lotteries have been used to distribute private school tuition subsidies; see Angrist et al. (2002).

that some qualified applicants fail to enlist at the last minute. Of course, the considerations that lead a qualified applicant to "drop out" of the enlistment process could be related to earnings potential, so the CIA is clearly not guaranteed even in this case.

### 3.2.3   Bad Control

We've made the point that control for covariates can increase the likelihood that regression estimates have a causal interpretation. But more control is not always better. Some variables are bad controls and should not be included in a regression model even when their inclusion might be expected to change the short regression coefficients. Bad controls are variables that are themselves outcome variables in the notional experiment at hand. That is, bad controls might just as well be dependent variables too. Good controls are variables that we can think of as having been fixed at the time the regressor of interest was determined.

The essence of the bad control problem is a version of selection bias, albeit somewhat more subtle than the selection bias discussed in chapter 2 and section 3.2.1. To illustrate, suppose we are interested in the effects of a college degree on earnings and that people can work in one of two occupations, white collar and blue collar. A college degree clearly opens the door to higher-paying white collar jobs. Should occupation therefore be seen as an omitted variable in a regression of wages on schooling? After all, occupation is highly correlated with both education and pay. Perhaps it's best to look at the effect of college on wages for those within an occupation, say white collar only. The problem with this argument is that once we acknowledge the fact that college affects occupation, comparisons of wages by college degree status within an occupation are no longer apples-to-apples comparisons, *even* if college degree completion is randomly assigned.

Here is a formal illustration of the bad control problem in the college/occupation example.[19] Let $w_i$ be a dummy variable that denotes white collar workers and let $y_i$ denote earnings.

---

[19] The same problem arises in conditional-on-positive comparisons, discussed in detail in section 3.4.2.

The realization of these variables is determined by college graduation status and potential outcomes that are indexed against $c_i$. We have

$$Y_i = c_i Y_{1i} + (1 - c_i) Y_{0i}$$
$$w_i = c_i w_{1i} + (1 - c_i) w_{0i},$$

where $c_i = 1$ for college graduates and is zero otherwise, $\{Y_{1i}, Y_{0i}\}$ denotes potential earnings, and $\{w_{1i}, w_{0i}\}$ denotes potential white collar status. We assume that $c_i$ is randomly assigned, so it is independent of all potential outcomes. We have no trouble estimating the causal effect of $c_i$ on either $Y_i$ or $w_i$ since independence gives us

$$E[Y_i | c_i = 1] - E[Y_i | c_i = 0] = E[Y_{1i} - Y_{0i}],$$
$$E[w_i | c_i = 1] - E[w_i | c_i = 0] = E[w_{1i} - w_{0i}].$$

In practice, we can estimate these average treatment effects by regressing $Y_i$ and $w_i$ on $c_i$.

Bad control means that a comparison of earnings conditional on $w_i$ does not have a causal interpretation. Consider the difference in mean earnings between college graduates and others, conditional on working at a white collar job. We can compute this in a regression model that includes $w_i$ or by regressing $Y_i$ on $c_i$ in the sample where $w_i = 1$. The estimand in the latter case is the difference in means with $c_i$ switched off and on, conditional on $w_i = 1$:

$$E[Y_i | w_i = 1, c_i = 1] - E[Y_i | w_i = 1, c_i = 0]$$
$$= E[Y_{1i} | w_{1i} = 1, c_i = 1] - E[Y_{0i} | w_{0i} = 1, c_i = 0].$$
(3.2.12)

By the joint independence of $\{Y_{1i}, w_{1i}, Y_{0i}, w_{0i}\}$ and $c_i$, we have

$$E[Y_{1i} | w_{1i} = 1, c_i = 1] - E[Y_{0i} | w_{0i} = 1, c_i = 0]$$
$$= E[Y_{1i} | w_{1i} = 1] - E[Y_{0i} | w_{0i} = 1].$$

This expression illustrates the apples-to-oranges nature of the bad control problem:

$$E[Y_{1i} | w_{1i} = 1] - E[Y_{0i} | w_{0i} = 1]$$
$$= \underbrace{E[Y_{1i} - Y_{0i} | w_{1i} = 1]}_{\text{Causal effect}} + \underbrace{\{E[Y_{0i} | w_{1i} = 1] - E[Y_{0i} | w_{0i} = 1]\}}_{\text{Selection bias}}.$$

In other words, the difference in wages between those with and those without a college degree conditional on working in a white collar job equals the causal effect of college on those with $w_{1i} = 1$ (people who work at a white collar job when they have a college degree) and a selection bias term that reflects the fact that college changes the composition of the pool of white collar workers.

The selection bias in this context can be positive or negative, depending on the relation between occupational choice, college attendance, and potential earnings. The main point is that even if $Y_{1i} = Y_{0i}$, so that there is no causal effect of college on wages, the conditional comparison in (3.2.12) will not tell us this (the regression of $Y_i$ on $w_i$ and $c_i$ has exactly the same problem). It is also incorrect to say that the conditional comparison captures the part of the effect of college that is "not explained by occupation." In fact, the conditional comparison does not tell us much that is useful without a more elaborate model of the links between college, occupation, and earnings.[20]

As an empirical illustration, we see that the addition of two-digit occupation dummies indeed reduces the schooling coefficient in the NLSY models reported in table 3.2.1, in this case from .087 to .066. However, it's hard to say what we should make of this decline. The change in schooling coefficients when we add occupation dummies may simply be an artifact of selection bias. So we would do better to control only for variables that are not themselves caused by education.

A second version of the bad control scenario involves *proxy control*, that is, the inclusion of variables that might partially control for omitted factors but are themselves affected by the variable of interest. A simple version of the proxy control story goes like this: Suppose you are interested in a long regression,

---

[20] In this example, selection bias is probably negative, that is, $E[Y_{0i}|w_{1i} = 1]$ $< E[Y_{0i}|w_{0i} = 1]$. It seems reasonable to think that any college graduate can get a white collar job, so $E[Y_{0i}|w_{1i} = 1]$ is not too far from $E[Y_{0i}]$. But someone who gets a white collar job without benefit of a college degree (i.e., $w_{0i} = 1$) is probably special, that is, has a better than average $Y_{0i}$.

similar to (3.2.10),

$$Y_i = \alpha + \rho s_i + \gamma a_i + e_i, \qquad (3.2.13)$$

where for the purposes of this discussion we've replaced the vector of controls $A_i$ with a scalar ability measure $a_i$. Think of this as an IQ score that measures innate ability in eighth grade, before any relevant schooling choices are made (assuming everyone completes eighth grade). The error term in this equation satisfies $E[s_i e_i] = E[a_i e_i] = 0$ by definition. Since $a_i$ is measured before $s_i$ is determined, it is a good control.

Equation (3.2.13) is the regression of interest, but unfortunately, data on $a_i$ are unavailable. However, you have a second ability measure collected later, after schooling is completed (say, the score on a test used to screen job applicants). Call this variable *late ability*, $a_{li}$. In general, schooling increases late ability relative to innate ability. To be specific, suppose

$$a_{li} = \pi_0 + \pi_1 s_i + \pi_2 a_i. \qquad (3.2.14)$$

By this, we mean to say that both schooling and innate ability increase late or measured ability. There is almost certainly some randomness in measured ability as well, but we can make our point more simply via the deterministic link, (3.2.14).

You're worried about OVB in the regression of $Y_i$ on $s_i$ alone, so you propose to regress $Y_i$ on $s_i$ and late ability, $a_{li}$, since the desired control, $a_i$, is unavailable. Using (3.2.14) to substitute for $a_i$ in (3.2.13), the regression on $s_i$ and $a_{li}$ is

$$Y_i = \left(\alpha - \gamma \frac{\pi_0}{\pi_2}\right) + \left(\rho - \gamma \frac{\pi_1}{\pi_2}\right) s_i + \frac{\gamma}{\pi_2} a_{li} + e_i. \qquad (3.2.15)$$

In this scenario, $\gamma$, $\pi_1$, and $\pi_2$ are all positive, so $\rho - \gamma \frac{\pi_1}{\pi_2}$ is too small unless $\pi_1$ turns out to be zero. In other words, use of a proxy control that is increased by the variable of interest generates a coefficient below the desired effect. But it is important to note that $\pi_1$ can be investigated to some extent: if the regression of $a_{li}$ on $s_i$ is zero, you might feel better about assuming that $\pi_1$ is zero in (3.2.14).

There is an interesting ambiguity in the proxy control story that is not present in the first bad control story. Control for outcome variables is simply misguided; you do not want to control for occupation in a schooling regression if the regression is to have a causal interpretation. In the proxy control scenario, however, your intentions are good. And while proxy control does not generate the regression coefficient of interest, it may be an improvement on no control at all. Recall that the motivation for proxy control is equation (3.2.13). In terms of the parameters in this model, the OVB formula tells us that a regression on $s_i$ with no controls generates a coefficient of $\rho + \gamma \delta_{as}$, where $\delta_{as}$ is the slope coefficient from a regression of $a_i$ on $s_i$. The schooling coefficient in (3.2.15) might be closer to $\rho$ than the coefficient you estimate with no control at all. Moreover, assuming $\delta_{as}$ is positive, you can safely say that the causal effect of interest lies between these two.

One moral of both the bad control and the proxy control stories is that when thinking about controls, timing matters. Variables measured before the variable of interest was determined are generally good controls. In particular, because these variables were determined before the variable of interest, they cannot themselves be outcomes in the causal nexus. Often, however, the timing is uncertain or unknown. In such cases, clear reasoning about causal channels requires explicit assumptions about what happened first, or the assertion that none of the control variables are themselves caused by the regressor of interest.[21]

## 3.3    Heterogeneity and Nonlinearity

As we saw in the previous section, a linear causal model in combination with the CIA leads to a linear CEF with a causal interpretation. Assuming the CEF is linear, the population

---

[21]Griliches and Mason (1972) is a seminal exploration of the use of early and late ability controls in schooling equations. See also Chamberlain (1977, 1978) for closely related studies. Rosenbaum (1984) offers an alternative discussion of the proxy control idea using very different notation, outside a regression framework.

regression function is it. In practice, however, the assumption of a linear CEF is not really necessary for a causal interpretation of regression. For one thing, as discussed in section 3.1.2, we can think of the regression of $Y_i$ on $X_i$ and $s_i$ as providing the best linear approximation to the underlying CEF, regardless of its shape. Therefore, if the CEF is causal, the fact that regression approximates it gives regression coefficients a causal flavor. This claim is a little vague, however, and the nature of the link between regression and the CEF is worth exploring further. This exploration leads us to an understanding of regression as a computationally attractive matching estimator.

### 3.3.1    Regression Meets Matching

The past decade or two has seen increasing interest in matching as an empirical tool. Matching as a strategy to control for covariates is typically motivated by the CIA, as with causal regression in the previous section. For example, Angrist (1998) used matching to estimate the effects of voluntary military service on the later earnings of soldiers. These matching estimates have a causal interpretation assuming that, conditional on the individual characteristics the military uses to select soldiers (age, schooling, test scores), veteran status is independent of potential earnings. Matching estimators are appealingly simple: at bottom, matching amounts to covariate-specific treatment-control comparisons, weighted together to produce a single overall average treatment effect.

An attractive feature of matching strategies is that they are typically accompanied by an explicit statement of the conditional independence assumption required to give matching estimates a causal interpretation. At the same time, we have just seen that the causal interpretation of a regression coefficient is based on exactly the same assumption. In other words, matching and regression are both control strategies. Since the core assumption underlying causal inference is the same for the two strategies, it's worth asking whether or to what extent matching really differs from regression. Our view is that regression can be motivated as a particular sort of weighted matching estimator, and therefore the differences between regression and matching estimates are unlikely to be of major empirical importance.

To flesh out this idea, it helps to look more deeply into the mathematical structure of the matching and regressions *estimands*, that is, the population quantities that these methods attempt to estimate. For regression, of course, the estimand is a vector of population regression coefficients. The matching estimand is typically a weighted average of contrasts or comparisons across cells defined by covariates. This is easiest to see in the case of discrete covariates, as in the military service example, and for a discrete regressor such as veteran status, which we denote here by the dummy $D_i$. Since treatment takes on only two values, we can use the notation $Y_{1i}$ and $Y_{0i}$ to denote potential outcomes. A parameter of primary interest in this context is the average effect of treatment on the treated, $E[Y_{1i} - Y_{0i}|D_i = 1]$. This tells us the difference between the average earnings of soldiers, $E[Y_{1i}|D_i = 1]$, an observable quantity, and the counterfactual average earnings they would have obtained if they had not served, $E[Y_{0i}|D_i = 1]$. Simple comparisons of earnings by veteran status give a biased measure of the effect of treatment on the treated unless $D_i$ is independent of $Y_{0i}$. Specifically,

$$E[Y_i|D_i = 1] - E[Y_i|D_i = 0]$$
$$= E[Y_{1i} - Y_{0i}|D_i = 1] + \{E[Y_{0i}|D_i = 1] - E[Y_{0i}|D_i = 0]\}.$$

In other words, the observed earnings difference by veteran status equals the average effect of treatment on the treated plus selection bias. This parallels the discussion of selection bias in chapter 2.

The CIA in this context says that

$$\{Y_{0i}, Y_{1i}\} \perp\!\!\!\perp D_i|X_i.$$

Given the CIA, selection bias disappears after conditioning on $X_i$, so the effect of treatment on the treated can be constructed by iterating expectations over $X_i$:

$$\delta_{TOT} \equiv E[Y_{1i} - Y_{0i}|D_i = 1]$$
$$= E\{E[Y_{1i} - Y_{0i}|X_i, D_i = 1]|D_i = 1\}$$
$$= E\{E[Y_{1i}|X_i, D_i = 1] - E[Y_{0i}|X_i, D_i = 1]|D_i = 1\}.$$

Of course, $E[Y_{0i}|X_i, D_i = 1]$ is counterfactual. By virtue of the CIA, however,

$$E[Y_{0i}|X_i, D_i = 0] = E[Y_{0i}|X_i, D_i = 1].$$

Therefore,

$$\delta_{TOT} = E\{E[Y_{1i}|X_i, D_i = 1] - E[Y_{0i}|X_i, D_i = 0]|D_i = 1\}$$
$$= E[\delta_X|D_i = 1], \qquad (3.3.1)$$

where

$$\delta_X \equiv E[Y_i|X_i, D_i = 1] - E[Y_i|X_i, D_i = 0],$$

is the difference in mean earnings by veteran status at each value of $X_i$. At a particular value, say $X_i = x$, we write $\delta_x$.

The matching estimator in Angrist (1998) uses the fact that $X_i$ is discrete to construct the sample analog of the right-hand side of (3.3.1). In the discrete case, the matching estimand can be written

$$E[Y_{1i} - Y_{0i}|D_i = 1] = \sum_x \delta_x P(X_i = x|D_i = 1), \qquad (3.3.2)$$

where $P(X_i = x|D_i = 1)$ is the probability mass function for $X_i$ given $D_i = 1$.[22] In this case, $X_i$ takes on values determined by all possible combinations of year of birth, test score group, year of application to the military, and educational attainment at the time of application. The test score in this case is from the AFQT, used by the military to categorize the mental abilities of applicants (we included this as a control in the schooling regression discussed in section 3.2.2). The Angrist (1998) matching estimator replaces $\delta_X$ by the sample veteran-nonveteran earnings difference for each combination of covariates and then combines these in a weighted average using the empirical distribution of covariates among veterans.

---

[22]This matching estimator is discussed by Rubin (1977) and used by Card and Sullivan (1988) to estimate the effect of subsidized training on employment.

Note also that we can just as easily construct the unconditional average treatment effect,

$$\delta_{ATE} = E\{E[Y_{1i}|X_i, D_i = 1] - E[Y_{0i}|X_i, D_i = 0]\}$$

$$= \sum_x \delta_x P(X_i = x) = E[Y_{1i} - Y_{0i}]. \qquad (3.3.3)$$

This is the expectation of $\delta_X$ using the marginal distribution of $X_i$ instead of the distribution among the treated. $\delta_{TOT}$ tells us how much the typical *soldier* gained or lost as a consequence of military service, while $\delta_{ATE}$ tells us how much the typical *applicant* to the military gained or lost (since the Angrist, 1998, population consists of applicants.)

The U.S. military tends to be fairly picky about its soldiers, especially after downsizing at the end of the cold war. For the most part, the military now takes only high school graduates with test scores in the upper half of the test score distribution. Applicant screening therefore generates positive selection bias in naive comparisons of veteran and nonveteran earnings. This can be seen in table 3.3.1, which reports differences-in-means, matching, and regression estimates of the effect of voluntary military service on the 1988–91 Social Security–taxable earnings of men who applied to join the military between 1979 and 1982. The matching estimates were constructed from the sample analog of (3.3.2). Although white veterans earned $1,233 more than white nonveterans, this estimated veteran effect becomes negative once differences in covariates are matched away. Similarly, while nonwhite veterans earned $2,449 more than nonwhite nonveterans, controlling for covariates reduces this difference to $840.

Table 3.3.1 also shows regression estimates of the effect of voluntary military service, controlling for the same set of covariates that were used to construct the matching estimates. These are estimates of $\delta_R$ in the equation

$$Y_i = \sum_x d_{ix}\alpha_x + \delta_R D_i + e_i, \qquad (3.3.4)$$

where $d_{ix} = 1[X_i = x]$ is a dummy variable that indicates $X_i = x$, $\alpha_x$ is a regression effect for $X_i = x$ and $\delta_R$ is the

TABLE 3.3.1
Uncontrolled, matching, and regression estimates of the effects of voluntary
military service on earnings

| Race | Average Earnings in 1988–1991 (1) | Differences in Means by Veteran Status (2) | Matching Estimates (3) | Regression Estimates (4) | Regression Minus Matching (5) |
|------|------|------|------|------|------|
| Whites | 14,537 | 1,233.4 (60.3) | −197.2 (70.5) | −88.8 (62.5) | 108.4 (28.5) |
| Non-whites | 11,664 | 2,449.1 (47.4) | 839.7 (62.7) | 1,074.4 (50.7) | 234.7 (32.5) |

Notes: Adapted from Angrist (1998, tables II and V). Standard errors are reported in parentheses. The table shows estimates of the effect of voluntary military service on the 1988–91 Social Security–taxable earnings of men who applied to enter the armed forces between 1979 and 1982. The matching and regression estimates control for applicants' year of birth, education at the time of application, and AFQT score. There are 128,968 whites and 175,262 nonwhites in the sample.

regression estimand. Note that this regression model allows a separate parameter for every value taken on by the covariates. This model can therefore be said to be saturated-in-$X_i$, since it includes a parameter for every value of $X_i$. It is not fully saturated, however, because there is a single additive effect for $D_i$ with no $D_i \cdot X_i$ interactions.

Despite the fact that the matching and regression estimates control for the same variables, the regression estimates in table 3.3.1 are somewhat larger for nonwhites and less negative for whites. In fact, the differences between the matching and regression results are statistically significant. At the same time, the two estimation strategies present a broadly similar picture of the effects of military service. The reason the regression and matching estimates are similar is that regression, too, can be seen as a sort of matching estimator: the regression estimand differs from the matching estimands only in the weights used to combine the covariate-specific effects, $\delta_X$, into a single average effect. In particular, while matching uses the distribution of covariates among the treated to weight covariate-specific estimates into an estimate of the effect of treatment on the treated, regression produces a variance-weighted average of these effects.

To see this, start by using the regression anatomy formula to write the coefficient on $D_i$ in the regression of $Y_i$ on $X_i$ and $D_i$ as

$$\delta_R = \frac{Cov(Y_i, \tilde{D}_i)}{V(\tilde{D}_i)} \qquad (3.3.5)$$

$$= \frac{E[(D_i - E[D_i|X_i])Y_i]}{E[(D_i - E[D_i|X_i])^2]}$$

$$= \frac{E\{(D_i - E[D_i|X_i])E[Y_i|D_i, X_i]\}}{E[(D_i - E[D_i|X_i])^2]}. \qquad (3.3.6)$$

The second equality in this set of expressions uses the fact that saturating the model in $X_i$ means $E[D_i|X_i]$ is linear. Hence, $\tilde{D}_i$, which is defined as the residual from a regression of $D_i$ on $X_i$, is the difference between $D_i$ and $E[D_i|X_i]$. The third equality uses the fact that the regression of $Y_i$ on $D_i$ and $X_i$ is the same as the regression of $Y_i$ on $E[Y_i|D_i,X_i]$ (this we know from the regression CEF theorem, 3.1.6).

To simplify further, we expand the CEF, $E[Y_i|D_i,X_i]$, to get

$$E[Y_i|D_i, X_i] = E[Y_i|D_i = 0, X_i] + \delta_X D_i,$$

and then substitute for $E[Y_i|D_i,X_i]$ in the numerator of (3.3.6). This gives

$$E\{(D_i - E[D_i|X_i])E[Y_i|D_i, X_i]\}$$
$$= E\{(D_i - E[D_i|X_i])E[Y_i|D_i = 0, X_i]\}$$
$$+ E\{(D_i - E[D_i|X_i])D_i\delta_X\}.$$

The first term on the right-hand side is zero because $E[Y_i|D_i = 0,X_i]$ is a function of $X_i$ only and is therefore uncorrelated with $(D_i - E[D_i|X_i])$. Similarly, the second term simplifies to

$$E\{(D_i - E[D_i|X_i])D_i\delta_X\} = E\{(D_i - E[D_i|X_i])^2\delta_X\}.$$

At this point, we've shown

$$\delta_R = \frac{E[(D_i - E[D_i|X_i])^2 \delta_X]}{E[(D_i - E[D_i|X_i])^2]}$$

$$= \frac{E\{E[(D_i - E[D_i|X_i])^2|X_i]\delta_X\}}{E\{E[(D_i - E[D_i|X_i])^2|X_i]\}} = \frac{E[\sigma_D^2(X_i)\delta_X]}{E[\sigma_D^2(X_i)]}, \quad (3.3.7)$$

where

$$\sigma_D^2(X_i) \equiv E[(D_i - E[D_i|X_i])^2|X_i]$$

is the conditional variance of $D_i$ given $X_i$. This establishes that the regression model, (3.3.4), produces a treatment-variance weighted average of $\delta_X$.

Because the regressor of interest, $D_i$, is a dummy variable, one last step can be taken. In this case, $\sigma_D^2(X_i) = P(D_i = 1|X_i)(1 - P(D_i = 1|X_i))$, so

$$\delta_R = \frac{\sum_x \delta_x[P(D_i = 1|X_i = x)(1 - P(D_i = 1|X_i = x))]P(X_i = x)}{\sum_x [P(D_i = 1|X_i = x)(1 - P(D_i = 1|X_i = x))]P(X_i = x)}.$$

This shows that the regression estimand weights each covariate-specific treatment effect by $[P(X_i = x|D_i = 1)(1 - P(X_i = x|D_i = 1))]P(X_i = x)$. In contrast, the matching estimand for the effect of treatment on the treated can be written

$$E[Y_{1i} - Y_{0i}|D_i = 1] = \sum_x \delta_x P(X_i = x|D_i = 1)$$

$$= \frac{\sum_x \delta_x P(D_i = 1|X_i = x)P(X_i = x)}{\sum_x P(D_i = 1|X_i = x)P(X_i = x)},$$

using the fact that

$$P(X_i = x|D_i = 1) = \frac{P(D_i = 1|X_i = x) \cdot P(X_i = x)}{P(D_i = 1)}.$$

So the weights used to construct $E[Y_{1i} - Y_{0i}|D_i = 1]$ are proportional to the probability of treatment at each value of the covariates. The regression and matching weighting schemes therefore differ unless treatment is independent of covariates.

An important point coming out of this derivation is that the treatment-on-the-treated estimand puts the most weight on covariate cells containing those who are most likely to be treated. In contrast, regression puts the most weight on covariate cells where the conditional variance of treatment status is largest. As a rule, treatment variance is maximized when $P(D_i = 1|X_i = x) = \frac{1}{2}$, in other words, for cells where there are equal numbers of treated and control observations. The difference in weighting schemes is of little importance if $\delta_x$ does not vary across cells (though weighting still affects the statistical efficiency of estimators). In this example, however, men who were most likely to serve in the military appear to benefit least from their service. This is probably because those most likely to serve were most qualified and therefore also had the highest civilian earnings potential. This fact leads matching estimates of the effect of military service to be smaller than regression estimates based on the same vector of control variables.[23]

Also important is the fact that neither the regression nor the covariate-matching estimands give any weight to covariate cells that do not contain both treated and control observations. Consider a value of $X_i$, say $x^*$, where either no one is treated or everyone is treated. Then, $\delta_{x^*}$ is undefined, while the regression weights, $[P(D_i = 1|X_i = x^*)(1 - P(D_i = 1|X_i = x^*))]$, are zero. In the language of the econometric literature on matching, with saturated control for covariates both the regression and matching estimands impose *common support*, that is, they are limited to covariate values where both treated and control observations are found.[24]

---

[23] It's no surprise that regression gives the most weight to cells where $P(D_i = 1|X_i = x) = \frac{1}{2}$ since regression is efficient for a homoskedastic constant effects linear model. We should expect an efficient estimator to give the most weight to cells where the common treatment effect is estimated most precisely. With homoskedastic residuals, the most precise treatment effects come from cells where the probability of treatment equals $\frac{1}{2}$.

[24] The *support* of a random variable is the set of realizations that occur with positive probability. See Heckman, Ichimura, Smith, and Todd (1998) and Smith and Todd (2001) for a discussion of common support in matching.

The step from estimand to estimator is a little more complicated. In practice, both regression and matching estimators are implemented using modeling assumptions that implicitly involve a certain amount of extrapolation across cells. For example, matching estimators often combine covariate cells with few observations. This violates common support if the cells being combined do not all have both treated and nontreated observations. Regression models that are not saturated in $X_i$ may also violate common support, since covariate cells without both treated and control observations can end up contributing to the estimates by extrapolation. Here, too, however, we see a symmetry between the matching and regression strategies: they are in the same class, in principle, and require the same sort of compromises in practice.[25]

### Even More on Regression and Matching: Ordered and Continuous Treatments★

Does the quasi-matching interpretation of regression outlined above for a binary treatment variable apply to models with ordered and continuous treatments? The long answer is fairly technical and may be more than you want to know. The short answer is, to one degree or another, yes.

As we've already discussed, the population OLS slope vector always provides the MMSE linear approximation to the CEF. This, of course, works for ordered and continuous regressors as well as for binary. A related property is the fact that regression coefficients have an "average derivative" interpretation. In multivariate regression models, this interpretation is unfortunately complicated by the fact that the OLS slope vector is a matrix-weighted average of the gradient of the

[25]Matching problems involving finely distributed $X$-variables are often solved by aggregating values to make coarser groupings or by pairing observations that have similar, though not necessarily identical, values. See Cochran (1965), Rubin (1973), or Rosenbaum (1995, chapter 3) for discussions of this approach. With continuously distributed covariates, matching estimators are biased because matches are imperfect. Abadie and Imbens (2008) have recently shown that a regression-based bias correction can eliminate the (asymptotic) bias from imperfect matches.

CEF. Matrix-weighted averages are difficult to interpret except in special cases (see Chamberlain and Leamer, 1976). An important special case when the average derivative property is relatively straightforward is in regression models for an ordered or continuous treatment with a saturated model for covariates. To avoid lengthy derivations, we simply explain the formulas. A derivation is sketched in the appendix to this chapter. For additional details, see the appendix to Angrist and Krueger (1999).

For the purposes of this discussion, the treatment intensity, $s_i$, is assumed to be a continuously distributed random variable, not necessarily non-negative. Suppose that the CEF of interest can be written $h(t) \equiv E[Y_i|s_i = t]$ with derivative $h'(t)$. Then

$$\frac{E[Y_i(s_i - E[s_i])]}{E[s_i(s_i - E[s_i])]} = \frac{\int h'(t)\mu_t dt}{\int \mu_t dt}, \qquad (3.3.8)$$

where

$$\mu_t \equiv \{E[s_i|s_i \geq t] - E[s_i|s_i < t]\}\{P(s_i \geq t)[1 - P(s_i \geq t)]\}, \qquad (3.3.9)$$

and the integrals in (3.3.8) run over the possible values of $s_i$. This formula (derived by Yitzhaki, 1996) weights each possible value of $s_i$ in proportion to the difference in the conditional mean of $s_i$ above and below that value. More weight is also given to points close to the median of $s_i$, since $P(s_i \geq t) \cdot [1 - P(s_i \geq t)]$ is maximized there.

With covariates, $X_i$, the weights in (3.3.8) become $X$-specific. A covariate-averaged version of the same formula applies to the multivariate regression coefficient of $Y_i$ on $s_i$, after partialing out $X_i$. In particular,

$$\frac{E[Y_i(s_i - E[s_i|X_i])]}{E[s_i(s_i - E[s_i|X_i])]} = \frac{E[\int h'_X(t)\mu_{tX}dt]}{E[\int \mu_{tX}dt]}, \qquad (3.3.10)$$

where $h'_X(t) \equiv \frac{\partial E[Y_i|X_i, s_i = t]}{\partial t}$ and

$$\mu_{tX} \equiv \{E[s_i|X_i, s_i \geq t] - E[s_i|X_i, s_i < t]\}$$
$$\times \{P(s_i \geq t|X_i)[1 - P(s_i \geq t|X_i)]\}.$$

Equation (3.3.10) reflects two types of averaging: an integral that averages *along* the length of a nonlinear CEF at fixed covariate values, and an expectation that averages *across* covariate cells. An important point in this context is that population regression coefficients contain no information about the effect of $s_i$ on the CEF for values of $X_i$ where $P(s_i \geq t|X_i)$ equals zero or one. This includes values of $X_i$ where $s_i$ is fixed. It's also worth noting that if $s_i$ is a dummy variable, we can extract equation (3.3.7) from the more general formula, (3.3.10).

Angrist and Krueger (1999) constructed the average weighting function for a schooling regression with state of birth and year of birth covariates. Although equations (3.3.8) and (3.3.10) may seem arcane or at least nonobvious, in this example the average weights, $E[\mu_{tX}]$, turn out to be a reasonably smooth symmetric function of $t$, centered at the mode of $s_i$.

The implications of (3.3.8) or (3.3.10) can be explored further given a model for the distribution of regressors. Suppose, for example, that $s_i$ is normally distributed. Let $z_i = \frac{s_i - E(s_i)}{\sigma_s}$, where $\sigma_s$ is the standard deviation of $s_i$, so that $z_i$ is standard normal. Then

$$E[s_i|s_i \geq t] = E(s_i) + \sigma_s E\left[z_i | z_i \geq \frac{t - E(s_i)}{\sigma_s}\right]$$
$$= E(s_i) + \sigma_s E[z_i|z_i \geq t^*].$$

From truncated normal formulas (see, e.g., Johnson and Kotz, 1970), we know that

$$E[z_i|z_i > t^*] = \frac{\phi(t^*)}{[1 - \Phi(t^*)]} \quad \text{and} \quad E[z_i|z_i < t^*] = \frac{-\phi(t^*)}{\Phi(t^*)}.$$

where $\phi(\cdot)$ and $\Phi(\cdot)$ are the standard normal density and distribution functions. Substituting in the formula for $\mu_t$, (3.3.9), we have

$$\mu_t = \sigma_s \left\{ \frac{\phi(t^*)}{[1 - \Phi(t^*)]} - \frac{-\phi(t^*)}{\Phi(t^*)} \right\} [1 - \Phi(t^*)]\Phi(t^*) = \sigma_s \phi(t^*).$$

We have therefore shown that

$$\frac{Cov(Y_i, s_i)}{V(s_i)} = E[h'(s_i)].$$

In other words, when $s_i$ is normal, the regression of $Y_i$ on $s_i$ is the unconditional average derivative, $E[h'(s_i)]$. Of course, this result is a special case of a special case.[26] Still, it seems reasonable to imagine that normality might not matter very much. And in our empirical experience, the average derivatives (also called "marginal effects") constructed from parametric nonlinear models (e.g., probit or Tobit) are usually indistinguishable from the corresponding regression coefficients, regardless of the distribution of regressors. We expand on this point in section 3.4.2.

### 3.3.2    Control for Covariates Using the Propensity Score

The most important result in regression theory is the OVB formula, which tells us that coefficients on included variables are unaffected by the omission of variables when the variables omitted are uncorrelated with the variables included. The propensity score theorem, due to Rosenbaum and Rubin (1983), extends this idea to estimation strategies that rely on matching instead of regression, where the causal variable of interest is a treatment dummy.[27]

The propensity score theorem says that if potential outcomes are independent of treatment status conditional on a multivariate covariate vector $X_i$, then potential outcomes are independent of treatment status conditional on a scalar function of covariates, the propensity score, defined as $p(X_i) \equiv E[D_i|X_i] = P[D_i = 1|X_i]$. Formally, we have the following theorem:

**Theorem 3.3.1** *The Propensity Score Theorem.*
*Suppose the CIA holds such that* $\{Y_{0i}, Y_{1i}\} \perp\!\!\!\perp D_i|X_i$. *Then* $\{Y_{0i}, Y_{1i}\} \perp\!\!\!\perp D_i|p(X_i)$.

---

[26] Other specialized results in this spirit appear in Yitzhaki (1996) and Ruud (1986), who considers distribution-free estimation of limited-dependent-variable models.

[27] Propensity score methods can be adapted to multivalued treatments, though this has yet to catch on. See Imbens (2000) for an effort in this direction.

**Proof.** It's enough to show that $P[D_i = 1 | Y_{ji}, p(X_i)]$ does not depend on $Y_{ji}$ for $j = 0, 1$:

$$\begin{aligned}
P[D_i = 1 | Y_{ji}, p(X_i)] &= E[D_i | Y_{ji}, p(X_i)] \\
&= E\{E[D_i | Y_{ji}, p(X_i), X_i] | Y_{ji}, p(X_i)\} \\
&= E\{E[D_i | Y_{ji}, X_i] | Y_{ji}, p(X_i)\} \\
&= E\{E[D_i | X_i] | Y_{ji}, p(X_i)\}, \text{by the CIA.}
\end{aligned}$$

But $E\{E[D_i | X_i] | Y_{ji}, p(X_i)\} = E\{p(X_i) | Y_{ji}, p(X_i)\}$, which is clearly just $p(X_i)$.

Like the OVB formula for regression, the propensity score theorem says that you need only control for covariates that affect the probability of treatment. But it also says something more: the only covariate you really need to control for is the probability of treatment itself. In practice, the propensity score theorem is usually used for estimation in two steps: first, $p(X_i)$ is estimated using some kind of parametric model, say, logit or probit. Then estimates of the effect of treatment are computed either by matching on the estimated score from this first step or using a weighting scheme described below (see Imbens, 2004, for an overview).

Direct propensity score matching works in the same way as covariate matching except that we match on the score instead of the covariates directly. By the propensity score theorem and the CIA,

$$\begin{aligned}
E[Y_{1i} - Y_{0i} | D_i = 1] & \\
= E\{E[Y_i | p(X_i), D_i = 1] &- E[Y_i | p(X_i), D_i = 0] | D_i = 1\}.
\end{aligned}$$

Estimates of the effect of treatment on the treated can therefore be obtained by stratifying on an estimate of $p(X_i)$ and substituting conditional sample averages for expectations or by matching each treated observation to controls with similar values of the propensity score (both of these approaches were used by Dehejia and Wahba, 1999). Alternatively, a model-based or nonparametric estimate of $E[Y_i | p(X_i), D_i]$ can be substituted for these conditional mean functions and the outer expectation replaced with a sum (as in Heckman, Ichimura, and Todd, 1998).

The somewhat niftier weighting approach to propensity score estimation skips the cumbersome matching step by exploiting the fact that the CIA implies $E\left[\frac{Y_i D_i}{p(X_i)}\right] = E[Y_{1i}]$ and $E\left[\frac{Y_i(1-D_i)}{(1-p(X_i))}\right] = E[Y_{0i}].$[28] Therefore, given a scheme for estimating $p(X_i)$, we can construct estimates of the average treatment effect from the sample analog of

$$E[Y_{1i} - Y_{0i}] = E\left[\frac{Y_i D_i}{p(X_i)} - \frac{Y_i(1 - D_i)}{1 - p(X_i)}\right]$$

$$= E\left[\frac{(D_i - p(X_i))Y_i}{p(X_i)(1 - p(X_i))}\right]. \qquad (3.3.11)$$

This last expression is an estimand of the form suggested by Newey (1990) and Robins, Mark, and Newey (1992). We can similarly calculate the effect of treatment on the treated from the sample analog of:

$$E[Y_{1i} - Y_{0i}|D_i = 1] = E\left[\frac{(D_i - p(X_i))Y_i}{(1 - p(X_i))P(D_i = 1)}\right]. \qquad (3.3.12)$$

The idea that you can correct for nonrandom sampling via weighting by the reciprocal of the probability of selection dates back to Horvitz and Thompson (1952). Of course, to make this approach feasible, and for the resulting estimates to be consistent, we need a consistent estimator of $p(X_i)$.

The Horvitz-Thompson version of the propensity score approach is appealing, since the estimator is essentially automated, with no cumbersome matching required. The Horvitz-Thompson approach also highlights the close link between propensity score matching and regression, much as discussed for covariate matching in section 3.3.1. Consider again the regression estimand, $\delta_R$, for the population regression of $Y_i$ on $D_i$, controlling for a saturated model for covariates. This estimand can be written

$$\delta_R = \frac{E[(D_i - p(X_i))Y_i]}{E[p(X_i)(1 - p(X_i))]}. \qquad (3.3.13)$$

---

[28]To see this, iterate over $X_i$: $E\left[\frac{Y_i D_i}{p(X_i)}\right] = E\left\{E\left[\frac{Y_i D_i}{p(X_i)}|X_i\right]\right\}$; $E\left[\frac{Y_i D_i}{p(X_i)}|X_i\right] = \frac{E[Y_i|D_i=1,X_i]p(X_i)}{p(X_i)} = E[Y_{1i}|D_i = 1, X_i] = E[Y_{1i}|X_i].$

The two Horvitz-Thompson matching estimands, (3.3.11) and (3.3.12), and the regression estimand are all in the class of weighted average estimands considered by Hirano, Imbens, and Ridder (2003):

$$E\left\{g(X_i)\left[\frac{Y_i D_i}{p(X_i)} - \frac{Y_i(1-D_i)}{(1-p(X_i))}\right]\right\}, \qquad (3.3.14)$$

where $g(X_i)$ is a known weighting function. (To go from estimand to estimator, replace $p(X_i)$ with a consistent estimator and replace expectations with sums.) For the average treatment effect, set $g(X_i) = 1$; for the effect on the treated, set $g(X_i) = \frac{p(X_i)}{P(D_i=1)}$; and for regression, set

$$g(X_i) = \frac{p(X_i)(1-p(X_i))}{E[p(X_i)(1-p(X_i))]}.$$

This similarity highlights once again the fact that regression and matching—including propensity score matching—are not really different animals, at least not until we specify a model for the propensity score.

A big question here is how best to model and estimate $p(X_i)$, or how much smoothing or stratification to use when estimating $E[Y_i|p(X_i), D_i]$, especially if the covariates are continuous. The regression analog of this question is how to parameterize the control variables (e.g., polynomials or main effects and interaction terms if the covariates are coded as discrete). The answer to this is inherently application-specific. A growing empirical literature suggests that a logit model for the propensity score with a few polynomial terms in continuous covariates works well in practice, though this cannot be a theorem, and inevitably, some experimentation will be required (see, e.g., Dehejia and Wahba, 1999).[29]

A developing theoretical literature has produced some thought-provoking theorems on the efficient use of the propensity score. First, from the point of view of asymptotic efficiency, there is usually a cost to matching on the propensity

[29] Andrea Ichino and Sascha Becker have posted Stata programs that implement various matching estimators; see Becker and Ichino (2002).

score instead of full covariate matching. We can get lower asymptotic standard errors by matching on any covariate that explains outcomes, whether or not it turns up in the propensity score. This we know from Hahn's (1998) investigation of the maximal precision of estimates of treatment effects under the CIA, with and without knowledge of the propensity score. For example, in Angrist (1998), there is an efficiency gain from matching on year of birth, even if the probability of serving in the military is unrelated to birth year, because earnings are related to birth year. A regression analog for this point is the result that even in a scenario with no OVB, the long regression generates more precise estimates of the coefficients on the variables included in a short regression whenever the omitted variables have some predictive power for outcomes (see section 3.1.3).

Hahn's (1998) results raise the question of why we should ever bother with estimators that use the propensity score. A philosophical argument is that the propensity score rightly focuses researcher attention on models for treatment assignment, something about which we may have reasonably good information, instead of the typically more complex and mysterious process determining outcomes. This view seems especially compelling when treatment assignment is the product of human institutions or government regulations, while the process determining outcomes is more anonymous (e.g., a market). For example, in a time series evaluation of the causal effects of monetary policy, Angrist and Kuersteiner (2004) argue that we know more about how the Federal Reserve sets interest rates than about the process determining GDP. In the same spirit, it may also be easier to validate a model for treatment assignment than to validate a model for outcomes (see Rosenbaum and Rubin, 1985, for a version of this argument).

A more precise though purely statistical argument for using the propensity score is laid out in Angrist and Hahn (2004). This paper shows that even though there is no *asymptotic* efficiency gain from the use of estimators based on the propensity score, there will often be a gain in precision in finite samples. Since all real data sets are finite, this result is empirically relevant. Intuitively, if the covariates omitted from the propensity score explain little of the variation in outcomes (in a purely statistical sense), it may be better to ignore them than to bear the statistical burden imposed by the need to estimate their effects. This is easy to see in studies using data sets such as the NLSY, where there are hundreds of covariates that might predict outcomes. In practice, we focus on a small subset of all possible covariates. This subset is usually chosen with an eye to what predicts treatment.

Finally, Hirano, Imbens, and Ridder (2003) provide an alternative asymptotic resolution of the "propensity score paradox" generated by Hahn's (1998) theorems. They show that even though estimates of treatment effects based on a known propensity score are inefficient, for models with continuous covariates, a Horvitz-Thompson-type weighting estimator is efficient when the weighting scheme uses a *nonparametric* estimate of the score. The facts that the propensity score is estimated and that it is estimated nonparametrically are both key for the Hirano, Imbens, and Ridder conclusions.

Do the Hirano, Imbens, and Ridder (2003) results resolve the propensity score paradox? For the moment, we prefer the finite-sample resolution given by Angrist and Hahn (2004). The latter result highlights the fact that it is the researchers' willingness to impose restrictions on the score that gives propensity score-based inference its conceptual and statistical power. In Angrist (1998), for example, an application with high-dimensional though discrete covariates, the unrestricted nonparametric estimator of the score is just the empirical probability of treatment in each covariate cell. With this nonparametric estimator plugged in for $p(X_i)$, it is straightforward to show that the sample analogs of (3.3.11) and (3.3.12) are algebraically equivalent to the corresponding full-covariate matching estimators. Hence, it's no surprise that score-based estimation comes out efficient, since full-covariate matching is the asymptotically efficient benchmark. An essential element of propensity score methods is the use of prior knowledge for dimension reduction. The statistical payoff is an improvement in finite-sample behavior. If you're not prepared to smooth, restrict, or otherwise reduce the dimensionality of the matching problem in a manner that has real empirical consequences, then you might as well go for full covariate matching or saturated regression control.

### 3.3.3  Propensity Score Methods versus Regression

Propensity score methods shift attention from the estimation of $E[Y_i|X_i,D_i]$ to the estimation of the propensity score, $p(X_i) \equiv E[D_i|X_i]$. This is attractive in applications where the latter is easier to model or motivate. For example, Ashenfelter (1978) showed that participants in government-funded training programs often have suffered a marked preprogram dip in earnings, a pattern found in many later studies. If this dip is the only thing that makes trainees special, then we can estimate the causal effect of training on earnings by controlling for past earnings dynamics. In practice, however, it's hard to match on earnings dynamics since earnings histories are both continuous and multidimensional. Dehejia and Wahba (1999) argue in this context that the causal effects of training programs are better estimated by conditioning on the propensity score than by conditioning on the earnings histories themselves.

The propensity score estimates reported by Dehejia and Wahba are remarkably close to the estimates from the randomized trial that constitute their benchmark. Nevertheless, we believe regression should be the starting point for most empirical projects. This is not a theorem; undoubtedly, there are circumstances in which propensity score matching provides more reliable estimates of average causal effects. The first reason we don't find ourselves on the propensity score bandwagon is practical: there are many details to be filled in when implementing propensity score matching, such as how to model the score and how to do inference; these details are not yet standardized. Different researchers might therefore reach very different conclusions, even when using the same data and covariates. Moreover, as we've seen with the Horvitz-Thompson estimands, there isn't very much theoretical daylight between regression and propensity score weighting. If the regression model for covariates is fairly flexible, say, close to saturated, regression can be seen as a type of propensity score weighting, so the difference is mostly in the implementation. In practice you may be far from saturation, but with the right covariates this shouldn't matter.

The face-off between regression and propensity score matching is illustrated here using the same National Supported Work (NSW) sample featured in Dehejia and Wahba (1999).[30] The NSW is a mid-1970s program that provided work experience to recipients with weak labor force attachment. Somewhat unusually for its time, the NSW was evaluated in a randomized trial. Lalonde's (1986) pathbreaking analysis compared the results from the NSW randomized study to econometric results using nonexperimental control groups drawn from the PSID and the CPS. He came away pessimistic because plausible non-experimental methods generated a wide range of results, many of which were far from the experimental estimates. More-over, Lalonde argued, an objective investigator, not knowing the results of the randomized trial, would be unlikely to pick the best econometric specifications and observational control groups.

In a striking second take on the Lalonde (1986) findings, Dehejia and Wahba (1999) found they could come close to the NSW experimental results by matching the NSW treatment group to observational control groups selected using the propensity score. They demonstrated this using various comparison groups. Following Dehejia and Wahba (1999), we look again at two of the CPS comparison groups, first, a largely unselected sample (CPS-1), and then a narrower comparison group selected from the recently unemployed (CPS-3).

Table 3.3.2 (columns 1–4 of which are a replication of table 1 in Dehejia and Wahba, 1999) reports descriptive statistics for the NSW treatment group, the randomly selected NSW control group, and our two observational control groups. The NSW treatment group and the randomly selected NSW control groups are younger, less educated, more likely to be nonwhite, and have much lower earnings than the general population represented by the CPS-1 sample. The CPS-3 sample matches the NSW treatment group more closely but still shows

[30] A more extended propensity-score face-off appears in the exchange between Smith and Todd (2005) and Dehejia (2005).

TABLE 3.3.2
Covariate means in the NSW and observational control samples

|  | NSW | | Full Comparison Samples | | P-Score Screened Comparison Samples | |
|---|---|---|---|---|---|---|
| Variable | Treated (1) | Control (2) | CPS-1 (3) | CPS-3 (4) | CPS-1 (5) | CPS-3 (6) |
| Age | 25.82 | 25.05 | 33.23 | 28.03 | 25.63 | 25.97 |
| Years of schooling | 10.35 | 10.09 | 12.03 | 10.24 | 10.49 | 10.42 |
| Black | .84 | .83 | .07 | .20 | .96 | .52 |
| Hispanic | .06 | .11 | .07 | .14 | .03 | .20 |
| Dropout | .71 | .83 | .30 | .60 | .60 | .63 |
| Married | .19 | .15 | .71 | .51 | .26 | .29 |
| 1974 earnings | 2,096 | 2,107 | 14,017 | 5,619 | 2,821 | 2,969 |
| 1975 earnings | 1,532 | 1,267 | 13,651 | 2,466 | 1,950 | 1,859 |
| Number of obs. | 185 | 260 | 15,992 | 429 | 352 | 157 |

Notes: Adapted from Dehejia and Wahba (1999), table 1. The samples in the first four columns are as described in Dehejia and Wahba (1999). The samples in the last two columns are limited to comparison group observations with a propensity score between .1 and .9. Propensity score estimates use all the covariates listed in the table.

some differences, particularly in terms of race and preprogram earnings.

Table 3.3.3 reports estimates of the NSW treatment effect. The dependent variable is annual earnings in 1978, a year or two after treatment. Rows of the table show results with alternative sets of controls: none; all the demographic variables in table 3.3.2; lagged (1975) earnings; demographics plus lagged earnings; demographics and two lags of earnings. All estimates are from regressions of 1978 earnings on a treatment dummy plus controls (the raw treatment-control difference appears in the first row).

Estimates using the experimental control group, reported in column 1, are on the order of $1,600–1,800. Not surprisingly, these estimates vary little across specifications. In contrast, the raw earnings gap between NSW participants and the CPS-1 sample, reported in column 2, is roughly −$8,500, suggesting this comparison is heavily contaminated by selection bias.

TABLE 3.3.3
Regression estimates of NSW training effects
using alternative controls

| Specification | Full Comparison Samples | | | P-Score Screened Comparison Samples | |
| --- | --- | --- | --- | --- | --- |
| | NSW (1) | CPS-1 (2) | CPS-3 (3) | CPS-1 (4) | CPS-3 (5) |
| Raw difference | 1,794 (633) | −8,498 (712) | −635 (657) | | |
| Demographic controls | 1,670 (639) | −3,437 (710) | 771 (837) | −3,361 (811) [139/497] | 890 (884) [154/154] |
| 1975 earnings | 1,750 (632) | −78 (537) | −91 (641) | No obs. [0/0] | 166 (644) [183/427] |
| Demographics, 1975 earnings | 1,636 (638) | 623 (558) | 1,010 (822) | 1,201 (722) [149/357] | 1,050 (861) [157/162] |
| Demographics, 1974 and 1975 earnings | 1,676 (639) | 794 (548) | 1,369 (809) | 1,362 (708) [151/352] | 649 (853) [147/157] |

Notes: The table reports regression estimates of training effects using the Dehejia-Wahba (1999) data with alternative sets of controls. The demographic controls are age, years of schooling, and dummies for black, Hispanic, high school dropout, and married. Standard errors are reported in parentheses. Observation counts are reported in brackets [treated/control]. There are no observations with an estimated propensity score in the interval [.1, .9] using only 1975 earnings as a covariate with CPS-1 data.

The addition of demographic controls and lagged earnings narrows the gap considerably; the estimated treatment effect reaches (positive) $800 in the last row. The results are even better in column 3, which uses the narrower CPS-3 comparison group. The characteristics of this group are much closer to those of NSW participants; consistent with this, the raw earnings difference is only −$635. The fully controlled estimate, reported in the last row, is close to $1,400, not far from the experimental treatment effect.

A drawback of the process taking us from CPS-1 to CPS-3 is the ad hoc nature of the rules used to construct the smaller and more carefully selected CPS-3 comparison group. The CPS-3 selection criteria can be motivated by the NSW program rules, which favor individuals with low earnings and weak labor-force attachment, but in practice, there are many ways to implement this. We'd therefore like a more systematic approach to prescreening. In a recent paper, Crump, Hotz, Imbens, and Mitnik (2009) suggest that the propensity score be used for systematic sample selection as a precursor to regression estimation. This contrasts with our earlier discussion of the propensity score as the basis for an estimator.

We implemented the Crump et al. (2009) suggestion by first estimating the propensity score on a pooled NSW-treatment and observational-comparison sample, and then picking only those observations with $0.1 < p(X_i) < 0.9$. In other words, the estimation sample is limited to observations with a predicted probability of treatment equal to at least 10 percent but no more than 90 percent. This ensures that regressions are estimated in a sample including only covariate cells where there are at least a few treated and control observations. Estimation using screened samples therefore requires no extrapolation to cells without "common support"—in other words, to cells where there is no overlap in the covariate distribution between treatment and controls. Descriptive statistics for samples screened on the score (estimated using the full set of covariates listed in the table) appear in the last two columns of table 3.3.2. The covariate means in the screened CPS-1 and CPS-3 samples are much closer to the NSW means in column 1 than are the covariate means from unscreened samples.

We explored the common support screener further using alternative sets of covariates, but with the same covariates used for both screening and the estimation of treatment effects at each iteration. The resulting estimates are displayed in the final two columns of table 3.3.3. Controlling for demographic variables or lagged earnings alone, these results differ little from those in columns 2 and 3. With both demographic variables and a single lag of earnings as controls, however, the screened CPS-1 estimates are quite a bit closer to the experimental estimates than are the unscreened results. Screened CPS-1 estimates with two lags of earnings are also close to the experimental benchmark. On the other hand, the common support screener improves the CPS-3 results only slightly with a single lag of earnings and seems to be a step backward with two.

This investigation boosts our (already strong) faith in regression. Regression control for the right covariates does a reasonably good job of eliminating selection bias in the CPS-1 sample despite a huge baseline gap. Restricting the sample using our knowledge of program admissions criteria yields even better regression estimates with CPS-3, about as good as Dehejia and Wahba's (1999) propensity score matching results with two lags of earnings. Systematic prescreening to enforce common support seems like a useful adjunct to regression estimation with CPS-1, a large and coarsely selected initial sample. The estimates in screened CPS-1 are as good as unscreened CPS-3. We note, however, that the standard errors for estimates using propensity score–screened samples have not been adjusted to reflect the sampling variance in our estimates of the score. An advantage of prescreening using prior information, as in the step from CPS-1 to CPS-3, is that no such adjustment is necessary.

## 3.4    Regression Details

### 3.4.1    Weighting Regression

Few things are as confusing to applied researchers as the role of sample weights. Even now, 20 years post-Ph.D., we read the section of the Stata manual on weighting with some dismay. Weights can be used in a number of ways, and how they are used may well matter for your results. Regrettably, however, the case for or against weighting is often less than clear-cut, as are the specifics of how the weights should be programmed. A detailed discussion of weighting pros and cons is beyond the scope of this book. See Pfefferman (1993) and Deaton (1997) for two perspectives. In this brief subsection, we provide a few guidelines and a rationale for our approach to weighting.

A simple rule of thumb for weighting regression is to use weights when they make it more likely that the regression you are estimating is close to the population target you are trying to estimate. If, for example, the target (or estimand) is the population regression function, and the sample to be used for estimation is nonrandom with sampling weights, $w_i$, equal to the inverse probability of sampling observation $i$, then it makes sense to use weighted least squares, weighting by $w_i$ (for this you can use Stata pweights or a SAS weight statement). Weighting by the inverse sampling probability generates estimates that are consistent for the population regression function even if the sample you have to work with is not a simple random sample.

A related weighting scenario involves grouped data. Suppose you would like to regress $Y_i$ on $X_i$ in a random sample, presumably because you want to learn about the population regression vector $\beta = E[X_i X_i']^{-1} E[X_i Y_i]$. Instead of a random sample, however, you have data grouped at the level of $X_i$. That is, you have estimates of $E[Y_i|X_i = x]$ for each $x$, estimated using data from a random sample. Let this average be denoted $\bar{y}_x$, and suppose you also know $n_x$, where $n_x/N$ is the relative frequency of the value $x$ in the underlying random sample. As we saw in section 3.1.2, the regression of $\bar{y}_x$ on $x$, weighted by $n_x$ is the same as the random sample microdata regression. Therefore, if your goal is to get back to the microdata regression, it makes sense to weight by group size. We note, however, that macroeconomists, accustomed to working with published averages (like per capita income) and ignoring the underlying microdata, might disagree, or perhaps take the point in principle but remain disinclined to buck tradition in their discipline, which favors the unweighted analysis of aggregate variables.

On the other hand, if the sole rationale for weighting is heteroskedasticity, as in many textbook discussions of weighting, we are even less sympathetic to weighting than the macroeconomists. The argument for weighting under heteroskedasticity goes roughly like this: suppose you are interested in a linear CEF, $E[Y_i|X_i] = X_i'\beta$. The error term, defined as $e_i \equiv Y_i - X_i'\beta$, may be heteroskedastic. That is, the conditional variance function $E[e_i^2|X_i]$ need not be constant. In this case, while the population regression function is still equal to $E[X_i X_i']^{-1} E[X_i Y_i]$, the sample analog is inefficient. A more precise estimator of the linear CEF is WLS—that is, the estimator that minimizes the sum of squared errors weighted by an estimate of $E[e_i^2|X_i]^{-1}$.

As noted in section 3.1.3, an inherently heteroskedastic scenario is the LPM, where $Y_i$ is a dummy variable. Assuming the CEF is in fact linear, as it will be if the model is saturated, then $P[Y_i = 1|X_i] = X_i'\beta$ and therefore $E[e_i^2|X_i] = X_i'\beta(1 - X_i'\beta)$, which is obviously a function of $X_i$. This is an example of model-based heteroskedasticity where estimates of the conditional variance function are easily constructed from estimates of the underlying regression function. The efficient WLS estimator for the LPM—a special case of generalized least squares (GLS)—is to weight by $[X_i'\beta(1 - X_i'\beta)]^{-1}$. Because the CEF has been assumed to be linear, these weights can be estimated in a first pass by OLS.

There are two reason why we prefer not to weight in this case (though we would use heteroskedasticity-consistent standard errors). First, in practice, the estimates of $E[e_i^2|X_i]$ may not be very good. If the conditional variance model is a poor approximation or if the estimates of it are very noisy, WLS estimates may have worse finite-sample properties than unweighted estimates. The inferences you draw based on asymptotic theory may therefore be misleading, and the hoped-for efficiency gain may not materialize.[31] Second, if the CEF is not linear, the WLS estimator is no more likely to estimate it than is the unweighted estimator. On the other hand, the unweighted estimator still estimates something easy to interpret: the MMSE linear approximation to the population CEF.

WLS estimators also provide some sort of approximation, but the nature of this approximation depends on the weights. At a minimum, this makes it harder to compare your results to estimates reported by other researchers, and opens up additional avenues for specification searches when results depend

---

[31] Altonji and Segal (1996) discuss this point in a generalized method-of-moments context.

on weighting. Finally, an old caution comes to mind: if it ain't broke, don't fix it. The interpretation of the population regression vector is unaffected by heteroskedasticity, so why worry about it? Any efficiency gain from weighting is likely to be modest, and incorrect or poorly estimated weights can do more harm than good.

### 3.4.2    *Limited Dependent Variables and Marginal Effects*

Many empirical studies involve dependent variables that take on only a limited number of values. An example is the Angrist and Evans (1998) investigation of the effect of childbearing on female labor supply, also discussed in the chapter on instrumental variables. This study is concerned with the causal effects of childbearing on parents' work and earnings. Because childbearing is likely to be correlated with potential earnings, Angrist and Evans report instrumental variables estimates based on sibling-sex composition and multiple births, as well as OLS estimates. Almost every outcome in this study is either binary (e.g., employment status) or non-negative (e.g., hours worked, weeks worked, and earnings). Should the fact that a dependent variable is limited affect empirical practice? Many econometrics textbooks argue that, while OLS is fine for continuous dependent variables, when the outcome of interest is a limited dependent variable (LDV), linear regression models are inappropriate and nonlinear models such as probit and Tobit are preferred. In contrast, our view of regression as inheriting its legitimacy from the CEF makes LDVness less central.

As always, a useful benchmark is a randomized experiment, where regression generates a simple treatment-control difference. Consider, for example, regressions of various outcome variables on a randomly assigned regressor that indicates one of the treatment groups in the RAND Health Insurance Experiment (HIE; Manning et al. 1987). In this ambitious experiment, probably the most expensive in American social science, the RAND Corporation set up a small health insurance company that charged no premium. Nearly 6,000 participants in the study were randomly assigned to health insurance plans with different features.

One of the most important features of any insurance plan is the portion of health care costs the insured individual is expected to pay. The HIE randomly assigned individuals to many different plans. One plan provided entirely free care, while the others included various combinations of copayments, expenditure caps, and deductibles, so that enrollees paid for some of their health care costs out-of-pocket. The main purpose of the experiment was to learn whether the use of medical care is sensitive to cost and, if so, whether this affects health. The HIE results showed that those offered free or low-cost medical care used more of it but were not, for the most part, any healthier as a result. These findings helped pave the way for cost-sensitive health insurance plans and managed care.

Most of the outcomes in the HIE are LDVs. These include dummies indicating whether an experimental subject incurred any medical expenditures or was hospitalized in a given year, and non-negative outcomes such as the number of face-to-face doctor visits and gross annual medical expenses (whether paid by patient or insurer). The expenditure variable is zero for about 20 percent of the sample. Results for two of the HIE treatment groups are reproduced in table 3.4.1, derived from the estimates reported in table 2 of Manning et al. (1987). Table 3.4.1 shows average outcomes in the free care and individual deductible groups. The latter group faced a deductible of $150 per person or $450 per family per year for outpatient care, after which all costs were covered (there was no charge for inpatient care). The overall sample size in these two groups was a little over 3,000.

To simplify the LDV discussion, suppose that the comparison between free care and deductible plans is the only comparison of interest and that treatment was determined by simple random assignment.[32] Let $D_i = 1$ denote assignment to the deductible group. By virtue of random assignment, the

---

[32]The HIE was considerably more complicated than described here. There were 14 different treatments, including assignment to a prepaid HMO-like service. The experimental design did not use simple random assignment but rather a more complicated stratified assignment scheme meant to ensure covariate balance across groups.

TABLE 3.4.1
Average outcomes in two of the HIE treatment groups

| Plan | Face-to-Face Visits | Outpatient Expenses (1984 $) | Admis-sions (%) | Prob. Any Medical (%) | Prob. Any Inpatient (%) | Total Expenses (1984 $) |
|---|---|---|---|---|---|---|
| Free | 4.55 | 340 | 12.8 | 86.8 | 10.3 | 749 |
| | (.17) | (10.9) | (.7) | (.8) | (.5) | (39) |
| Deductible | 3.02 | 235 | 11.5 | 72.3 | 9.6 | 608 |
| | (.17) | (11.9) | (.8) | (1.5) | (.6) | (46) |
| Deductible | −1.53 | −105 | −1.3 | −14.5 | −0.7 | −141 |
| minus free | (.24) | (16.1) | (1.0) | (1.7) | (.7) | (60) |

*Notes*: Adapted from Manning et al. (1987), table 2. All standard errors (shown in parentheses) are corrected for intertemporal and intrafamily correlations. Amounts are in June 1984 dollars. Visits are face-to-face contacts with health providers; visits solely for radiology, anesthesiology, or pathology services are excluded. Visits and expenses exclude dental care and outpatient psychotherapy.

difference in means between those with $D_i = 1$ and $D_i = 0$ gives the unconditional average treatment effect. As in our earlier discussion of experiments (chapter 2):

$$E[Y_i|D_i = 1] - E[Y_i|D_i = 0] \qquad (3.4.1)$$
$$= E[Y_{1i}|D_i = 1] - E[Y_{0i}|D_i = 1]$$
$$= E[Y_{1i} - Y_{0i}]$$

because $D_i$ is independent of potential outcomes. Also, as before, $E[Y_i|D_i = 1] - E[Y_i|D_i = 0]$ is the slope coefficient in a regression of $Y_i$ on $D_i$.

Equation (3.4.1) suggests that the estimation of causal effects in experiments presents no special challenges whether $Y_i$ is binary, non-negative, or continuously distributed. Although the interpretation of the right-hand side changes for different sorts of dependent variables, you do not need to *do* anything special to get the average causal effect. For example, one of the HIE outcomes is a dummy denoting any medical expenditure. Since the outcome here is a Bernoulli trial, we have

$$E[Y_{1i} - Y_{0i}] = E[Y_{1i}] - E[Y_{0i}]$$
$$= P[Y_{1i} = 1] - P[Y_{0i} = 1]. \qquad (3.4.2)$$

This might affect the language we use to describe results, but not the underlying calculation. In the HIE, for example, comparisons across experimental groups, as on the left-hand side of (3.4.1), show that 87 percent of those assigned to the free-care group used at least some care in a given year, while only 72 percent of those assigned to the deductible plan used care. The relatively modest \$150 deductible therefore had a marked effect on use of care. The difference between these two rates, $-.15$ is an estimate of $E[Y_{1i} - Y_{0i}]$, where $Y_i$ is a dummy indicating any medical expenditure. Because the outcome here is a dummy variable, the average causal effect is also a causal effect on usage rates or probabilities.

Recognizing that the medical usage outcome variable is a probability, suppose instead that you use probit to fit the CEF in this case. No harm in trying! The probit model is usually motivated by the assumption that participation is determined by a latent variable, $Y_i^*$, that satisfies

$$Y_i^* = \beta_0^* + \beta_1^* D_i - \nu_i, \qquad (3.4.3)$$

where $\nu_i$ is distributed $N(0, \sigma_\nu^2)$. Note that this latent variable cannot be actual medical expenditure since expenditure is non-negative and therefore non-normal, while normally distributed random variables are continuously distributed on the real line and can therefore be negative. Given the latent index model,

$$Y_i = 1[Y_i^* > 0],$$

so the CEF for $Y_i$ can be written

$$E[Y_i|D_i] = \Phi\left[\frac{\beta_0^* + \beta_1^* D_i}{\sigma_\nu}\right],$$

where $\Phi[\cdot]$ is the normal CDF. Therefore

$$E[Y_i|D_i] = \Phi\left[\frac{\beta_0^*}{\sigma_\nu}\right] + \left\{\Phi\left[\frac{\beta_0^* + \beta_1^*}{\sigma_\nu}\right] - \Phi\left[\frac{\beta_0^*}{\sigma_\nu}\right]\right\} D_i.$$

This is a linear function of the regressor, $D_i$, so the slope coefficient in the linear regression, of $Y_i$ on $D_i$ is just the difference in probit fitted values, $\Phi\left[\frac{\beta_0^* + \beta_1^*}{\sigma_v}\right] - \Phi\left[\frac{\beta_0^*}{\sigma_v}\right]$. But the probit coefficients, $\frac{\beta_0^*}{\sigma_v}$ and $\frac{\beta_1^*}{\sigma_v}$ do not give us the size of the effect of $D_i$ on participation until we feed them back into the normal CDF (though they do have the right sign). Regression, in contrast, gives us what we need with or without the probit distributional assumptions.

One of the most important outcomes in the HIE is gross medical expenditure, in other words, health care costs. Did subjects who faced a deductible use less care, as measured by the cost? In the HIE, the average difference in expenditures between the deductible and free-care groups was $-141$ dollars, about 19 percent of the expenditure level in the free-care group. This calculation suggests that making patients pay a portion of costs reduces expenditures quite a bit, though the estimate is not very precise.

Because expenditure outcomes are non-negative random variables, and sometimes equal to zero, their expectation can be written

$$E[Y_i|D_i] = E[Y_i|Y_i > 0, D_i]P[Y_i > 0|D_i].$$

The difference in expenditure outcomes across treatment groups is

$$E[Y_i|D_i = 1] - E[Y_i|D_i = 0] \qquad\qquad (3.4.4)$$
$$= E[Y_i|Y_i > 0, D_i = 1]P[Y_i > 0|D_i = 1]$$
$$- E[Y_i|Y_i > 0, D_i = 0]P[Y_i > 0|D_i = 0]$$
$$= \underbrace{\{P[Y_i > 0|D_i = 1] - P[Y_i > 0|D_i = 0]\}}_{\text{Participation effect}}E[Y_i|Y_i > 0, D_i = 1]$$
$$+ \underbrace{\{E[Y_i|Y_i > 0, D_i = 1] - E[Y_i|Y_i > 0, D_i = 0]\}}_{\text{COP effect}}$$
$$\times P[Y_i > 0|D_i = 0].$$

So, the overall difference in average expenditure can be broken up into two parts: the difference in the probability that expenditures are positive (often called a participation effect) and the difference in means conditional on participation, a conditional-on-positive (COP) effect. Again, however, this has no special implications for the estimation of causal effects; equation (3.4.1) remains true: the regression of $Y_i$ on $D_i$ gives the unconditional average treatment effect for expenditures.

### Good COP, Bad COP: Conditional-on-Positive Effects

Because causal effects on a non-negative random variable such as expenditure have two parts, some applied researchers feel they should look at these parts separately. In fact, many use a two-part model, in which the first part is an evaluation of the effect on participation and the second part looks at COP effects (see, e.g., Duan et al., 1983 and 1984, for such models applied to the HIE). The first part of (3.4.4) raises no special issues, because, as noted above, the fact that $Y_i$ is a dummy means only that average treatment effects are also differences in probabilities. The problem with the two-part model is that the COP effects do not have a causal interpretation, even in a randomized trial. This complication can be understood as the same selection problem described in section 3.2.3, on bad control.

To analyze the COP effect further, write

$$E[Y_i|Y_i > 0, D_i = 1] - E[Y_i|Y_i > 0, D_i = 0] \qquad (3.4.5)$$
$$= E[Y_{1i}|Y_{1i} > 0] - E[Y_{0i}|Y_{0i} > 0]$$
$$= \underbrace{E[Y_{1i} - Y_{0i}|Y_{1i} > 0]}_{\text{Causal effect}} + \underbrace{\{E[Y_{0i}|Y_{1i} > 0] - E[Y_{0i}|Y_{0i} > 0]\}}_{\text{Selection bias}},$$

where the second line uses the random assignment of $D_i$. This decomposition shows that the COP effect is composed of two terms: a causal effect for the subpopulation that uses medical care with a deductible and the difference in $Y_{0i}$ between those who use medical care when they have to pay something and when it is free. This second term is a form of selection bias, though it is more subtle than the selection bias in chapter 2.

Here selection bias arises because the experiment changes the composition of the group with positive expenditures. The $Y_{0i} > 0$ population probably includes some low-cost users who would opt out of care if they had to pay a deductible. In other words, this group is larger and probably has lower costs on average than the $Y_{1i} > 0$ group. The selection bias term is therefore positive, with the result that COP effects are closer to zero than the presumably negative causal effect, $E[Y_{1i} - Y_{0i}|Y_{1i} > 0]$. This is a version of the bad control problem from section 3.2.3: in a causal effects setting, $Y_i > 0$ is an outcome variable and therefore unkosher for conditioning unless the treatment has no effect on the likelihood that $Y_i$ is positive.

One resolution of the noncausality of COP effects relies on censored regression models like Tobit. These models postulate a latent expenditure outcome for nonparticipants (e.g., Hay and Olsen, 1984). A traditional Tobit formulation for the expenditure problem stipulates that the observed $Y_i$ is generated by

$$Y_i = 1[Y_i^* > 0]Y_i^*,$$

where $Y_i^*$ is a normally distributed latent expenditure variable that can take on negative values. Because $Y_i^*$ is not an LDV, Tobit proponents feel comfortable linking this to $D_i$ using a traditional linear model, say, equation (3.4.3). In this case, $\beta_1^*$ is the causal effect of $D_i$ on latent expenditure, $Y_i^*$. This equation is defined for everyone, whether $Y_i$ is positive or not. There is no COP-style selection problem if we are happy to study effects on $Y_i^*$.

But we are not happy with effects on $Y_i^*$. The first problem is that "latent health care expenditure" is a puzzling construct. Health care expenditure really is zero for some people; this is not a statistical artifact or due to some kind of censoring. So the notion of latent and potentially negative $Y_i^*$ is hard to grasp. There are no data on $Y_i^*$ and there never will be. A second problem is that the link between the parameter $\beta_1^*$ in the latent model and causal effects on the observed outcome, $Y_i$, turns on distributional assumptions about the latent variable. To establish this link we evaluate the expectation of $Y_i$ given $D_i$ to find

$$E[Y_i|D_i] = \Phi\left[\frac{\beta_0^* + \beta_1^* D_i}{\sigma_\nu}\right][\beta_0^* + \beta_1^* D_i]$$
$$+ \sigma_\nu \phi\left[\frac{\beta_0^* + \beta_1^* D_i}{\sigma_\nu}\right], \qquad (3.4.6)$$

(see, e.g., McDonald and Moffitt, 1980). This expression is derived using the normality and homoskedasticity of $v_i$ and the assumption that $Y_i$ can be represented as $1[Y_i^* > 0]Y_i^*$.

The Tobit CEF provides us with an expression for the average treatment effect on observed expenditure. Specifically,

$$E[Y_i|D_i = 1] - E[Y_i|D_i = 0]$$

$$= \left\{ \Phi\left[\frac{\beta_0^* + \beta_1^*}{\sigma_v}\right][\beta_0^* + \beta_1^*] + \sigma\phi\left[\frac{\beta_0^* + \beta_1^*}{\sigma_v}\right] \right\}$$

$$- \left\{ \Phi\left[\frac{\beta_0}{\sigma_v}\right][\beta_0^*] + \sigma_v\phi\left[\frac{\beta_0^*}{\sigma_v}\right] \right\} \qquad (3.4.7)$$

a rather daunting formula. But since the only regressor is a dummy variable, $D_i$, none of this is necessary for the estimation of $E[Y_i|D_i = 1] - E[Y_i|D_i = 0]$. The slope coefficient from an OLS regression of $Y_i$ on $D_i$ recovers the CEF difference on the left-hand side of (3.4.7) whether or not you adopt a Tobit model to explain the underlying structure.[33]

COP effects are sometimes motivated by a researcher's sense that when the outcome distribution has a mass point—that is, when it piles up on a particular value, such as zero—or has a heavily skewed distribution, or both, then an analysis of effects on averages misses something. Analyses of effects on averages indeed miss some things, such as changes in the probability of specific values or a shift in quantiles away from the median. But why not look at these distribution effects directly? Distribution outcomes include the likelihood that annual medical expenditures exceed zero, 100 dollars, 200 dollars, and so on. In other words, put $1[Y_i > c]$ for different choices of $c$ on the left-hand side of the regression of interest. Econometrically, these outcomes are all in the category of (3.4.2). The idea of looking directly at distribution effects with linear probability models is illustrated by Angrist (2001), in an analysis of the effects of childbearing on hours worked. Alternatively, if

---

[33] A generalization of Tobit is the sample selection model, where the latent variable determining participation differs from the latent expenditure variable. See, for example, Maddala (1983). The same conceptual problems related to the interpretation of effects on latent variables arise in the sample selection model as with Tobit.

quantiles provide a focal point, we can use quantile regression to model them. Chapter 7 discusses this idea in detail.

Do Tobit-type latent variable models ever make sense? Yes, if the data you are working with are truly censored. True censoring means the latent variable has an empirical counterpart that is the outcome of primary interest. A leading example from labor economics is CPS earnings data, which topcodes (censors) very high values of earnings to protect respondent confidentiality. Typically, we're interested in the causal effect of schooling on earnings as it appears on respondents' tax returns, not their CPS-topcoded earnings. Chamberlain (1994) shows that in some years, CPS topcoding reduces the measured returns to schooling considerably, and proposes an adjustment for censoring based on a Tobit-style adaptation of quantile regression. The use of quantile regression to model censored data is also discussed in chapter 7.[34]

### Covariates Lead to Nonlinearity

True censoring as with the CPS topcode is rare, a fact that leaves limited scope for constructive applications of Tobit-type models in applied work. At this point, however, we have to hedge a bit. Part of the neatness in the discussion of experiments comes from the fact that $E[Y_i | D_i]$ is necessarily a linear function of $D_i$, so that regression and the CEF are one and the same. In fact, this CEF is linear for any function of $Y_i$, including the distribution indicators, $1[Y_i > c]$. In practice, of course, the explanatory variable of interest isn't always a dummy, and there are usually additional covariates in the CEF, in which case $E[Y_i | X_i, D_i]$ for LDVs is almost certainly nonlinear. Intuitively, as predicted means get close to the dependent variable boundaries, the derivatives of the CEF

---

[34]We should note that our favorite regression example, a regression of log wages on schooling, may have a COP problem since the sample of log wages naturally omits those with zero earnings. This leads to COP-style selection bias if education affects the probability of working. In practice, therefore, we focus on samples of prime-age males, whose participation rates are high and reasonably stable across schooling groups (e.g., white men aged 40–49 in figure 3.1.1).

for LDVs get smaller (think, for example, of how the normal CDF flattens at extreme values).

The upshot is that in LDV models with covariates, regression need not fit the CEF perfectly. It remains true, however, that the underlying CEF has a causal interpretation if the CIA holds. And if the CEF has a causal interpretation, it seems fair to say that regression has a causal interpretation as well, because it still provides the MMSE approximation to the CEF. Moreover, if the model for covariates is saturated, then regression also estimates a weighted average treatment effect similar to (3.3.1) and (3.3.3). Likewise, if the regressor of interest is multivalued or continuous, we get a weighted average derivative, as described by the formulas at the end of subsection 3.3.1.

And yet, we may not have enough data for the saturated-covariate regression specification to be very attractive. Regression will therefore miss some features of the CEF. For one thing, it may generate fitted values outside the LDV boundaries. This fact bothers some researchers and has generated a lot of bad press for the linear probability model. One attractive feature of nonlinear models like probit and Tobit is that they produce CEFs that respect LDV boundaries. In particular, probit fitted values are always between zero and one, while Tobit fitted values are positive (this is not obvious from equation (3.4.6)). We might therefore prefer nonlinear models on simple curve-fitting grounds.

Point conceded. It's important to emphasize, however, that the output from nonlinear models must be converted into *marginal effects* to be useful. Marginal effects are the (average) changes in CEF implied by a nonlinear model. Without marginal effects, it's hard to talk about the impact on observed dependent variables. If we continue to assume the regressor of interest is the dummy variable, $D_i$, marginal effects can be constructed either by differencing

$$E\{E[Y_i|X_i, D_i = 1] - E[Y_i|X_i, D_i = 0]\},$$

or, by differentiation, $E\{\frac{\partial E[Y_i|X_i, D_i]}{\partial D_i}\}$. Most people use derivatives when dealing with continuous or multivalued regressors.

How close do OLS regression estimates come to the marginal effects induced by a nonlinear model like probit or Tobit? We first derive the marginal effects, and then show an empirical example. The probit CEF for a model with covariates is

$$E[Y_i|X_i, D_i] = \Phi \left[ \frac{X_i'\beta_0^* + \beta_1^* D_i}{\sigma_\nu} \right].$$

The average finite difference is therefore

$$E\left\{ \Phi \left[ \frac{X_i'\beta_0^* + \beta_1^*}{\sigma_\nu} \right] - \Phi \left[ \frac{X_i'\beta_0^*}{\sigma_\nu} \right] \right\}. \qquad (3.4.8)$$

In practice, this can be approximated by the average derivative,

$$E\left\{ \phi \left[ \frac{X_i'\beta_0^* + \beta_1^* D_i}{\sigma_\nu} \right] \right\} \cdot \left( \frac{\beta_1^*}{\sigma_\nu} \right)$$

(Stata computes marginal effects both ways but defaults to (3.4.8) for dummy regressors).

Similarly, generalizing equation (3.4.6) to a model with covariates, we have

$$E[Y_i|X_i, D_i] = \Phi \left[ \frac{X_i'\beta_0^* + \beta_1^* D_i}{\sigma_\nu} \right] [X_i'\beta_0^* + \beta_1^* D_i]$$
$$+ \sigma_\nu \phi \left[ \frac{X_i'\beta_0^* + \beta_1^* D_i}{\sigma_\nu} \right]$$

for a non-negative LDV. Tobit marginal effects are almost always cast in terms of the average derivative, which can be shown to be the surprisingly simple expression

$$E\left\{ \Phi \left[ \frac{X_i'\beta_0^* + \beta_1^* D_i}{\sigma_\nu} \right] \right\} \cdot \beta_1^* \qquad (3.4.9)$$

(see, e.g., Wooldridge, 2006). One immediate implication of (3.4.9) is that the Tobit coefficient, $\beta_1^*$, is always too big relative to the effect of $D_i$ on $Y_i$. Intuitively, this is because, given the linear model for latent $Y_i^*$, the latent outcome always changes when $D_i$ switches on or off. But real $Y_i$ need not change: for many people, it's zero either way.

Table 3.4.2 compares OLS estimates and nonlinear marginal effects for regressions of female employment and hours of work, both LDVs, on measures of fertility. These estimates were constructed using one of the 1980 census samples used by Angrist and Evans (1998). This sample includes married women aged 21–35 with at least two children. The childbearing variables consist of a dummy indicating women with more than two children or the total number of births. The covariates include linear terms in mother's age, age at first birth, race dummies (black and Hispanic), and mother's education (dummies for high school graduates, some college, and college graduates). The covariate model is not saturated; rather, there are additive terms and no interactions, though the underlying CEF in this example is surely nonlinear.

Probit marginal effects for the impact of a dummy variable indicating more than two children are indistinguishable from OLS estimates of the same relation. This can be seen in columns 2, 3, and 4 of table 3.4.2, the first row of which compares the estimates from different methods for the full 1980 sample. The OLS estimate of the effect of a third child is $-.162$, while the corresponding probit marginal effects are $-.163$ and $-.162$. These were estimated using (3.4.8) in the first case and

$$E\left\{\Phi\left[\frac{X_i'\beta_0^* + \beta_1^*}{\sigma_\nu}\right] - \Phi\left[\frac{X_i'\beta_0^*}{\sigma_\nu}\right]\Bigg| D_i = 1\right\}$$

in the second (hence, a marginal effect on the treated).

Tobit marginal effects for the relation between fertility and hours worked are quite close to the corresponding OLS estimates, though not indistinguishable. This can be seen in columns 5 and 6. Compare, for example, the Tobit estimates of $-6.56$ and $-5.87$ with the OLS estimate of $-5.92$ in column 2. Although one Tobit estimate is 10 percent larger in absolute value, this seems unlikely to be of substantive importance. The remaining columns of the table compare OLS estimates to marginal effects for an ordinal childbearing variable instead of a dummy. These calculations all use derivatives to compute marginal effects (labeled MFX). Here, too, the OLS and

TABLE 3.4.2
Comparison of alternative estimates of the effect of childbearing on LDVs

| | | More than Two Children | | | | | Number of Children | | | |
| | | Probit | | | Tobit | | | Probit MFX | Tobit MFX | |
| Dependent Variable | Mean (1) | OLS (2) | Avg. Effect, Full Sample (3) | Avg. Effect on Treated (4) | Avg. Effect, Full Sample (5) | Avg. Effect on Treated (6) | OLS (7) | Avg. Effect, Full Sample (8) | Avg. Effect, Full Sample (9) | Avg. Effect on Treated (10) |
|---|---|---|---|---|---|---|---|---|---|---|
| A. Full sample | | | | | | | | | | |
| Employment | .528 (.499) | −.162 (.002) | −.163 (.002) | −.162 (.002) | — | — | −.113 (.001) | −.114 (.001) | — | — |
| Hours worked | 16.7 (18.3) | −5.92 (.074) | — | — | −6.56 (.081) | −5.87 (.073) | −4.07 (.047) | — | −4.66 (.054) | −4.23 (.049) |
| B. Nonwhite college attenders over age 30, first birth before age 20 | | | | | | | | | | |
| Employment | .832 (.374) | −.061 (.028) | −.064 (.028) | −.070 (.031) | — | — | −.054 (.016) | −.048 (.013) | — | — |
| Hours worked | 30.8 (16.0) | −4.69 (1.18) | — | — | −4.97 (1.33) | −4.90 (1.31) | −2.83 (.645) | — | −3.20 (.670) | −3.15 (.659) |

*Notes:* The table reports OLS estimates, average treatment effects, and marginal effects (MFX) for the effect of childbearing on mothers' labor supply. The sample in panel A includes 254,654 observations and is the same as the 1980 census sample of married women used by Angrist and Evans (1998). Covariates include age, age at first birth, and dummies for boys at first and second birth. The sample in panel B includes 746 nonwhite women with at least some college aged over 30 whose first birth was before age 20. Standard deviations are reported in parentheses in column 1. Standard errors are shown in parentheses in other columns. The sample used to estimate average effects on the treated in columns 4, 6, and 10 includes women with more than two children.

nonlinear marginal effects estimates are similar for both probit and Tobit.

It is sometimes said that probit models can be expected to generate marginal effects close to OLS when the predicted probabilities are close to .5 because the underlying nonlinear CEF is roughly linear in the middle. With predictions close to zero or one, however, we might expect a larger gap. We therefore replicated the comparison of OLS and marginal effects in a subsample with relatively high average employment rates, nonwhite women over age 30 who attended college and whose first birth was before age 20. Although the average employment rate is 83 percent in this group, the OLS estimates and marginal effects are again similar.

The upshot of this discussion is that while a nonlinear model may fit the CEF for LDVs more closely than a linear model, when it comes to marginal effects, this probably matters little. This optimistic conclusion is not a theorem, but, as in the empirical example here, it seems to be fairly robustly true.

Why, then, should we bother with nonlinear models and marginal effects? One answer is that the marginal effects are easy enough to compute now that they are automated in packages like Stata. But there are a number of decisions to make along the way (e.g., the weighting scheme, derivatives versus finite differences), while OLS is standardized. Nonlinear life also gets considerably more complicated when we work with instrumental variables and panel data. Finally, extra complexity comes into the inference step as well, since we need standard errors for marginal effects. The principle of Occam's razor advises, "Entities should not be multiplied unnecessarily." In this spirit, we quote our former teacher, Angus Deaton (1997), pondering the nonlinear regression function generated by Tobit-type models:

> Absent knowledge of $F$ [the distribution of the errors], this regression function does not even identify the $\beta$'s [Tobit coefficients]—see Powell (1989)—but more fundamentally, we should ask how it has come about that we have to deal with such an awkward, difficult, and non-robust object.

### 3.4.3   Why Is Regression Called Regression, and What Does Regression to the Mean Mean?

The term *regression* originates with Francis Galton's (1886) study of height. Galton, who is pictured visiting his tailor on page 26, worked with samples of roughly normally distributed data on parents and children. He noted that the CEF of a child's height conditional on his parents' height is linear, with parameters given by the bivariate regression slope and intercept. Since height is stationary (its distribution does not change much over time), the bivariate regression slope is also the correlation coefficient, that is, between zero and one.

The single regressor in Galton's setup, $x_i$, is average parent height and the dependent variable, $Y_i$, is the height of adult children. The regression slope coefficient, as always, is $\beta_1 = \frac{Cov(Y_i, x_i)}{V(x_i)}$, and the intercept is $\alpha = E[Y_i] - \beta_1 E[X_i]$. But because height is not changing across generations, the mean and variance of $Y_i$ and $x_i$ are the same. Therefore,

$$\beta_1 = \frac{Cov(Y_i, x_i)}{V(x_i)} = \frac{Cov(Y_i, x_i)}{\sqrt{V(x_i)}\sqrt{V(Y_i)}} = \rho_{xy}$$

$$\alpha = E[Y_i] - \beta_1 E[X_i] = \mu(1 - \beta_1) = \mu(1 - \rho_{xy}),$$

where $\rho_{xy}$ is the intergenerational correlation coefficient in height and $\mu = E[Y_i] = E[X_i]$ is the population average height. From this we get the linear CEF

$$E[Y_i | x_i] = \mu(1 - \rho_{xy}) + \rho_{xy} x_i,$$

so the height of a child given his parents' height is a weighted average of his parents' height and the population average height. The child of tall parents will therefore not be as tall as they are, on average. Likewise, for the short. To be specific, Pischke, who is six feet three inches tall, can expect his children to be tall, though not as tall as he is. Thankfully, however, Angrist, who is five feet six inches tall, can expect his children to be taller than he is. Galton called this property "regression toward mediocrity in hereditary stature." Today we call it regression to the mean.

Galton, who was Charles Darwin's cousin, is also remembered for having founded the Eugenics Society, dedicated to breeding better people. Indeed, his interest in regression came largely from this quest. We conclude from this that the value of scientific ideas should not be judged by their author's politics.

Galton does not seem to have shown much interest in multiple regression, our chief concern in this chapter. The regressions in Galton's work are mechanical features of distributions of stationary random variables; they work just as well for the regression of parents' height on childrens' height and are certainly not causal. Galton would have said so himself, because he objected to the Lamarckian idea (later promoted in Stalin's Russia) that acquired traits can be inherited.

The idea that regression can be used for statistical control in pursuit of causality satisfyingly originates in an inquiry into the determinants of poverty rates by George Udny Yule (1899). Yule, a statistician and student of Karl Pearson (Pearson was Galton's protégé), realized that Galton's regression coefficient could be extended to multiple variables by solving the least squares normal equations that had been derived long before by Legendre and Gauss. Yule's (1899) paper appears to be the first publication containing multivariate regression estimates. His model links changes in poverty rates in an area to changes in the local administration of the English Poor Laws, while controlling for population growth and the age distribution in the area. He was particularly interested in whether out-relief, the practice of providing income support for poor people without requiring them to move to the poorhouse, did not itself contribute to higher poverty rates. This is a well-defined causal question of a sort that still occupies us today.[35]

Finally, we note that the history of regression is beautifully detailed in the book by Steven Stigler (1986). Stigler is a famous statistician at the University of Chicago, but not quite

[35] Yule's first applied paper on the poor laws was published in 1895 in the *Economic Journal*, where Pischke is proud to serve as co-editor. The theory of multiple regression that goes along with this appears in Yule (1897).

as famous as his father, the economist and Nobel laureate, George Stigler.

## 3.5    Appendix: Derivation of the Average Derivative Weighting Function

Begin with the regression of $Y_i$ on $s_i$:

$$\frac{Cov(Y_i, s_i)}{V(s_i)} = \frac{E[h(s_i)(s_i - E[s_i])]}{E[s_i(s_i - E[s_i])]}.$$

Let $\kappa_{-\infty} = \lim_{t \to -\infty} h(t)$, which we assume exists. By the fundamental theorem of calculus, we have:

$$h(s_i) = \kappa_{-\infty} + \int_{-\infty}^{s_i} h'(t)dt.$$

Substituting for $h(s_i)$, the numerator becomes

$$E[h(s_i)(s_i - E[s_i])] = \int_{-\infty}^{+\infty} \int_{-\infty}^{u} h'(t)(u - E[s_i])g(u)dt\,du,$$

where $g(u)$ is the density of $s_i$ at $u$. Reversing the order of integration, we have

$$E[h(s_i)(s_i - E[s_i])] = \int_{-\infty}^{+\infty} h'(t) \int_{t}^{+\infty} (u - E[s_i])g(u)du\,dt.$$

The inner integral is equal to $\mu_t \equiv \{E[s_i|s_i \geq t] - E[s_i|s_i < t]\}$ $\{P(s_i \geq t)[1 - P(s_i \geq t)]\}$, the weighting function in (3.3.9), which is clearly non-negative. Setting $s_i = Y_i$, the denominator can similarly be shown to be the integral of these weights. We therefore have a weighted average derivative representation of the bivariate regression coefficient, $\frac{Cov(Y_i, s_i)}{V(s_i)}$. A similar formula for a regression with covariates is derived in the appendix to Angrist and Krueger (1999).

Chapter 4

# Instrumental Variables in Action:
# Sometimes You Get What You Need

Anything that happens, happens.
Anything that, in happening, causes something else to happen,
causes something else to happen.
Anything that, in happening,
causes itself to happen again, happens again.
It doesn't necessarily do it in chronological order, though.
  Douglas Adams, *Mostly Harmless*

wo things distinguish the discipline of econometrics from the older sister field of statistics. One is a lack of shyness about causality. Causal inference has always been the name of the game in applied econometrics. Statistician Paul Holland (1986) cautions that there can be "no causation without manipulation," a maxim that would seem to rule out causal inference from nonexperimental data. Less thoughtful observers fall back on the truism that "correlation is not causality." Like most people who work with data for a living, we believe that correlation can sometimes provide pretty good evidence of a causal relation, even when the variable of interest has not been manipulated by a researcher or experimenter.[1]

The second thing that distinguishes us from most statisticians—and indeed from most other social scientists— is an arsenal of statistical tools that grew out of early

---

[1]Recent years have seen an increased willingness by statisticians to discuss statistical models for observational data in an explicitly causal framework; see, for example, Freedman's (2005) review.

econometric research on the problem of how to estimate the parameters in a system of linear simultaneous equations. The most powerful weapon in this arsenal is the method of instrumental variables (IV), the subject of this chapter. As it turns out, the IV method does more than allow us to consistently estimate the parameters in a system of simultaneous equations, though it allows us to do that as well.

Studying agricultural markets in the 1920s, the father-and-son research team of Phillip and Sewall Wright were interested in a challenging problem of causal inference: how to estimate the slope of supply and demand curves when observed data on prices and quantities are determined by the intersection of these two curves. In other words, equilibrium prices and quantities—the only ones we get to observe—solve these two stochastic equations at the same time. On which curve, therefore, does the observed scatterplot of prices and quantities lie? The fact that population regression coefficients do not capture the slope of any one equation in a set of simultaneous equations had been understood by Phillip Wright for some time. The IV method, first laid out in Wright (1928), solves the statistical simultaneous equations problem by using variables that appear in one equation to shift this equation and trace out the other. The variables that do the shifting came to be known as *instrumental variables* (Reiersol, 1941).

In a separate line of inquiry, IV methods were pioneered to solve the problem of bias from measurement error in regression models.[2] One of the most important results in the statistical theory of linear models is that a regression coefficient is biased toward zero when the regressor of interest is measured with random errors (to see why, imagine the regressor contains only random error; then it will be uncorrelated with the dependent variable, and hence the regression of $Y_i$ on this variable will be zero). Instrumental variables methods can be used to eliminate this sort of bias.

Simultaneous equations models (SEMs) have been enormously important in the history of econometric thought. At

---

[2]Key historical references here are Wald (1940) and Durbin (1954), both discussed later in this chapter.

the same time, few of today's most influential applied papers rely on an orthodox SEM framework, though the technical language used to discuss IV methods still comes from this framework. Today, we are more likely to find IV methods used to address measurement error problems than to estimate the parameters of an SEM. Undoubtedly, however, the most important contemporary use of IV methods is to solve the problem of omitted variables bias (OVB). IV methods solve the problem of missing or unknown control variables, much as a randomized trial obviates extensive controls in a regression.[3]

## 4.1    IV and Causality

We like to tell the IV story in two iterations, first in a restricted model with constant effects, then in a framework with unrestricted heterogeneous potential outcomes, in which case causal effects must also be heterogeneous. The introduction of heterogeneous effects enriches the interpretation of IV estimands without changing the mechanics of the core statistical methods we are most likely to use in practice (typically, two-stage least squares, or 2SLS). An initial focus on constant effects allows us to explain the mechanics of IV with a minimum of fuss.

To motivate the constant effects setup as a framework for the causal link between schooling and wages, suppose, as before, that potential outcomes can be written

$$Y_{si} \equiv f_i(s),$$

and that

$$f_i(s) = \alpha + \rho s + \eta_i, \qquad (4.1.1)$$

as in the discussion of regression and causality in section 3.2. Also, as in the earlier discussion, we imagine that there is a

---

[3] See Angrist and Krueger (2001) for a brief exposition of the history and uses of IV, Stock and Trebbi (2003) for a detailed account of the birth of IV, and Morgan (1990) for an extended history of econometric ideas, including the simultaneous equations model.

vector of control variables, $A_i$, called "ability," that gives a selection-on-observables story:

$$\eta_i = A_i'\gamma + v_i,$$

where $\gamma$ is again a vector of population regression coefficients, so that $v_i$ and $A_i$ are uncorrelated by construction. For now, the variables $A_i$, are assumed to be the only reason why $\eta_i$ and $s_i$ are correlated, so that

$$E[s_i v_i] = 0.$$

In other words, if $A_i$ were observed, we would be happy to include it in the regression of wages on schooling; thereby producing a long regression that can be written

$$Y_i = \alpha + \rho s_i + A_i'\gamma + v_i. \tag{4.1.2}$$

Equation (4.1.2) is a version of the linear causal model (3.2.9). The error term in this equation is the random part of potential outcomes, $v_i$, left over after controlling for $A_i$. This error term is uncorrelated with schooling by assumption. If this assumption turns out to be correct, the population regression of $Y_i$ on $s_i$ and $A_i$ produces the coefficients in (4.1.2).

The problem we initially want to tackle is how to estimate the long regression coefficient, $\rho$, when $A_i$ is unobserved. Instrumental variables methods can be used to accomplish this when the researcher has access to a variable (the instrument, which we'll call $z_i$), that is correlated with the causal variable of interest, $s_i$, but uncorrelated with any other determinants of the dependent variable. Here, the phrase "uncorrelated with any other determinants of the dependent variables" is like saying $Cov(\eta_i, z_i) = 0$, or, equivalently, $z_i$ is uncorrelated with both $A_i$ and $v_i$. This statement is called an *exclusion restriction*, since $z_i$ can be said to be excluded from the causal model of interest.

Given the exclusion restriction, it follows from (4.1.2) that

$$\rho = \frac{Cov(Y_i, z_i)}{Cov(s_i, z_i)} = \frac{Cov(Y_i, z_i)/V(z_i)}{Cov(s_i, z_i)/V(z_i)}. \tag{4.1.3}$$

The second equality in (4.1.3) is useful because it's usually easier to think in terms of regression coefficients than in terms of covariances. The coefficient of interest, $\rho$, is the ratio of the population regression of $y_i$ on $z_i$ (called the reduced form) to the population regression of $s_i$ on $z_i$ (called the first stage). The IV estimator is the sample analog of expression (4.1.3). Note that the IV estimand is predicated on the notion that the first stage is not zero, but this is something you can check in the data. As a rule, if the first stage is only marginally significantly different from zero, the resulting IV estimates are unlikely to be informative, a point we return to later.

It's worth recapping the assumptions needed for the ratio of covariances in (4.1.3) to equal the casual effect, $\rho$. First, the instrument must have a clear effect on $s_i$. This is the first stage. Second, the only reason for the relationship between $y_i$ and $z_i$ is the first stage. For the moment, we're calling this second assumption the exclusion restriction, though as we'll see in the discussion of models with heterogeneous effects, this assumption really has two parts: the first is the statement that the instrument is as good as randomly assigned (i.e., independent of potential outcomes, conditional on covariates, like the CIA in chapter 3), and the second is that the instrument has no effect on outcomes other than through the first-stage channel.

So, where can you find an instrumental variable? Good instruments come from a combination of institutional knowledge and ideas about the processes determining the variable of interest. For example, the economic model of education suggests that schooling decisions are based on the costs and benefits of alternative choices. Thus, one possible source of instruments for schooling is differences in costs due to loan policies or other subsidies that vary independently of ability or earnings potential. A second source of variation in schooling is institutional constraints. A set of institutional constraints relevant for schooling is compulsory schooling laws. Angrist and Krueger (1991) exploit the variation induced by compulsory schooling in a paper that typifies the use of "natural experiments" to try to eliminate OVB.

The starting point for the Angrist and Krueger (1991) quarter-of-birth strategy is the observation that most states require students to enter school in the calendar year in which they turn 6. School start age is therefore a function of date of birth. Specifically, those born late in the year are young for their grade. In states with a December 31 birthday cutoff, children born in the fourth quarter enter school shortly before they turn 6, while those born in the first quarter enter school at around age $6\frac{1}{2}$. Furthermore, because compulsory schooling laws typically require students to remain in school only until their 16th birthday, these groups of students will be in different grades, or through a given grade to a different degree, when they reach the legal dropout age. The combination of school start-age policies and compulsory schooling laws creates a natural experiment in which children are compelled to attend school for different lengths of time, depending on their birthdays.

Angrist and Krueger looked at the relationship between educational attainment and quarter of birth using U.S. census data. Panel A of figure 4.1.1 (adapted from Angrist and Krueger, 1991) displays the education quarter-of-birth pattern for men in the 1980 census who were born in the 1930s. The figure clearly shows that men born earlier in the calendar year tended to have lower average schooling levels. Panel A of figure 4.1.1 is a graphical depiction of the first stage. The first stage in a general IV framework is the regression of the causal variable of interest on covariates and instruments. The plot summarizes this regression because average schooling by year and quarter of birth is what you get for fitted values from a regression of schooling on a full set of year-of-birth dummies (covariates) and quarter-of-birth dummies (instruments).

Panel B of figure 4.1.1 displays average earnings by quarter of birth for the same sample used to construct panel A. This panel illustrates the reduced-form relationship between the instruments and the dependent variable. The reduced form is the regression of the dependent variable on any covariates in the model and the instruments. Panel B shows that older cohorts tend to have higher earnings, because earnings rise with work experience. The figure also shows that men born in early quarters almost always earned less, on average, than those born later in the year, even after adjusting for year of birth, a covariate in the Angrist and Krueger (1991) setup. Importantly, this reduced-form relation parallels the

**A. AVERAGE EDUCATION BY QUARTER OF BIRTH (FIRST STAGE)**

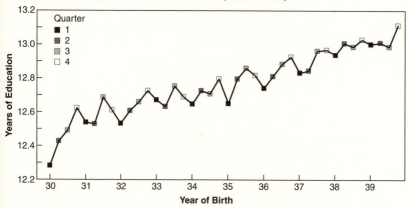

**B. AVERAGE WEEKLY WAGE BY QUARTER OF BIRTH (REDUCED FORM)**

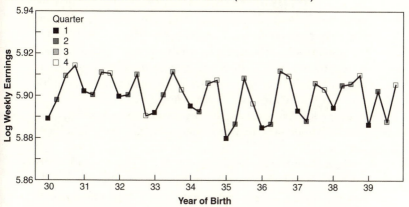

**Figure 4.1.1**   Graphical depiction of the first stage and reduced form for IV estimates of the economic return to schooling using quarter-of-birth instruments (from Angrist and Krueger, 1991).

quarter-of-birth pattern in schooling, suggesting the two patterns are closely related. Because an individual's date of birth is probably unrelated to his or her innate ability, motivation, or family connections, it seems credible to assert that the only reason for the up-and-down quarter-of-birth pattern in earnings is the up-and-down quarter-of-birth pattern in schooling.

This is the critical assumption that drives the quarter-of-birth IV story.[4]

A mathematical representation of the story told by figure 4.1.1 comes from the first-stage and reduced-form regression equations, spelled out below:

$$s_i = X_i'\pi_{10} + \pi_{11}z_i + \xi_{1i} \tag{4.1.4a}$$

$$Y_i = X_i'\pi_{20} + \pi_{21}z_i + \xi_{2i}. \tag{4.1.4b}$$

The parameter $\pi_{11}$ in equation (4.1.4a) captures the first-stage effect of $z_i$ on $s_i$, adjusting for covariates, $X_i$. The parameter $\pi_{21}$ in equation (4.1.4b) captures the reduced-form effect of $z_i$ on $Y_i$, adjusting for these same covariates. In Angrist and Krueger (1991), the instrument $z_i$ is quarter of birth (or a dummy indicating quarter of birth) and the covariates are dummies for year of birth and state of birth. In the language of the SEM, the dependent variables in these two equations are said to be the *endogenous variables* (determined jointly within the system), while the variables on the right-hand side are said to be the *exogenous variables* (determined outside the system). The instruments $z_i$ are a subset of the exogenous variables. The exogenous variables that are not instruments are said to be *exogenous covariates*. Although we're not estimating a traditional supply-and-demand system in this case, these SEM variable labels are still widely used in empirical practice.

The covariate-adjusted IV estimator is the sample analog of the ratio $\frac{\pi_{21}}{\pi_{11}}$. To see this, note that the denominators of the reduced-form and first-stage coefficients are the same. Hence, their ratio is

$$\rho = \frac{\pi_{21}}{\pi_{11}} = \frac{Cov(Y_i, \tilde{z}_i)}{Cov(s_i, \tilde{z}_i)}, \tag{4.1.5}$$

---

[4] Other explanations are possible, the most likely being some sort of family background effect associated with season of birth (see, e.g., Bound, Jaeger, and Baker, 1995). Weighing against the possibility of omitted family background effects is the fact that the quarter-of-birth pattern in average schooling is most pronounced at the schooling levels most affected by compulsory attendance laws.

where $\tilde{z}_i$ is the residual from a regression of $z_i$ on the exogenous covariates, $X_i$. The right-hand side of (4.1.5) therefore swaps $\tilde{z}_i$ for $z_i$ in the IV formula, (4.1.3). Econometricians call the sample analog of equation (4.1.5) an indirect least squares (ILS) estimator of $\rho$ in the causal model with covariates,

$$Y_i = \alpha'X_i + \rho s_i + \eta_i, \qquad (4.1.6)$$

where $\eta_i$ is the compound error term, $A_i'\gamma + v_i$. It's easy to use equation (4.1.6) to confirm directly that $Cov(Y_i, \tilde{z}_i) = \rho Cov(s_i, \tilde{z}_i)$, since $\tilde{z}_i$ is uncorrelated with $X_i$ by construction and with $\eta_i$ by assumption.

### 4.1.1   Two-Stage Least Squares

The reduced-form equation, (4.1.4b), can be derived by substituting the first-stage equation, (4.1.4a), into the causal relation of interest, (4.1.6), which is also called a "structural equation" in simultaneous equations language. We have:

$$\begin{aligned} Y_i &= \alpha'X_i + \rho[X_i'\pi_{10} + \pi_{11}z_i + \xi_{1i}] + \eta_i \qquad (4.1.7) \\ &= X_i'[\alpha + \rho\pi_{10}] + \rho\pi_{11}z_i + [\rho\xi_{1i} + \eta_i] \\ &= X_i'\pi_{20} + \pi_{21}z_i + \xi_{2i}, \end{aligned}$$

where $\pi_{20} \equiv \alpha + \rho\pi_{10}$, $\pi_{21} \equiv \rho\pi_{11}$, and $\xi_{2i} \equiv \rho\xi_{1i} + \eta_i$ in equation (4.1.4b). Equation (4.1.7) again shows why $\rho = \frac{\pi_{21}}{\pi_{11}}$. Note also that a slight rearrangement of (4.1.7) gives

$$Y_i = \alpha'X_i + \rho[X_i'\pi_{10} + \pi_{11}z_i] + \xi_{2i}, \qquad (4.1.8)$$

where $[X_i'\pi_{10} + \pi_{11}z_i]$ is the population fitted value from the first-stage regression of $s_i$ on $X_i$ and $z_i$. Because $z_i$ and $X_i$ are uncorrelated with the reduced-form error, $\xi_{2i}$, the coefficient on $[X_i'\pi_{10} + \pi_{11}z_i]$ in the population regression of $Y_i$ on $X_i$ and $[X_i'\pi_{10} + \pi_{11}z_i]$ equals $\rho$.

In practice, of course, we almost always work with data from samples. Given a random sample, the first-stage fitted values are consistently estimated by

$$\hat{s}_i = X_i'\hat{\pi}_{10} + \hat{\pi}_{11}z_i,$$

where $\hat{\pi}_{10}$ and $\hat{\pi}_{11}$ are OLS estimates from equation (4.1.4a). The coefficient on $\hat{s}_i$ in the regression of $Y_i$ on $X_i$ and $\hat{s}_i$ is called the two-stage least squares (2SLS) estimator of $\rho$. In other words, 2SLS estimates can be constructed by OLS estimation of the "second-stage equation,"

$$Y_i = \alpha' X_i + \rho \hat{s}_i + [\eta_i + \rho(s_i - \hat{s}_i)], \qquad (4.1.9)$$

This is called 2SLS because it can be done in two steps, the first estimating $\hat{s}_i$ using equation (4.1.4a) and the second estimating equation (4.1.9). The resulting estimator is consistent for $\rho$ because the covariates and first-stage fitted values are uncorrelated with both $\eta_i$ and $(s_i - \hat{s}_i)$.

The 2SLS name notwithstanding, we don't usually construct 2SLS estimates in two steps. For one thing, the resulting standard errors are wrong, as we discuss later. Typically, we let specialized software routines (such as are available in SAS or Stata) do the calculation for us. This gets the standard errors right and helps to avoid other mistakes (see section 4.6.1). Still, the fact that the 2SLS estimator can be computed by a sequence of OLS regressions is one way to remember why it works. Intuitively, conditional on covariates, 2SLS retains only the variation in $s_i$ that is generated by quasi-experimental variation—that is, generated by the instrument $z_i$.

2SLS is a many-splendored thing. For one, it is an IV estimator: the 2SLS estimate of $\rho$ in (4.1.9) is the sample analog of $\frac{Cov(Y_i, \hat{s}_i^*)}{Cov(s_i, \hat{s}_i^*)}$, where $\hat{s}_i^*$ is the residual from a regression of $\hat{s}_i$ on $X_i$. This follows from the multivariate regression anatomy formula and the fact that $Cov(s_i, \hat{s}_i^*) = V(\hat{s}_i^*)$. It is also easy to show that, in a model with a single endogenous variable and a single instrument, the 2SLS estimator is the same as the corresponding ILS estimator.[5]

---

[5] Note that $\hat{s}_i^* = \tilde{z}_i \hat{\pi}_{11}$, where $\tilde{z}_i$ is the residual from a regression of $z_i$ on $X_i$, so that the 2SLS estimator is the sample analog of $\left[\frac{Cov(Y_i, \tilde{z}_i)}{V(\tilde{z}_i)}\right](\hat{\pi}_{11})^{-1}$. But the sample analog of the numerator, $\frac{Cov(Y_i, \tilde{z}_i)}{V(\tilde{z}_i)}$, is the OLS estimate of $\pi_{21}$ in the reduced form, (4.1.4b), while $\hat{\pi}_{11}$ is the OLS estimate of the first-stage effect, $\pi_{11}$, in (4.1.4a). Hence, 2SLS with a single instrument is ILS, that is, the ratio of the reduced-form effect of the instrument to the corresponding first-stage effect where both the first-stage and reduced-form equations include covariates.

The link between 2SLS and IV warrants a bit more elaboration in the multi-instrument case. Assuming each instrument captures the same causal effect (a strong assumption that is relaxed below), we might want to combine these alternative IV estimates into a single more precise estimate. In models with multiple instruments, 2SLS accomplishes this by combining multiple instruments into a single instrument. Suppose, for example, we have three instrumental variables, $z_{1i}$, $z_{2i}$, and $z_{3i}$. In the Angrist and Krueger (1991) application, these are dummies for first-, second-, and third-quarter births. The first-stage equation then becomes

$$s_i = X_i'\pi_{10} + \pi_{11}z_{1i} + \pi_{12}z_{2i} + \pi_{13}z_{3i} + \xi_{1i}, \qquad (4.1.10a)$$

while the 2SLS second stage is the same as (4.1.9), except that the fitted values are from (4.1.10a) instead of (4.1.4a). The IV interpretation of this 2SLS estimator is the same as before: the instrument is the residual from a regression of first-stage fitted values on exogenous covariates. The exclusion restriction in this case is the claim that the quarter-of-birth dummies in (4.1.10a) are uncorrelated with $\eta_i$ in equation (4.1.6).

The results of 2SLS estimation of the economic returns to schooling using quarter-of-birth dummies as instruments are shown in table 4.1.1, which reports OLS and 2SLS estimates of models similar to those estimated by Angrist and Krueger (1991). Each column in the table contains OLS and 2SLS estimates of $\rho$ from an equation like (4.1.6), estimated with different combinations of instruments and control variables. The OLS estimate in column 1 is from a regression of log wages with no control variables, while the OLS estimates in column 2 are from a model adding dummies for year of birth and state of birth as control variables. In both cases, the estimated return to schooling is around .075.

The first pair of IV estimates, reported in columns 3 and 4, are from models without exogenous covariates. The instrument used to construct the estimate in column 3 is a single dummy for first-quarter births, while the instruments used to construct the estimate in column 4 are three dummies indicating first-, second-, and third-quarter births. These estimates range from .10 to .11. The results from models including year-of-birth and state-of-birth dummies as exogenous covariates

TABLE 4.1.1
2SLS estimates of the economic returns to schooling

| | OLS | | 2SLS | | | | | |
|---|---|---|---|---|---|---|---|---|
| | (1) | (2) | (3) | (4) | (5) | (6) | (7) | (8) |
| Years of education | .071 (.0004) | .067 (.0004) | .102 (.024) | .13 (.020) | .104 (.026) | .108 (.020) | .087 (.016) | .057 (.029) |
| *Exogenous Covariates* | | | | | | | | |
| Age (in quarters) | | | | | ✓ | ✓ | ✓ | ✓ |
| Age (in quarters) squared | | | | | ✓ | ✓ | ✓ | ✓ |
| 9 year-of-birth dummies | | ✓ | ✓ | ✓ | ✓ | ✓ | ✓ | ✓ |
| 50 state-of-birth dummies | | ✓ | | ✓ | | ✓ | | ✓ |
| *Instruments* | | | | | | | | |
| dummy for QOB = 1 | | | ✓ | ✓ | ✓ | ✓ | ✓ | ✓ |
| dummy for QOB = 2 | | | ✓ | ✓ | ✓ | ✓ | ✓ | ✓ |
| dummy for QOB = 3 | | | ✓ | ✓ | ✓ | ✓ | ✓ | ✓ |
| QOB dummies interacted with year-of-birth dummies (30 instruments total) | | | | | | | ✓ | ✓ |

*Notes:* The table reports OLS and 2SLS estimates of the returns to schooling using the Angrist and Krueger (1991) 1980 census sample. This sample includes native-born men, born 1930–39, with positive earnings and nonallocated values for key variables. The sample size is 329,509. Robust standard errors are reported in parentheses. QOB denotes quarter of birth.

(reported in columns 5 and 6) are similar, not surprisingly, since quarter of birth is not closely related to either of these controls. Overall, the 2SLS estimates are mostly a bit larger than the corresponding OLS estimates. This suggests that the observed association between schooling and earnings is not driven by omitted variables such as ability and family background.

Column 7 in table 4.1.1 shows the results of adding inter-action terms to the instrument list. In particular, this speci-fication adds three quarter-of-birth dummies interacted with nine dummies for year of birth (the sample includes cohorts born in 1930–39), for a total of 30 excluded instruments. The first-stage equation becomes

$$s_i = X_i' \pi_{10} + \pi_{11} Z_{1i} + \pi_{12} Z_{2i} + \pi_{13} Z_{3i} \qquad (4.1.10b)$$
$$+ \sum_j (B_{ij} Z_{1i}) \kappa_{1j} + \sum_j (B_{ij} Z_{2i}) \kappa_{2j} + \sum_j (B_{ij} Z_{3i}) \kappa_{3j} + \xi_{1i},$$

where $B_{ij}$ is a dummy equal to one if individual $i$ was born in year $j$ for $j$ equal to 1931–39. The coefficients $\kappa_{1j}, \kappa_{2j}, \kappa_{3j}$ are the corresponding quarter and year interaction terms. The rationale for adding these interaction terms is an increase in precision that comes from increasing the first-stage $R^2$, which goes up because the quarter-of-birth pattern in schooling dif-fers across cohorts. In this example, the addition of interaction terms to the instrument list leads to a modest gain in precision; the standard error declines from .019 to .016 as we move from column 6 to column 7.[6] (The first-stage and reduced-form effects plotted in figure 4.1.1 are from this fully interacted specification.)

The last 2SLS model reported in table 4.1.1 adds controls for linear and quadratic terms in age in quarters to the list of exogenous covariates. In other words, someone who was born in the first quarter of 1930 is recorded as being 50 years old on census day (April 1), 1980, while someone born in the fourth quarter is recorded as being 49.25 years old. This

---

[6] This gain may not be without cost, as the use of many additional instrum-ents opens up the possibility of increased bias, an issue discussed in sec-tion 4.6.4.

finely coded age variable provides a partial control for the fact that small differences in age may be an omitted variable that confounds the quarter-of-birth identification strategy. As long as the effects of age are reasonably smooth, the quadratic age-in-quarters model will pick them up.

Columns 7 and 8 in table 4.1.1 illustrate the interplay between identification and estimation. (In traditional SEM theory, a parameter is said to be *identified* if we can figure it out from the reduced form.) For the 2SLS procedure to work, there must be some variation in the first-stage fitted values conditional on whatever exogenous covariates are included in the model. If the first-stage fitted values are a linear combination of the included covariates, then the 2SLS estimate simply does not exist. In equation (4.1.9) this would be manifest by perfect multicollinearity (i.e., linear dependence between $X_i$ and $\hat{s}_i$). 2SLS estimates with quadratic age controls exist, but the variability "left over" in the first-stage fitted values is reduced when the covariates include variables such as age in quarters that are closely related to the instruments (quarter-of-birth dummies). Because this variability is the primary determinant of 2SLS standard errors, the estimate in column 8 is markedly less precise than that in column 7, though it is still close to the corresponding OLS estimate.

### Recap of IV and 2SLS Lingo

As we've seen, the *endogenous variables* are the dependent variable and the independent variable(s) to be instrumented; in a simultaneous equations model, endogenous variables are determined by solving a system of stochastic linear equations. To *treat an independent variable as endogenous* is to instrument it, in other words, to replace it with fitted values in the second stage of a 2SLS procedure. The independent endogenous variable in the Angrist and Krueger (1991) study is schooling. The *exogenous variables* include the *exogenous covariates* that are not instrumented and the instruments themselves. In a simultaneous equations model, exogenous variables are determined outside the system. The exogenous covariates in the Angrist and Krueger (1991) study are dummies for year of birth and state of birth. We think of exogenous covariates as controls. 2SLS aficionados live in a world of mutually exclusive labels: in any empirical study involving IV, the random variables to be studied are either dependent variables, independent endogenous variables, instrumental variables, or exogenous covariates. Sometimes we shorten this to dependent and endogenous variables, instruments, and covariates (fudging the fact that the dependent variable is also endogenous in a traditional SEM).

### 4.1.2    The Wald Estimator

The simplest IV estimator uses a single dummy instrument to estimate a model with one endogenous regressor and no covariates. Without covariates, the causal regression model is

$$Y_i = \alpha + \rho s_i + \eta_i, \qquad (4.1.11)$$

where $\eta_i$ and $s_i$ may be correlated. Given the further simplification that $z_i$ is a dummy variable that equals one with probability $p$, we can easily show that

$$Cov(Y_i, z_i) = \{E[Y_i|z_i = 1] - E[Y_i|z_i = 0]\}p(1 - p),$$

with an analogous formula for $Cov(s_i, z_i)$. It therefore follows that

$$\rho = \frac{E[Y_i|z_i = 1] - E[Y_i|z_i = 0]}{E[s_i|z_i = 1] - E[s_i|z_i = 0]}. \qquad (4.1.12)$$

A direct route to this result uses (4.1.11) and the fact that $E[\eta_i|z_i] = 0$, so we have

$$E[Y_i|z_i] = \alpha + \rho E[s_i|z_i]. \qquad (4.1.13)$$

Solving this equation for $\rho$ produces (4.1.12).

Equation (4.1.12) is the population analog of the landmark *Wald estimator* for a bivariate regression with mismeasured regressors.[7] In our context, the Wald formula provides an appealingly transparent implementation of the IV strategy for the elimination of OVB. The principal claim that motivates IV estimation of causal effects is that the *only* reason for any relation between the dependent variable and the instrument is the effect of the instrument on the causal variable of interest. In the context of a dummy instrument, it therefore seems natural to divide—or rescale—the reduced-form difference in means by the corresponding first-stage difference in means.

The Angrist and Krueger (1991) study using quarter of birth to estimate the economic returns to schooling shows the Wald estimator in action. Table 4.1.2 displays the ingredients behind a Wald estimate constructed using the 1980 census. The difference in earnings between men born in the first and fourth quarters of the year is −.0135, while the corresponding difference in schooling is −.151. The ratio of these two differences is a Wald estimate of the economic value of schooling in per-year terms. This comes out to be .089. Not surprisingly, this estimate is not too different from the 2SLS estimates in table 4.1.1. The reason we should expect the Wald and 2SLS estimates to be similar is that both are constructed from the same information: differences in earnings by season of birth.

The Angrist (1990) study of the effects of Vietnam-era military service on the earnings of veterans also shows the Wald estimator in action. In the 1960s and early 1970s, young American men were at risk of being drafted for military service. Concerns about the fairness of the U.S. conscription policy led to the institution of a draft lottery in 1970 that was used to determine priority for conscription. A promising instrument for Vietnam veteran status is therefore draft eligibility, since this was determined by a lottery over birthdays. Specifically,

---

[7]As noted in the introduction to this chapter, measurement error in regressors tends to shrink regression coefficients toward zero. To eliminate this bias, Wald (1940) suggested that the data be divided in a manner independent of the measurement error, and the coefficient of interest estimated as a ratio of differences in means, as in (4.1.12). Durbin (1954) showed that Wald's method of fitting straight lines is an IV estimator where the instrument is a dummy marking Wald's division of the data. Hausman (2001) provides an overview of econometric strategies for dealing with measurement error.

TABLE 4.1.2
Wald estimates of the returns to schooling using
quarter-of-birth instruments

|  | (1) Born in 1st Quarter of Year | (2) Born in 4th Quarter of Year | (3) Difference (Std. Error) (1) – (2) |
|---|---|---|---|
| ln (weekly wage) | 5.892 | 5.905 | −.0135 (.0034) |
| Years of education | 12.688 | 12.839 | −.151 (.016) |
| Wald estimate of return to education |  |  | .089 (.021) |
| OLS estimate of return to education |  |  | .070 (.0005) |

*Notes*: From Angrist and Imbens (1995). The sample includes native-born men with positive earnings from the 1930–39 birth cohorts in the 1980 census 5 percent file. The sample size is 162,515.

in each year from 1970 to 1972, random sequence numbers (RSNs) were randomly assigned to each birth date in cohorts of 19-year-olds. Men with lottery numbers below a cutoff were eligible for the draft, while men with numbers above the cutoff could not be drafted. In practice, many draft-eligible men were still exempted from service for health or other reasons, while many men who were draft-exempt nevertheless volunteered for service. So veteran status was not completely determined by randomized draft eligibility, but draft eligibility provides a dummy instrument highly correlated with Vietnam-era veteran status.

Among white men who were at risk of being drafted in the 1970 draft lottery, draft eligibility is clearly associated with lower earnings in the years after the lottery. This is documented in table 4.1.3, which reports the effect of random-ized draft eligibility status on Social Security–taxable earnings in column 2. Column 1 shows average annual earnings for purposes of comparison. For men born in 1950, there are

TABLE 4.1.3
Wald estimates of the effects of military service on the earnings of white men born in 1950

| | Earnings | | Veteran Status | | |
| --- | --- | --- | --- | --- | --- |
| Earnings Year | Mean (1) | Eligibility Effect (2) | Mean (3) | Eligibility Effect (4) | Wald Estimate of Veteran Effect (5) |
| 1981 | 16,461 | −435.8 (210.5) | .267 | .159 (.040) | −2,741 (1,324) |
| 1971 | 3,338 | −325.9 (46.6) | | | −2,050 (293) |
| 1969 | 2,299 | −2.0 (34.5) | | | |

*Notes*: Adapted from Angrist (1990), tables 2 and 3. Standard errors are shown in parentheses. Earnings data are from Social Security administrative records. Figures are in nominal dollars. Veteran status data are from the Survey of Income and Program Participation. There are about 13,500 individuals in the sample.

significant negative effects of eligibility status on earnings in 1971, when these men were mostly just beginning their military service, and, perhaps more surprisingly, in 1981, ten years later. In contrast, there is no evidence of an association between draft eligibility status and earnings in 1969, the year the lottery drawing for men born in 1950 was held but before anyone born in 1950 was actually drafted.

Because eligibility status was randomly assigned, the claim that the estimates in column 2 represent the casual effect of draft eligibility on earnings seems uncontroversial. The information required to go from draft eligibility effects to veteran status effects is the denominator of the Wald estimator, which is the effect of draft eligibility on the probability of serving in the military. This information is reported in column 4 of table 4.1.3, which shows that draft-eligible men were almost 16 percentage points more likely to have served in the Vietnam era. The Wald estimate of the effect of military service on 1981 earnings, reported in column 4, amounts to about 15 percent of the mean. Effects were even larger in 1971 (in percentage terms), when affected soldiers were still in the army.

An important feature of the Wald/IV estimator is that the identifying assumptions are easy to assess and interpret. Let $D_i$ denote Vietnam-era veteran status and $z_i$ indicate draft eligibility. The fundamental claim justifying our interpretation of the Wald estimator as capturing the causal effect of $D_i$ is that the only reason why $E[Y_i|z_i]$ changes as $z_i$ changes is the variation in $E[D_i|z_i]$. A simple check on this is to look for an association between $z_i$ and personal characteristics that should not be affected by $D_i$, for example race, sex, or any other characteristic that was determined before $D_i$ was determined. Another useful check is to look for an association between the instrument and outcomes in samples where there is no relationship between $D_i$ and $z_i$. If the only reason for draft eligibility effects on earnings is veteran status, then draft eligibility effects on earnings should be zero in samples where draft eligibility status is unrelated to veteran status.

This idea is illustrated in Angrist's (1990) study of the draft lottery by looking at 1969 earnings, an estimate repeated in the last row of table 4.1.3. It's comforting that the draft eligibility treatment effect on 1969 earnings is zero, since 1969 earnings predate the 1970 draft lottery. A second variation on this idea looks at the cohort of men born in 1953. Although there was a lottery drawing that assigned RSNs to the 1953 birth cohort in February 1972, no one born in 1953 was actually drafted (the draft officially ended in July 1973). The first-stage relationship between draft eligibility and veteran status for men born in 1953 (defined using the 1952 lottery cutoff of 95) therefore shows only a small difference in the probability of serving by eligibility status. There is also no significant relationship between earnings and draft eligibility status for men born in 1953, a result that supports the claim that the only reason for draft eligibility effects is military service.

We conclude the discussion of Wald estimators with a set of IV estimates of the effect of family size on mothers' employment and work. Like the schooling and military service studies, these estimates are used for illustration elsewhere in the book. The relationship between fertility and labor supply has long been of interest to labor economists, while the case for omitted variables bias in this context is clear: mothers with weak labor force attachment or low earnings potential may be more likely to have children than mothers with strong labor force attachment or high earnings potential. This makes the observed association between family size and employment hard to interpret, since mothers who have big families probably would have worked less anyway. Angrist and Evans (1998) solve this omitted variables problem using two instrumental variables, both of which lend themselves to Wald-type estimation strategies.

The first Wald estimator uses multiple births, an identification strategy for the effects of family size pioneered by Rosenzweig and Wolpin (1980). The twins instrument in Angrist and Evans (1998) is a dummy for a multiple second birth in a sample of mothers with at least two children. The twins first-stage is .625, an estimate reported in column 3 of table 4.1.4. This means that 37.5 percent of mothers with two or more children would have had a third birth anyway; a multiple third birth increases this proportion to 1. The twins instrument rests on the idea that the occurrence of a multiple birth is essentially random, unrelated to potential outcomes or family background.

The second Wald estimator in table 4.1.4 uses sibling sex composition, an instrument motivated by the fact that American parents with two children are much more likely to have a third child if the first two are of the same sex than if the sex composition is mixed. This is illustrated in column 5 of table 4.1.4, which shows that parents of same-sex sibling birth are 6.7 percentage points more likely to have a third birth (the probability of a third birth among parents with a mixed-sex sibship is .38). The same-sex instrument is based on the claim that sibling sex composition is essentially random and affects family labor supply solely by increasing fertility.

Twins and sex composition instruments both suggest that the birth of a third child has a large effect on employment rates and on weeks and hours worked. Wald estimates using twins instruments show a precisely estimated employment reduction of about .08, while weeks worked fall by 3.8 and hours per week fall by 3.4. These results, which appear in column 4 of table 4.1.4, are smaller in absolute value than the corresponding OLS estimates reported in column 2. This suggests

TABLE 4.1.4

Wald estimates of the effects of family size on labor supply

| | | | IV Estimates Using | | | |
|---|---|---|---|---|---|---|
| | | | Twins | | Sex Composition | |
| Dependent Variable | Mean (1) | OLS (2) | First Stage (3) | Wald Estimates (4) | First Stage (5) | Wald Estimates (6) |
| Employment | .528 | −.167 (.002) | .625 (.011) | −.083 (.017) | .067 (.002) | −.135 (.029) |
| Weeks worked | 19.0 | −8.05 (.09) | | −3.83 (.76) | | −6.23 (1.29) |
| Hours/week | 16.7 | −6.02 (.08) | | −3.39 (.64) | | −5.54 (1.08) |

Note: The table reports OLS and Wald estimates of the effects of a third birth on labor supply using twins and sex composition instruments. Data are from the Angrist and Evans (1998) extract including married women aged 21–35 with at least two children in the 1980 census. OLS models include controls for mother's age, age at first birth, dummies for the sex of first and second births, and dummies for race. The first stage is the same for all dependent variables.

the latter are exaggerated by selection bias. Interestingly, the Wald estimates constructed using a same-sex dummy, reported in column 6, are larger than the twins estimates (showing an employment reduction of .135, for example). The juxtaposition of twins and sex composition instruments in table 4.1.4 suggests that different instruments need not generate similar estimates of causal effects even if both are valid. We expand on this important point in section 4.4. For now, however, we stick with a constant effects framework.

### 4.1.3    Grouped Data and 2SLS

The Wald estimator is the mother of all IV estimators because more complicated 2SLS estimators can typically be constructed from an underlying set of Wald estimators. The link between Wald and 2SLS is grouped data: 2SLS using dummy instruments is the same thing as GLS on a set of group means. GLS in turn can be understood as a linear combination of all the Wald estimators that can be constructed from pairs of means. The generality of this link might appear to be limited by the presumption that the instruments at hand are dummies. Not all instrumental variables are dummies, or even discrete, but this is not really important. For one thing, many instruments can be thought of as defining categories, such as quarter of birth. Moreover, instrumental variables that appear more continuous (such as draft lottery numbers, which range from 1 to 365) can usually be grouped without much loss of information (e.g., a single dummy for draft eligibility status, or dummies for groups of 25 lottery numbers).[8]

To explain the Wald-grouping-2SLS nexus more fully, we stick with the draft lottery study. Earlier we noted that draft eligibility is a promising instrument for Vietnam-era veteran status. The draft eligibility ceilings were RSN 195 for men born in 1950, RSN 125 for men born in 1951, and RSN 95 for men born in 1952. In practice, however, there is a richer link between draft lottery numbers (which we'll call $R_i$, short for RSN) and veteran status ($D_i$) than draft eligibility status alone. Although men with numbers above the eligibility ceiling were not drafted, the ceiling was unknown in advance. Some men therefore volunteered in the hope of serving under better terms and gaining some control over the timing of their service. The pressure to become a draft-induced volunteer was high for men with low lottery numbers but low for men with high numbers. As a result, there is variation in $P[D_i = 1|R_i]$ even for values strictly above or below the draft eligibility cutoff. For example, men born in 1950 with lottery numbers 200–225 were more likely to serve than those with lottery numbers 226–250, though ultimately no one in either group was drafted.

The Wald estimator using draft eligibility as an instrument for men born in 1950 compares the earnings of men with $R_i < 195$ to the earnings of men with $R_i > 195$. But the previous

---

[8]An exception is the classical measurement error model, where both the variable to be instrumented and the instrument are assumed to be continuous. Here, we have in mind IV scenarios involving OVB.

discussion suggests the possibility of many more comparisons, for example men with $R_i \leq 25$ versus men with $R_i \in [26 - 50]$, men with $R_i \in [51 - 75]$ versus men with $R_i \in [76 - 100]$, and so on, until these 25-number intervals are exhausted. We might also make the intervals finer, comparing, say, men in five-number or single-number intervals instead of 25-number intervals. The result of this expansion in the set of comparisons is a set of Wald estimators. These sets are complete in that the intervals partition the support of the underlying instrument, while the individual estimators are linearly independent in the sense that their numerators are linearly independent. Finally, each of these Wald estimators consistently estimates the same causal effect, assumed here to be constant, as long as $R_i$ is independent of potential outcomes and correlated with veteran status (i.e., the Wald denominators are not zero).

The possibility of constructing multiple Wald estimators for the same causal effect naturally raises the question of what to do with all of them. We would like to come up with a single estimate that somehow combines the information in the individual Wald estimates efficiently. As it turns out, the most efficient linear combination of a full set of linearly independent Wald estimates is produced by fitting a line through the group means used to construct these estimates.

The grouped data estimator can be motivated directly as follows. As in (4.1.11), we work with a bivariate constant effects model, which in this case can be written

$$Y_i = \alpha + \rho D_i + \eta_i, \qquad (4.1.14)$$

where $\rho = Y_{1i} - Y_{0i}$ is the causal effect of interest and $Y_{0i} = \alpha + \eta_i$. Because $R_i$ was randomly assigned and lottery numbers are assumed to have no effect on earnings other than through veteran status, $E[\eta_i | R_i] = 0$. It therefore follows that

$$E[Y_i | R_i] = \alpha + \rho P[D_i = 1 | R_i], \qquad (4.1.15)$$

since $P[D_i = 1 | R_i] = E[D_i | R_i]$. In other words, the slope of the line connecting average earnings given lottery number with the average probability of service by lottery number is equal to the effect of military service, $\rho$. This is in spite of the fact that the regression $Y_i$ on $D_i$—in this case, the difference in means by veteran status—almost certainly differs from $\rho$, since $Y_{0i}$ and $D_i$ are likely to be correlated.

Equation (4.1.15) suggests we estimate $e$ by fitting a line to the sample analog of $E[Y_i|R_i]$ and $P[D_i = 1|R_i]$. Suppose that $R_i$ takes on values $j = 1, \ldots, J$. In principle, $j$ might run from 1 to 365, but in Angrist (1990), lottery number information was aggregated to 69 five-number intervals, plus a 70th interval for numbers 346–365. We can therefore think of $R_i$ as running from 1 to 70. Let $\bar{y}_j$ and $\hat{p}_j$ denote estimates of $E[Y_i|R_i = j]$ and $P[D_i = 1|R_i = j]$, while $\bar{\eta}_j$ denotes the average error in (4.1.14). Because sample moments converge to population moments, it follows that OLS estimates of $\rho$ in the grouped equation

$$\bar{y}_j = \alpha + \rho\hat{p}_j + \bar{\eta}_j \qquad (4.1.16)$$

are consistent. In practice, however, generalized least squares (GLS) may be preferable, since a grouped equation is heteroskedastic with a known variance structure. The efficient GLS estimator for grouped data in a constant effects linear model is WLS, weighted by the variance of $\bar{\eta}_j$ (see, e.g., Prais and Aitchison, 1954, or Wooldridge, 2006). Assuming the microdata residual is homoskedastic with variance $\sigma_\eta^2$, this variance is $\frac{\sigma_\eta^2}{n_j}$, where $n_j$ is the group size. Therefore, we should weight by the group size, as discussed in a different context in section 3.4.1.

The GLS (or WLS) estimator of $\rho$ in equation (4.1.16) is especially important for two reasons. First, the GLS slope estimate constructed from J grouped observations is an asymptotically efficient linear combination of any full set of $J - 1$ linearly independent Wald estimators (Angrist, 1991). This can be seen without any mathematics: GLS and any linear combination of Wald estimators are both linear combinations of the grouped dependent variable. Moreover, GLS is the asymptotically efficient linear estimator for grouped data. Therefore we can conclude that there is no better (i.e., asymptotically more efficient) linear combination of Wald estimators than GLS (again, a maintained assumption here is that $\rho$ is constant). The formula for constructing the GLS estimator from a full set of linearly independent Wald estimators appears in Angrist (1988).

Second, just as each Wald estimator is also an IV estimator, the GLS estimator of equation (4.1.16) is 2SLS. The instruments in this case are a full set of dummies to indicate each lottery number cell. To see why, define the set of dummy instruments $Z_i \equiv \{r_{ji} = 1[\text{R}_i = j]; j = 1, \ldots J - 1\}$, where $1[\cdot]$ denotes the indicator function used to construct dummy variables. Now, consider the first-stage regression of $\text{D}_i$ on $Z_i$ plus a constant. Since this first stage is saturated, the fitted values will be the sample conditional means, $\hat{p}_j$, repeated $n_j$ times for each $j$. The second-stage slope estimate is therefore the same as the slope from WLS estimation of the grouped equation, (4.1.16), weighted by the cell size, $n_j$.

The connection between grouped data and 2SLS is of both conceptual and practical importance. On the conceptual side, any 2SLS estimator using a set of dummy instruments can be understood as a linear combination of all the Wald estimators generated by using these instruments one at a time. The Wald estimator in turn provides a simple framework used later in this chapter to interpret IV estimates in the more realistic world of heterogeneous potential outcomes.

Although not all instruments are inherently discrete and therefore immediately amenable to a Wald or grouped data interpretation, many are. Examples include the draft lottery number, quarter of birth, twins, and sibling sex composition instruments we've already discussed. (See also the recent studies by Bennedsen et al., 2007, and Ananat and Michaels, 2008, both of which use dummies for male first births as instruments.) Moreover, instruments that have a continuous flavor can often be fruitfully turned into discrete variables. For example, Angrist, Graddy, and Imbens (2000) recode continuous weather-based instruments into three dummy variables, *stormy, mixed,* and *clear,* which they then use to estimate the demand for fish. This dummy variable parameterization seems to capture the main features of the relationship between weather conditions and the price of fish.[9]

On the practical side, the grouped data equivalent of 2SLS gives us a simple tool that can be used to explain and evaluate any IV strategy. In the case of the draft lottery, for example, the grouped model embodies the assumption that the only reason average earnings vary with lottery numbers is the variation in probability of military service across lottery number groups. If the underlying causal relation is linear with constant effects, then equation (4.1.16) should fit the group means well, something we can assess by inspection and, as discussed in the next section, with the machinery of formal statistical inference.

Sometimes labor economists refer to grouped data plots for discrete instruments as visual instrumental variables (VIV).[10] An example appears in Angrist (1990), reproduced here as figure 4.1.2. This figure shows the relationship between average earnings in five-number RSN cells and the probability of service in these cells, for the 1981–84 earnings of white men born in 1950–53. The slope of the line through these points is an IV estimate of the earnings loss due to military service, in this case about $2,400, not very different from the Wald estimates discussed earlier but with a lower standard error (in this case, about $800).

## 4.2    Asymptotic 2SLS Inference

### 4.2.1    The Asymptotic Distribution of the 2SLS Coefficient Vector

We can derive the limiting distribution of the 2SLS coefficient vector using an argument similar to that used in section 3.1.3 for OLS. In this case, let $V_i \equiv [X_i'\ \hat{s}_i]'$ denote the vector of regressors in the 2SLS second stage, equation (4.1.9). The 2SLS

[9]Continuous instruments recoded as dummies can be seen as providing a parsimonious nonparametric model for the underlying first-stage relation, $E[D_i|z_i]$. In homoskedastic models with constant coefficients, $E[D_i|z_i]$ is the asymptotically efficient instrument (Newey, 1990).

[10]See, for example, the preface to Borjas (2005).

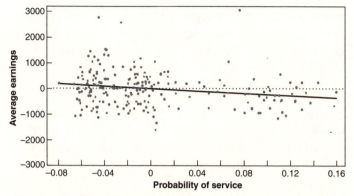

**Figure 4.1.2**  The relationship between average earnings and the probability of military service (from Angrist, 1990). This is a VIV plot of average 1981–84 earnings by cohort and five-RSN lottery number group against conditional probabilities of veteran status in the same cells. The sample includes white men born in 1950–53. Plotted points consist of average residuals (over four years of earnings) from regressions on period and cohort effects. The slope of the least squares regression line drawn through the points is −2,384, with a standard error of 778.

estimator can then be written

$$\hat{\Gamma}_{2SLS} \equiv \left[ \sum_i V_i V_i' \right]^{-1} \sum_i V_i Y_i,$$

where $\Gamma \equiv [\alpha' \ \rho]'$ is the corresponding coefficient vector. Note that

$$\hat{\Gamma}_{2SLS} = \Gamma + \left[ \sum_i V_i V_i' \right]^{-1} \sum_i V_i [\eta_i + \rho(s_i - \hat{s}_i)]$$

$$= \Gamma + \left[ \sum_i V_i V_i' \right]^{-1} \sum_i V_i \eta_i, \qquad (4.2.1)$$

where the second equality comes from the fact that the first-stage residuals, $s_i - \hat{s}_i$, are orthogonal to $V_i$ in the sample. The asymptotic distribution of the 2SLS coefficient vector is therefore the asymptotic distribution of $\left[\sum_i V_i V_i'\right]^{-1} \sum_i V_i \eta_i$. This quantity is a little harder to work with than the corresponding OLS quantity, because the regressors in this case involve estimated fitted values, $\hat{s}_i$. A Slutsky-type argument shows, however, that we get the same limiting distribution replacing estimated fitted values with the corresponding population fitted values (i.e., replacing $\hat{s}_i$ with $[X_i' \pi_{10} + \pi_{11} z_i]$). It therefore follows that $\hat{\Gamma}_{2SLS}$ has an asymptotically normal distribution, with probability limit $\Gamma$, and a covariance matrix estimated consistently by $\left[\sum_i V_i V_i'\right]^{-1} \left[\sum_i V_i V_i' \eta_i^2\right] \left[\sum_i V_i V_i'\right]^{-1}$. This is a sandwich formula like the one for OLS standard errors (White, 1982). Much as with OLS, if $\eta_i$ is conditionally homoskedastic given covariates and instruments, the consistent covariance matrix estimator simplifies to $\left[\sum_i V_i V_i'\right]^{-1} \sigma_\eta^2$.

There is little new here, but there is one tricky point. It seems natural to construct 2SLS estimates manually by estimating the first stage (4.1.4a) and then plugging the fitted values into equation (4.1.9) and estimating this by OLS. That's fine as far as the coefficient estimates go, but the resulting standard errors are wrong. Conventional regression software does not know that you are trying to construct a 2SLS estimate. When constructing standard errors, the software computes the residual variance of the equation you estimate by OLS in the manual second stage:

$$Y_i - [\alpha' X_i + \rho \hat{s}_i] = [\eta_i + \rho(s_i - \hat{s}_i)],$$

replacing the coefficients $\alpha$ and $\rho$ with the corresponding second-stage estimates. The correct residual variance estimator, however, uses the original endogenous regressor to construct residuals and not the first-stage fitted values, $\hat{s}_i$. In other words, the residual you want is the estimated $Y_i - [\alpha' X_i + \rho s_i] = \eta_i$, so as to consistently estimate $\sigma_\eta^2$, and not the variance of $\eta_i + \rho(s_i - \hat{s}_i)$. Although this problem is easy to fix (you can construct the appropriate residual variance estimator in a separate calculation), software designed for 2SLS gets this right automatically, and may help you avoid other common 2SLS mistakes.

### 4.2.2  Overidentification and the 2SLS Minimand⋆

Constant effects models with more instruments than endogenous variables are said to be *overidentified*. (Models with the same number of instruments and endogenous variables are said to be *just-identified*.) With more instruments than needed to identify the parameters of interest, overidentified models impose a set of restrictions that can be evaluated as part of a process of specification testing. This process amounts to asking whether the line plotted in a VIV-type picture fits the relevant conditional means tightly enough, given the precision with which these means are estimated. The details behind this useful idea are easiest to spell out using matrix notation.

Let $Z_i \equiv [X_i'\ z_{1i} \cdots z_{Qi}]'$ denote the vector formed by concatenating the exogenous covariates and $Q$ instrumental variables, and let $W_i \equiv [X_i'\ s_i]'$ denote the vector formed by concatenating the covariates and the single endogenous variable of interest. In the quarter-of-birth study, for example, the covariates are year-of-birth and state-of-birth dummies, the instruments are quarter-of-birth dummies, and the endogenous variable is schooling. The coefficient vector is still $\Gamma \equiv [\alpha'\ \rho]'$, as in the previous subsection. The residuals for the causal (second-stage) model can be defined as a function of $\Gamma$ using

$$\eta_i(\Gamma) \equiv Y_i - \Gamma'W_i = Y_i - [\alpha'X_i + \rho s_i].$$

This residual is assumed to be uncorrelated with the instrument vector, $Z_i$. In other words, $\eta_i$ satisfies the orthogonality condition,

$$E[Z_i \eta_i(\Gamma)] = 0. \qquad (4.2.2)$$

In any sample, however, this equation will not hold exactly because there are more moment conditions than there are elements of $\Gamma$.[11] The sample analog of (4.2.2) is the sum over $i$,

$$\frac{1}{N} \sum Z_i \eta_i(\Gamma) \equiv m_N(\Gamma). \qquad (4.2.3)$$

[11] With a single endogenous variable and more than one instrument, $\Gamma$ is $[K+1] \times 1$, while $Z_i$ is $[K+Q] \times 1$ for $Q > 1$. Hence the resulting linear system cannot be solved exactly unless there is a linear dependency that makes some of the instruments (moment equations) redundant.

2SLS can be understood as a generalized method of moments (GMM) estimator that chooses a value for $\Gamma$ by making (4.2.3) as close to zero as possible.

By the central limit theorem, the sample moment vector $\sqrt{N}m_N(\Gamma)$ has an asymptotic covariance matrix equal to $E[Z_iZ_i'\eta_i(\Gamma)^2]$, a matrix we'll call $\Lambda$. Although somewhat intimidating at first blush, this is just a matrix of fourth moments, as in the sandwich formula used to construct robust standard errors, (3.1.7). As shown by Hansen (1982), the optimal GMM estimator based on (4.2.2) minimizes a quadratic form in the sample moment vector, $m_N(\hat{g})$, where $\hat{g}$ is a candidate estimator of $\Gamma$. The optimal weighting matrix in the middle of the GMM quadratic form is $\Lambda^{-1}$. In practice, of course, $\Lambda$ is unknown and must be estimated. A feasible version of the GMM procedure uses a consistent estimator of $\Lambda$ in the weighting matrix. Since the estimators using known and estimated $\Lambda$ have the same asymptotic distribution, we'll ignore this distinction for now. The quadratic form to be minimized can therefore be written,

$$J_N(\hat{g}) \equiv Nm_N(\hat{g})'\Lambda^{-1}m_N(\hat{g}), \qquad (4.2.4)$$

where the $N$-term out front comes from $\sqrt{N}$ normalization of the sample moments. As shown immediately below, when the residuals are conditionally homoskedastic, the minimizer of $J_N(\hat{g})$ is the 2SLS estimator. Without homoskedasticity, the GMM estimator that minimizes (4.2.4) is White's (1982) two-stage IV (a generalization of 2SLS), so it makes sense to call $J_N(\hat{g})$ the 2SLS minimand.

Here are some of the details behind the GMM interpretation of 2SLS.[12] Conditional homoskedasticity means that

$$\Lambda = E[Z_iZ_i'\eta_i(\Gamma)^2] = E[Z_iZ_i']\sigma_\eta^2.$$

Substituting for $\Lambda^{-1}$ and using $y, Z,$ and $W$ to denote sample data vectors and matrices, the quadratic form to be minimized

---

[12]More detail can be found in Newey (1985), Newey and West (1987), the advanced text by Amemiya (1985), and the original Hansen (1982) GMM paper.

becomes

$$J_N(\hat{g}) = \frac{1}{N\sigma_\eta^2}(y - W\hat{g})'ZE[Z_iZ_i']^{-1}Z'(y - W\hat{g}). \quad (4.2.5)$$

Finally, substituting the sample cross-product matrix $[\frac{Z'Z}{N}]$ for $E[Z_iZ_i']$, we have

$$\hat{J}_N(\hat{g}) = \frac{1}{\sigma_\eta^2}(y - W\hat{g})'P_Z(y - W\hat{g}),$$

where $P_Z = Z(Z'Z)^{-1}Z$. From here, we get the solution

$$\hat{g} = \hat{\Gamma}_{2SLS} = [W'P_ZW]^{-1}W'P_Zy.$$

Since the projection operator, $P_Z$, produces fitted values (i.e., $P_ZW$ gives the fitted values from a regression of $W$ on $Z$), and $P_Z$ is an idempotent matrix, this can be seen to be the OLS estimator of the second-stage equation, (4.1.9), written in matrix notation. More generally, even without homoskedasticity we can obtain a feasible efficient 2SLS-type estimator by minimizing (4.2.4) and using a consistent estimator of $E[Z_iZ_i'\eta_i(\Gamma)^2]$ to form $\hat{J}_N(\hat{g})$. Typically, we'd use the empirical fourth moments, $\sum Z_iZ_i'\hat{\eta}_i^2$, where $\hat{\eta}_i$ is the regular 2SLS residual computed without worrying about heteroskedasticity (see White, 1982, for distribution theory and other details).

The overidentification test statistic is given by the minimized 2SLS minimand. Intuitively, this statistic tells us whether the sample moment vector, $m_N(\hat{g})$, is close enough to zero for the assumption that $E[Z_i\eta_i] = 0$ to be plausible. In particular, under the null hypothesis that the residuals and instruments are indeed uncorrelated, the minimized $J_N(\hat{g})$ has a $\chi^2(Q-1)$ distribution. We can therefore compare the empirical value of the 2SLS minimand with chi-square tables in a formal test for $H_0: E[Z_i\eta_i] = 0$.

We're especially interested in the 2SLS minimand when the instruments are a full set of mutually exclusive dummy variables, as for the Wald estimators and grouped data estimation strategies discussed above. In this important special case, 2SLS becomes WLS estimation of a grouped equation like (4.1.16), while the 2SLS minimand is the weighted sum of squares being minimized. To see this, note that regression on a full set of mutually exclusive dummy variables for an instrument that takes on J values produces an $N \times 1$ vector of fitted values equal to the J conditional means at each value of the instrument (included covariates are counted as instruments), each one of these $n_j$ times, where $n_j$ is the group size and $\sum n_j = N$. The cross-product matrix $[Z'Z]$ in this case is a $J \times J$ diagonal matrix with elements $n_j$. Simplifying, we then have

$$\hat{J}_N(\hat{g}) = \frac{1}{\sigma_\eta^2} \sum_j n_j(\bar{y}_j - \hat{g}' \bar{W}_j)^2, \qquad (4.2.6)$$

where $\bar{W}_j$ is the sample mean of the rows of matrix $W$ in group $j$. Thus, $\hat{J}_N(\hat{g})$ is the GLS minimand for estimation of the regression of $\bar{y}_j$ on $\bar{W}_j$. With a little more work (here we skip the details), we can similarly show that the efficient two-step IV procedure without homoskedasticity minimizes

$$\hat{J}_N(\hat{g}) = \sum_j \left(\frac{n_j}{\sigma_j^2}\right) (\bar{y}_j - \hat{g}' \bar{W}_j)^2, \qquad (4.2.7)$$

where $\sigma_j^2$ is the variance of $\eta_i$ in group $j$. Estimation using (4.2.7) is feasible because we can estimate $\sigma_j^2$ in a first step, using an inefficient but still consistent 2SLS estimator that ignores heteroskedasticity. Efficient two-step IV estimators are constructed in Angrist (1990, 1991).

The GLS structure of the 2SLS minimand allows us to interpret the overidentification test statistic for dummy instruments as a measure of the goodness of fit of the line connecting $\bar{y}_j$ and $\bar{W}_j$. In other words, this is the chi-square goodness-of-fit statistic for the regression line in a VIV plot like that shown in figure 4.1.2. The chi-square degrees of freedom parameter is given by the difference between the number of instruments (groups) and the number of parameters being estimated.[13]

---

[13]If, for example, the instrument takes on three values, one of which is assigned to the constant, and the model includes a constant and a single endogenous variable only, the test statistic has 1 degree of freedom.

As with the 2SLS estimator, there are many roads to the test statistic, (4.2.7). Here are two further paths that are worth knowing. First, the test statistic based on the GMM minimand for IV, whether the instruments are group dummies or not, is the same as the overidentification test statistic discussed in widely used econometric references on simultaneous equations models. For example, this statistic features in Hausman's (1983) chapter on simultaneous equations in the *Handbook of Econometrics*. Hausman also proposes a simple computational procedure: in homoskedastic models, the minimized 2SLS minimand is the sample size times the $R^2$ from a regression of the 2SLS residuals on the instruments (and the exogenous covariates). The formula for this is $N[\frac{\hat{\eta}' P_Z \hat{\eta}}{\hat{\eta}' \hat{\eta}}]$, where $\hat{\eta} = \text{Y} - \text{W}\hat{\Gamma}_{2SLS}$ is the vector of 2SLS residuals.

Second, it's worth emphasizing that the overidentification idea can be said to be "more than one way to skin the same econometric cat." In other words, given more than one instrument for the same causal relation, we might construct just-identified IV estimators one at a time and compare them. This comparison checks overidentification directly: if each just-identified estimator is consistent, the differences between them should be small relative to sampling variance, and should shrink as the sample size and hence the precision of these estimates increases. In fact, a formal test of the equality of all possible just-identified estimators is said to generate a Wald test of this null hypothesis, while the test statistic based on the 2SLS minimand is said to be a Lagrange multiplier (LM) test because it can be related to the score vector in a maximum likelihood version of the IV setup.[14]

In the grouped data version of IV, the Wald test amounts to a test for equality of the set of all possible linearly independent Wald estimators. If, for example, draft lottery numbers are divided into four groups based on various cohorts' eligibility cutoffs (RSN 1–95, 96–125, 126–195, and the rest), then

---

[14]The Wald estimator and Wald test are named after the same man, Abraham Wald, but the latter reference is Wald (1943). Wald, who died tragically in a plane crash at the age of 48, was a giant of econometrics as well as mathematical statistics.

three linearly independent Wald estimators can be constructed. Alternatively, the efficient grouped data estimator can be constructed by running GLS on these four conditional means. Four groups means there are three possible Wald estimators and two nonredundant equality restrictions on these three; hence, the relevant *Wald statistic* has 2 degrees of freedom. On the other hand, four groups means three instruments and a constant are available to estimate a model with two parameters (the constant and the causal effect of military service). So the 2SLS minimand generates an overidentification test statistic with $4 - 2 = 2$ degrees of freedom. And, provided you use the same method of estimating the weighting matrix in the relevant quadratic forms, these two test statistics not only test the same thing, they are numerically equivalent. This makes sense, since 2SLS is the efficient linear combination of Wald estimators.[15]

Finally, a caveat regarding overidentification tests in practice. Because $J_N(\hat{g})$ measures variance-normalized goodness of fit, the overidentification test statistic tends to be low when the underlying estimates are imprecise. Since IV estimates are very often imprecise, we cannot take much satisfaction from the fact that one estimate is within sampling variance of another, even if the individual estimates appear precise enough to be informative. On the other hand, in cases where the underlying IV estimates are quite precise, the fact that the overidentification test statistic rejects need not point to an identification failure. Rather, this may be evidence of treatment effect heterogeneity, a possibility we discuss further below. On the conceptual side, however, an understanding of the anatomy of the 2SLS minimand is invaluable, for it once again highlights

---

[15] The fact that Wald and LM testing procedures for the same null are equivalent in linear models was established by Newey and West (1987). Angrist (1991) gives a more formal statement of the argument in this paragraph. An interesting econometric question in this context, first raised by Deaton (1985), is how many groups are optimal when this can be varied. The analogy between grouping and IV means that more groups equals more instruments, and hence greater asymptotic efficiency at the cost of more bias (see chapter 8). Devereux (2007) proposes a simple bias-corrected IV estimator for grouped data with many groups.

the important link between grouped data and IV. This link takes the mystery out of estimation and testing with instrumental variables and focuses our attention on the raw moments that provide the foundation for causal inference.

## 4.3    Two-Sample IV and Split-Sample IV★

The GMM interpretation of 2SLS highlights the fact that IV estimates can be constructed from sample moments alone, with no microdata. Returning to the sample moment condition, (4.2.3), and rearranging slightly produces a regression-like equation involving second moments:

$$\frac{Z'Y}{N} = \frac{Z'W}{N}\Gamma + \frac{Z'\eta}{N} \qquad (4.3.1)$$

GLS estimates of $\Gamma$ in (4.3.1) are consistent because $E[\frac{Z'Y}{N}] = E[\frac{Z'W}{N}]\Gamma$.

The 2SLS minimand can be thought of as GLS applied to (4.3.1), after multiplying by $\sqrt{N}$ to keep the residual from disappearing as the sample size gets large. In other words, 2SLS minimizes a quadratic form in the residuals from (4.3.1) with a (possibly nondiagonal) weighting matrix. An important insight that comes from writing the 2SLS problem in this way is that we do not need individual observations to estimate (4.3.1). Just as with the OLS coefficient vector, which can be constructed from the sample conditional mean function, IV estimates can also be constructed from sample moments. The necessary moments are $\frac{Z'Y}{N}$ and $\frac{Z'W}{N}$. The dependent variable, $\frac{Z'Y}{N}$, is a vector of dimension $[\kappa + Q] \times 1$. The regressor matrix, $\frac{Z'W}{N}$, is of dimension $[\kappa + Q] \times [\kappa + 1]$. The IV second-moment equation cannot be solved exactly unless $Q = 1$, so it makes sense to make the fit as close as possible by minimizing a quadratic form in the residuals. The most efficient weighting matrix for this purpose is the asymptotic covariance matrix of $\frac{Z'\eta}{\sqrt{N}}$. This again produces the 2SLS minimand, $\hat{J}_N(\hat{g})$.

A related insight is the fact that the moment matrices on the left- and right-hand side of the equals sign in equation (4.3.1) need not come from the same data sets, provided these data sets are drawn from the same population. This observation leads to the two-sample instrumental variables (TSIV) estimator used by Angrist (1990) and developed formally in Angrist and Krueger (1992).[16] Briefly, let $Z_1$ and $Y_1$ denote the instrument/covariate matrix and dependent variable vectors in data set 1 of size $N_1$ and let $Z_2$ and $W_2$ denote the instrument/covariate matrix and endogenous variable/covariate matrix in data set 2 of size $N_2$. Assuming $plim(\frac{Z_2'W_2}{N_2}) = plim(\frac{Z_1'W_1}{N_1})$, GLS estimates of the two-sample moment equation

$$\frac{Z_1'Y_1}{N_1} = \frac{Z_2'W_2}{N_2}\Gamma + \left\{ \left[ \frac{Z_1'W_1}{N_1} - \frac{Z_2'W_2}{N_2} \right] \Gamma + \frac{Z_1'\eta_1}{N_1} \right\}$$

are consistent for $\Gamma$. The asymptotic distribution of this estimator is obtained by normalizing by $\sqrt{N_1}$ and assuming $plim(\frac{N_2}{N_1})$ is a constant.

The utility of TSIV comes from the fact that it widens the scope for IV estimation to situations where observations on dependent variables, instruments, and the endogenous variable of interest are hard to find in a single sample. It may be easier to find one data set that has information on outcomes and instruments, with which the reduced form can be estimated, and another data set that has information on endogenous variables and instruments, with which the first stage can be estimated. For example, in Angrist (1990), administrative records from the Social Security Administration (SSA) provide information on the dependent variable (annual earnings) and the instruments (draft lottery numbers coded from dates of birth, as well as covariates for race and year of birth). The SSA does not, however, track participants' veteran status. This information was taken from military records, which also contain dates of birth that can used to code lottery numbers.

---

[16] Applications of TSIV include Bjorklund and Jantti (1997), Jappelli, Pischke, and Souleles (1998), Currie and Yelowitz (2000), and Dee and Evans (2003). In a recent paper, Inoue and Solon (2009) compare the asymptotic distributions of alternative TSIV estimators and introduce a maximum likelihood (LIML-type) version of TSIV. They also correct a mistake in the distribution theory in Angrist and Krueger (1995), discussed later in this section.

Angrist (1990) used these military records to construct $\frac{Z_2'W_2}{N_2}$, the first-stage correlation between lottery numbers and veteran status conditional on race and year of birth, while the SSA data were used to construct $\frac{Z_1'Y_1}{N_1}$.

Two further simplifications make TSIV especially easy to use. First, as noted previously, when the instruments consist of a full set of mutually exclusive dummy variables, as in Angrist (1990) and Angrist and Krueger (1992), the second moment equation, (4.3.1), simplifies to a model for conditional means. In particular, the 2SLS minimand for the two-sample problem becomes

$$\hat{J}_N(\hat{g}) = \sum_j \omega_j (\bar{y}_{1j} - \hat{g}'\bar{W}_{2j})^2, \qquad (4.3.2)$$

where $\bar{y}_{1j}$ is the mean of the dependent variable at instrument/covariate value $j$ in one sample, $\bar{W}_{2j}$ is the mean of endogenous variables and covariates at instrument/covariate value $j$ in a second sample, and $\omega_j$ is an appropriate weight. This amounts to WLS estimation of the VIV equation, except that the dependent and independent variables do not come from the same sample. Again, Angrist (1990) and Angrist and Krueger (1992) provide illustrations. The optimal weights for asymptotically efficient TSIV are given by the variance of $\bar{y}_{1j} - \hat{g}'\bar{W}_{2j}$. This variance is easy to compute if the two samples used for TSIV are independent.

Second, Angrist and Krueger (1995) introduced a computationally attractive TSIV-type estimator that requires no matrix manipulation and can be implemented with ordinary regression software. This estimator, called split-sample IV (SSIV), works as follows.[17] The first-stage estimates in data set 2 are $(Z_2'Z_2)^{-1}Z_2'W_2$. These are carried over to data set 1 by constructing *cross-sample fitted values*, $\hat{W}_{12} \equiv Z_1(Z_2'Z_2)^{-1}Z_2'W_2$.

---

[17]Angrist and Krueger called this estimator SSIV because they were concerned with a scenario where a single data set is deliberately split in two. As discussed in section 4.6.4, the resulting estimator may have less bias than conventional 2SLS. Inoue and Solon (2009) refer to the estimator Angrist and Krueger (1995) called SSIV as two-sample 2SLS, or TS2SLS.

The SSIV second stage is a regression of $Y_1$ on $\hat{W}_{12}$. The correct asymptotic distribution for this estimator is derived in Inoue and Solon (2009), who show that the distribution presented in Angrist and Krueger (1992) requires the assumption that $Z_1'Z_1 = Z_2'Z_2$ (as would be true if the marginal distribution of the instruments and covariates is fixed in repeated samples). It's worth noting, however, that the limiting distributions of SSIV and 2SLS are the same when the coefficient on the endogenous variable is zero. The standard errors for this special case are simple to construct and probably provide a reasonably good approximation to the general case.[18]

## 4.4   IV with Heterogeneous Potential Outcomes

The discussion of IV up to this point postulates a constant causal effect. In the case of a dummy variable such as veteran status, this means $Y_{1i} - Y_{0i} = \rho$ for all $i$, while with a multivalued treatment such as schooling, this means $Y_{si} - Y_{s-1,i} = \rho$ for all $s$ and all $i$. Both are highly stylized views of the world, especially the multivalued case, which imposes linearity as well as homogeneity. To focus on one thing at a time in a heterogeneous effects model, we start with a zero-one causal variable, like a treatment dummy. In this context, we'd like to allow for treatment effect heterogeneity, in other words, a distribution of causal effects across individuals.

---

[18]This shortcut formula uses the standard errors from the manual SSIV second stage. The correct asymptotic covariance matrix formula, from Inoue and Solon (2005), is

$$\{B'[(\sigma_{11} + \kappa \Gamma' \Sigma_{22} \Gamma)A]^{-1}B\}^{-1},$$

where   $B = plim\left(\frac{Z_2'W_2}{N_2}\right) = plim\left(\frac{Z_1'W_1}{N_1}\right)$,    $A = plim\left(\frac{Z_1'Z_1}{N_1}\right) = plim\left(\frac{Z_2'Z_2}{N_2}\right)$, $plim\left(\frac{N_2}{N_1}\right) = \kappa, \sigma_{11}$ is the variance of the reduced-form residual in data set 1, and $\Sigma_{22}$ is the variance of the first-stage residual in data set 2. In principle, these pieces are easy enough to calculate. Other approaches to SSIV inference include those of Dee and Evans (2003), who calculate standard errors for just-identified models using the delta method, and Bjorklund and Jantti (1997), who use a bootstrap.

Why is treatment effect heterogeneity important? The answer lies in the distinction between the two types of validity that characterize a research design. *Internal validity* is the question of whether a given design successfully uncovers causal effects for the population being studied. A randomized clinical trial, or for that matter a good IV study, has a strong claim to internal validity. *External validity* is the predictive value of the study's findings in a different context. For example, if the study population in a randomized trial is especially likely to benefit from treatment, the resulting estimates may have little external validity. Likewise, draft lottery estimates of the effects of conscription for service in the Vietnam era need not be a good measure of the consequences of voluntary military service. An econometric framework with heterogeneous treatment effects helps us to assess both the internal and external validity of IV estimates.[19]

### 4.4.1   Local Average Treatment Effects

In an IV framework, the engine that drives causal inference is the instrument $z_i$, but the variable of interest is still $D_i$. This feature of the IV setup leads us to adopt a generalized potential outcomes concept, indexed against both instruments and treatment status. Let $Y_i(d, z)$ denote the potential outcome of individual $i$ were this person to have treatment status $D_i = d$ and instrument value $z_i = z$. This tells us, for example, what the earnings of $i$ would be given alternative combinations of veteran status and draft eligibility status. The causal effect of veteran status given $i$'s realized draft eligibility status is $Y_i(1, z_i) - Y_i(0, z_i)$, while the causal effect of draft eligibility status given $i$'s veteran status is $Y_i(D_i, 1) - Y_i(D_i, 0)$.

We can think of instrumental variables as initiating a causal chain where the instrument $z_i$ affects the variable of interest, $D_i$, which in turn affects outcomes, $Y_i$. To make this precise, we introduce notation to express the idea that the instrument

---

[19]The distinction between internal and external validity has a long history in social science. See, for example, the chapter-length discussion in Shadish, Cook, and Campbell (2002), the successor to a classic text on research methods by Campbell and Stanley (1963).

has a causal effect on $D_i$. Let $D_{1i}$ be $i$'s treatment status when $z_i = 1$, while $D_{0i}$ is $i$'s treatment status when $z_i = 0$. Observed treatment status is therefore

$$D_i = D_{0i} + (D_{1i} - D_{0i})z_i = \pi_0 + \pi_{1i}z_i + \xi_i. \quad (4.4.1)$$

In random coefficients notation, $\pi_0 \equiv E[D_{0i}]$ and $\pi_{1i} \equiv (D_{1i} - D_{0i})$, so $\pi_{1i}$ is the heterogeneous causal effect of the instrument on $D_i$. As with potential outcomes, only one of the potential treatment assignments, $D_{1i}$ and $D_{0i}$, is ever observed for any one person. In the draft lottery example, $D_{0i}$ tells us whether $i$ would serve in the military if he drew a high (draft-ineligible) lottery number, while $D_{1i}$ tells us whether $i$ would serve if he drew a low (draft-eligible) lottery number. We get to see one or the other of these potential assignments depending on $z_i$. The average causal effect of $z_i$ on $D_i$ is $E[\pi_{1i}]$.

The first assumption in the heterogeneous effects framework is that the instrument is as good as randomly assigned: it is independent of the vector of potential outcomes and potential treatment assignments. Formally, this can be written as

$$[\{Y_i(d,z); \forall\, d, z\}, D_{1i}, D_{0i}] \perp\!\!\!\perp z_i. \quad (4.4.2)$$

This *independence assumption* is sufficient for a causal interpretation of the reduced form, that is, the regression of $Y_i$ on $z_i$. Specifically,

$$E[Y_i|z_i = 1] - E[Y_i|z_i = 0]$$
$$= E[Y_i(D_{1i}, 1)|z_i = 1] - E[Y_i(D_{0i}, 0)|z_i = 0]$$
$$= E[Y_i(D_{1i}, 1) - Y_i(D_{0i}, 0)],$$

the causal effect of the instrument on $Y_i$. Independence also means that

$$E[D_i|z_i = 1] - E[D_i|z_i = 0] = E[D_{1i}|z_i = 1] - E[D_{0i}|z_i = 0]$$
$$= E[D_{1i} - D_{0i}].$$

In other words, the first stage from our earlier discussion of 2SLS captures the causal effect of $z_i$ on $D_i$.

The second key assumption in the heterogeneous effects framework is the presumption that $Y_i(d, z)$ is a function only of $d$. To be specific, while draft eligibility clearly affects veteran status, an individual's potential earnings as a veteran or nonveteran are assumed to be unchanged by draft eligibility status. In general, the claim that an instrument operates through a single known causal channel is called an *exclusion restriction*. Formally, the exclusion restriction says that

$$Y_i(d, 0) = Y_i(d, 1) \text{ for } d = 0, 1.$$

In a linear model with constant effects, the exclusion restriction is expressed by the omission of instruments from the causal equation of interest and by saying that $E[z_i \eta_i] = 0$ in an equation like (4.1.14) in section 4.1. It's worth noting however, that the traditional error term notation used for simultaneous equations models doesn't lend itself to a clear distinction between independence and exclusion. We need $z_i$ and $\eta_i$ to be uncorrelated, but the reasoning that lies behind this assumption is unclear until we consider the independence and exclusion restrictions as distinct propositions.

The exclusion restriction fails for draft lottery instruments if men with low draft lottery numbers were affected in some way other than through an increased likelihood of military service. For example, Angrist and Krueger (1992) looked for an association between draft lottery numbers and schooling. Their idea was that educational draft deferments could have led men with low lottery numbers to stay in college longer than they would have otherwise desired. If so, draft lottery numbers are correlated with earnings for at least two reasons: an increased likelihood of military service and an increased likelihood of college attendance. The fact that the lottery number is randomly assigned (and therefore satisfies the independence assumption) does not make this possibility less likely. The exclusion restriction is distinct from the claim that the instrument is (as good as) randomly assigned. Rather, it is a claim about a unique channel for causal effects of the instrument.[20]

---

[20] As it turns out, there is not much of a relationship between schooling and lottery numbers in the Angrist and Krueger (1992) data, probably because educational deferments were phased out during the lottery period. On the other hand, in a recent paper, Angrist and Chen (2007) argue that Vietnam veterans end up with more schooling because of veterans benefits (known as the GI Bill). Extra schooling via the GI Bill does not violate the exclusion restriction because veterans' benefits are a downstream consequence of military service.

Using the exclusion restriction, we can define potential outcomes indexed solely against treatment status using the single index $(Y_{1i}, Y_{0i})$ notation we have been using all along. In particular,

$$Y_{1i} \equiv Y_i(1, 1) = Y_i(1, 0);$$
$$Y_{0i} \equiv Y_i(0, 1) = Y_i(0, 0). \qquad (4.4.3)$$

The observed outcome, $Y_i$, can therefore be written in terms of potential outcomes as:

$$Y_i = Y_i(0, z_i) + [Y_i(1, z_i) - Y_i(0, z_i)]D_i \qquad (4.4.4)$$
$$= Y_{0i} + (Y_{1i} - Y_{0i})D_i.$$

Random coefficients notation for this is

$$Y_i = \alpha_0 + \rho_i D_i + \eta_i,$$

a compact version of (4.4.4) with $\alpha_0 \equiv E[Y_{0i}]$ and $\rho_i \equiv Y_{1i} - Y_{0i}$.

A final assumption needed for heterogeneous IV models is that either $\pi_{1i} \geq 0$ for all $i$ or $\pi_{1i} \leq 0$ for all $i$. This *monotonicity assumption*, introduced by Imbens and Angrist (1994), means that while the instrument may have no effect on some people, all those who are affected are affected in the same way. In other words, either $D_{1i} \geq D_{0i}$ or $D_{1i} \leq D_{0i}$ for all $i$. In what follows, we assume monotonicity holds with $D_{1i} \geq D_{0i}$. In the draft lottery example, this means that although draft eligibility may have had no effect on the probability of military service for some men, there is no one who was actually kept out of the military by being draft eligible. Without monotonicity, IV estimators are not guaranteed to estimate a weighted average of the underlying individual causal effects, $Y_{1i} - Y_{0i}$.

Given the exclusion restriction, the independence of instruments and potential outcomes, the existence of a first stage, and monotonicity, the Wald estimand can be interpreted as the effect of veteran status on those whose treatment status can be changed by the instrument. This parameter is called the local average treatment effect (LATE; Imbens and Angrist, 1994). Here is a formal statement:

**Theorem 4.4.1** *The LATE Theorem. Suppose*

    *(A1, Independence)* $\{Y_i(D_{1i}, 1), Y_i(D_{0i}, 0), D_{1i}, D_{0i}\} \perp\!\!\!\perp Z_i$;

    *(A2, Exclusion)* $Y_i(d, 0) = Y_i(d, 1) \equiv Y_{di}$ *for* $d = 0, 1$;

    *(A3, First stage)* $E[D_{1i} - D_{0i}] \neq 0$;

    *(A4, Monotonicity)* $D_{1i} - D_{0i} \geq 0 \; \forall i$, *or vice versa;*

*Then*

$$\frac{E[Y_i|Z_i = 1] - E[Y_i|Z_i = 0]}{E[D_i|Z_i = 1] - E[D_i|Z_i = 0]} = E[Y_{1i} - Y_{0i}|D_{1i} > D_{0i}]$$

$$= E[\rho_i|\pi_{1i} > 0].$$

**Proof.** Use the exclusion restriction to write $E[Y_i|Z_i = 1] = E[Y_{0i} + (Y_{1i} - Y_{0i})D_i|Z_i = 1]$, which equals $E[Y_{0i} + (Y_{1i} - Y_{0i})D_{1i}]$ by independence.[21] Likewise $E[Y_i|Z_i = 0] = E[Y_{0i} + (Y_{1i} - Y_{0i})D_{0i}]$, so the numerator of the Wald estimator is $E[(Y_{1i} - Y_{0i})(D_{1i} - D_{0i})]$. Monotonicity means $D_{1i} - D_{0i}$ equals one or zero, so

$$E[(Y_{1i} - Y_{0i})(D_{1i} - D_{0i})] = E[Y_{1i} - Y_{0i}|D_{1i} > D_{0i}]P[D_{1i} > D_{0i}].$$

A similar argument shows

$$E[D_i|Z_i = 1] - E[D_i|Z_i = 0] = E[D_{1i} - D_{0i}] = P[D_{1i} > D_{0i}].$$

This theorem says that an instrument that is as good as randomly assigned, affects the outcome through a single known channel, has a first stage, and affects the causal channel of interest only in one direction can be used to estimate the average causal effect on the affected group. Thus, IV estimates of effects of military service using the draft lottery capture the effect of military service on men who served because they were draft eligible but who would not otherwise have served. This excludes volunteers and men who were exempted from military service for medical reasons, but it includes men for whom draft policy was binding.

How useful is LATE? No theorem answers this question, but it's always worth discussing. Part of the interest in the effects of

---

[21]Note that the statement of independence in A1 has been simplified from (4.4.2) to cover only those values of $Y_i(d, z)$ that we might see, specifically, $Y_i(D_{z_i}, Z_i)$.

Vietnam-era service has to do with the question of whether veterans (especially conscripts) were adequately compensated for their service. Internally valid draft lottery estimates answer this question. Draft lottery estimates of the effects of Vietnam-era conscription may also be relevant for discussions of any future conscription policy. On the other hand, while draft lottery instruments produce internally valid estimates of the causal effect of Vietnam-era conscription, the external validity—that is, the predictive value of these estimates for military service in other times and places—is not directly addressed by the IV framework. There is nothing in IV formulas to explain *why* Vietnam-era service affects earnings; for that, you need a theory.[22]

You might wonder why we need monotonicity for the LATE theorem, an assumption that plays no role in the traditional simultaneous equations framework with constant effects. A failure of monotonicity means the instrument pushes some people into treatment while pushing others out. Angrist, Imbens, and Rubin (1996) call the latter group *defiers*. Defiers complicate the link between LATE and the reduced form. To see why, go back to the step in the proof of the LATE theorem that shows the reduced form is

$$E[Y_i|z_i = 1] - E[Y_i|z_i = 0] = E[(Y_{1i} - Y_{0i})(D_{1i} - D_{0i})].$$

Without monotonicity, this is equal to

$$E[Y_{1i} - Y_{0i}|D_{1i} > D_{0i}]P[D_{1i} > D_{0i}]$$
$$- E[Y_{1i} - Y_{0i}|D_{1i} < D_{0i}]P[D_{1i} < D_{0i}].$$

We might therefore have a scenario where treatment effects are positive for everyone yet the reduced form is zero because effects on compliers are canceled out by effects on defiers. This doesn't come up in a constant effects model because the reduced form is always the constant effect times the first

---

[22] Angrist (1990) interprets draft lottery estimates as the penalty for lost labor market experience. This suggests draft lottery estimates should have external validity for the effects of conscription in other periods, a conjecture born out by the results for World War II draftees in Angrist and Krueger (1994).

stage, regardless of whether the first stage includes defiant behavior.[23]

A deeper understanding of LATE can be had by linking it to a workhorse of contemporary econometrics, the latent index model for dummy endogenous variables such as assignment to treatment. Latent index models describe individual choices as being determined by a comparison of partly observed and partly unknown ("latent") utilities and costs (see, e.g., Heckman, 1978). Typically, these unobservables are thought of as being related to outcomes, in which case the treatment variable is said to be endogenous (though it is not really endogenous in a simultaneous equations sense). For example, we can model veteran status as

$$D_i = \begin{cases} 1 & \text{if } \gamma_0 + \gamma_1 z_i > v_i \\ 0 & \text{otherwise} \end{cases}$$

where $v_i$ is a random factor involving unobserved costs and benefits of military service assumed to be independent of $z_i$. This latent index model characterizes potential treatment assignments as

$$D_{0i} = 1[\gamma_0 > v_i] \text{ and } D_{1i} = 1[\gamma_0 + \gamma_1 > v_i].$$

Note that in this model, monotonicity is automatically satisfied since $\gamma_1$ is a constant. Assuming $\gamma_1 > 0$, LATE can be written

$$E[Y_{1i} - Y_{0i} | D_{1i} > D_{0i}] = E[Y_{1i} - Y_{0i} | \gamma_0 + \gamma_1 > v_i > \gamma_0],$$

which is a function of the latent first-stage parameters, $\gamma_0$ and $\gamma_1$, as well as the joint distribution of $Y_{1i} - Y_{0i}$ and $v_i$. This is not, in general, the same as the unconditional average treatment effect, $E[Y_{1i} - Y_{0i}]$, or the effect on the treated,

---

[23]With a constant effect, $\rho$,

$$E[Y_{1i} - Y_{0i} | D_{1i} > D_{0i}] P[D_{1i} > D_{0i}] - E[Y_{1i} - Y_{0i} | D_{1i} < D_{0i}] P[D_{1i} < D_{0i}]$$
$$= \rho\{P[D_{1i} > D_{0i}] - P[D_{1i} < D_{0i}]\}$$
$$= \rho\{E[D_{1i} - D_{0i}]\}.$$

So a zero reduced-form effect means either the first stage is zero or $\rho = 0$.

$E[Y_{1i} - Y_{0i}|D_i = 1]$. We explore the distinction between different average causal effects in the next section.

### 4.4.2   The Compliant Subpopulation

The LATE framework partitions any population with an instrument into a set of three instrument-dependent subgroups, defined by the manner in which members of the population react to the instrument:

**Definition 4.4.1** *Compliers. The subpopulation with* $D_{1i} = 1$ *and* $D_{0i} = 0$.
*Always-takers. The subpopulation with* $D_{1i} = D_{0i} = 1$.
*Never-takers. The subpopulation with* $D_{1i} = D_{0i} = 0$.

LATE is the effect of treatment on the population of compliers. The term "compliers" comes from an analogy with randomized trials where some experimental subjects comply with the randomly assigned treatment protocol (e.g., take their medicine) but some do not, while some control subjects obtain access to the experimental treatment even though they are not supposed to. Those who don't take their medicine when randomly assigned to do so are never-takers, while those who take the medicine even when put into the control group are always-takers. Without adding further assumptions (e.g., constant causal effects), LATE is not informative about effects on never-takers and always-takers because, by definition, treatment status for these two groups is unchanged by the instrument. The analogy between IV and a randomized trial with partial compliance is more than allegorical: IV solves the problem of causal inference in a randomized trial with partial compliance. This important point merits a separate subsection, below.

Before turning to this important special case, we make a few general points. First, the average causal effect on compliers is not usually the same as the average treatment effect on the treated. From the simple fact that $D_i = D_{0i} + (D_{1i} - D_{0i})Z_i$, we learn that the treated population consists of two nonoverlapping groups. By monotonicity, we cannot have both $D_{0i} = 1$

and $D_{1i} - D_{0i} = 1$, since $D_{0i} = 1$ implies $D_{1i} = 1$. The treated therefore have *either* $D_{0i} = 1$ or $D_{1i} - D_{0i} = 1$ and $z_i = 1$, and hence $D_i$ can be written as the sum of two mutually exclusive dummies, $D_{i0}$ and $(D_{1i} - D_{0i})z_i$. In other words, the treated consist of either always-takers or of compliers with the instrument switched on. Since the instrument is as good as randomly assigned, compliers with the instrument switched on are representative of all compliers. From here we get

$$\underbrace{E[Y_{1i} - Y_{0i} | D_i = 1]}_{\text{Effect on the treated}}$$

$$= \underbrace{E[Y_{1i} - Y_{0i} | D_{0i} = 1]}_{\text{Effect on always-takers}} P[D_{0i} = 1 | D_i = 1]$$

$$+ \underbrace{E[Y_{1i} - Y_{0i} | D_{1i} > D_{0i}]}_{\text{Effect on compliers}} P[D_{1i} > D_{0i}, z_i = 1 | D_i = 1].$$

$$(4.4.5)$$

Since $P[D_{0i} = 1 | D_i = 1]$ and $P[D_{1i} > D_{0i}, z_i = 1 | D_i = 1]$ add up to one, this means that the effect of treatment on the treated is a weighted average of effects on always-takers and compliers.

Likewise, LATE is not the average causal effect of treatment on the nontreated, $E[Y_{1i} - Y_{0i} | D_i = 0]$. In the draft lottery example, the average effect on the nontreated is the average causal effect of military service on the population of nonveterans from Vietnam-era cohorts. The average effect of treatment on the nontreated is a weighted average of effects on never-takers and compliers. In particular,

$$\underbrace{E[Y_{1i} - Y_{0i} | D_i = 0]}_{\text{Effect on the nontreated}}$$

$$= \underbrace{E[Y_{1i} - Y_{0i} | D_{1i} = 0]}_{\text{Effect on never-takers}} P[D_{1i} = 0 | D_i = 0]$$

$$+ \underbrace{E[Y_{1i} - Y_{0i} | D_{1i} > D_{0i}]}_{\text{Effect on compliers}} P[D_{1i} > D_{0i}, z_i = 0 | D_i = 0],$$

$$(4.4.6)$$

where we use the fact that, by monotonicity, those with $D_{1i} = 0$ must be never-takers.

Finally, averaging (4.4.5) and (4.4.6) using

$$E[Y_{1i} - Y_{0i}] = E[Y_{1i} - Y_{0i}|D_i = 1]P[D_i = 1]$$
$$+ E[Y_{1i} - Y_{0i}|D_i = 0]P[D_i = 0]$$

shows the unconditional average treatment effect to be a weighted average of effects on compliers, always-takers, and never-takers. Of course, this is a conclusion we could have reached directly given monotonicity and definition (4.4.1).

Because an IV is not directly informative about effects on always-takers and never-takers, instruments do not usually capture the average causal effect on all of the treated or on all of the nontreated. There are important exceptions to this rule, however: instrumental variables that allow no always-takers or no never-takers. Although this scenario is not typical, it is an important special case. One example is the twins instrument for fertility, used by Rosenzweig and Wolpin (1980), Bronars and Grogger (1994), Angrist and Evans (1998), and Angrist, Lavy, and Schlosser (2006). Another is Oreopoulos's (2006) recent study using changes in compulsory attendance laws as instruments for schooling in Britain.

To see how this special case works with twins instruments, let $T_i$ be a dummy variable indicating multiple second births. Angrist and Evans (1998) used this instrument to estimate the causal effect of having three children on earnings in the population of women with at least two children. The third child is especially interesting because reduced fertility for American wives in the 1960s and 1970s meant a switch from three children to two. Multiple second births provide quasi-experimental variation on this margin. Let $Y_{0i}$ denote potential earnings if a woman has only two children while $Y_{1i}$ denotes her potential earnings if she has three, an event indicated by $D_i$. Assuming that $T_i$ is as good as randomly assigned, that fertility increases by at most one child in response to a multiple birth, and that multiple births affect outcomes only by increasing fertility, LATE using the twins instrument $T_i$ is also $E[Y_{1i} - Y_{0i}|D_i = 0]$, the average causal effect on women who are not treated (i.e., have two children only). This is because all women who have a multiple second birth end up with three children, that is, there are no never-takers in response to the twins instrument.

Oreopoulos (2006) also uses IV to estimate an average causal effect of treatment on the nontreated. His study estimates the economic returns to schooling using an increase in the British compulsory attendance age from 14 to 15. Compliance with the Britain's new compulsory attendance law was near perfect, though many teens would previously have dropped out of school at age 14. The causal effect of interest in this case is the earnings premium for an additional year of high school. Finishing this year can be thought of as the treatment. Since everybody in Oreopoulos's British sample finished an additional year when compulsory schooling laws were made stricter, there are no never-takers. Oreopoulos's IV strategy therefore captures the average causal effect of obtaining one more year of high school on all those who leave school at 14. This turns on the fact that British teens are remarkably law-abiding people—Oreopoulos's IV strategy wouldn't estimate the effect of treatment on the nontreated in, say, Israel, where teenagers get more leeway when it comes to compulsory school attendance. Israeli econometricians using changes in compulsory attendance laws as instruments must therefore make do with LATE.

### 4.4.3   IV in Randomized Trials

The language of the LATE framework is based on an analogy between IV and randomized trials. But some instruments really do come from randomized trials. If the instrument is a randomly assigned offer of treatment, then LATE is the effect of treatment on those who comply with the offer but are not treated otherwise. An especially important case is when the instrument is generated by a randomized trial with one-sided noncompliance. In many randomized trials, participation is voluntary among those randomly assigned to receive treatment. On the other hand, no one in the control group has access to the experimental intervention. Since the group that receives (i.e., complies with) the assigned treatment is a self-selected subset of those offered treatment, a comparison between those actually treated and the control group is misleading. The selection bias in this case is almost always positive: those who take their medicine in a randomized trial tend to be healthier; those who take advantage of randomly assigned economic interventions such as training programs tend to earn more anyway.

IV using randomly assigned treatment intended as an instrumental variable for treatment received solves this sort of compliance problem. Moreover, LATE is the effect of treatment on the treated in this case. Suppose the instrument $z_i$ is a dummy variable indicating random assignment to a treatment group, while $D_i$ is a dummy indicating whether treatment was actually received. In practice, because of noncompliance, $D_i$ is not equal to $z_i$. An example is the randomized evaluation of the JTPA training program, where only 60 percent of those assigned to be trained received training, while roughly 2 percent of those assigned to the control group received training anyway (Bloom et al., 1997; see also section 7.2.1). Noncompliance in the JTPA arose from lack of interest among participants and the failure of program operators to encourage participation. Since the compliance problem in this case was largely confined to the treatment group, LATE using random assignment, $z_i$, as an instrument for treatment received, $D_i$, is the effect of treatment on the treated.

The use of IV to solve compliance problems is illustrated in table 4.4.1, which presents results from the JTPA experiment. The outcome variable of primary interest in the JTPA experiment is total earnings in the 30-month period after random assignment. Columns 1 and 2 of the table show the difference in earnings between those who were trained and those who were not (the OLS estimates in column 2 are from a regression model that adjusts for a number of individual characteristics measured at the beginning of the experiment). The contrast reported in columns 1 and 2 is on the order of \$4,000 for men and \$2,200 for women, in both cases a large treatment difference that amounts to about 20 percent of average earnings. But these estimates are misleading because they compare individuals according to $D_i$, the actual treatment received. Since individuals assigned to the treatment group were free to

TABLE 4.4.1

Results from the JTPA experiment: OLS and IV estimates of training impacts

| | Comparisons by Training Status (OLS) | | Comparisons by Assignment Status (ITT) | | Instrumental Variable Estimates (IV) | |
|---|---|---|---|---|---|---|
| | Without Covariates (1) | With Covariates (2) | Without Covariates (3) | With Covariates (4) | Without Covariates (5) | With Covariates (6) |
| A. Men | 3,970 | 3,754 | 1,117 | 970 | 1,825 | 1,593 |
| | (555) | (536) | (569) | (546) | (928) | (895) |
| B. Women | 2,133 | 2,215 | 1,243 | 1,139 | 1,942 | 1,780 |
| | (345) | (334) | (359) | (341) | (560) | (532) |

*Notes*: Authors' tabulation of JTPA study data. The table reports OLS, ITT, and IV estimates of the effect of subsidized training on earnings in the JTPA experiment. Columns 1 and 2 show differences in earnings by training status; columns 3 and 4 show differences by random-assignment status. Columns 5 and 6 report the result of using random-assignment status as an instrument for training. The covariates used for columns 2, 4, and 6 are high school or GED, black, Hispanic, married, worked less than 13 weeks in past year, AFDC (for women), plus indicators for the JTPA service strategy recommended, age group, and second follow-up survey. Robust standard errors are shown in parentheses. There are 5,102 men and 6,102 women in the sample.

decline (and 40 percent did so), this comparison throws away the random assignment unless the decision to comply was itself independent of potential outcomes. This seems unlikely.

Columns 3 and 4 of table 4.4.1 compare individuals according to whether they were *offered* treatment. In other words, this comparison is based on randomly assigned $z_i$. In the language of clinical trials, the contrast in columns 3 and 4 is known as an *intention-to-treat* (ITT) effect. The ITT effects in the table are on the order of $1,200 (somewhat less with covariates). Since $z_i$ was randomly assigned, ITT effects have a causal interpretation: they tell us the causal effect of the offer of treatment, building in the fact that many of those offered have declined to participate. For this reason, the ITT effect is too small relative to the average causal effect on those who were in fact treated. Columns 5 and 6 put the pieces together and give us the most interesting effect: ITT divided by the difference in compliance rates between treatment and control groups as originally assigned (about .6). These figures, roughly $1,800, measure the effect of treatment on the treated.

How do we know that ITT divided by compliance is the effect of treatment on the treated? We can recognize ITT as the reduced-form effect of the randomly assigned offer of treatment, our instrument in this case. The compliance rate is the first stage associated with this instrument, and the Wald estimand, as always, is the reduced form divided by the first stage. In general, this equals LATE, but because we have (almost) no always-takers, the treated population consists (almost) entirely of compliers. The IV estimates in columns 5 and 6 of table 4.4.1 are therefore consistent estimates of the effect of treatment on the treated.

This conclusion is important enough that it warrants an alternative derivation. To the best of our knowledge, the first person to point out that the IV formula can be used to estimate the effect of treatment on the treated in a randomized trial with one-sided noncompliance was Howard Bloom (1984). Here is Bloom's result with a simple direct proof.

**Theorem 4.4.2** *The Bloom Result. Suppose the assumptions of the LATE theorem hold, and* $E[D_i|z_i = 0] = P[D_i = 1|z_i = 0] = 0$. *Then*

$$\frac{E[Y_i|z_i = 1] - E[Y_i|z_i = 0]}{P[D_i = 1|z_i = 1]} = E[Y_{1i} - Y_{0i}|D_i = 1].$$

**Proof.** $E[Y_i|z_i = 1] = E[Y_{0i}|z_i = 1] + E[(Y_{1i} - Y_{0i})D_i|z_i = 1]$, while $E[Y_i|z_i = 0] = E[Y_{0i}|z_i = 0]$ because $z_i = 0$ implies $D_i = 0$. Therefore

$$E[Y_i|z_i = 1] - E[Y_i|z_i = 0] = E[(Y_{1i} - Y_{0i})D_i|z_i = 1],$$

since $E[Y_{0i}|z_i = 0] = E[Y_{0i}|z_i = 1]$ by independence. But

$$E[(Y_{1i} - Y_{0i})D_i|z_i = 1]$$
$$= E[Y_{1i} - Y_{0i}|D_i = 1, z_i = 1]P[D_i = 1|z_i = 1],$$

while $D_i = 1$ implies $z_i = 1$, since no one with $z_i = 0$ is treated. Hence, $E[Y_{1i} - Y_{0i}|D_i = 1, z_i = 1] = E[Y_{1i} - Y_{0i}|D_i = 1]$.

In addition to telling us how to analyze randomized trials with noncompliance, the LATE framework opens the door to cleverly designed randomized experiments in settings where it's impossible or unethical to compel treatment compliance. A creative example from the field of criminology is the Minneapolis Domestic Violence Experiment (MDVE). The MDVE was a pioneering effort to determine the best police response to domestic violence (Sherman and Berk, 1984). In general, police use a number of strategies in response to a domestic violence call. These include referral to counseling, separation orders, and arrest. A vigorous debate swirls around the question of whether a hard-line response—arrest and at least temporary incarceration—is productive, especially in view of the fact that domestic assault charges are frequently dropped.

As a result of this debate, the city of Minneapolis authorized a randomized trial where the police response to a domestic disturbance call was determined in part by random assignment. The research design used randomly shuffled color-coded report forms telling the responding officers to arrest some perpetrators while referring others to counseling or merely separating the parties. In practice, however, the police were free to overrule the random assignment. For example, an especially dangerous or drunk offender was arrested no matter what. As a result, the actual response often deviated from the randomly assigned response, though the two are highly correlated.

Most published analyses of the MDVE data recognize this compliance problem and focus on ITT effects, that is, they use the original random assignment and not the treatment actually delivered. But the MDVE data can also be used to get the average causal effect on compliers, in this case those who were not arrested because they were randomly assigned to be treated differently but would have been arrested otherwise. The MDVE is analyzed in this spirit in Angrist (2006). Because everyone in the MDVE who was assigned to be arrested was in fact arrested, there are no never-takers. This is an interesting twist and the flip side of the Bloom scenario: here we have $D_{1i} = 1$ for everybody. Consequently, LATE is the effect of treatment on the nontreated, that is,

$$E[Y_{1i} - Y_{0i}|D_{1i} > D_{0i}] = E[Y_{1i} - Y_{0i}|D_i = 0],$$

where $D_i$ indicates arrest. The IV estimates using MDVE data show that the average causal effect of arrest is to reduce repeat offenses sharply, in this case, among the subpopulation not arrested.[24]

### 4.4.4    Counting and Characterizing Compliers

We've seen that, except in special cases, each instrumental variable identifies a unique causal parameter, one specific to the subpopulation of compliers for that instrument. Different valid instruments for the same causal relation therefore estimate different things, at least in principle (an important exception being instruments that allow for perfect compliance on one side or the other). Although different IV estimates are implicitly weighted up by 2SLS to produce a single average causal effect, overidentification testing of the sort discussed in section 4.2.2, where multiple instruments are validated according to whether or not they estimate the same thing, is out the window in a fully heterogeneous world.

Differences in compliant subpopulations might explain variability in treatment effects from one instrument to another. We would therefore like to learn as much as we can about the compliers for different instruments. Moreover, if the compliant subpopulation is similar to other populations of interest, the case for extrapolating estimated causal effects to these other populations is stronger. In this spirit, Acemoglu and Angrist (2000) argue that quarter-of-birth instruments and state compulsory attendance laws (specifically, the minimum schooling required before leaving school in your state of birth) affect essentially the same group of people and for the same reasons. We therefore expect IV estimates of the returns to

---

[24]The Krueger (1999) study discussed in chapter 2 also uses IV to analyze data from a randomized trial. Specifically, this study uses randomly assigned class size as an instrument for actual class size with data from the Tennessee STAR experiment. For students in first grade and higher, actual class size differs from randomly assigned class size because parents and teachers moved students around in years after the experiment began. Krueger (1999) also illustrates 2SLS applied to a model with variable treatment intensity, as discussed in section 4.5.3.

schooling from quarter-of-birth and compulsory schooling instruments to be similar. We might also expect the quarter-of-birth estimates to predict the impact of contemporary proposals to strengthen compulsory attendance laws.

On the other hand, if the compliant subpopulations associated with two or more instruments are very different, yet the IV estimates they generate are similar, we might be prepared to adopt homogeneous effects as a working hypothesis. This revives the overidentification idea but puts it at the service of external validity.[25] This reasoning is illustrated in a study of the effects of family size on children's education by Angrist, Lavy, and Schlosser (2006). The Angrist, Lavy, and Schlosser study was motivated by the observation that children from larger families typically end up with less education than those from smaller families. A longstanding concern in research on fertility is whether the observed negative correlation between larger families and worse outcomes is causal. As it turns out, IV estimates of the effect of family size using a number of different instruments, each with very different compliant subpopulations, all generate results showing no effect of family size. Angrist, Lavy, and Schlosser (2006) argue that their results point to a common family size effect of zero for just about everybody in the Israeli population they studied.[26]

We have already seen that the size of a complier group is easy to measure. This is just the Wald first stage, since, given monotonicity, we have

$$P[\mathrm{D}_{1i} > \mathrm{D}_{0i}] = E[\mathrm{D}_{1i} - \mathrm{D}_{0i}]$$
$$= E[\mathrm{D}_{1i}] - E[\mathrm{D}_{0i}]$$
$$= E[\mathrm{D}_i|z_i = 1] - E[\mathrm{D}_i|z_i = 0].$$

We can also tell what proportion of the treated are compliers since, for compliers, treatment status is completely determined

[25] In fact, maintaining the hypothesis that all instruments in an overidentified model are valid, the traditional overidentification test statistic becomes a formal test for treatment effect homogeneity.

[26] See also Black, Devereux, and Salvones (2005) for similar results from Norway.

by $z_i$. Start with the definition of conditional probability:

$$P[\text{D}_{1i} > \text{D}_{0i}|\text{D}_i = 1] = \frac{P[\text{D}_i = 1|\text{D}_{1i} > \text{D}_{0i}]P[\text{D}_{1i} > \text{D}_{0i}]}{P[\text{D}_i = 1]}$$

$$= \frac{P[z_i = 1](E[\text{D}_i|z_i = 1] - E[\text{D}_i|z_i = 0])}{P[\text{D}_i = 1]}. \qquad (4.4.7)$$

The second equality uses the facts that $P[\text{D}_i = 1|\text{D}_{1i} > \text{D}_{0i}] = P[z_i = 1|\text{D}_{1i} > \text{D}_{0i}]$ and that $P[z_i = 1|\text{D}_{1i} > \text{D}_{0i}] = P[z_i = 1]$ by independence. In other words, the proportion of the treated who are compliers is given by the first stage, times the probability the instrument is switched on, divided by the proportion treated.

Formula (4.4.7) is illustrated here by calculating the proportion of veterans who are draft lottery compliers. The ingredients are reported in the first two rows of table 4.4.2. For example, for white men born in 1950, the first stage is .159, the probability of draft eligibility is $\frac{195}{365}$, and the marginal probability of treatment is .267. From these statistics, we compute that the compliant subpopulation is .32 of the veteran population in this group. The proportion of veterans who were draft lottery compliers falls to 20 percent for nonwhite men born in 1950. This is not surprising, since the draft lottery first stage is considerably weaker for nonwhites. The last column of the table reports the proportion of *nonveterans* who would have served if they had been draft eligible. This ranges from about 3 percent of nonwhites to 10 percent of whites, reflecting the fact that most nonveterans were deferred, ineligible, or unqualified for military service.

The effect of compulsory military service is the parameter of primary interest in the Angrist (1990) study, so the fact that draft eligibility compliers are a minority of veterans is not really a limitation of this study. Even in the Vietnam era, most soldiers were volunteers, a little appreciated fact about Vietnam-era veterans. The LATE interpretation of IV estimates using the draft lottery highlights the fact that other identification strategies are needed to estimate the effects of military service on volunteers (some of these are implemented in Angrist, 1998).

TABLE 4.4.2
Probabilities of compliance in instrumental variables studies

| Source (1) | Endogenous Variable (D) (2) | Instrument (z) (3) | Sample (4) | $P[D=1]$ (5) | First Stage, $P[D_1 > D_0]$ (6) | $P[z=1]$ (7) | Compliance Probabilities | | |
|---|---|---|---|---|---|---|---|---|---|
| | | | | | | | $P[D_1 > D_0|D=1]$ (8) | $P[D_1 > D_0|D=0]$ (9) |
| Angrist (1990) | Veteran status | Draft eligibility | White men born in 1950 | .267 | .159 | .534 | .318 | .101 |
| | | | Non-white men born in 1950 | .163 | .060 | .534 | .197 | .033 |
| Angrist and Evans (1998) | More than two children | Twins at second birth | Married women aged 21–35 with two or more children in 1980 | .381 | .603 | .008 | .013 | .966 |
| | | First two children are same sex | | .381 | .060 | .506 | .080 | .048 |
| Angrist and Krueger (1991) | High school graduate | Third- or fourth-quarter birth | Men born between 1930 and 1939 | .770 | .016 | .509 | .011 | .034 |
| Acemoglu and Angrist (2000) | High school graduate | State requires 11 or more years of school attendance | White men aged 40–49 | .617 | .037 | .300 | .018 | .068 |

*Notes*: The table computes the absolute and relative size of the complier population for a number of instrumental variables. The first stage, reported in column 6, gives the absolute size of the complier group. Columns 8 and 9 show the size of the complier population relative to the treated and untreated populations.

The remaining rows in table 4.4.2 show the size of the compliant subpopulation for the twins and sibling sex composition instruments used by Angrist and Evans (1998) to estimate the effects of childbearing and for the quarter-of-birth instruments and compulsory attendance laws used by Angrist and Krueger (1991) and Acemoglu and Angrist (2000) to estimate the returns to schooling. In each of these studies, the compliant subpopulation is a small fraction of the treated group. For example, less than 2 percent of those who graduated from high school did so because of compulsory attendance laws or by virtue of having been born in a late quarter.

The question of whether a small compliant subpopulation is a cause for worry is context-specific. In some cases, it seems fair to say, "you get what you need." With many policy interventions, for example, it is a marginal group that is of primary interest, a point emphasized in McClellan, McNeil, and Newhouse's (1994) landmark IV study of the effects of surgery on heart attack patients. They used the relative distance to cardiac care facilities to construct instruments for whether an elderly heart attack patient was treated with a surgical intervention. Most patients get the same treatment either way, but for some, the proper course of action (or at least the received wisdom as to the proper course of action) is uncertain. In such cases, health care providers or patients opt for a more invasive strategy only if a well-equipped surgical facility is close by. McClellan et al. found little benefit from surgical procedures for this marginal group. Similarly, an increase in the compulsory attendance cut-off to age 18 is clearly irrelevant for the majority of American high school students, but affects some who would otherwise drop out. IV estimates suggest the economic returns to schooling for this marginal group are substantial.

The last column of table 4.4.2 illustrates the special feature of twins instruments alluded to at the end of section 4.4.2. As before, let $D_i = 0$ for women with two children in a sample of women with at least two children and 1 for women who have more than two. Because there are no never-takers in response to the event of a multiple birth—all mothers who have twins at second birth end up with (at least) three children—the probability of compliance among those with $D_i = 0$ is virtually one (the table shows an entry of .97). LATE is therefore the effect on the nontreated, $E[Y_{1i} - Y_{0i}|D_i = 0]$, in this case.

Unlike the size of the complier group, information on the *characteristics* of compliers seems like a tall order because the compliers cannot be individually identified. Because we can't see both $D_{1i}$ and $D_{0i}$ for each individual, we can't just list those with $D_{1i} > D_{0i}$ and then calculate the distribution of characteristics for this group. Nevertheless, in spite of the fact that compliers cannot be listed or named, it's easy to describe the distribution of complier characteristics. To simplify, we focus here on characteristics, such as race or degree completion, that can be described by dummy variables. In this case, everything we need to know can be learned from variation in the first stage across covariate groups.

Let $x_{1i}$ be a Bernoulli-distributed characteristic, say a dummy indicating college graduates. Are sex composition compliers more or less likely to be college graduates than other women with two children? This question is answered by the following calculation:

$$
\begin{aligned}
\frac{P[x_{1i} = 1|D_{1i} > D_{0i}]}{P[x_{1i} = 1]} &= \frac{P[D_{1i} > D_{0i}|x_{1i} = 1]}{P[D_{1i} > D_{0i}]} \\
&= \frac{E[D_i|z_i = 1, x_{1i} = 1] - E[D_i|z_i = 0, x_{1i} = 1]}{E[D_i|z_i = 1] - E[D_i|z_i = 0]}.
\end{aligned} \quad (4.4.8)
$$

In other words, the relative likelihood a complier is a college graduate is given by the ratio of the first stage for college graduates to the overall first stage.[27]

---

[27] A general method for constructing the mean or other features of the distribution of covariates for compliers uses Abadie's (2003) kappa-weighting scheme. For example,

$$
E[X_i|D_{1i} > D_{0i}] = \frac{E[\kappa_i X_i]}{E[\kappa_i]},
$$

where

$$
\kappa_i = 1 - \frac{D_i(1 - z_i)}{1 - P(z_i = 1|X_i)} - \frac{(1 - D_i)z_i}{P(z_i = 1|X_i)}.
$$

This works because the weighting function, $\kappa_i$, "finds compliers," in a sense discussed in section 4.5.2.

TABLE 4.4.3

Complier characteristics ratios for twins and sex composition instruments

| | | Twins at Second Birth | | First Two Children Are Same Sex | |
|---|---|---|---|---|---|
| Variable | $P[x_{1i} = 1]$ (1) | $P[x_{1i} = 1\|$ $D_{1i} > D_{0i}]$ (2) | $P[x_{1i} = 1\|D_{1i} > D_{0i}]/$ $P[x_{1i} = 1]$ (3) | $P[x_{1i} = 1\|$ $D_{1i} > D_{0i}]$ (4) | $P[x_{1i} = 1\|D_{1i} > D_{0i}]/$ $P[x_{1i} = 1]$ (5) |
| Age 30 or older at first birth | .0029 | .004 | 1.39 | .0023 | .995 |
| Black or hispanic | .125 | .103 | .822 | .102 | .814 |
| High school graduate | .822 | .861 | 1.048 | .815 | .998 |
| College graduate | .132 | .151 | 1.14 | .0904 | .704 |

Notes: The table reports an analysis of complier characteristics for twins and sex composition instruments. The ratios in columns 3 and 5 give the relative likelihood that compliers have the characteristic indicated at left. Data are from the 1980 census 5 percent sample, including married mothers aged 21–35 with at least two children, as in Angrist and Evans (1998). The sample size is 254,654 for all columns.

This calculation is illustrated in table 4.4.3, which reports compliers' characteristics ratios for age at first birth, non-white race, and degree completion using twins and same-sex instruments. The table was constructed from the Angrist and Evans (1998) extract from the 1980 census containing married women aged 21–35 with at least two children. Twins compliers are much more likely to be over 30 than the average mother in the sample, reflecting the fact that younger women who had a multiple birth were more likely to go on to have additional children anyway (though over-30 first births are rare for all women in the Angrist-Evans sample). Twins compliers are also more educated than the average mother, while sex composition compliers are less educated. This helps to explain the smaller 2SLS estimates generated by twins instruments (reported here in table 4.1.4), since Angrist and Evans (1998) show that the labor supply consequences of childbearing decline with mother's schooling.

## 4.5    Generalizing LATE

The LATE theorem applies to a stripped-down causal model in which a single dummy instrument is used to estimate the impact of a dummy treatment with no covariates. We can generalize this in three important ways: multiple instruments (e.g., a set of quarter-of-birth dummies), models with covariates (e.g., controls for year of birth), and models with variable and continuous treatment intensity (e.g., years of schooling). In all three cases, the IV estimand is a weighted average of causal effects for instrument-specific compliers. The econometric tool remains 2SLS and the interpretation remains fundamentally similar to the basic LATE result, with a few bells and whistles. 2SLS with multiple instruments produces a causal effect that averages IV estimands using the instruments one at a time; 2SLS with covariates produces an average of covariate-specific LATEs; 2SLS with variable or continuous treatment intensity produces a weighted average derivative along the length of a possibly nonlinear causal response function. These results provide a simple casual interpretation for 2SLS in most empirically relevant settings.

### 4.5.1   LATE with Multiple Instruments

The multiple-instruments extension is easy to see. This is essentially the same as a result we discussed in the grouped data context. Consider a pair of dummy instruments, $z_{1i}$ and $z_{2i}$. Without loss of generality, assume these dummies are mutually exclusive (if not, then we can work with a mutually exclusive set of three dummies, $z_{1i}(1 - z_{2i})$, $z_{2i}(1 - z_{1i})$, and $z_{1i}z_{2i}$). The two dummies can be used to construct Wald estimators. Again without loss of generality, assume monotonicity is satisfied for each with a positive first stage (if not, we can recode the dummies so this is true). Both therefore estimate a version of $E[Y_{1i} - Y_{0i}|D_{1i} > D_{0i}]$, though the population with $D_{1i} > D_{0i}$ differs for $z_{1i}$ and $z_{2i}$.

Instead of Wald estimators, we can use $z_{1i}$ and $z_{2i}$ together in a 2SLS procedure. Since these two dummies and a constant exhaust the information in the instrument set, this 2SLS procedure is the same as grouped data estimation using conditional means defined given $z_{1i}$ and $z_{2i}$ (whether or not the instruments are correlated). As in Angrist (1991), the resulting grouped data estimator is a linear combination of the underlying Wald estimators. In other words, it is a linear combination of the instrument-specific LATEs using the instruments one at a time (in fact, it is the efficient linear combination in a traditional homoskedastic linear constant effects model).

This argument is not quite complete, since we haven't shown that the linear combination of LATEs produced by 2SLS is also a weighted average (i.e., the weights are non-negative and sum to one). The relevant weighting formulas appear in Imbens and Angrist (1994) and Angrist and Imbens (1995). The general formulas are a little messy, so here we lay out a simple version based on the two-instrument example. The example shows that 2SLS using $z_{1i}$ and $z_{2i}$ together is a weighted average of IV estimates using $z_{1i}$ and $z_{2i}$ one at a time. Let

$$\rho_j = \frac{Cov(Y_i, z_{ji})}{Cov(D_i, z_{ji})}; j = 1, 2$$

denote the two IV estimands using $z_{1i}$ and $z_{2i}$.

The (population) first-stage fitted values for 2SLS are $\hat{D}_i = \pi_{11}z_{1i} + \pi_{12}z_{2i}$, where $\pi_{11}$ and $\pi_{12}$ are positive numbers. By virtue of the IV interpretation of 2SLS, the 2SLS estimand is

$$
\begin{aligned}
\rho_{2SLS} &= \frac{Cov(Y_i, \hat{D}_i)}{Cov(D_i, \hat{D}_i)} = \frac{\pi_{11}Cov(Y_i, z_{1i})}{Cov(D_i, \hat{D}_i)} + \frac{\pi_{12}Cov(Y_i, z_{2i})}{Cov(D_i, \hat{D}_i)} \\
&= \left[\frac{\pi_{11}Cov(D_i, z_{1i})}{Cov(D_i, \hat{D}_i)}\right]\left[\frac{Cov(Y_i, z_{1i})}{Cov(D_i, z_{1i})}\right] \\
&\quad + \left[\frac{\pi_{12}Cov(D_i, z_{2i})}{Cov(D_i, \hat{D}_i)}\right]\left[\frac{Cov(Y_i, z_{2i})}{Cov(D_i, z_{2i})}\right] \\
&= \psi\rho_1 + (1-\psi)\rho_2,
\end{aligned}
$$

where $\psi_1$ is LATE using $z_{1i}$ and $\rho_2$ is LATE using $z_{2i}$, and

$$\psi = \frac{\pi_{11}Cov(D_i, z_{1i})}{\pi_{11}Cov(D_i, z_{1i}) + \pi_{12}Cov(D_i, z_{2i})}$$

is a number between zero and one that depends on the relative strength of each instrument in the first stage. Thus, we have shown that 2SLS is a weighted average of causal effects for instrument-specific compliant subpopulations. Suppose, for example, that $z_{1i}$ denotes twin births and $z_{2i}$ indicates (nontwin) same-sex sibships in families with two or more children, both instruments for family size, as in Angrist and Evans (1998). A multiple second birth increases the likelihood of having a third child by about .6, while a same-sex sibling pair increases the likelihood of a third birth by about .07. When these two instruments are used together, the resulting 2SLS estimates are a weighted average of the Wald estimates produced by using the instruments one at a time.[28]

### 4.5.2   Covariates in the Heterogeneous Effects Model

You might be wondering where the covariates have gone. After all, covariates played a starring role in our earlier discussion of regression and matching. Yet the LATE theorem does not involve covariates. This stems from the fact that when we see instrumental variables as a type of (natural or man-made) randomized trial, covariates take a back seat. If the instrument is randomly assigned, it is likely to be independent of covariates. Not all instruments have this property, however. As with covariates in the regression models in the previous chapter, the main reason why covariates are included in causal analyses using instrumental variables is that the conditional independence and exclusion restrictions underlying IV estimation may be more likely to be valid after conditioning on covariates. Even randomly assigned instruments, like draft eligibility status, may be valid only after conditioning on covariates. In the case of draft eligibility, older cohorts were more likely to be draft eligible because the draft eligibility cutoffs were higher. Because there are year-of-birth (or age) differences in earnings,

---

[28]Using twins instruments alone, the IV estimate of the effect of a third child on female labor force participation is $-.084$. The corresponding same-sex estimate is $-.138$. Using both instruments produces a 2SLS estimate of $-.098$. The 2SLS weight in this case is .74 for twins, .26 for same sex, due to the much stronger twins first stage.

draft eligibility is a valid instrument only after conditioning on year of birth.

More formally, IV estimation with covariates may be justified by a *conditional* independence assumption

$$\{Y_{1i}, Y_{0i}, D_{1i}, D_{0i}\} \perp\!\!\!\perp Z_i | X_i \qquad (4.5.1)$$

In other words, we think of the instrumental variables as being "as good as randomly assigned," conditional on covariates $X_i$ (here we are implicitly maintaining the exclusion restriction as well). A second reason for incorporating covariates is that conditioning on covariates may reduce some of the variability in the dependent variable. This can lead to more precise 2SLS estimates.

A benchmark constant effects model with covariates imposes functional form restrictions as follows:

$E[Y_{0i}|X_i] = X_i'\alpha^*$ for a $K \times 1$ vector of coefficients, $\alpha^*$;

$Y_{1i} - Y_{0i} = \rho$.

In combination with (4.5.1), this motivates 2SLS estimation of an equation like (4.1.6), as discussed in section 4.1.

A straightforward generalization of the constant effects model allows

$$Y_{1i} - Y_{0i} = \rho(X_i),$$

where $\rho(X_i)$ is a deterministic function of $X_i$. This model can be estimated by adding interactions between $Z_i$ and $X_i$ to the first stage and (the same) interactions between $D_i$ and $X_i$ to the second stage. There are now multiple endogenous variables and hence multiple first-stage equations. These can be written

$$D_i = X_i'\pi_{00} + \pi_{01}Z_i + Z_iX_i'\pi_{02} + \xi_{0i} \qquad (4.5.2a)$$
$$D_iX_i = X_i'\pi_{10} + \pi_{11}Z_i + Z_iX_i'\pi_{12} + \xi_{1i}. \qquad (4.5.2b)$$

Although (4.5.2b) is written as if $D_iX_i$ is a scalar, there should be a first stage like this for each element of $D_iX_i$. The second-stage equation in this case is

$$Y_i = \alpha'X_i + \rho_0D_i + D_iX_i'\rho_1 + \eta_i,$$

so $\rho(X_i) = \rho_0 + \rho_1' X_i$. Alternatively, a nonparametric version of $\rho(X_i)$ can be estimated by 2SLS in subsamples stratified on $X_i$.

The heterogeneous effects model underlying the LATE theorem allows for identification based on conditional independence as in (4.5.1), though the interpretation is a little more complicated than for LATE without covariates. For each value of $X_i$, we define covariate-specific LATE,

$$\lambda(X_i) \equiv E[Y_{1i} - Y_{0i} | X_i, D_{1i} > D_{0i}].$$

The "saturate and weight" approach to estimation with covariates, which generates a weighted average of $\lambda(X_i)$, is spelled out in the following theorem (from Angrist and Imbens, 1995).

**Theorem 4.5.1** *Saturate and Weight. Suppose the assumptions of the LATE theorem hold conditional on $X_i$. That is,*
  *(CA1, Independence)* $\{Y_i(D_{1i}, 1), Y_{0i}(D_{0i}, 0), D_{1i}, D_{0i}\} \perp\!\!\!\perp Z_i | X_i$;
  *(CA2, Exclusion)* $P[Y_i(d, 0) = Y_i(d, 1) | X_i] = 1$ *for* $d = 0, 1$;
  *(CA3, First Stage)* $E[D_{1i} - D_{0i} | X_i] \neq 0$.
*We also assume monotonicity (A4) holds as before. Consider the 2SLS estimand based on the first-stage equation*

$$D_i = \pi_X + \pi_{1X} Z_i + \xi_{1i} \qquad (4.5.3)$$

*and the second-stage equation*

$$Y_i = \alpha_X + \rho_c D_i + \eta_i,$$

*where $\pi_X$ and $\alpha_X$ denote saturated models for covariates (a full set of dummies for all values of $X_i$) and $\pi_{1X}$ denotes a first-stage effect of $Z_i$ for every value of $X_i$. Then $\rho_c = E[\omega(X_i)\lambda(X_i)]$, where*

$$\omega(X_i) = \frac{V\{E[D_i | X_i, Z_i] | X_i\}}{E[V\{E[D_i | X_i, Z_i] | X_i\}]} \qquad (4.5.4)$$

*and*

$$V\{E[D_i | X_i, Z_i] | X_i\} = E\{E[D_i | X_i, Z_i](E[D_i | X_i, Z_i] - E[D_i | X_i]) | X_i\}.$$

This theorem says that 2SLS with a fully saturated first stage and a saturated model for covariates in the second stage produces a weighted average of covariate-specific LATEs. The weights are proportional to the average conditional variance of the population first-stage fitted value, $E[D_i|X_i,z_i]$, at each value of $X_i$.[29] The theorem comes from the fact that the first stage coincides with $E[D_i|X_i,z_i]$ when (4.5.3) is saturated (i.e., the first-stage regression recovers the CEF).

In practice, we may not want to work with a model with a first-stage parameter for each value of the covariates. First, there is the risk of bias, as we discuss at the end of this chapter, and second, a big pile of individually imprecise first-stage estimates is not pretty to look at. It seems reasonable to imagine that models with fewer parameters, say a restricted first stage imposing a constant $\pi_{1X}$, nevertheless approximate some kind of covariate-averaged LATE. This turns out to be true, but the argument is surprisingly indirect. The vision of 2SLS as providing a MMSE approximation to an underlying causal relation was developed by Abadie (2003).

The Abadie approach begins by defining the object of interest to be $E[Y_i|D_i, X_i, D_{1i} > D_{0i}]$, the CEF for $Y_i$ given treatment status and covariates, for compliers. An important feature of this CEF is that when the conditions of the LATE theorem hold conditional on $X_i$, it has a causal interpretation. In other words, *for compliers*, treatment-control contrasts conditional on $X_i$ are equal to conditional-on-$X_i$ LATEs:

$$E[Y_i|D_i = 1, X_i, D_{1i} > D_{0i}] - E[Y_i|D_i = 0, X_i, D_{1i} > D_{0i}]$$
$$= E[Y_{1i} - Y_{0i}|X_i, D_{1i} > D_{0i}]$$
$$= \lambda(X_i).$$

This follows immediately from the facts that $D_i = z_i$ for compliers and, given (4.5.1), potential outcomes are independent of $z_i$ given $X_i$ and $D_{1i} > D_{0i}$. The upshot is that a regression of $Y_i$ on $D_i$ and $X_i$ in the complier population also has a causal interpretation. Although this regression might not

---

[29] Note that the variability in $E[D_i|X_i,z_i]$ conditional on $X_i$ comes from $z_i$. So the weighting formula gives more weight to covariate values where the instrument creates more variation in fitted values.

give us the CEF of interest (unless it is linear or the model is saturated), it will, as always, provide the MMSE approximation to it. That is, a regression of $Y_i$ on $D_i$ and $X_i$ in the complier population approximates $E[Y_i | D_i, X_i, D_{1i} > D_{0i}]$, just as OLS approximates $E[Y_i | D_i, X_i]$. Alas, we do not know who the compliers are, so we cannot sample them. Nevertheless, they can be found, in the following sense.

**Theorem 4.5.2** *Abadie Kappa. Suppose the assumptions of the LATE theorem hold conditional on covariates, $X_i$. Let $g(Y_i, D_i, X_i)$ be any measurable function of $(Y_i, D_i, X_i)$ with finite expectation. Define*

$$\kappa_i = 1 - \frac{D_i(1 - z_i)}{1 - P(z_i = 1 | X_i)} - \frac{(1 - D_i)z_i}{P(z_i = 1 | X_i)}.$$

*Then*

$$E[g(Y_i, D_i, X_i) | D_{1i} > D_{0i}] = \frac{E[\kappa_i g(Y_i, D_i, X_i)]}{E[\kappa_i]}.$$

This can be proved by direct calculation using the fact that, given the assumptions of the LATE theorem, any expectation is a weighted average of means for always-takers, never-takers, and compliers. By monotonicity, those with $D_i(1 - z_i) = 1$ are always-takers because they have $D_{0i} = 1$, while those with $(1 - D_i)z_i = 1$ are never-takers because they have $D_{1i} = 0$. Hence, the compliers are the left-out group.

The Abadie theorem has a number of important implications; for example, it crops up again in the discussion of quantile treatment effects. Here, we use it to approximate $E[Y_i | D_i, X_i, D_{1i} > D_{0i}]$ by linear regression. Specifically, let $\alpha_c$ and $\beta_c$ solve

$$(\alpha_c, \beta_c) = \underset{a,b}{\arg\min} \, E\{(E[Y_i | D_i, X_i, D_{1i} > D_{0i}]$$

$$- aD_i - X_i'b)^2 | D_{1i} > D_{0i}\}.$$

In other words, $\alpha_c D_i + X_i' \beta_c$ gives the MMSE approximation to $E[Y_i | D_i, X_i, D_{1i} > D_{0i}]$, or fits it exactly if it's linear. A consequence of Abadie's theorem is that this approximating function can be obtained by solving

$$(\alpha_c, \beta_c) = \underset{a,b}{\arg \min}\, E\{\kappa_i(Y_i - aD_i - X_i'b)^2\}, \qquad (4.5.5)$$

the kappa-weighted least squares minimand.[30]

Abadie proposes an estimation strategy (and develops distribution theory) for a procedure that involves first-step estimation of $\kappa_i$ using parametric or semiparametric models for $P(z_i = 1|X_i)$. The estimates from the first step are then plugged into the sample analog of (4.5.5) in the second step. Not surprisingly, when the only covariate is a constant, Abadie's procedure simplifies to the Wald estimator. More surprisingly, minimization of (4.5.5) produces the traditional 2SLS estimator as long as a linear model is used for $P(z_i = 1|X_i)$ in the construction of $\kappa_i$. In other words, if $P(z_i = 1|X_i) = X_i'\pi$ is used when constructing an estimate of $\kappa_i$, the Abadie estimand is 2SLS. Thus, we can conclude that whenever $P(z_i = 1|X_i)$ can be fit or closely approximated by a linear model, it makes sense to view 2SLS as an approximation to the complier causal response function, $E[Y_i|D_i, X_i, D_{1i} > D_{0i}]$. On the other hand, $\alpha_a$ is not, in general, the 2SLS estimand, and $\beta_a$ is not, in general, the vector of covariate effects produced by 2SLS. Still, the equivalence to 2SLS for linear $P(z_i = 1|X_i)$ leads us to think that Abadie's method and 2SLS are likely to produce similar estimates in most applications.

The Angrist (2001) reanalysis of Angrist and Evans (1998) is an example where estimates based on (4.5.5) are indistinguishable from 2SLS estimates. Using twins instruments to estimate the effect of a third child on female labor supply generates a 2SLS estimate of $-.088$, while the corresponding Abadie estimate is $-.089$. Similarly, 2SLS and Abadie estimates of the effect on hours worked are identical at $-3.55$. This is not a strike against Abadie's procedure. Rather, it supports

---

[30]The class of approximating functions needn't be linear. Instead of $\alpha_c D_i + X_i'\beta_c$, it might make sense to use a nonlinear function such as an exponential (if the dependent variable is non-negative) or probit (if the dependent variable is zero-one). We return to this point at the end of this chapter. As noted in section 4.4.4, the kappa-weighting scheme can be used to characterize covariate distributions for compliers as well as to estimate outcome distributions.

the notion that 2SLS approximates the causal relation of interest.[31]

### 4.5.3  Average Causal Response with Variable Treatment Intensity★

An important difference between the causal effects of a dummy variable and those of a variable that takes on the values $\{0, 1, 2, \ldots\}$ is that in the first case, there is only one causal effect for any one person, while in the latter there are many: the effect of going from 0 to 1, the effect of going from 1 to 2, and so on. The potential outcomes notation we used for schooling recognizes this. Here it is again. Let

$$Y_{si} \equiv f_i(s)$$

denote the potential (or latent) earnings that person $i$ would receive after obtaining $s$ years of education. Note that the function $f_i(s)$ has an "$i$" subscript on it but $s$ does not. The function $f_i(s)$ tells us what $i$ would earn for *any* value of schooling, $s$, and not just for the realized value, $s_i$. In other words, $f_i(s)$ answers causal "what if" questions for multinomial $s_i$.

Suppose that $s_i$ takes on values in the set $\{0, 1, \ldots, \bar{s}\}$. Then there are $\bar{s}$ unit causal effects, $Y_{si} - Y_{s-1,i}$. A linear causal model assumes these are the same for all $s$ and for all $i$, obviously unrealistic assumptions. But we need not take these assumptions literally. Rather, 2SLS provides a computational device that generates a weighted average of unit causal effects, with a weighting function we can estimate and study, so as to learn

---

[31] The Abadie estimator can be computed by weighting conventional linear or nonlinear regression software. The trick is to first construct a weighting scheme with positive weights. This is accomplished by iterating expectations in (4.5.5), so that $\kappa_i$ (which is negative for always-takers and never-takers) can be replaced by the always-positive average weight,

$$E[\kappa_i | X_i, D_i, Y_i] = 1 - \frac{D_i(1 - E[z_i | X_i, D_i, Y_i])}{1 - P(z_i = 1 | X_i)} - \frac{(1 - D_i)E[z_i | X_i, D_i, Y_i]}{P(z_i = 1 | X_i)}.$$

(See also the discussion in section 7.2.1.) Abadie (2003) gives formulas for standard errors and Alberto Abadie has posted software to compute them, as well as the corresponding parameter estimates. Standard errors for the Abadie estimator can also be estimated using a bootstrap.

where the action is coming from with a particular instrument. This weighting function tells us how the compliers are distributed over the range of $s_i$. It tells us, for example, that the returns to schooling estimated using quarter of birth or compulsory schooling laws come from shifts in the distribution of grades completed in high school. Other instruments, such as the distance instruments used by Card (1995), act elsewhere on the schooling distribution and therefore capture a different sort of return.

To flesh this out, suppose that a single binary instrument, $z_i$, a dummy for having been born in a state with restrictive compulsory attendance laws, is to be used to estimate the returns to schooling (as in Acemoglu and Angrist, 2000). Also, let $s_{1i}$ denote the schooling $i$ would get if $z_i = 1$, and let $s_{0i}$ denote the schooling $i$ would get if $z_i = 0$. The theorem below, from Angrist and Imbens (1995), offers an interpretation of the Wald estimand with variable treatment intensity in this case. Note that here we combine the independence and exclusion restrictions by simply stating that potential outcomes indexed by $s$ are independent of the instruments.

**Theorem 4.5.3** *Average Causal Response. Suppose*
*(ACR1, Independence and Exclusion)* $\{Y_{0i}, Y_{1i}, \ldots, Y_{\bar{s}i}; s_{0i}, s_{1i}\} \perp\!\!\!\perp z_i;$
*(ACR2, First Stage)* $E[s_{1i} - s_{0i}] \neq 0;$
*(ACR3, Monotonicity)* $s_{1i} - s_{0i} \geq 0 \, \forall i,$ *or vice versa; assume the first.*
*Then*

$$\frac{E[Y_i|z_i = 1] - E[Y_i|z_i = 0]}{E[s_i|z_i = 1] - E[s_i|z_i = 0]}$$

$$= \sum_{s=1}^{\bar{s}} \omega_s E[Y_{si} - Y_{s-1,i}|s_{1i} \geq s > s_{0i}],$$

*where*

$$\omega_s = \frac{P[s_{1i} \geq s > s_{0i}]}{\sum_{j=1}^{\bar{s}} P[s_{1i} \geq j > s_{0i}]}.$$

*The weights $\omega_s$ are non-negative and sum to one.*

The average causal response (ACR) theorem says that the Wald estimator with variable treatment intensity is a weighted average of the *unit causal response* along the length of the potentially nonlinear causal relation described by $f_i(s)$. The unit causal response, $E[Y_{si} - Y_{s-1,i}|s_{1i} \geq s > s_{0i}]$, is the average difference in potential outcomes for *compliers at point s*, that is, individuals driven by the instrument from a treatment intensity less than $s$ to at least $s$. For example, the quarter-of-birth instruments used by Angrist and Krueger (1991) push some people from 11th grade to finishing 12th or higher, and others from 10th grade to finishing 11th or higher. The Wald estimator using quarter-of-birth instruments combines all these effects into a single ACR.

The size of the group of compliers at point $s$ is $P[s_{1i} \geq s > s_{0i}]$. By monotonicity, this must be non-negative and is given by the difference in the CDF of $s_i$ at point $s$. To see this, note that

$$P[s_{1i} \geq s > s_{0i}] = P[s_{1i} \geq s] - P[s_{0i} \geq s]$$
$$= P[s_{0i} < s] - P[s_{1i} < s],$$

which is non-negative since monotonicity requires $s_{1i} \geq s_{0i}$. Moreover,

$$P[s_{0i} < s] - P[s_{1i} < s] = P[s_i < s|z_i = 0] - P[s_i < s|z_i = 1]$$

by independence. Finally, note that because the mean of a non-negative random variable is the sum (or integral) of one minus the CDF, we have,

$$E[s_i|z_i = 1] - E[s_i|z_i = 0]$$
$$= \sum_{j=1}^{\bar{s}} (P[s_i < j|z_i = 0] - P[s_i < j|z_i = 1])$$
$$= \sum_{j=1}^{\bar{s}} P[s_{1i} \geq j > s_{0i}]$$

Thus, the ACR weighting function can be consistently estimated by comparing the CDFs of the endogenous variable (treatment intensity) with the instrument switched off and on. The weighting function is normalized by the first stage.

The ACR theorem helps us understand what we are learning from a 2SLS estimate. For example, instrumental variables derived from compulsory attendance and child labor laws capture the causal effect of increases in schooling in the 6–12 grade range, but tell us little about the effects of postsecondary schooling. This is illustrated in figure 4.5.1, taken from Acemoglu and Angrist (2000).

The figure plots differences in the probability that educational attainment is at or exceeds the grade level on the $x$-axis (i.e., one minus the CDF). The differences are between men exposed to different child labor laws and compulsory schooling laws in the sample of white men aged 40–49 drawn from the 1960, 1970, and 1980 censuses. The instruments are coded as the number of years of schooling required either to work (panel A) or to leave school (panel B) in the year the respondent was age 14. Men exposed to the least restrictive laws are the reference group. Each instrument (e.g., a dummy for seven years of schooling required before work is allowed) can be used to construct a Wald estimator by making comparisons with the reference group.

The top panel of figure 4.5.1 shows that men exposed to more restrictive child labor laws were one to six percentage points more likely to complete grades 8–12. The intensity of the shift depends on whether the laws required seven, eight, or nine-plus years of schooling before work was allowed. But in all cases, the CDF differences decline at lower grades, and drop off sharply after grade 12. The bottom panel shows a similar pattern for compulsory attendance laws, though the effects are a little smaller and the action here is at somewhat higher grades, consistent with the fact that compulsory attendance laws are typically binding in higher grades than child labor laws. Interestingly, the child labor and compulsory attendance instruments generate similar 2SLS estimates of about .08–.10.

Before wrapping up our discussion of LATE generalizations, it's worth noting that most of the elements covered here work in combination. For example, models with multiple instruments and variable treatment intensity generate a weighted average of the ACR for each instrument. Likewise, the saturate

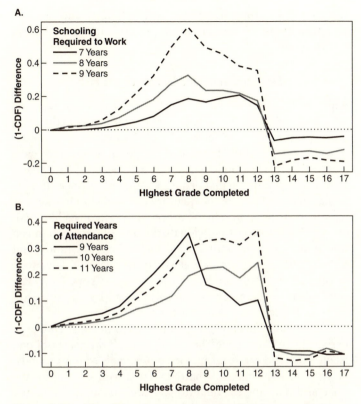

**Figure 4.5.1** The effect of compulsory schooling instruments on education (from Acemoglu and Angrist 2000). The figures show the instrument-induced difference in the probability that schooling is greater than or equal to the grade level on the $x$-axis. The reference group is six or fewer years of required schooling in the top panel and eight or fewer years in the bottom panel. The top panel shows the CDF difference by severity of child labor laws. The bottom panel shows the CDF difference by severity of compulsory attendance laws.

and weight theorem applies to models with variable treatment intensity (though we do not yet have an extension of Abadie's kappa for models with variable treatment intensity). A final important extension covers the scenario where the causal variable of interest is continuous and we can therefore think of the causal response function as having derivatives.

### So Long, and Thanks for All the Fish

Suppose, as with the schooling problem, that counterfactuals are generated by an underlying functional relation. In this case, however, the causal variable of interest can take on any non-negative value and the functional relation is assumed to have a derivative. An example where this makes sense is a demand curve, the quantity demanded as a function of price. In particular, let $q_i(p)$ denote the quantity demanded in market $i$ at hypothetical price $p$. This is a potential outcome, like $f_i(s)$, except that instead of individuals the unit of observation is a time or a location or both. For example, Angrist, Graddy, and Imbens (2000) estimate the elasticity of quantity demanded at the Fulton wholesale fish market in New York City. The slope of this demand curve is $q_i'(p)$; if quantity and price are measured in logs, this is an elasticity.

The instruments in Angrist, Graddy, and Imbens (2000) are derived from data on weather conditions off the coast of Long Island, not too far from major commercial fishing grounds. Stormy weather makes it hard to catch fish, driving up the price and reducing the quantity demanded. Angrist, Graddy, and Imbens use dummy variables such as $stormy_i$, a dummy indicating periods with high wind and waves, to estimate the demand for fish. The data consist of daily observations on wholesale purchases of whiting, a cheap fish used for fish cakes and things like that.

The Wald estimator using the $stormy_i$ instrument can be interpreted using

$$\frac{E[q_i|stormy_i = 1] - E[q_i|stormy_i = 0]}{E[p_i|stormy_i = 1] - E[p_i|stormy_i = 0]}$$

$$= \frac{\int E[q_i'(t)| \; \mathrm{P}_{1i} \geq t > \mathrm{P}_{0i}]P[\mathrm{P}_{1i} \geq t > \mathrm{P}_{0i}]dt}{\int P[\mathrm{P}_{1i} \geq t > \mathrm{P}_{0i}]dt}, \quad (4.5.6)$$

where $p_i$ is the price in market (day) $i$ and $\mathrm{P}_{1i}$ and $\mathrm{P}_{0i}$ are potential prices indexed by *stormy$_i$*. This is a weighted average derivative with weighting function $P[\mathrm{P}_{1i} \geq t > \mathrm{P}_{0i}] = P[p_i < t|stormy_i = 0] - P[p_i < t|stormy_i = 1]$ at price $t$. In other words, IV estimation using *stormy$_i$* produces an average of the derivative $q_i'(t)$, with weight given to each possible price (indexed by $t$) in proportion to the instrument-induced change in the cumulative distribution function (CDF) of prices at that point. This is the same sort of averaging as in the ACR theorem except that now the underlying causal response is a derivative instead of a one-unit difference.

The continuous ACR formula, (4.5.6), comes from the fact that

$$E[q_i|stormy_i = 1] - E[q_i|stormy_i = 0] = E\left[\int_{\mathrm{P}_{0i}}^{\mathrm{P}_{1i}} q_i'(t)dt\right],$$

$$(4.5.7)$$

by the independence assumption and the fundamental theorem of calculus. Two interesting special cases fall neatly out of (4.5.7). The first is when the causal response function is linear, that is, $q_i(p) = \alpha_{0i} + \alpha_{1i}p$, for some random coefficients, $\alpha_{0i}$ and $\alpha_{1i}$. Then, we have

$$\frac{E[q_i|stormy_i = 1] - E[q_i|stormy_i = 0]}{E[p_i|stormy_i = 1] - E[p_i|stormy_i = 0]} = \frac{E[\alpha_{1i}(\mathrm{P}_{1i} - \mathrm{P}_{0i})]}{E[\mathrm{P}_{1i} - \mathrm{P}_{0i}]},$$

$$(4.5.8)$$

a weighted average of the random coefficient, $\alpha_{1i}$. The weights are proportional to the price change induced by the weather in market $i$.

The second special case is when we can write quantity demanded as

$$q_i(p) = Q(p) + \eta_i, \qquad (4.5.9)$$

where $Q(p)$ is a nonstochastic function and $\eta_i$ is an additive random error. By this we mean $q_i'(p) = Q'(p)$ every day or in every market. In this case, the average causal response function becomes

$$\int Q'(t)\omega(t)dt, \text{ where } \omega(t) = \frac{P[\text{P}_{1i} \geq t > \text{P}_{0i}]}{\int P[\text{P}_{1i} \geq r > \text{P}_{0i}]dr}$$

where $r$ is the integrating variable in the denominator.

These special cases highlight the two types of averaging wrapped up in the ACR theorem and its continuous corollary, (4.5.6). First, there is averaging *across* markets, with weights proportional to the first-stage impact on prices in each market. Markets where prices are highly sensitive to the weather contribute the most. Second, there is averaging *along* the length of the causal response function in a given market. IV recovers the average derivative over the range of prices where the instruments shift the CDF of prices most sharply.

## 4.6    IV Details

### 4.6.1    2SLS Mistakes

2SLS estimates are easy to compute, especially since software packages like SAS and Stata will do it for you. Occasionally, however, you might be tempted to do it yourself just to see if it really works. Or you may be stranded on the planet Krikkit with all of your software licenses expired (Krikkit is encased in a slo-time envelope, so it will take you a long time to get licenses renewed). Manual 2SLS is for just such emergencies. In the manual 2SLS procedure, you estimate the first stage yourself (which in any case you should be looking at) and plug the fitted values into the second-stage equation, which is then estimated by OLS. Returning to the system at the beginning of this chapter, the first and second stages are

$$s_i = \text{X}_i'\pi_{10} + \pi_{11}'\text{Z}_i + \xi_{1i}$$
$$\text{Y}_i = \alpha'\text{X}_i + \rho\hat{s}_i + [\eta_i + \rho(s_i - \hat{s}_i)],$$

where $\text{X}_i$ is a set of covariates, $\text{Z}_i$ is a set of excluded instruments, and the first-stage fitted values are $\hat{s}_i = \text{X}_i'\hat{\pi}_{10} + \hat{\pi}_{11}'\text{Z}_i$.

Manual 2SLS takes some of the mystery out of canned 2SLS and may be useful in a software crisis, but it opens the door to mistakes. For one thing, as we discussed earlier, the OLS standard errors from the manual second stage will not be correct (the OLS residual variance is the variance of $\eta_i + \rho(s_i - \hat{s}_i)$, while for proper 2SLS standard errors you want the variance of $\eta_i$ only). There are more subtle risks as well.

## Covariate Ambivalence

Suppose the covariate vector contains two sorts of variables, some (say, $X_{0i}$) that you are comfortable with, and others (say, $X_{1i}$) about which you are ambivalent. Griliches and Mason (1972) faced this scenario when constructing 2SLS estimates of a wage equation that treats AFQT scores (an ability test used by the armed forces) as an endogenous variable to be instrumented. The instruments for AFQT are early schooling (completed before military service), race, and family background variables. They estimated a system that can be described like this:

$$s_i = X'_{0i}\pi_{10} + \pi'_{11}Z_i + \xi_{1i}$$
$$Y_i = \alpha'_0 X_{0i} + \alpha'_1 X_{1i} + \rho\hat{s}_i + [\eta_i + \rho(s_i - \hat{s}_i)].$$

This looks a lot like manual 2SLS.

A closer look, however, reveals an important difference between the equations above and the usual 2SLS procedure: the covariates in the first and second stages are not the same. For example, Griliches and Mason included age in the second stage but not in the first, a fact noted by Cardell and Hopkins (1977) in a comment on their paper. This was a mistake. Griliches and Mason's second-stage estimates are not the same as 2SLS. What's worse, they are inconsistent where 2SLS might have been fine. To see why, note that the first-stage residual, $s_i - \hat{s}_i$, is uncorrelated with $X_{0i}$ by construction, since OLS residuals are always uncorrelated with included regressors. But because $X_{1i}$ is not included in the first stage it is likely to be correlated with the first-stage residuals (e.g., age is probably correlated with the AFQT residual from the Griliches and Mason (1972) first stage). The inconsistency from this correlation spills over to all coefficients in the second stage. The moral of the story: Put the same exogenous covariates in your first and second stage. If a covariate is good enough for the second stage, it's good enough for the first.

## Forbidden Regressions

Forbidden regressions were forbidden by MIT professor Jerry Hausman in 1975, and while they occasionally resurface in an undersupervised thesis, they are still technically off-limits. A forbidden regression crops up when researchers apply 2SLS reasoning directly to nonlinear models. A common scenario is a dummy endogenous variable. Suppose, for example, that the causal model of interest is

$$Y_i = \alpha' X_i + \rho D_i + \eta_i, \qquad (4.6.1)$$

where $D_i$ is a dummy variable for veteran status. The usual 2SLS first stage is

$$D_i = \pi'_{10} X_i + \pi'_{11} Z_i + \xi_{1i}, \qquad (4.6.2)$$

a linear regression of $D_i$ on covariates and a vector of instruments, $Z_i$.

Because $D_i$ is a dummy variable, the CEF associated with this first stage, $E[D_i | X_i, Z_i]$, is probably nonlinear. So the usual OLS first stage is an approximation to the underlying nonlinear CEF. We might, therefore, use a nonlinear first stage in an attempt to come closer to the CEF. Suppose that we use probit to model $E[D_i | X_i, Z_i]$. The probit first stage is $\Phi[\pi'_{p0} X_i + \pi'_{p1} Z_i]$, where $\pi_{p0}$ and $\pi_{p1}$ are probit coefficients and the fitted values are $\hat{D}_{pi} = \Phi[\hat{\pi}'_{p0}, X_i + \hat{\pi}'_{p1} Z_i]$. The forbidden regression in this case is the second-stage equation created by substituting $\hat{D}_{pi}$ for $D_i$:

$$Y_i = \alpha' X_i + \rho \hat{D}_{pi} + [\eta_i + \rho(D_i - \hat{D}_{pi})]. \qquad (4.6.3)$$

The problem with (4.6.3) is that only OLS estimation of (4.6.2) is guaranteed to produce first-stage residuals that are uncorrelated with fitted values and covariates. If $E[D_i | X_i, Z_i] = \Phi[X'_i \pi_{p0} + \pi'_{p1} Z_i]$, then residuals from the nonlinear model will be asymptotically uncorrelated with $X_i$ and $\hat{D}_{pi}$, but who is to say that the first-stage CEF is really probit? In contrast, with garden variety 2SLS, we do not need to worry about whether the first-stage CEF is really linear.[32]

A simple alternative to the forbidden second step, (4.6.3), avoids problems due to an incorrect nonlinear first stage. Instead of plugging in nonlinear fitted values, we can use the nonlinear fitted values as instruments. In other words, use $\hat{D}_{pi}$ as an instrument for $D_i$ in (4.6.1) in a conventional 2SLS procedure (as always, the exogenous covariates, $X_i$, should also be in the instrument list). Use of fitted values as instruments is the same as plugging in fitted values when the first stage is estimated by OLS, but not in general. Using nonlinear fits as instruments has the further advantage that, if the nonlinear model gives a better approximation to the first-stage CEF than the linear model, the resulting 2SLS estimates will be more efficient than those using a linear first stage (Newey, 1990).

But here, too, there is a drawback. The procedure using nonlinear fitted values as instruments implicitly uses nonlinearities in the first stage as a source of identifying information. To see this, suppose the causal model of interest includes the vector of instruments, $Z_i$:

$$Y_i = \alpha'X_i + \gamma'Z_i + \rho D_i + \eta_i. \qquad (4.6.4)$$

Now, with the first stage given by (4.6.2), the model is unidentified, and conventional 2SLS estimates of (4.6.4) don't exist. In fact, 4.6.4 violates the exclusion restriction. But 2SLS estimates using $X_i$, $Z_i$, and $\hat{D}_{pi}$ as instruments do exist, because $\hat{D}_{pi}$ is a nonlinear function of $X_i$ and $Z_i$ that is excluded from the second stage. Should you use this nonlinearity as a source of identifying information? We usually prefer to avoid this sort of back-door identification since it's not clear what the underlying experiment really is.

---

[32]The insight that consistency of 2SLS estimates in a traditional SEM does not depend on correct specification of the first-stage CEF goes back to Kelejian (1971). Use of a nonlinear plug-in first stage may not do too much damage in practice—a probit first stage can be pretty close to linear—but why take a chance when you don't have to?

As a rule, naively plugging in first-stage fitted values in nonlinear models is a bad idea. This includes models with a nonlinear second stage as well as those where the CEF for the first stage is nonlinear. Suppose, for example, that you believe the causal relation between schooling and earnings is approximately quadratic but otherwise homogeneous (as in Card's (1995) structural model). In other words, the model of interest is

$$Y_i = \alpha' X_i + \rho_1 s_i + \rho_2 s_i^2 + \eta_i. \qquad (4.6.5)$$

Given two instruments, it's easy enough to estimate (4.6.5), treating both $s_i$ and $s_i^2$ as endogenous. In this case, there are two first-stage equations, one for $s_i$ and one for $s_i^2$. Although you need at least two instruments for this to work, it's natural to use the original instrument and its square (unless the only instrument is a dummy, in which case you'll need a better idea).

You might be tempted, however, to work with a single first stage, say equation (4.6.2), and estimate the following second stage manually:

$$Y_i = \alpha' X_i + \rho_1 \hat{s}_i + \rho_2 \hat{s}_i^2 + [\eta_i + \rho_1(s_i - \hat{s}_i) + \rho_2(s_i^2 - \hat{s}_i^2)].$$

This is a mistake, since $\hat{s}_i$ can be correlated with $s_i^2 - \hat{s}_i^2$ while $\hat{s}_i^2$ can be correlated with both $s_i - \hat{s}_i$ and $s_i^2 - \hat{s}_i^2$. In contrast, as long as $X_i$ and $Z_i$ are uncorrelated with $\eta_i$ in (4.6.5) and you have enough instruments in $Z_i$, 2SLS estimation of (4.6.5) is straightforward.

### 4.6.2    Peer Effects

A vast literature in social science is concerned with peer effects. Loosely speaking, this means the causal effect of group characteristics on individual outcomes. Sometimes regression is used in an attempt to uncover these effects. In practice, the use of regression models to estimate peer effects is fraught with peril. Although this is not really an IV issue per se, the language and algebra of 2SLS help us understand why peer effects are hard to identify.

Broadly speaking, there are two types of peer effects. The first concerns the effect of group characteristics such as the average schooling in a state or city on individual outcomes as described by another variable. For example, Acemoglu and Angrist (2000) ask whether a given individual's earnings are affected by the average schooling in his or her state of residence. The theory of human capital externalities suggests that living in a state with a more educated workforce may make everyone in the state more productive, not just those who are more educated. This kind of spillover is said to be a *social return* to schooling: human capital that benefits everyone, whether or not they are more educated.

A causal model that allows for such externalities can be written

$$Y_{ijt} = \mu_j + \lambda_t + \gamma \bar{S}_{jt} + \rho s_i + u_{jt} + \eta_{ijt}, \qquad (4.6.6)$$

where $Y_{ijt}$ is the log weekly wage of individual $i$ in state $j$ in year $t$, $u_{jt}$ is a state-year error component, and $\eta_{ijt}$ is an individual error term. The controls $\mu_j$ and $\lambda_t$ are state-of-residence and year effects. The coefficient $\rho$ is the returns to schooling for an individual, while the coefficient $\gamma$ is meant to capture the effect of average schooling, $\bar{S}_{jt}$, in state $j$ and year $t$.

In addition to the usual concerns about $s_i$, the most important identification problem raised by equation (4.6.6) is omitted variables bias from correlation between average schooling and other state-year effects embodied in the error component $u_{jt}$. For example, public university systems may expand during cyclical upturns, generating a common trend in state average schooling levels and state average earnings. Acemoglu and Angrist (2000) attempt to solve this problem using instrumental variables derived from historical compulsory attendance laws that are correlated with $\bar{S}_{jt}$ but uncorrelated with contemporaneous $u_{jt}$ and $\eta_i$.

While omitted state-year effects are the primary concern motivating Acemoglu and Angrist's (2000) IV estimation, the fact that one regressor, $\bar{S}_{jt}$, is the average of another regressor, $s_i$, also complicates the interpretation of OLS estimates of equation (4.6.6). To see this, consider a simpler version of (4.6.6) with a cross-section dimension only. This can be written

$$Y_{ij} = \mu + \pi_0 s_i + \pi_1 \bar{S}_j + v_{ij}; \qquad (4.6.7)$$

where $Y_{ij}$ is the log weekly wage of individual $i$ in state $j$ and $\bar{S}_j$ is average schooling in the state. The coefficients $\pi_0$ and $\pi_1$ are defined so that the error, $v_{ij}$, is uncorrelated with both regressors. Now, let $\rho_0$ denote the coefficient from a bivariate regression of $Y_{ij}$ on $s_i$ only and let $\rho_1$ denote the coefficient from a bivariate regression of $Y_{ij}$ on $\bar{S}_j$ only. From the discussion of grouping and 2SLS earlier in this chapter, we know that $\rho_1$ is the 2SLS estimate of the coefficient on $s_i$ in a bivariate regression of $Y_{ij}$ on $s_i$ using a full set of state dummies as instruments. The appendix uses this fact to show that the parameters in equation (4.6.7) can be written in terms of $\rho_0$ and $\rho_1$ as

$$\pi_0 = \rho_1 + \phi(\rho_0 - \rho_1) \qquad (4.6.8)$$
$$\pi_1 = \phi(\rho_1 - \rho_0),$$

where $\phi = \frac{1}{1-R^2} > 1$, and $R^2$ is the first-stage $R^2$ when state dummies are used as instruments for $s_i$.

The upshot of (4.6.8) is that if, for any reason, OLS estimates of the bivariate regression of wages on individual schooling differ from 2SLS estimates using state dummy instruments, the coefficient on average schooling in (4.6.7) will be nonzero. For example, if instrumenting with state dummies corrects for attenuation bias due to measurement error in $s_i$, we have $\rho_1 > \rho_0$ and the spurious appearance of positive social returns. In contrast, if instrumenting with state dummies eliminates the bias from positive correlation between $s_i$ and unobserved earnings potential, we have $\rho_1 < \rho_0$, and the appearance of negative social returns.[33] In practice, therefore, it is very difficult to isolate social effects by OLS estimation of

---

[33]The coefficient on average schooling in an equation with individual schooling can be interpreted as the Hausman (1978) test statistic for the equality of OLS estimates and 2SLS estimates of private returns to schooling using state dummies as instruments. Borjas (1992) discusses a similar problem affecting the estimation of ethnic-background effects.

an equation like (4.6.6), though more sophisticated IV strategies where both the individual and group averages are treated as endogenous may work.

A second and even more difficult peer effect to uncover is the effect of the group average of a variable on the individual level of this same variable. This is not really an IV problem; it takes us back to basic regression issues. To see this point, suppose that $\bar{S}_j$ is the high school graduation rate in school $j$, and we would like to know whether students are more likely to graduate from high school when everyone around them is more likely to graduate from high school. To uncover the peer effect on high school graduation rates, we might work with a regression model like:

$$s_{ij} = \mu + \pi_2 \bar{S}_j + v_{ij}, \qquad (4.6.9)$$

where $s_{ij}$ is individual $i$'s high school graduation status and $\bar{S}_j$ is the average high school graduation rate in school $j$, which $i$ attends.

At first blush, equation (4.6.9) seems like a sensible formulation of a well-defined causal question, but in fact it is nonsense. The regression of $s_{ij}$ on $\bar{S}_j$ *always* has a coefficient of 1, a conclusion that can be drawn immediately once you recognize $\bar{S}_j$ as the first-stage fitted value from a regression of $s_{ij}$ on a full set of school dummies.[34] Thus, an equation like (4.6.9) cannot possibly be informative about causal effects. A modestly improved version of this bad peer regression changes (4.6.9) to

$$s_{ij} = \mu + \pi_3 \bar{S}_{(i)j} + v_{ij}, \qquad (4.6.10)$$

[34]Here is a direct proof that the regression of $s_{ij}$ on $\bar{S}_j$ is always unity:

$$\frac{\displaystyle\sum_j \sum_i s_{ij}(\bar{S}_j - \bar{S})}{\displaystyle\sum_j n_j(\bar{S}_j - \bar{S})^2} = \frac{\displaystyle\sum_j (\bar{S}_j - \bar{S}) \sum_i s_{ij}}{\displaystyle\sum_j n_j(\bar{S}_j - \bar{S})^2}$$

$$= \frac{\displaystyle\sum_j (\bar{S}_j - \bar{S})(n_j \bar{S}_j)}{\displaystyle\sum_j n_j(\bar{S}_j - \bar{S})^2} = 1.$$

where $\overline{S}_{(i)j}$ is the mean of $s_{ij}$ in school $j$, excluding student $i$. This is a step in the right direction—$\pi_3$ is no longer automatically equal to 1—but still problematic because $s_{ij}$ and $\overline{S}_{(i)j}$ are both affected by school-level random shocks that are implicitly part of $v_{ij}$. The presence of random group effects in the error term raises important issues for statistical inference, issues discussed at length in chapter 8. But in an equation like (4.6.10), group-level random shocks are more than a problem for standard errors: any shock common to the group (school) creates spurious peer effects. For example, particularly effective school principals may raise graduation rates for everyone in the schools at which they work. This looks like a peer effect, since it induces correlation between $s_{ij}$ and $\overline{S}_{(i)j}$ even if there is no causal link between peer means and individual student achievement. We therefore prefer not to see regressions like (4.6.10) either.

The best shot at a causal investigation of peer effects focuses on variation in ex ante peer characteristics, that is, some measure of peer quality that predates the outcome variable and is therefore unaffected by common shocks. A recent example is Ammermueller and Pischke (2006), who studied the link between classmates' family background, as measured by the number of books in their homes, and student achievement in European primary schools. The Ammermueller and Pischke regressions are versions of

$$s_{ij} = \mu + \pi_4 \overline{B}_{(i)j} + v_{ij},$$

where $\overline{B}_{(i)j}$ is the average number of books in the home of student $i$'s peers. This looks like (4.6.10), but with an important difference. The variable $\overline{B}_{(i)j}$ is a feature of the home environment that predates test scores and is therefore unaffected by school-level random shocks.

Angrist and Lang (2004) provide another example of an attempt to link student achievement with the ex ante characteristics of peers. The Angrist and Lang study looked at the impact of bused-in low-achieving newcomers on high-achieving residents' test scores. The regression of interest in this case is a version of

$$s_{ij} = \mu + \pi_5 \overline{m}_j + v_{ij}, \qquad (4.6.11)$$

where $\overline{m}_j$ is the number of bused-in low achievers in school $j$ and $s_{ij}$ is resident student $i$'s test score. Spurious correlation due to common shocks is not a concern in this context, for two reasons. First, $\overline{m}_j$ is a feature of the school population determined by students outside the sample used to estimate (4.6.11). Second, the number of low achievers is an ex ante variable biased on information about where the students come from and not the outcome variable, $s_{ij}$. School-level random effects that are part of $v_{ij}$ remain an important issue for inference, however, since $\overline{m}_j$ is a group-level variable.

### 4.6.3  Limited Dependent Variables Reprise

In section 3.4.2, we discussed the consequences of limited dependent variables for regression models. When the dependent variable is binary or non-negative—say, employment status or hours worked—the CEF is typically nonlinear. Most nonlinear LDV models are built around a nonlinear transformation of a linear latent index. Examples include probit, logit, and Tobit. These models capture features of the associated CEFs (e.g., probit fitted values are guaranteed to be between zero and one, while Tobit fitted values are non-negative). Yet we saw that the added complexity and extra work required to interpret the results from latent index models may not be worth the trouble.

An important consideration in favor of OLS is a conceptual robustness that structural models often lack. OLS always gives a MMSE linear approximation to the CEF. In fact, we can think of OLS as a scheme for computing marginal effects—a scheme that has the virtue of simplicity, automation, and comparability across studies. Nonlinear latent index models are more like GLS: they provide an efficiency gain when taken literally, but require a commitment to functional form and distributional assumptions, about which we do not usually feel strongly.[35] A second consideration is the distinction between the latent index parameters at the heart of nonlinear models and the average causal effects that we believe should be the objects of primary interest in most research projects.

The arguments in favor of conventional OLS with LDVs apply with equal force to 2SLS and models with endogenous variables. IV methods capture local average treatment effects regardless of whether the dependent variable is binary, nonnegative, or continuously distributed. With covariates, we can think of 2SLS as estimating LATE averaged across covariate cells. In models with variable or continuous treatment intensity, 2SLS gives us the average causal response or an average derivative. Although Abadie (2003) has shown that 2SLS does not, in general, provide the MMSE approximation to the complier causal response function, in practice, 2SLS estimates come out remarkably close to estimates using the more rigorously grounded Abadie procedure (and with a saturated model for covariates, 2SLS and Abadie are the same). Moreover, 2SLS estimates LATE directly; there is no intermediate step involving the calculation of marginal effects.

2SLS is not the only way to go. An alternative, more elaborate approach tries to build up a causal story by describing the process generating LDVs in detail. A good example is bivariate probit, which can be applied to the Angrist and Evans (1998) example like this. Suppose that a woman decides to

---

[35] The analogy between nonlinear LDV models and GLS is more than rhetorical. Consider a probit model with nonlinear CEF, $E[y_i|X_i] = \Phi\left[\frac{X_i'\beta^*}{\sigma}\right] \equiv r_i$. The first-order conditions for maximum likelihood estimation of this model are

$$\sum_i \frac{(y_i - r_i)X_i}{r_i(1 - r_i)} = 0.$$

Maximum likelihood is asymptotically the same as GLS estimation of the nonlinear regression model

$$y_i = \Phi\left[\frac{X_i'\beta^*}{\sigma}\right] + \xi_i,$$

since the conditional variance of $y_i$ is $r_i(1 - r_i)$. The only difference is that GLS is done in two steps.

have a third child by comparing costs and benefits using a net benefit function or latent index that is linear in covariates and excluded instruments, with a random error term, $v_i$. The bivariate probit first stage can be written

$$D_i = 1[X_i' \gamma_0^* + \gamma_1^* z_i > v_i], \qquad (4.6.12)$$

where $z_i$ is an instrumental variable that increases the benefit of a third child, conditional on covariates, $X_i$. For example, American parents appear to value a third child more when they have had either two boys or two girls, a sort of portfolio diversification phenomenon that can be understood as increasing the benefit of a third child in families with same-sex sibships.

An outcome variable of primary interest in this context is employment status, a Bernoulli random variable with a conditional mean between zero and one. To complete the model, suppose that employment status, $Y_i$, is determined by the latent index

$$Y_i = 1[X_i' \beta_0^* + \beta_1^* D_i > \varepsilon_i], \qquad (4.6.13)$$

where $\varepsilon_i$ is a second random component or error term. This latent index can be seen as arising from a comparison of the costs and benefits of working.

The source of omitted variables bias in the bivariate probit setup is correlation between $v_i$ and $\varepsilon_i$. In other words, unmeasured random determinants of childbearing are correlated with unmeasured random determinants of employment. The model is identified by assuming $z_i$ is independent of these components, and that the random components are normally distributed. Given normality, the parameters in (4.6.12) and (4.6.13) can be estimated by maximum likelihood. The log likelihood function is

$$\sum Y_i \ln \Phi_b \left( \frac{X_i' \beta_0^* + \beta_1^* D_i}{\sigma_\varepsilon}, \frac{X_i' \gamma_0^* + \gamma_1^* z_i}{\sigma_v}; \rho_{\varepsilon v} \right)$$
$$+ (1 - Y_i) \ln \left[ 1 - \Phi_b \left( \frac{X_i' \beta_0^* + \beta_1^* D_i}{\sigma_\varepsilon}, \frac{X_i' \gamma_0^* + \gamma_1^* z_i}{\sigma_v}; \rho_{\varepsilon v} \right) \right],$$

$$(4.6.14)$$

where $\Phi_b(\cdot, \cdot; \rho_{\varepsilon v})$ is the bivariate normal distribution function with correlation coefficient $\rho_{\varepsilon v}$. Note, however, that we can multiply the latent index coefficients and error standard deviations $(\sigma_\varepsilon, \sigma_v)$ by a positive constant without changing the likelihood. The object of estimation is therefore the ratio of the index coefficients to the error standard deviations (e.g., $\beta_1^*/\sigma_\varepsilon$).

The potential outcomes defined by the bivariate probit model are

$$\mathrm{Y}_{0i} = 1[\mathrm{X}_i'\beta_0^* > \varepsilon_i] \text{ and } \mathrm{Y}_{1i} = 1[\mathrm{X}_i'\beta_0^* + \beta_1^* > \varepsilon_i],$$

while potential treatment assignments are

$$\mathrm{D}_{0i} = 1[\mathrm{X}_i'\gamma_0^* > v_i] \text{ and } \mathrm{D}_{1i} = 1[\mathrm{X}_i'\gamma_0^* + \gamma_1^* > v_i].$$

As usual, only one potential outcome and one potential assignment are observed for any one person. It's also clear from this representation that correlation between $v_i$ and $\varepsilon_i$ is the same thing as correlation between potential treatment assignments and potential outcomes.

The latent index coefficients do not themselves tell us anything about the size of the causal effect of childbearing on employment other than the sign. To see this, note that the average causal effect of childbearing is

$$E[\mathrm{Y}_{1i} - \mathrm{Y}_{0i}] = E\{1[\mathrm{X}_i'\beta_0^* + \beta_1^* > \varepsilon_i] - 1[\mathrm{X}_i'\beta_0^* > \varepsilon_i]\},$$

while the average effect on the treated is

$$E[\mathrm{Y}_{1i} - \mathrm{Y}_{0i}|\mathrm{D}_i = 1]$$
$$= E\{1[\mathrm{X}_i'\beta_0^* + \beta_1^* > \varepsilon_i] - 1[\mathrm{X}_i'\beta_0^* > \varepsilon_i]|\mathrm{X}_i'\gamma_0^* + \gamma_1^*\mathrm{z}_i > v_i\}.$$

Given alternative distributional assumptions for $v_i$ and $\varepsilon_i$, these can be anything. (If the error terms are heteroskedastic, then even the sign of these expressions is indeterminate.)

By virtue of normality, the average causal effects generated by the bivariate probit model are easy to evaluate. The average treatment effect is

$$E\{1[X_i'\beta_0^* + \beta_1^* > \varepsilon_i] - 1[X_i'\beta_0^* > \varepsilon_i]\} \qquad (4.6.15)$$
$$= E\left\{\Phi\left[\frac{X_i'\beta_0^* + \beta_1^*}{\sigma_\epsilon}\right] - \Phi\left[\frac{X_i'\beta_0^*}{\sigma_\epsilon}\right]\right\},$$

where $\Phi[\cdot]$ is the normal CDF. The effect on the treated is a little more complicated since it involves the bivariate normal CDF:

$$E[Y_{1i} - Y_{0i}|D_i = 1]$$
$$= E\left\{\frac{\Phi_b\left(\frac{X_i'\beta_0^* + \beta_1^*}{\sigma_\varepsilon}, \frac{X_i'\gamma_0^* + \gamma_1^* z_i}{\sigma_v}; \rho_{\varepsilon v}\right) - \Phi_b\left(\frac{X_i'\beta_0^*}{\sigma_\varepsilon}, \frac{X_i'\gamma_0^* + \gamma_1^* z_i}{\sigma_v}; \rho_{\varepsilon v}\right)}{\Phi\left(\frac{X_i'\gamma_0^* + \gamma_1^* z_i}{\sigma_v}\right)}\right\}.$$
$$(4.6.16)$$

The bivariate normal CDF is a canned function in many software packages, so this is easy enough to calculate in practice.

Bivariate probit probably qualifies as harmless in the sense that it's not very complicated and easy to get right using packaged software routines. Still, it shares the disadvantages of nonlinear latent index modeling discussed in section 3.4.2. First, some researchers become distracted by an effort to estimate index coefficients instead of average causal effects. For example, a large literature in econometrics is concerned with the estimation of index coefficients without the need for distributional assumptions. Applied researchers interested in causal effects can safely ignore this work.[36]

[36] Suppose the latent error term has an unknown distribution, with CDF $\Lambda[\cdot]$. The average causal effect in this case is

$$E\{\Lambda[X_i'\beta_0^* + \beta_1^*] - \Lambda[X_i'\beta_0^*]\} = \Lambda'[X_i'\beta_0^* + \tilde{\beta}_1]\beta_1^*,$$

where (by the mean value theorem) $\tilde{\beta}_1$ is a number in $[0, \beta_1^*]$. This always depends on the shape of $\Lambda[\cdot]$, so it is never enough to know the index coefficients alone.

A second vice in this context is also a virtue. Bivariate probit and other models of this sort can be used to estimate unconditional average causal effects and/or effects on the treated. In contrast, 2SLS does not promise you average causal effects, only *local* average causal effects. But it should be clear from (4.6.15) that the assumed normality of the latent index error terms is essential for this. As always, the best you can do without a distributional assumption is LATE, the average causal effect for compliers. For bivariate probit, we can write LATE as

$$
\begin{aligned}
E[Y_{1i} &- Y_{0i}|D_{1i} > D_{0i}] \\
&= E\{1[X_i'\beta_0^* + \beta_1^* > \varepsilon_i] \\
&\quad - 1[X_i'\beta_0^* > \varepsilon_i]|X_i'\gamma_0^* + \gamma_1^* > v_i > X_i'\gamma_0^*\},
\end{aligned}
$$

which, like (4.6.16), can be evaluated using joint normality of $v_i$ and $\varepsilon_i$. But you needn't bother using normality to evaluate $E[Y_{1i} - Y_{0i}|D_{1i} > D_{0i}]$, since LATE can be estimated by IV for each $X_i$ and averaged using the histogram of the covariates. Alternately, do 2SLS and settle for a variance-weighted average of covariate-specific LATEs, as described by the saturate and weight theorem in section 4.5.3.

You might be wondering whether LATE is enough. Perhaps you would like to estimate the unconditional average treatment effect or the effect of treatment on the treated and are willing to make a few extra assumptions to do so. That's all well and good, but in our experience you can't get blood from a stone, even with heroic assumptions. Since local information is all that's in the data, in practice, the average causal effects produced by bivariate probit are likely to be similar to 2SLS estimates, provided the model for covariates is sufficiently flexible. This is illustrated in table 4.6.1, which reports 2SLS and bivariate probit estimates of the effects of a third child on female labor supply using the Angrist-Evans (1998) same-sex instruments and the same 1980 census sample of married women with two or more children used in their paper. The dependent variable is a dummy for having worked the previous year; the endogenous variable is a dummy for

TABLE 4.6.1
2SLS, Abadie, and bivariate probit estimates of the effects of a third child on female labor supply

|  | Abadie Estimates | | Bivariate Probit | | |
|---|---|---|---|---|---|
| 2SLS (1) | Linear (2) | Probit (3) | MFX (4) | ATE (5) | TOT (6) |
| A. No Covariates | | | | | |
| −.138 | −.138 | −.137 | −.138 | −.139 | −.139 |
| (.029) | (.030) | (.030) | (.029) | (.029) | (.029) |
| B. Some covariates (no age controls) | | | | | |
| −.132 | −.132 | −.131 | −.135 | −.135 | −.135 |
| (.029) | (.029) | (.028) | (.028) | (.028) | (.028) |
| C. Some covariates plus age at first birth | | | | | |
| −.129 | −.129 | −.129 | −.133 | −.133 | −.133 |
| (.028) | (.028) | (.028) | (.026) | (.026) | (.026) |
| D. Some covariates plus age at first birth and a dummy for age > 30 | | | | | |
| −.124 | −.125 | −.125 | −.131 | −.131 | −.131 |
| (.028) | (.029) | (.029) | (.025) | (.025) | (.025) |
| E. Some covariates plus age at first birth and age | | | | | |
| −.120 | −.121 | −.121 | −.171 | −.171 | −.171 |
| (.028) | (.026) | (.026) | (.023) | (.023) | (.023) |

*Notes*: Adapted from Angrist (2001). The table compares 2SLS estimates to alternative estimates of the effect of childbearing on labor supply using nonlinear models. All models use same-sex instruments. Standard errors for the Abadie estimates were bootstrapped using 100 replications of subsamples of size 20,000. MFX denotes marginal effects; ATE is the unconditional average treatment effect; TOT is the average effect of treatment on the treated.

having a third child. The first-stage effect of a same-sex sibship on the probability of a third birth is about 7 percentage points.

Panel A of table 4.6.1 reports estimates from a model with no covariates. The 2SLS estimate of −.138 in column 1 is numerically identical to the Abadie causal effect estimated using a linear model in column 2, as it should be in this case. Without covariates, the 2SLS slope coefficient provides the best linear approximation to the complier causal response function as does Abadie's kappa-weighting procedure. The marginal effect changes little if, instead of a linear approximation, we use nonlinear least squares with a probit CEF. The marginal effect estimated by minimizing

$$E\left\{\kappa_i\left(\mathrm{Y}_i - \Phi\left[\frac{\beta_0^* + \beta_1^*\mathrm{D}_i}{\sigma_\varepsilon}\right]\right)^2\right\}$$

is $-.137$, reported in column 3. This is not surprising, since the model without covariates imposes no functional form assumptions.

Perhaps more surprising is the fact that marginal effects and the average treatment effects calculated using (4.6.15) and (4.6.16) are also the same as the 2SLS and Abadie estimates. These results are reported in columns 4–6. The marginal effect calculated using a derivative to approximate to the finite difference in (4.6.15) is $-.138$ (in column 4, labeled MFX for marginal effects), while both average treatment effects are $-.139$ in columns 5 and 6. Adding a few covariates has little effect on the estimates, as can be seen in panel B. In this case, the covariates are all dummy variables, three for race (black, Hispanic, other), and two indicating first- and second-born boys (the excluded instrument is the interaction of these two). Panels C and D show that adding a linear term in age at first birth and a dummy for maternal age also leaves the estimates unchanged.

The invariance to covariates seems desirable: because the same-sex instrument is essentially independent of covariates, control for covariates is unnecessary to eliminate bias and should primarily affect precision. Yet, as panel E shows, the marginal effects generated by bivariate probit are sensitive to the list of covariates. Swapping a dummy indicating mothers over 30 with a linear age term increases the bivariate probit estimates markedly, to $-.171$, while leaving 2SLS and the Abadie estimators unchanged. This probably reflects the fact that the linear age term induces an extrapolation into cells where there is little data. Although there is no harm in reporting the bivariate probit effects in panel E, it's hard to see why the more robust 2SLS and Abadie estimators should not be preferred.[37]

## 4.6.4    The Bias of 2SLS⋆

It is a fortunate fact that the OLS estimator is not only consistent, it is also unbiased (as we briefly noted at the end of section 3.1.3). This means that in a sample of any size, the estimated OLS coefficient vector has a distribution that is centered on the population coefficient vector.[38] The 2SLS estimator, in contrast, is consistent, but biased. This means that the 2SLS estimator only promises to be close to the causal effect of interest in large samples. In small samples, 2SLS estimates can differ systematically from the target parameter.

For many years, applied researchers lived with the knowledge that 2SLS is biased without losing too much sleep. Neither of us heard much about the bias of 2SLS in our graduate econometrics classes. A series of papers in the early 1990s changed this, however. These papers show that 2SLS estimates can be highly misleading in cases relevant for empirical practice.[39]

The 2SLS estimator is most biased when the instruments are "weak," meaning the correlation with endogenous regressors is low, and when there are many overidentifying restrictions. When the instruments are both many and weak, the 2SLS estimator is biased toward the probability limit of the corresponding OLS estimate. In the worst-case scenario, when the instruments are so weak that there is no first stage in the population, the 2SLS sampling distribution is centered on the

---

[37] Angrist (2001) makes the same point using twins instruments and reports a similar pattern in a comparison of 2SLS, Abadie, and nonlinear structural estimates of models for hours worked.

[38] A more precise statement is that OLS is unbiased when either (1) the CEF is linear or (2) the regressors are nonstochastic, that is, fixed in repeated samples. In practice, these qualifications do not seem to matter much. As a rule, the sampling distribution of $\hat{\beta} = [\sum_i X_i X_i']^{-1} \sum_i X_i Y_i$, tends to be centered on the population analog, $\beta = E[X_i X_i']^{-1} E[X_i Y_i]$, in samples of any size, whether or not the CEF is linear or the regressors are stochastic.

[39] Key references are Nelson and Startz (1990a,b), Buse (1992), Bekker (1994), and especially Bound, Jaeger, and Baker (1995).

probability limit of OLS. The theory behind this result is a little technical, but the basic idea is easy to see. The source of the
bias in 2SLS estimates is the randomness in estimates of the
first-stage fitted values. In practice, the first-stage estimates
reflect some of the randomness in the endogenous variable,
since the first-stage coefficients come from a regression of the
endogenous variable on the instruments. If the population first
stage is zero, then all randomness in the first stage is due to the
endogenous variable. This randomness generates finite-sample
correlation between first-stage fitted values and second-stage
errors, since the endogenous variable is correlated with the
second-stage errors (or else you wouldn't be instrumenting in
the first place).

A more formal derivation of 2SLS bias goes like this. To
streamline the discussion we use matrices and vectors and a
simple constant-effects model (it's difficult to discuss bias in a
heterogeneous effects world, since the target parameter may
change as the number of instruments changes). Suppose you
are interested in estimating the effect of a single endogenous
regressor, stored in a vector $x$, on a dependent variable, stored
in the vector $y$, with no other covariates. The causal model of
interest can then be written

$$y = \beta x + \eta. \tag{4.6.17}$$

The $N \times Q$ matrix of instrumental variables is $Z$, with the
associated first-stage equation

$$x = Z\pi + \xi. \tag{4.6.18}$$

OLS estimates of (4.6.17) are biased because $\eta_i$ is correlated with $\xi_i$. The instruments $Z_i$ are uncorrelated with $\xi_i$ by
construction and uncorrelated with $\eta_i$ by assumption.

The 2SLS estimator is

$$\hat{\beta}_{2SLS} = (x'P_Z x)^{-1} x'P_Z y = \beta + (x'P_Z x)^{-1} x'P_Z \eta,$$

where $P_Z = Z(Z'Z)^{-1}Z'$ is the projection matrix that produces
fitted values from a regression of $x$ on $Z$. Substituting for $x$ in

$x'P_Z\eta$, we get

$$\hat{\beta}_{2SLS} - \beta = (x'P_Zx)^{-1}(\pi'Z' + \xi')P_Z\eta$$
$$= (x'P_Zx)^{-1}\pi'Z'\eta + (x'P_Zx)^{-1}\xi'P_Z\eta. \quad (4.6.19)$$

The bias in 2SLS comes from the nonzero expectation of terms on the right-hand side.

The expectation of (4.6.19) is hard to evaluate because the expectation operator does not pass through the inverse $(x'P_Zx)^{-1}$, a nonlinear function. It's possible to show, however, that the expectation of the ratios on the right-hand side of (4.6.19) can be closely approximated by the ratio of expectations. In other words,

$$E[\hat{\beta}_{2SLS} - \beta] \approx (E[x'P_Zx])^{-1}E[\pi'Z'\eta] + (E[x'P_Zx])^{-1}E[\xi'P_Z\eta].$$

This approximation is much better than the usual asymptotic approximation invoked in large-sample theory, so we think of it as giving us a good measure of the finite-sample behavior of the 2SLS estimator.[40] Furthermore, because $E[\pi'Z'\xi] = 0$ and $E[\pi'Z'\eta] = 0$, we have

$$E[\hat{\beta}_{2SLS} - \beta] \approx [E(\pi'Z'Z\pi) + E(\xi'P_Z\xi)]^{-1}E(\xi'P_Z\eta).$$
$$(4.6.20)$$

The approximate bias of 2SLS therefore comes from the fact that $E(\xi'P_Z\eta)$ is not zero unless $\eta_i$ and $\xi_i$ are uncorrelated. But correlation between $\eta_i$ and $\xi_i$ is what led us to use IV in the first place.

Further manipulation of (4.6.20) generates an expression that is especially useful:

$$E[\hat{\beta}_{2SLS} - \beta] \approx \frac{\sigma_{\eta\xi}}{\sigma_\xi^2}\left[\frac{E(\pi'Z'Z\pi)/Q}{\sigma_\xi^2} + 1\right]^{-1}$$

---

[40] See Bekker (1994) and Angrist and Krueger (1995). This is also called a group-asymptotic approximation because it can be derived from an an asymptotic sequence that lets the number of instruments go to infinity at the same time as the number of observations goes to infinity, keeping the number of observations per instrument (group) constant.

(see the appendix for a derivation). The term $(1/\sigma_\xi^2)E(\pi'Z'Z\pi)/$ Q is the $F$-statistic for the joint significance of all regressors in the first stage regression.[41] Call this statistic $F$, so that we can write

$$E[\hat{\beta}_{2SLS} - \beta] \approx \frac{\sigma_{\eta\xi}}{\sigma_\xi^2}\frac{1}{F+1}. \qquad (4.6.21)$$

From this we see that as the first stage $F$-statistic gets small, the bias of 2SLS approaches $\sigma_{\eta\xi}/\sigma_\xi^2$. The bias of the OLS estimator is $\sigma_{\eta\xi}/\sigma_x^2$, which also equals $\sigma_{\eta\xi}/\sigma_\xi^2$ if $\pi = 0$. Thus, we have shown that 2SLS is centered on the same point as OLS when the first stage is zero. More generally, we can say 2SLS estimates are "biased toward OLS estimates" when there isn't much of a first stage. On the other hand, the bias of 2SLS vanishes when $F$ gets large, as should happen in large samples when $\pi \neq 0$.

When the instruments are weak, the $F$-statistic varies inversely with the number of instruments. To see why, consider adding useless instruments to your 2SLS model, that is, instruments with no effect on the first-stage $R^2$. The model sum of squares, $E(\pi'Z'Z\pi)$, and the residual variance, $\sigma_\xi^2$, will both stay the same while Q goes up. The $F$-statistic becomes smaller as a result. From this we learn that the addition of many weak instruments increases bias.

Intuitively, the bias in 2SLS is a consequence of the fact that the first-stage is estimated. If the first stage coefficients were known, we could use $\hat{x}_{pop} = Z\pi$ for the first-stage fitted values. These fitted values are uncorrelated with the second-stage error. In practice, however, we use $\hat{x} = P_Z x = Z\pi + P_Z\xi$, which differs from $\hat{x}_{pop}$ by the term $P_Z\xi$. The bias in 2SLS arises from the fact that $P_Z\xi$ is correlated with $\eta$, so some of

---

[41]Sort of; the actual $F$-statistic is $(1/\hat{\sigma}_\xi^2)\hat{\pi}'Z'Z\hat{\pi}/Q$, where hats denote estimates. $(1/\sigma_\xi^2)E(\pi'Z'Z\pi)/Q$ is therefore sometimes called the population $F$-statistic since it's the $F$-statistic we'd get in an infinitely large sample. In practice, the distinction between population and sample $F$ matters little in this context. Some econometricians prefer to multiply the first-stage $F$ by the number of instruments when summarizing instrument strength. This product is called the "concentration parameter."

the correlation between errors in the first and second stages seeps into our 2SLS estimates through the sampling variability in $\hat{\pi}$. Asymptotically, this correlation disappears, but real life does not play out in asymptopia.

Formula (4.6.21) shows that, other things equal, the bias in 2SLS is an increasing function of the number of instruments, so bias is least in the just-identified case when the number of instruments is as low as it can get. In fact, just-identified 2SLS (say, the simple Wald estimator) is approximately *unbiased*. This is hard to show formally because just-identified 2SLS has no moments (i.e., the sampling distribution has fat tails). Nevertheless, even with weak instruments, just-identified 2SLS is approximately centered where it should be. We therefore say that just-identified 2SLS is median-unbiased. This is not to say that you can happily use weak instruments in just-identified models. With a weak instrument, just-identified estimates tend to be too imprecise to be useful.

The limited information maximum likelihood (LIML) estimator is approximately median-unbiased for overidentified constant effects models, and therefore provides an attractive alternative to just-identified estimation using one instrument at a time (see, e.g., Davidson and MacKinnon, 1993, and Mariano, 2001). LIML has the advantage of having the same asymptotic distribution as 2SLS (under constant effects) while providing a finite-sample bias reduction. A number of other estimators also reduce the bias in overidentified 2SLS models. But an extensive Monte Carlo study by Flores-Lagunes (2007) suggests that LIML does at least as well as the alternatives in a wide range of circumstances (in terms of bias, mean absolute error, and the empirical rejection rates for $t$-tests). Another advantage of LIML is that many statistical packages compute it, while other estimators typically require some programming.[42]

---

[42]LIML is available in SAS and in STATA 10. With weak instruments, LIML standard errors are not quite right, but Bekker (1994) gives a simple fix for this. Why is LIML unbiased? Expression (4.6.21) shows that the approximate bias of 2SLS is proportional to the bias of OLS. From this we conclude that there is a linear combination of OLS and 2SLS that is approximately

We use a small Monte Carlo experiment to illustrate some of the theoretical results from the discussion above. The simulated data are drawn from the following model,

$$y_i = \beta x_i + \eta_i$$

$$x_i = \sum_{j=1}^{Q} \pi_j z_{ij} + \xi_i,$$

with $\beta = 1, \pi_1 = 0.1, \pi_j = 0$ for $j = 2, \ldots, Q$; and

$$\begin{pmatrix} \eta_i \\ \xi_i \end{pmatrix} \bigg| Z \sim N \left( \begin{pmatrix} 0 \\ 0 \end{pmatrix}, \begin{pmatrix} 1 & 0.8 \\ 0.8 & 1 \end{pmatrix} \right),$$

where the $z_{ij}$ are independent, normally distributed random variables with mean zero and unit variance. This simulates a scenario with one good instrument and $Q - 1$ worthless instruments. The sample size is 1000.

Figure 4.6.1 shows the Monte Carlo cumulative distribution functions of four estimators: OLS, just-identified IV (i.e., 2SLS with $Q = 1$, labeled IV; first-stage $F = 11.1$), 2SLS with two instruments ($Q = 2$, labeled 2SLS; first-stage $F = 6.0$), and LIML with $Q = 2$. The OLS estimator is biased and centered around a value of about 1.79. IV is centered around 1, the value of $\beta$. 2SLS with one weak and one uninformative instrument is moderately biased toward OLS (the median is 1.07). The distribution function for LIML with $Q = 2$ is indistinguishable from that for just-identified IV, even though the LIML estimator also uses an uninformative instrument.

Figure 4.6.2 reports simulation results where we set $Q = 20$. Thus, in addition to the one informative but weak instrument,

---

unbiased. LIML turns out to be just such a "combination estimator." Like the bias of 2SLS, the approximate unbiasedness of LIML can be shown using a Bekker-style group-asymptotic sequence that fixes the ratio of instruments to sample size. It is worth mentioning, however, that LIML is biased in models with a certain type of heteroskedasticity. See Bekker and van der Ploeg (2005) and Hausman, et al. (2008) for details. Unlike LIML, the Jackknife IV Estimator (JIVE: see, e.g., Angrist, Imbens, and Krueger, 1999) is Bekker-unbiased under heteroskedasticity. Ackerberg and Devereux (2007) recently introduced an improved version of JIVE with lower variance.

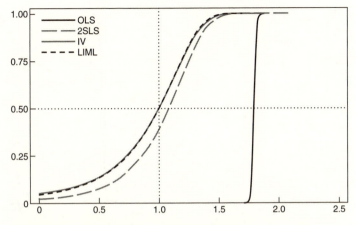

**Figure 4.6.1**  Monte Carlo cumulative distribution functions of OLS, IV ($Q = 1$), 2SLS ($Q = 2$), and LIML ($Q = 2$) estimators.

we added 19 worthless instruments (first-stage $F = 1.51$). The figure again shows OLS, 2SLS, and LIML distributions. The bias in 2SLS is now much worse (the median is 1.53, close to the OLS median). The sampling distribution of the 2SLS estimator is also much tighter than in the $Q = 2$ case. LIML

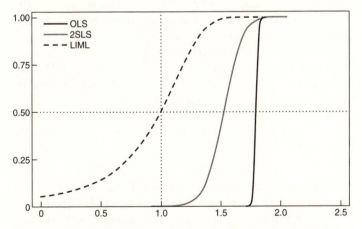

**Figure 4.6.2**  Monte Carlo cumulative distribution functions of OLS, 2SLS, and LIML estimators with $Q = 20$ instruments.

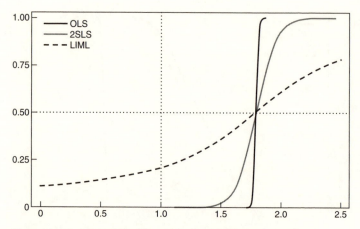

**Figure 4.6.3** Monte Carlo cumulative distribution functions of OLS, 2SLS, and LIML estimators with $Q = 20$ worthless instruments.

again performs well and is centered around $\beta = 1$, with a bit more dispersion than in the $Q = 2$ case.

Finally, figure 4.6.3 reports simulation results from a model that is truly unidentified. In this case, we set $\pi_j = 0$; $j = 1, \ldots, 20$ (first-stage $F = 1.0$). Not surprisingly, all the sampling distributions are centered around the same value as OLS. On the other hand, the 2SLS sampling distribution is much tighter than the LIML distribution. We would say advantage LIML in this case because the widely dispersed LIML sampling distribution correctly reflects the fact that the data are uninformative about the parameter of interest.

What does this mean in practice? Besides retaining a vague sense of worry about your first stage, we recommend the following:

1. Report the first stage and think about whether it makes sense. Are the magnitude and sign as you would expect, or are the estimates too big or wrong-signed? If so, perhaps your hypothesized first-stage mechanism isn't really there, rather, you simply got lucky.

2. Report the $F$-statistic on the excluded instruments. The bigger this is, the better. Stock, Wright, and Yogo (2002) suggest that $F$-statistics above about 10 put you in the safe zone, though obviously this cannot be a theorem.

3. Pick your single best instrument and report just-identified estimates using this one only. Just-identified IV is median-unbiased and therefore unlikely to be subject to a weak instruments critique.

4. Check overidentified 2SLS estimates with LIML. LIML is less precise than 2SLS but also less biased. If the results come out similar, be happy. If not, worry, and try to find stronger instruments or reduce the degree of overidentification.

5. Look at the coefficients, $t$-statistics, and $F$-statistics for excluded instruments in the reduced-form regression of dependent variables on instruments. Remember that the reduced form is proportional to the causal effect of interest. Moreover, the reduced-form estimates, since they are OLS, are unbiased. As Angrist and Krueger (2001) note, if you can't see the causal relation of interest in the reduced form, it's probably not there.[43]

We illustrate some of this reasoning in a reanalysis of data from the Angrist and Krueger (1991) quarter-of-birth study. Bound, Jaeger, and Baker (1995) argued that bias is a major concern when using quarter of birth as an instrument for schooling, even though the sample size exceeds 300,000. ("Small sample" is clearly relative.) Earlier in the chapter, we saw that the quarter-of-birth pattern in schooling is reflected in the reduced form, so there would seem to be little cause for concern. On the other hand, Bound, Jaeger, and Baker (1995) argue that the most relevant models have additional controls not included in these reduced forms. Table 4.6.2 reproduces some of the specifications from Angrist and Krueger (1991) as well as other specifications in the spirit of Bound, Jaeger, and Baker (1995).

---

[43] A recent paper by Chernozhukov and Hansen (2008) formalizes this maxim.

TABLE 4.6.2
Alternative IV estimates of the economic returns to schooling

|  | (1) | (2) | (3) | (4) | (5) | (6) |
|---|---|---|---|---|---|---|
| 2SLS | .105 | .435 | .089 | .076 | .093 | .091 |
|  | (.020) | (.450) | (.016) | (.029) | (.009) | (.011) |
| LIML | .106 | .539 | .093 | .081 | .106 | .110 |
|  | (.020) | (.627) | (.018) | (.041) | (.012) | (.015) |
| F-statistic (excluded instruments) | 32.27 | .42 | 4.91 | 1.61 | 2.58 | 1.97 |
| *Controls* |  |  |  |  |  |  |
| Year of birth | ✓ | ✓ | ✓ | ✓ | ✓ | ✓ |
| State of birth |  |  |  |  | ✓ | ✓ |
| Age, age squared |  | ✓ |  | ✓ |  | ✓ |
| *Excluded instruments* |  |  |  |  |  |  |
| Quarter-of-birth dummies | ✓ | ✓ |  |  |  |  |
| Quarter of birth*year of birth |  |  | ✓ | ✓ | ✓ | ✓ |
| Quarter of birth*state of birth |  |  |  |  | ✓ | ✓ |
| Number of excluded instruments | 3 | 2 | 30 | 28 | 180 | 178 |

*Notes*: The table compares 2SLS and LIML estimates using alternative sets of instruments and controls. The age and age squared variables measure age in quarters. The OLS estimate corresponding to the models reported in columns 1–4 is .071; the OLS estimate corresponding to the models reported in columns 5 and 6 is .067. Data are from the Angrist and Krueger (1991) 1980 census sample. The sample size is 329,509. Standard errors are reported in parentheses.

The first column in the table reports 2SLS and LIML estimates of a model using three quarter-of-birth dummies as instruments, with year-of-birth dummies as covariates. The OLS estimate for this specification is 0.071, while the 2SLS estimate is a bit higher, at 0.105. The first-stage $F$-statistic is over 32, well out of the danger zone. Not surprisingly, the LIML estimate is almost identical to 2SLS in this case.

Angrist and Krueger (1991) experimented with models that include age and age squared measured in quarters as additional controls. These controls are meant to pick up omitted age effects that might confound the quarter-of-birth instruments. The addition of age and age squared reduces the number of instruments to two, since age in quarters, year of birth, and quarter of birth are linearly dependent. As shown in column 2, the first-stage $F$-statistic drops to 0.4 when age and age squared are included as controls, a sure sign of trouble. But the 2SLS standard error is high enough that we would not draw any substantive conclusions from this estimate. The LIML estimate is even less precise. This model is effectively unidentified.

Columns 3 and 4 report the results of adding interactions between quarter-of-birth dummies and year-of-birth dummies to the instrument list, so that there are 30 instruments, or 28 when the age and age squared variables are included. The first-stage $F$-statistics are 4.9 and 1.6 in these two specifications. The 2SLS estimates are a bit lower than in column 1 and hence closer to OLS. But LIML is not too far away from 2SLS. Although the LIML standard error is pretty big in column 4, it is not so large that the estimate is uninformative. On balance, there seems to be little cause for worry about weak instruments in 30-instrument models, even with the age quadratic included.

The most worrisome specifications are those reported in columns 5 and 6. These estimates were constructed by adding 150 interactions between quarter of birth and state of birth to the 30 interactions between quarter of birth and year of birth. The rationale for the inclusion of state-of-birth interactions in the instrument list is to exploit differences in compulsory schooling laws across states. But this leads to highly overidentified models with 180 (or 178) instruments, many of which are weak. The first stage $F$-statistics for these models are only 2.6 and 2.0. On the plus side, the LIML estimates again look fairly similar to 2SLS. Moreover, the LIML standard errors are not too far above the 2SLS standard errors in this case. This suggests that you can't always determine instrument relevance using a mechanical rule, such as "$F > 10$." In some cases, a low $F$ may not be fatal.[44]

Finally, it's worth noting that in applications with multiple endogenous variables, the conventional first-stage $F$ is no longer appropriate. To see why, suppose there are two instruments for two endogenous variables and that the first instrument is strong and predicts both endogenous variables

[44] Cruz and Moreira (2005) similarly conclude that low $F$-statistics notwithstanding, there is little bias in the Angrist and Krueger (1991) 180-instrument specifications.

well, while the second instrument is weak. The first-stage
$F$-statistics in each of the two first-stage equations are likely
to be high, but the model is weakly identified, because one
instrument is not enough to capture two causal effects. A simple modification of the first-stage $F$ for this case is given in the
appendix.

## 4.7  Appendix

### Derivation of Equation (4.6.8)

Rewrite equation (4.6.7) as follows

$$Y_{ij} = \mu + \pi_0 \tau_i + (\pi_0 + \pi_1)\overline{S}_j + \nu_{ij}$$

where $\tau_i \equiv s_i - \overline{S}_j$. Since $\tau_i$ and $\overline{S}_j$ are uncorrelated by construction, we have:

$$\rho_1 = \pi_0 + \pi_1.$$
$$\pi_0 = \frac{Cov(\tau_i, Y_{ij})}{V(\tau_i)}.$$

Expanding the second line,

$$\pi_0 = \frac{Cov[(s_i - \overline{S}_j), Y_{ij}]}{[V(s_i) - V(\overline{S}_j)]}$$

$$= \left[\frac{Cov(s_i, Y_{ij})}{V(s_i)}\right]\left[\frac{V(s_i)}{V(s_i) - V(\overline{S}_j)}\right]$$

$$+ \left[\frac{Cov(\overline{S}_j, Y_{ij})}{V(\overline{S}_j)}\right]\left[\frac{-V(\overline{S}_j)}{V(s_i) - V(\overline{S}_j)}\right]$$

$$= \rho_0\phi + \rho_1(1 - \phi) = \rho_1 + \phi(\rho_0 - \rho_1),$$

where $\phi \equiv \frac{V(s_i)}{V(s_i)-V(\overline{S}_j)}$ is a positive number. Solving for $\pi_1$, we
also have

$$\pi_1 = \rho_1 - \pi_0 = \phi(\rho_1 - \rho_0).$$

### Derivation of the Approximate Bias of 2SLS

Start with (4.6.20):

$$E[\hat{\beta}_{2SLS} - \beta] \approx [E(\pi'Z'Z\pi) + E(\xi'P_Z\xi)]^{-1}E(\xi'P_Z\eta).$$

The magic of linear algebra helps us simplify this expression: the term $\xi'P_Z\eta$ is a scalar and therefore equal to its trace; the trace function is a linear operator that passes through expectations and is invariant to cyclic permutations; finally, the trace of $P_Z$, an idempotent matrix, is equal to its rank, Q. Using these facts, and iterating expectations over $Z$, we have

$$
\begin{aligned}
E(\xi'P_Z\eta|Z) &= E[\text{tr}(\xi'P_Z\eta)|Z] \\
&= E[\text{tr}(P_Z\eta\xi')|Z] \\
&= \text{tr}(P_Z E[\eta\xi'|Z]) \\
&= \text{tr}(P_Z \sigma_{\eta\xi} I) \\
&= \sigma_{\eta\xi} \text{tr}(P_Z) \\
&= \sigma_{\eta\xi} Q,
\end{aligned}
$$

where we have assumed that $\eta_i$ and $\xi_i$ are homoskedastic. Similarly, applying the trace trick to $E[\xi'P_Z\xi]$ shows that this term is equal to $\sigma_\xi^2 Q$. Therefore,

$$
\begin{aligned}
E[\hat{\beta}_{2SLS} - \beta] &\approx \sigma_{\eta\xi} Q[E(\pi'Z'Z\pi) + \sigma_\xi^2 Q]^{-1} \\
&= \frac{\sigma_{\eta\xi}}{\sigma_\xi^2} \left[ \frac{E(\pi'Z'Z\pi)/Q}{\sigma_\xi^2} + 1 \right]^{-1}.
\end{aligned}
$$

### Multivariate First-Stage F-Statistics

Assume any exogenous covariates have been partialed out of the instrument list and there are two endogenous variables, $x_1$ and $x_2$, with coefficients $\delta_1$ and $\delta_2$. We are interested in the bias of the 2SLS estimator of $\delta_2$ when $x_1$ is also treated as endogenous. The second-stage equation is

$$y = P_Z x_1 \delta_1 + P_Z x_2 \delta_2 + [\eta + (x_1 - P_Z x_1)\delta_1 + (x_2 - P_Z x_2)\delta_2],$$
$$(4.7.1)$$

where $P_Z x_1$ and $P_Z x_2$ are the first-stage fitted values from regressions of $x_1$ and $x_2$ on $Z$. By the multivariate regression anatomy formula, $\delta_2$ in (4.7.1) is the bivariate regression of $y$ on the residual from a regression of $P_Z x_2$ on $P_Z x_1$. This residual is

$$[I - P_Z x_1 (x_1' P_Z x_1)^{-1} x_1' P_Z] P_Z x_2 = M_{1z} P_Z x_2,$$

where $M_{1z} = [I - P_Z x_1 (x_1' P_Z x_1)^{-1} x_1' P_Z]$ is the relevant residual-maker matrix. Note also that $M_{1z} P_Z x_2 = P_Z[M_{1z} x_2]$.

From here we conclude that the 2SLS estimator of $\delta_2$ is the OLS regression on $P_Z[M_{1z} x_2]$, in other words, OLS on the fitted values from a regression of $M_{1z} x_2$ on $Z$. This is the same as 2SLS using $Z$ to instrument $M_{1z} x_2$. So the 2SLS estimator of $\delta_2$ can be written

$$[x_2' M_{1z} P_Z M_{1z} x_2]^{-1} x_2' M_{1z} P_Z y$$
$$= \delta_2 + [x_2' M_{1z} P_Z M_{1z} x_2]^{-1} x_2' M_{1z} P_Z \eta.$$

The first-stage sum of squares (numerator of the $F$-statistic) that determines the bias of the 2SLS estimator of $\delta_2$ is therefore the expectation of $[x_2' M_{1z} P_Z M_{1z} x_2]$, while 2SLS bias comes from the fact that the expectation $E[\xi' M_{1z} P_Z \eta]$ is nonzero when $\eta$ and $\xi$ are correlated.

Here's how to compute this $F$-statistic in practice: (1) Regress the first-stage fitted values for the regressor of interest, $P_Z x_2$, on the other first-stage fitted values and any exogenous covariates. Save the residuals from this step. (2) Construct the $F$-statistic for excluded instruments in a first-stage regression of the residuals from (1) on the excluded instruments. Note that you should get the 2SLS coefficient of interest in a 2SLS procedure where the residuals from (1) are instrumented using $Z$, with no other covariates or endogenous variables. Use this fact to check your calculations.

Chapter 5

# Parallel Worlds: Fixed Effects, Differences-in-Differences, and Panel Data

‖‖‖‖‖‖‖‖‖‖‖‖‖‖‖‖‖‖‖‖‖‖‖‖‖‖‖‖‖‖‖‖‖‖‖■◆■‖‖‖‖‖‖‖‖‖‖‖‖‖‖‖‖‖‖‖‖‖‖‖‖‖‖‖‖‖‖‖

The first thing to realize about parallel universes ... is that
they are not parallel.
   Douglas Adams, *Mostly Harmless*

The key to causal inference in chapter 3 is control for
observed confounding factors. If important confounders
are unobserved, we might try to get at causal effects using
instrumental variables, as discussed in chapter 4. Good instruments are hard to find, however, so we'd like to have other
tools to deal with unobserved confounders. This chapter considers a variation on the control theme: strategies that use data
with a time or cohort dimension to control for unobserved but
fixed omitted variables. These strategies punt on comparisons
in levels while requiring the counterfactual *trend* behavior of
treatment and control groups to be the same. We also discuss
the idea of controlling for lagged dependent variables, another
strategy that exploits timing.

## 5.1   Individual Fixed Effects

One of the oldest questions in labor economics is the connection between union membership and wages. Do workers
whose wages are set by collective bargaining earn more
because of this, or would they earn more anyway, perhaps

because they are more experienced or skilled? To set this question up, let $Y_{it}$ equal the (log) earnings of worker $i$ at time $t$, and let $D_{it}$ denote his union status. The observed $Y_{it}$ is either $Y_{0it}$ or $Y_{1it}$, depending on union status. Suppose further that

$$E[Y_{0it}|A_i, X_{it}, t, D_{it}] = E[Y_{0it}|A_i, X_{it}, t],$$

where $X_{it}$ is a vector of observed time-varying covariates and $A_i$ is a vector of unobserved but fixed confounders that we'll call ability.

In other words, union status is as good as randomly assigned conditional on $A_i$ and observed covariates, such as age, schooling, and region of residence.

The key to fixed effects estimation is the assumption that the unobserved $A_i$ appears without a time subscript in a linear model for $E(Y_{0it}|A_i, X_{it}, t)$:

$$E[Y_{0it}|A_i, X_{it}, t] = \alpha + \lambda_t + A_i'\gamma + X_{it}'\beta, \qquad (5.1.1)$$

We also assume that the causal effect of union membership is additive and constant:

$$E[Y_{1it}|A_i, X_{it}, t] = E[Y_{0it}|A_i, X_{it}, t] + \rho.$$

Together with (5.1.1), this implies

$$E[Y_{it}|A_i, X_{it}, t, D_{it}] = \alpha + \lambda_t + \rho D_{it} + A_i'\gamma + X_{it}'\beta, \quad (5.1.2)$$

where $\rho$ is the causal effect of interest. The set of assumptions leading to (5.1.2) is more restrictive than those we used to motivate regression in chapter 3; we need the linear, additive functional form to make headway on the problem of unobserved confounders using panel data with no instruments.[1]

---

[1] In some cases, we can allow heterogeneous treatment effects so that

$$E(Y_{1it} - Y_{0it}|A_i, X_{it}, t) = \rho_i.$$

See, for example, Wooldridge (2005), who discusses estimators for the average of $\rho_i$.

Equation (5.1.2) implies

$$Y_{it} = \alpha_i + \lambda_t + \rho D_{it} + X'_{it}\beta + \varepsilon_{it}, \qquad (5.1.3)$$

where $\varepsilon_{it} \equiv Y_{0it} - E[Y_{0it}|A_i, x_{it}, t]$ and

$$\alpha_i \equiv \alpha + A'_i\gamma.$$

This is a fixed effects model. Given panel data (repeated observations on individuals), the causal effect of union status on wages can be estimated by treating $\alpha_i$, the fixed effect, as a parameter to be estimated. The year effect, $\lambda_t$, is also treated as a parameter to be estimated. The unobserved individual effects are coefficients on dummies for each individual, while the year effects are coefficients on time dummies.[2]

It might seem that there are a lot of parameters to be estimated in the fixed effects model. For example, the Panel Survey of Income Dynamics, a widely used panel data set, includes data on about 5,000 working-age men observed for about 20 years. So there are roughly 5,000 fixed effects. In practice, however, this doesn't matter. Treating the individual effects as parameters to be estimated is algebraically the same as estimation in deviations from means. In other words, first we calculate the individual averages,

$$\overline{Y}_i = \alpha_i + \overline{\lambda} + \rho\overline{D}_i + \overline{X}'_i\beta + \overline{\varepsilon}_i.$$

Subtracting this from (5.1.3) gives

$$Y_{it} - \overline{Y}_i = \lambda_t - \overline{\lambda} + \rho(D_{it} - \overline{D}_i) + (X_{it} - \overline{X}_i)'\beta + (\varepsilon_{it} - \overline{\varepsilon}_i), \qquad (5.1.4)$$

---

[2] An alternative to the fixed effects specification is random effects (see, e.g., Wooldridge, 2006). The random effects model assumes that $\alpha_i$ is uncorrelated with the regressors. Because the omitted variable in a random effects model is uncorrelated with included regressors, there is no bias from ignoring it—in effect, it becomes part of the residual. The most important consequence of random effects is that the residuals for a given person are correlated across periods. Chapter 8 discusses the implications of this for OLS standard errors. Random effects models can be estimated by GLS, which promises to be more efficient if the assumptions of the random effects model are satisfied. However, as in chapter 3, we prefer fixing OLS standard errors to GLS. GLS requires stronger assumptions than OLS, and the resulting asymptotic efficiency gain is likely to be modest, while finite-sample properties may be worse.

so deviations from means kills the unobserved individual effects.[3]

An alternative to deviations from means is differencing. In other words, we estimate,

$$\Delta Y_{it} = \Delta\lambda_t + \rho\Delta D_{it} + \Delta X'_{it}\beta + \Delta\varepsilon_{it}, \qquad (5.1.5)$$

where the $\Delta$ prefix denotes the change from one year to the next. For example, $\Delta Y_{it} = Y_{it} - Y_{it-1}$. With two periods, differencing is algebraically the same as deviations from means, but not otherwise. Both should work, although with homoskedastic and serially uncorrelated $\varepsilon_{it}$ and more than two periods, deviations from means is more efficient. You might find differencing more convenient if you have to do it by hand, though the differenced standard errors should be adjusted for the fact that the differenced residuals are serially correlated.

Some regression packages automate the deviations from means estimator, with an appropriate standard error adjustment for the degrees of freedom lost in estimating $N$ individual means. This is all that's needed to get the standard errors right with a homoskedastic, serially uncorrelated residual. The deviations from means estimator has many names, including the "within estimator" and "analysis of covariance." Estimation in deviations from means form is also called *absorbing* the fixed effects.[4]

Freeman (1984) uses four data sets to estimate union wage effects under the assumption that selection into union status is based on unobserved but fixed individual characteristics. Table 5.1.1 displays some of his estimates. For each data set,

[3] Why is deviations from means the same as estimating each fixed effect in (5.1.3)? Because, by the regression anatomy formula, (3.1.3), any set of multivariate regression coefficients can be estimated in two steps. To get the multivariate coefficient on one set of variables, first regress them on all the other included variables, then regress the original dependent variable on the residuals from this first step. The residuals from a regression on a full set of person-dummies in a person-year panel are deviations from person means.

[4] The fixed effects are not estimated consistently in a panel where the number of periods $T$ is fixed while $N \to \infty$. This is called the incidental parameters problem, a name that reflects the fact that the number of parameters grows with the sample size. Nevertheless, other parameters in the fixed effects model—the ones we care about—are consistently estimated.

TABLE 5.1.1
Estimated effects of union status on wages

| Survey | Cross Section Estimate | Fixed Effects Estimate |
|---|---|---|
| May CPS, 1974–75 | .19 | .09 |
| National Longitudinal Survey of Young Men, 1970–78 | .28 | .19 |
| Michigan PSID, 1970–79 | .23 | .14 |
| QES, 1973–77 | .14 | .16 |

*Notes*: Adapted from Freeman (1984). The table reports cross section and panel (fixed effects) estimates of the union relative wage effect. The estimates were calculated using the surveys listed in the left-hand column. The cross section estimates include controls for demographic and human capital variables.

the table displays results from a fixed effects estimator and the corresponding cross section estimates. The cross section estimates are typically higher (ranging from .14 to .28) than the fixed effects estimates (ranging from .09 to .19). This may indicate positive selection bias in the cross section estimates, though selection bias is not the only explanation for the lower fixed effects estimates.

Although they control for a certain type of omitted variable, fixed effects estimates are notoriously susceptible to attenuation bias from measurement error. On one hand, economic variables such as union status tend to be persistent (a worker who is a union member this year is most likely a union member next year). On the other hand, measurement error often changes from year to year (union status may be misreported or miscoded this year but not next year). Therefore, while union status may be misreported or miscoded for only a few workers in any single year, the observed year-to-year changes in union status may be mostly noise. In other words, there is more measurement error in the differenced regressors in an equation like (5.1.4) or (5.1.5) than in the levels of the regressors. This fact may account for smaller fixed effects estimates.[5]

---

[5] See Griliches and Hausman (1986) for a more complete discussion of measurement error in panel data.

A variant on the measurement error problem in panel data arises from that fact that the differencing and deviations from means estimators used to control for fixed effects typically remove both good and bad variation. In other words, these transformations may kill some of the omitted variables bias bathwater, but they also remove much of the useful information in the baby, the variable of interest. An example is the use of twins to estimate the causal effect of schooling on wages. Although there is no time dimension to this problem, the basic idea is the same as the union problem discussed above: twins have similar but largely unobserved family and genetic backgrounds. We can therefore control for their common family background by including a family fixed effect in samples of pairs of twins.

Ashenfelter and Krueger (1994) and Ashenfelter and Rouse (1998) estimate the returns to schooling using samples of twins, controlling for family fixed effects. Because there are two twins from each family, this is the same as regressing differences in earnings within twin pairs on differences in schooling. Surprisingly, the within-family estimates come out larger than OLS estimates. But how do differences in schooling come about between individuals who are otherwise so much alike? Bound and Solon (1999) point out that there are small differences between twins, with first-borns typically having higher birth weight and higher IQ scores (here differences in birth timing are measured in minutes). While these within-twin differences are not large, neither is the difference in their schooling. Hence, small unobserved ability differences between twins could be responsible for substantial bias in the resulting estimates.

What should be done about measurement error and related problems in models with fixed effects? A possible solution to measurement error is to use IV methods. Ashenfelter and Krueger (1994) use cross-sibling reports to construct instruments for schooling differences between twins. For example, they use each twin's report of his brother's schooling as an instrument for self-reports. A second approach is to bring in external information on the extent of measurement error and adjust naive estimates accordingly. In a study of union wage effects, Card (1996) uses external information from a separate validation survey to adjust panel data estimates for measurement error in reported union status. But data from multiple reports and repeated measures of the sort used by Ashenfelter and Krueger (1994) and Card (1996) are unusual. At a minimum, therefore, it's important to avoid overly strong claims when interpreting fixed effects estimates (never bad advice for an applied econometrician in any case).

## 5.2    Differences-in-Differences: Pre and Post, Treatment and Control

The fixed effects strategy requires panel data, that is, repeated observations on the same individuals (or firms, or whatever the unit of observation might be). Often, however, the regressor of interest varies only at a more aggregate or group level, such as state or cohort. For example, state policies regarding health care benefits for pregnant workers may change over time but are fixed across workers within states. The source of OVB when evaluating these policies must therefore be unobserved variables at the state and year level. In some cases, group-level omitted variables can be captured by group-level fixed effects, an approach that leads to the differences-in-differences (DD) identification strategy.

The DD idea was probably pioneered by physician John Snow (1855), who studied cholera epidemics in London in the mid-nineteenth century. Snow wanted to establish that cholera is transmitted by contaminated drinking water (as opposed to "bad air," the prevailing theory at the time). To show this, Snow compared changes in death rates from cholera in districts serviced by two water companies, the Southwark and Vauxhall Company and the Lambeth Company. In 1849 both companies obtained their water supply from the dirty Thames in central London. In 1852, however, the Lambeth Company moved its water works upriver to an area relatively free of sewage. Death rates in districts supplied by Lambeth fell sharply in comparison to the change in death rates in districts supplied by Southwark and Vauxhall.

To make matters more concrete, let us return to an example from economics. Suppose we are interested in the effect of the minimum wage on employment, a classic question in labor economics. In a competitive labor market, increases in the minimum wage move us up a downward-sloping labor demand curve. Higher minimums therefore reduce employment, perhaps hurting the very workers minimum wage policies were designed to help. Card and Krueger (1994) use a dramatic change in the New Jersey state minimum wage to see if this is true.[6]

On April 1, 1992, New Jersey raised the state minimum from \$4.25 to \$5.05. Card and Krueger collected data on employment at fast food restaurants in New Jersey in February 1992 and again in November 1992. These restaurants (Burger King, Wendy's, and so on) are big minimum wage employers. Card and Krueger also collected data from the same type of restaurants in eastern Pennsylvania, just across the Delaware River. The minimum wage in Pennsylvania stayed at \$4.25 throughout this period. They used their data set to compute differences-in-differences (DD) estimates of the effects of the New Jersey minimum wage increase. That is, they compared the February-to-November change in employment in New Jersey to the change in employment in Pennsylvania over the same period.

DD is a version of fixed effects estimation using aggregate data. To see this, let $Y_{1ist}$ be fast food employment at restaurant $i$ in state $s$ and period $t$ if there is a high state minimum wage, and let $Y_{0ist}$ be fast food employment at restaurant $i$ in state $s$ and period $t$ if there is a low state minimum wage. These are potential outcomes; in practice, we only get to see one or the other. For example, we see $Y_{1ist}$ in New Jersey in November 1992. The heart of the DD setup is an additive structure for potential outcomes in the no-treatment state. Specifically, we assume that

$$E[Y_{0ist}|s,t] = \gamma_s + \lambda_t, \qquad (5.2.1)$$

---

[6]The DD idea was first used to study the effects of minimum wages by Obenauer and von der Nienburg (1915), writing for the U.S. Bureau of Labor Statistics.

where $s$ denotes state (New Jersey or Pennsylvania) and $t$ denotes period (February, before the minimum wage increase, or November, after the increase). This equation says that in the absence of a minimum wage change, employment is determined by the sum of a time-invariant state effect and a year effect that is common across states. The additive state effect plays the role of the unobserved individual effect in section 5.1.

Let $D_{st}$ be a dummy for high-minimum-wage states and periods. Assuming that $E[Y_{1ist} - Y_{0ist}|s, t]$ is a constant, denoted $\delta$, observed employment, $Y_{ist}$, can be written:

$$Y_{ist} = \gamma_s + \lambda_t + \delta D_{st} + \varepsilon_{ist}, \qquad (5.2.2)$$

where $E(\varepsilon_{ist}|s, t) = 0$. From here, we get

$$E[Y_{ist}|s = PA, t = Nov] - E[Y_{ist}|s = PA, t = Feb]$$
$$= \lambda_{Nov} - \lambda_{Feb}$$

and

$$E[Y_{ist}|s = NJ, t = Nov] - E[Y_{ist}|s = NJ, t = Feb]$$
$$= \lambda_{Nov} - \lambda_{Feb} + \delta.$$

The population difference-in-differences,

$$\{E[Y_{ist}|s = NJ, t = Nov] - E[Y_{ist}|s = NJ, t = Feb]\}$$
$$- \{E[Y_{ist}|s = PA, t = Nov] - E[Y_{ist}|s = PA, t = Feb]\} = \delta,$$

is the causal effect of interest. This is easily estimated using the sample analog of the population means.

Table 5.2.1 (based on table 3 in Card and Krueger, 1994) shows average employment at fast food restaurants in New Jersey and Pennsylvania before and after the change in the New Jersey minimum wage. There are four cells in the first two rows and columns, while the margins show state differences in each period, the changes over time in each state, and the difference-in-differences. Employment in Pennsylvania restaurants is somewhat higher than in New Jersey in February but falls by November. Employment in New Jersey, in contrast, increases slightly. These two changes produce

TABLE 5.2.1
Average employment in fast food restaurants before and after the
New Jersey minimum wage increase

| Variable | PA (i) | NJ (ii) | Difference, NJ – PA (iii) |
|---|---|---|---|
| 1. FTE employment before, all available observations | 23.33 (1.35) | 20.44 (.51) | −2.89 (1.44) |
| 2. FTE employment after, all available observations | 21.17 (.94) | 21.03 (.52) | −.14 (1.07) |
| 3. Change in mean FTE employment | −2.16 (1.25) | .59 (.54) | 2.76 (1.36) |

*Notes*: Adapted from Card and Krueger (1994), table 3. The table reports average full-time-equivalent (FTE) employment at restaurants in Pennsylvania and New Jersey before and after a minimum wage increase in New Jersey. The sample consists of all restaurants with data on employment. Employment at six closed restaurants is set to zero. Employment at four temporarily closed restaurants is treated as missing. Standard errors are reported in parentheses.

a positive difference-in-differences, the opposite of what we might expect if a higher minimum wage pushed businesses up the labor demand curve.

How convincing is this evidence against the standard labor demand story? The key identifying assumption here is that employment *trends* would be the same in both states in the absence of treatment. Treatment induces a deviation from this common trend, as illustrated in figure 5.2.1. Although the treatment and control states can differ, this difference is meant to be captured by the state fixed effect, which plays the same role as the unobserved individual effect in (5.1.3).[7]

---

[7]The common trends assumption can be applied to transformed data, for example,

$$E[\ln Y_{0ist}|s,t] = \gamma_s + \lambda_t.$$

Note, however, that common trends in logs rule out common trends in levels and vice versa. Athey and Imbens (2006) introduce a semiparametric DD estimator that allows for common trends after an unspecified transformation of the dependent variable. Poterba, Venti, and Wise (1995) and Meyer, Viscusi, and Durbin (1995) discuss DD-type models for quantiles.

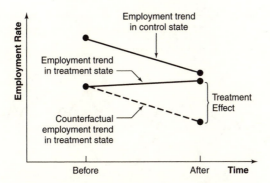

**Figure 5.2.1**   Causal effects in the DD model.

The common trends assumption can be investigated using data on multiple periods. In an update of their original minimum wage study, Card and Krueger (2000) obtained administrative payroll data for restaurants in New Jersey and a number of Pennsylvania counties. These data are shown here in figure 5.2.2, similar to figure 2 in their follow-up study. The vertical lines indicate the dates when the original Card and Krueger surveys were conducted, and the third vertical line indicates the October 1996 increase in the federal minimum wage to $4.75, which affected Pennsylvania but not New Jersey. These data give us an opportunity to look at a new minimum wage experiment.

As in the original Card and Krueger survey, the administrative data show a slight decline in employment from February to November 1992 in Pennsylvania, and little change in New Jersey over the same period. However, the data also reveal substantial year-to-year employment variation in other periods. These swings often seem to differ substantially in the two states. In particular, while employment levels in New Jersey and Pennsylvania were similar at the end of 1991, employment in Pennsylvania fell relative to employment in New Jersey over the next three years (especially in the 14-county group), mostly before the 1996 increase in the federal minimum wage. So Pennsylvania may not provide a very good measure of counterfactual employment rates in New Jersey in the absence of a minimum wage change.

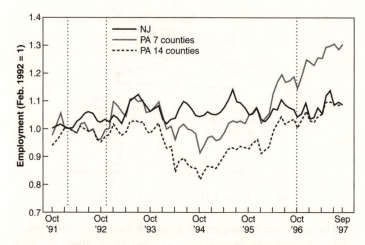

**Figure 5.2.2**   Employment in New Jersey and Pennsylvania fast food restaurants, October 1991 to September 1997 (from Card and Krueger 2000). Vertical lines indicate dates of the original Card and Krueger (1994) survey and the October 1996 federal minimum wage increase.

A more encouraging example comes from Pischke (2007), who looked at the effect of school term length on student performance using variation generated by a sharp policy change in Germany. Until the 1960s, children in all German states except Bavaria started school in the spring. Beginning in the 1966–67 school year, the spring starters moved to start school in the fall. The transition to a fall start required two short school years for affected cohorts, 24 weeks long instead of 37. Students in these cohorts effectively had their time in school compressed relative to cohorts on either side and relative to students in Bavaria, which already had a fall start.

Figure 5.2.3 plots the likelihood of grade repetition for the 1962–73 cohorts of second graders in Bavaria and affected states (there are no repetition data for 1963–65). Repetition rates in Bavaria were reasonably flat from 1966 on at around 2.5 percent. Repetition rates are higher in the short-school-year (SSY) states, at around 4–4.5 percent in 1962 and 1966, before the change in term length. But repetition rates jump up by about a percentage point for the two affected cohorts

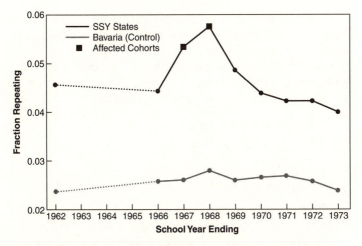

**Figure 5.2.3**  Average grade repetition rates in second grade for treatment and control schools in Germany (from Pischke, 2007). The data span a period before and after a change in term length for students outside Bavaria (SSY states).

in these states, a bit more so for the second cohort than for the first, before falling back to the baseline level. This graph provides strong visual evidence of treatment and control states with a common underlying trend, and a treatment effect that induces a sharp but transitory deviation from this trend. A shorter school year seems to have increased repetition rates for affected cohorts.

### 5.2.1  Regression DD

As with the fixed effects model, we can use regression to estimate equations like (5.2.2). Let $NJ_s$ be a dummy for restaurants in New Jersey and $d_t$ be a time dummy that switches on for observations obtained in November (i.e., after the minimum wage change). Then

$$Y_{ist} = \alpha + \gamma NJ_s + \lambda d_t + \delta(NJ_s \cdot d_t) + \varepsilon_{ist} \qquad (5.2.3)$$

is the same as (5.2.2) where $NJ_s \cdot d_t = D_{st}$. In the language of section 3.1.4, this model includes two main effects for state and year and an interaction term that marks observations from New Jersey in November. This is a saturated model, since the conditional mean function $E(Y_{ist}|s,t)$ takes on four possible values and there are four parameters. The link between the parameters in the regression equation, (5.2.3), and those in the DD model for the conditional mean function, (5.2.2), is

$$\alpha = E[Y_{ist}|s = PA, t = Feb] = \gamma_{PA} + \lambda_{Feb}$$
$$\gamma = E[Y_{ist}|s = NJ, t = Feb] - E[Y_{ist}|s = PA, t = Feb]$$
$$= \gamma_{NJ} - \gamma_{PA}$$
$$\lambda = E[Y_{ist}|s = PA, t = Nov] - E[Y_{ist}|s = PA, t = Feb]$$
$$= \lambda_{Nov} - \lambda_{Feb}$$
$$\delta = \{E[Y_{ist}|s = NJ, t = Nov] - E[Y_{ist}|s = NJ, t = Feb]\}$$
$$- \{E[Y_{ist}|s = PA, t = Nov] - E[Y_{ist}|s = PA, t = Feb]\}.$$

The regression formulation of the DD model offers a convenient way to construct DD estimates and standard errors. It's also easy to add additional states or periods to the regression setup. We might, for example, add additional control states and pretreatment periods to the New Jersey-Pennsylvania sample. The resulting generalization of (5.2.3) includes a dummy for each state and period but is otherwise unchanged.

A second advantage of regression DD is that it facilitates the study of policies other than those that can be described by dummy variables. Instead of New Jersey and Pennsylvania in 1992, for example, we might look at all state minimum wages in the United States. Some of these are a little higher than the federal minimum (which covers everyone regardless of where they live), some are a lot higher, and some are the same. The minimum wage is therefore a variable with differing treatment intensity across states and over time. Moreover, in addition to statutory variation in state minima, the local importance of a minimum wage varies with average state wage levels. For example, the early 1990s federal minimum wage of $4.25 an hour was probably irrelevant in Connecticut, with high average wages, but a big deal in Mississippi.

Card (1992) exploits regional variation in the impact of the federal minimum wage. His approach is motivated by an equation like

$$Y_{ist} = \gamma_s + \lambda_t + \delta(\text{FA}_s \cdot d_t) + \varepsilon_{ist}, \qquad (5.2.4)$$

where the variable $\text{FA}_s$ is a measure of the fraction of teenagers likely to be affected by a minimum wage increase in each state and $d_t$ is a dummy for observations in 1990, when the federal minimum wage increased from \$3.35 to \$3.80. The $\text{FA}_s$ variable measures the baseline (pre-increase) proportion of each state's teen labor force earning less than \$3.80.

As in the New Jersey-Pennsylvania study, Card (1992) works with data from two periods, before and after, in this case 1989 and 1990. But this study uses 51 states (including the District of Columbia), for a total of 102 state-year observations. Since there are no individual-level covariates in (5.2.4), this is the same as estimation with microdata (provided the group-level estimates are weighted by cell size). Note that $\text{FA}_s \cdot d_t$ is an interaction term, like $NJ_s \cdot d_t$ in (5.2.3), though here the interaction term takes on a distinct value for each observation in the data set. Finally, because Card (1992) analyzes data for only two periods, the reported estimates are from an equation in first differences:

$$\Delta \bar{Y}_s = \lambda^* + \delta \text{FA}_s + \Delta \bar{\varepsilon}_s,$$

where $\Delta \bar{Y}_s$ is the change in average teen employment in state $s$ and $\Delta \bar{\varepsilon}_s$ is the error term in the differenced equation.[8]

Table 5.2.2, based on table 3 in Card (1992), shows that wages increased more in states where the minimum wage increase is likely to have had more bite (see the estimate of .15 in column 1). This is an important step in Card's analysis—it verifies the notion that the $\text{FA}_s$ (fraction of affected teens) variable is a good predictor of the wage changes induced by an increase in the federal minimum. Employment, on the other

---

[8] Other specifications in the spirit of (5.2.4) put a normalized function of state and federal minimum wages on the right-hand side instead of $\text{FA}_s \cdot d_t$. See, for example, Neumark and Wascher (1992), who work with the difference between state and federal minima, adjusted for minimum wage coverage provisions, and normalized by state average hourly wage rates.

TABLE 5.2.2
Regression DD estimates of minimum wage effects on teens,
1989 to 1990

| Explanatory Variable | Change in Mean Log Wage | | Change in Teen Employment-Population Ratio | |
|---|---|---|---|---|
| | (1) | (2) | (3) | (4) |
| 1. Fraction of affected teens (FA$_s$) | .15 (.03) | .14 (.04) | .02 (.03) | −.01 (.03) |
| 2. Change in overall emp./pop. ratio | — | .46 (.60) | — | 1.24 (.60) |
| 3. $R^2$ | .30 | .31 | .01 | .09 |

*Notes*: Adapted from Card (1992). The table reports estimates from a regression of the change in average teen employment by state on the fraction of teens affected by a change in the federal minimum wage in each state. Data are from the 1989 and 1990 CPS. Regressions are weighted by the CPS sample size for each state.

hand, seems largely unrelated to FA$_s$, as can be seen in column 3. Thus, the results in Card (1992) are in line with the results from the New Jersey-Pennsylvania study.

Card's (1992) analysis illustrates a further advantage of regression DD: it's easy to add additional covariates in this framework. For example, we might like to control for adult employment as a source of omitted state-specific trends. In other words, we can model counterfactual employment in the absence of a change in the minimum wage as

$$E[Y_{0ist}|s, t, X_{st}] = \gamma_s + \lambda_t + X'_{st}\beta.$$

where $X_{st}$ is a vector of state- and time-varying covariates, including adult employment (though this may not be kosher if adult employment also responds to the minimum wage change, in which case it's bad control; see section 3.2.3). As it turns out, the addition of an adult employment control has little effect on Card's estimates, as can be seen in columns 2 and 4 in table 5.2.2.

It's worth emphasizing that Card (1992) analyzes state averages instead of individual data. He might have used a pooled multiyear sample of microdata from the CPS to estimate an equation like

$$Y_{ist} = \gamma_s + \lambda_t + \delta(\text{FA}_s \cdot d_t) + X'_{ist}\beta + \varepsilon_{ist}, \qquad (5.2.5)$$

where $X_{ist}$ can include individual level characteristics such as race as well as time-varying variables measured at the state level. Only the latter are likely to be a source of omitted variables bias, but individual-level controls can increase precision, a point we noted in section 2.3. Inference is a little more complicated in a framework that combines microdata on dependent variables with group-level regressors, however. The key issue is how best to adjust standard errors for possible group-level random effects, as we discuss in chapter 8.

When the sample includes many years, the regression-DD model lends itself to a test for causality in the spirit of Granger (1969). The Granger idea is to see whether causes happen before consequences, and not vice versa (though as we know from the epigraph at the beginning of chapter 4, this alone is not sufficient for causal inference). Suppose the policy variable of interest, $D_{st}$, changes at different times in different states. In this context, Granger causality testing means a check on whether, conditional on state and year effects, past $D_{st}$ predicts $Y_{ist}$ while future $D_{st}$ does not. If $D_{st}$ causes $Y_{ist}$ but not vice versa, then dummies for future policy changes should not matter in an equation like

$$Y_{ist} = \gamma_s + \lambda_t + \sum_{\tau=0}^{m} \delta_{-\tau} D_{s,t-\tau} + \sum_{\tau=1}^{q} \delta_{+\tau} D_{s,t+\tau} + X'_{ist}\beta + \varepsilon_{ist},$$

$$(5.2.6)$$

where the sums on the right-hand side allow for $m$ lags ($\delta_{-1}$, $\delta_{-2}, \ldots, \delta_{-m}$) or posttreatment effects and $q$ leads ($\delta_{+1}, \delta_{+2}, \ldots, \delta_{+q}$) or anticipatory effects. The pattern of lagged effects is usually of substantive interest as well. We might, for example, believe that causal effects should grow or fade as time passes.

Autor (2003) implements the Granger test in an investigation of the effect of employment protection on firms' use of temporary help. In the U.S., employment protection is a type of labor law—promulgated by state legislatures or, more typically, through common law as made by state courts—that makes it harder to fire workers. As a rule, U.S. labor law allows employment at will, which means that workers can be fired for just cause or no cause, at the employer's whim. But some state courts have allowed a number of exceptions to the employment-at-will doctrine, leading to lawsuits for unjust dismissal. Autor is interested in whether fear of employee lawsuits makes firms more likely to use temporary workers for tasks for which they would otherwise have increased their workforce. Temporary workers are employed by someone else besides the firm for which they are executing tasks. As a result, firms using them cannot be sued for unjust dismissal when they let temporary workers go.

Autor's empirical strategy relates the employment of temporary workers in a state to dummy variables indicating state court rulings that allow exceptions to the employment-at-will doctrine. His regression-DD model includes both leads and lags, as in equation (5.2.6). The estimated leads and lags, running from two years ahead to four years behind, are plotted in figure 5.2.4, a reproduction of figure 3 from Autor (2003). The estimates show no effects in the two years before the courts adopted an exception, with sharply increasing effects on temporary employment in the first few years after the adoption, which then appear to flatten out with a permanently higher rate of temporary employment in affected states. This pattern seems consistent with a causal interpretation of Autor's results.

An alternative check on the DD identification strategy adds state-specific time trends to the list of controls. In other words, we estimate

$$Y_{ist} = \gamma_{0s} + \gamma_{1s}t + \lambda_t + \delta D_{st} + X'_{ist}\beta + \varepsilon_{ist}, \qquad (5.2.7)$$

where $\gamma_{0s}$ is a state-specific intercept, as before, and $\gamma_{1s}$ is a state-specific trend coefficient multiplying the time trend variable, $t$. This allows treatment and control states to follow different trends in a limited but potentially revealing way. It's heartening to find that the estimated effects of interest are unchanged by the inclusion of these trends, and discouraging

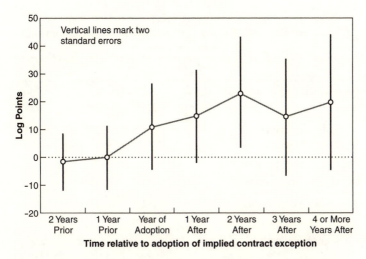

**Figure 5.2.4** The estimated impact of implied-contract exceptions to the employment-at-will doctrine on the use of temporary workers (from Autor, 2003). The dependent variable is the log of state temporary help employment in 1979–1995. Estimates are from a model that allows for effects before, during, and after exceptions were adopted.

otherwise. Note, however, that we need at least three periods to estimate a model with state-specific trends. Moreover, in practice, three periods is typically inadequate to pin down both the trends and the treatment effect. As a rule, DD estimation with state-specific trends is likely to be more robust and convincing when the pretreatment data establish a clear trend that can be extrapolated into the posttreatment period.

In a study of the effects of labor regulation on businesses in Indian states, Besley and Burgess (2004) use state trends as a robustness check. Different states change regulatory regimes at different times, giving rise to a DD research design. As in Card (1992), the unit of observation in Besley and Burgess (2004) is a state-year average. Table 5.2.3 (based on table IV in their paper) reproduces the key results.

The estimates in column 1, from a regression DD model without state-specific trends, suggest that labor regulation leads to lower output per capita. The models used to construct

TABLE 5.2.3
Estimated effects of labor regulation on the performance of firms
in Indian states

|  | (1) | (2) | (3) | (4) |
|---|---|---|---|---|
| Labor regulation (lagged) | −.186 | −.185 | −.104 | .0002 |
|  | (.064) | (.051) | (.039) | (.020) |
| Log development | | .240 | .184 | .241 |
| expenditure per capita | | (.128) | (.119) | (.106) |
| Log installed electricity | | .089 | .082 | .023 |
| capacity per capita | | (.061) | (.054) | (.033) |
| Log state population | | .720 | 0.310 | −1.419 |
|  | | (.96) | (1.192) | (2.326) |
| Congress majority | | | −.0009 | .020 |
|  | | | (.01) | (.010) |
| Hard left majority | | | −.050 | −.007 |
|  | | | (.017) | (.009) |
| Janata majority | | | .008 | −.020 |
|  | | | (.026) | (.033) |
| Regional majority | | | .006 | .026 |
|  | | | (.009) | (.023) |
| State-specific trends | No | No | No | Yes |
| Adjusted $R^2$ | .93 | .93 | .94 | .95 |

*Notes*: Adapted from Besley and Burgess (2004), table IV. The table reports
regression DD estimates of the effects of labor regulation on productivity. The
dependent variable is log manufacturing output per capita. All models include
state and year effects. Robust standard errors clustered at the state level are
reported in parentheses. State amendments to the Industrial Disputes Act are
coded 1 = pro-worker, 0 = neutral, −1 = pro-employer and then cumulated
over the period to generate the labor regulation measure. Log of installed
electrical capacity is measured in kilowatts, and log development expenditure
is real per capita state spending on social and economic services. Congress,
hard left, Janata, and regional majority are counts of the number of years
for which these political groupings held a majority of the seats in the state
legislatures. The data are for the sixteen main states for the period 1958–92.
There are 552 observations.

the estimates in columns 2 and 3 add time-varying state-specific covariates, such as government expenditure per capita and state population. This is in the spirit of Card's (1992) addition of state-level adult employment rates as a control in the minimum wage study. The addition of controls affects the Besley and Burgess estimates little. But the addition of state-specific trends kills the labor regulation effect, as can be seen in column 4. Apparently, labor regulation in India increased in states where output was declining anyway. Control for this trend therefore drives the estimated regulation effect to zero.

## Picking Controls

We've labeled the two dimensions in the DD setup *states* and *time* because this is the archetypical DD example in applied econometrics. But the DD idea is much more general. Instead of states, the subscript *s* might denote demographic groups, some of which are affected by a policy and others are not. For example, Kugler, Jimeno, and Hernanz (2005) look at the effects of age-specific employment protection policies in Spain. Likewise, instead of time, we might group data by cohort or other types of characteristics. An example is Angrist and Evans (1999), who studied the effect of changes in state abortion laws on teen pregnancy using variation by state and year of birth. Regardless of the group labels, however, DD designs always set up an implicit treatment-control comparison. The question of whether this comparison is a good one deserves careful consideration.

One potential pitfall in this context arises when the composition of the treatment and control groups changes as a result of treatment. Going back to a design based on state and time comparisons, suppose we're interested in the effects of the generosity of public assistance on labor supply. Historically, U.S. states have offered widely varying welfare payments to poor unmarried mothers. Labor economists have long been interested in the effects of such income maintenance policies: how much of an increase in living standards they facilitate, and whether they make work less attractive (see, e.g., Meyer and Rosenbaum, 2001, for a recent study). A concern here, emphasized in a review of research on welfare by Moffitt (1992), is that poor people who would in any case have weak labor force attachment might move to states with more generous welfare benefits. In a DD research design, this sort of program-induced migration tends to make generous welfare programs look worse for labor supply than they really are.

Migration problems can usually be fixed if we know where an individual starts out. Say we know state of residence in the period before treatment, or state of birth. State of birth or previous state of residence are unchanged by the treatment but are still highly correlated with current state of residence. The problem of migration is therefore eliminated in comparisons using these dimensions instead of state of residence. This introduces a new problem, however, which is that individuals who do move are incorrectly located. In practice, however, this is easily addressed with the IV methods discussed in chapter 4 (state of birth or previous residence can be used to construct instruments for current location).

A modification of the two-by-two DD setup with possibly improved control groups uses higher-order contrasts to draw causal inferences. An example is the extension of Medicaid coverage in the United States, studied by Yelowitz (1995). Eligibility for Medicaid, the massive U.S. health insurance program for the poor, was once tied to eligibility for Aid for Families with Dependent Children (AFDC), a large cash welfare program. At various times in the 1980s, however, some states extended Medicaid coverage to children in families ineligible for AFDC. Yelowitz was interested in how this expansion of publicly provided health insurance for children affected, among other things, mothers' labor force participation and earnings.

In addition to state and time, children's age provides a third dimension on which Medicaid policy varies. Yelowitz exploits this variation by estimating

$$Y_{iast} = \gamma_{st} + \lambda_{at} + \theta_{as} + \delta D_{ast} + X'_{iast}\beta + \varepsilon_{iast},$$

where $s$ index states, $t$ indexes time, and $a$ is the age of the youngest child in a family. This model provides full nonparametric control for state-specific time effects that are common across age groups ($\gamma_{st}$), time-varying age effects ($\lambda_{at}$), and state-specific age effects ($\theta_{as}$). The regressor of interest, $D_{ast}$, indicates families with children in affected age groups in states and periods where Medicaid coverage is provided. This triple-differences model may generate a more convincing set of results than a traditional DD analysis that exploits differences by state and time alone.

## 5.3   Fixed Effects versus Lagged Dependent Variables

Fixed effects and DD estimators are based on the presumption of time-invariant (or group-invariant) omitted variables. Suppose, for example, we are interested in the effects of participation in a subsidized training program, as in the Dehejia and Wahba (1999) and Lalonde (1986) studies discussed in section 3.3.3. The key identifying assumption motivating fixed effects estimation in this case is

$$E[Y_{0it}|\alpha_i, X_{it}, D_{it}] = E[Y_{0it}|\alpha_i, X_{it}], \qquad (5.3.1)$$

where $\alpha_i$ is an unobserved personal characteristic that determines, along with covariates, $X_{it}$, whether individual $i$ gets training. To be concrete, $\alpha_i$ might be a measure of vocational skills, though a strike against the fixed effects setup is the fact that the exact nature of the unobserved variables typically remains somewhat mysterious. In any case, coupled with a linear model for $E(Y_{0it}|\alpha_i, X_{it})$, assumption (5.3.1) leads to simple estimation strategies involving differences or deviations from means.

For many causal questions, the notion that the most important omitted variables are time invariant doesn't seem plausible. The evaluation of training programs is a case in point. It's likely that people looking to improve their labor market options by participating in a government-sponsored training program have suffered some kind of setback. Many training programs explicitly target people who have suffered a recent setback, such as men who recently lost their jobs. Consistent with this, Ashenfelter (1978) and Ashenfelter and Card

(1985) find that training participants typically have earnings histories that exhibit a preprogram dip. Past earnings is a time-varying confounding variable that cannot be subsumed in a time-invariant omitted variable like $\alpha_i$.

The distinctive earnings histories of trainees motivates an estimation strategy that controls for past earnings directly and dispenses with fixed effects. To be precise, instead of (5.3.1), we might base causal inference on the conditional independence assumption,

$$E[Y_{0it}|Y_{it-h}, X_{it}, D_{it}] = E[Y_{0it}|Y_{it-h}, X_{it}]. \qquad (5.3.2)$$

This is like saying that what makes trainees special is their earnings $h$ periods ago. We can then use panel data to estimate

$$Y_{it} = \alpha + \theta Y_{it-h} + \lambda_t + \delta D_{it} + X_{it}'\beta + \varepsilon_{it}, \qquad (5.3.3)$$

where the causal effect of training is $\delta$. To make this more general, $Y_{it-h}$ can be a vector including lagged earnings for multiple periods.[9]

Applied researchers using panel data are often faced with the challenge of choosing between fixed effects and lagged dependent variables models, that is, between causal inferences based on (5.3.1) and (5.3.2). One solution to this dilemma is to work with a model that includes both lagged dependent variables and unobserved individual effects. In other words, identification might be based on

$$E[Y_{0it}|\alpha_i, Y_{it-h}, X_{it}, D_{it}] = E[Y_{0it}|\alpha_i, Y_{it-h}, X_{it}], \qquad (5.3.4)$$

which requires conditioning on both $\alpha_i$ and $Y_{it-h}$. We can then try to estimate causal effects using a specification like

$$Y_{it} = \alpha_i + \theta Y_{it-h} + \lambda_t + \delta D_{it} + X_{it}'\beta + \varepsilon_{it}. \qquad (5.3.5)$$

---

[9] Abadie, Diamond, and Hainmueller (2007) develop a semiparametric version of the lagged dependent variables model, more flexible than the traditional regression setup. As in 5.3.2, the key assumption in this model is independence of treatment status and potential outcomes conditional on lagged earnings. The Abadie, Diamond, and Hainmuller approach works for microdata and for data with a group structure. The Dehejia and Wahba (1999) matching strategy also uses lagged dependent variables.

Unfortunately, the conditions for consistent estimation of $\delta$ in equation (5.3.5) are much more demanding than those required with fixed effects or lagged dependent variables alone. This can be seen in a simple example where the lagged dependent variable is $Y_{it-1}$. We kill the fixed effect by differencing, which produces

$$\Delta Y_{it} = \theta \Delta Y_{it-1} + \Delta \lambda_t + \delta \Delta D_{it} + \Delta X_{it}' \beta + \Delta \varepsilon_{it}. \quad (5.3.6)$$

The problem here is that the differenced residual, $\Delta \varepsilon_{it}$, is necessarily correlated with the lagged dependent variable, $\Delta Y_{it-1}$, because both are a function of $\varepsilon_{it-1}$. Consequently, OLS estimates of (5.3.6) are not consistent for the parameters in (5.3.5), a problem first noted by Nickell (1981). This problem can be solved, though the solution requires strong assumptions. The easiest solution is to use $Y_{it-2}$ as an instrument for $\Delta Y_{it-1}$ in (5.3.6).[10] But this requires that $Y_{it-2}$ be uncorrelated with the differenced residuals, $\Delta \varepsilon_{it}$. This seems unlikely, since residuals are the part of earnings left over after accounting for covariates. Most people's earnings are highly correlated from one year to the next, so that past earnings are also likely to be correlated with $\Delta \varepsilon_{it}$. If $\varepsilon_{it}$ is serially correlated, there may be no consistent estimator for (5.3.6). (Note also that the IV strategy using $Y_{it-2}$ as an instrument requires at least three periods, so we get data for $t$, $t-1$, and $t-2$.)

Given the difficulties that arise when trying to estimate (5.3.6), we might ask whether the distinction between fixed effects and lagged dependent variables matters. The answer, unfortunately, is yes. The fixed effects and lagged dependent variables models are not nested, which means we cannot hope to estimate one and get the other as a special case if need be.

So what's an applied guy to do? One answer, as always, is to check the robustness of your findings using alternative identifying assumptions. That means that you would like to find broadly similar results using plausible alternative models. Fixed effects and lagged dependent variables estimates also have a useful bracketing property. The appendix to this

[10] See Holtz-Eakin, Newey, and Rosen (1988), Arellano and Bond (1991), and Blundell and Bond (1998) for details and examples.

chapter shows that if (5.3.2) is correct, but you mistakenly use fixed effects, estimates of a positive treatment effect will tend to be too big. On the other hand, if (5.3.1) is correct and you mistakenly estimate an equation with lagged outcomes, such as (5.3.3), estimates of a positive treatment effect will tend to be too small. You can therefore think of fixed effects and lagged dependent variables as bounding the causal effect of interest (given some assumptions about the nature of selection bias). Guryan (2004) illustrates this sort of reasoning in a study estimating the effects of court-ordered busing on black students' high school graduation rates.

## 5.4    Appendix: More on Fixed Effects and Lagged Dependent Variables

To simplify, we ignore covariates, intercepts, and year effects and assume there are only two periods, with treatment equal to zero for everyone in the first period (the punch line is the same in a more general setup). The causal effect of interest, $\delta$, is positive. Suppose first that treatment (training status) is correlated with an unobserved individual effect, $\alpha_i$, uncorrelated with lagged outcome residuals, $\varepsilon_{it-1}$, and that outcomes can be described by

$$Y_{it} = \alpha_i + \delta D_{it} + \varepsilon_{it}, \qquad (5.4.1)$$

where $\varepsilon_{it}$ is serially uncorrelated, and also uncorrelated with $\alpha_i$ and $D_{it}$. We also have

$$Y_{it-1} = \alpha_i + \varepsilon_{it-1},$$

where $\alpha_i$ and $\varepsilon_{it-1}$ are uncorrelated. You mistakenly estimate the effect of $D_{it}$ in a model that controls for $Y_{it-1}$ but ignores fixed effects. The resulting estimator has probability limit $\frac{Cov(Y_{it}, \tilde{D}_{it})}{V(\tilde{D}_{it})}$, where $\tilde{D}_{it} = D_{it} - \gamma Y_{it-1}$ is the residual from a regression of $D_{it}$ on $Y_{it-1}$.

Now substitute $\alpha_i = Y_{it-1} - \varepsilon_{it-1}$ in (5.4.1) to get

$$Y_{it} = Y_{it-1} + \delta D_{it} + \varepsilon_{it} - \varepsilon_{it-1}.$$

From here, we get

$$\frac{Cov(Y_{it}, \tilde{D}_{it})}{V(\tilde{D}_{it})} = \delta - \frac{Cov(\varepsilon_{it-1}, \tilde{D}_{it})}{V(\tilde{D}_{it})}$$

$$= \delta - \frac{Cov(\varepsilon_{it-1}, D_{it} - \gamma Y_{it-1})}{V(\tilde{D}_{it})} = \delta + \frac{\gamma \sigma_\varepsilon^2}{V(\tilde{D}_{it})},$$

where $\sigma_\varepsilon^2$ is the variance of $\varepsilon_{it-1}$. Since trainees have low $Y_{it-1}$, $\gamma < 0$, and the resulting estimate of $\delta$ is too small.

Suppose instead that treatment is determined by low $Y_{it-1}$. Causal effects can be estimated using a simplified version of (5.3.3), say

$$Y_{it} = \alpha + \theta Y_{it-1} + \delta D_{it} + \varepsilon_{it}, \qquad (5.4.2)$$

where $\varepsilon_{it}$ is serially uncorrelated and uncorrelated with $D_{it}$. You mistakenly estimate a first-differenced equation in an effort to kill fixed effects. This ignores the lagged dependent variable. In this simple example, where $D_{it-1} = 0$ for everyone, the first-differenced estimator has probability limit

$$\frac{Cov(Y_{it} - Y_{it-1}, D_{it} - D_{it-1})}{V(D_{it} - D_{it-1})} = \frac{Cov(Y_{it} - Y_{it-1}, D_{it})}{V(D_{it})}. \qquad (5.4.3)$$

Subtracting $Y_{it-1}$ from both sides of (5.4.2), we have

$$Y_{it} - Y_{it-1} = \alpha + (\theta - 1)Y_{it-1} + \delta D_{it} + \varepsilon_{it}.$$

Substituting this in (5.4.3), the inappropriately differenced model yields

$$\frac{Cov(Y_{it} - Y_{it-1}, D_{it})}{V(D_{it})} = \delta + (\theta - 1) \left[ \frac{Cov(Y_{it-1}, D_{it})}{V(D_{it})} \right].$$

In general, we think $\theta$ is a positive number less than one, otherwise $Y_{it}$ is nonstationary (i.e., an explosive time series process). Therefore, since trainees have low $Y_{it-1}$, the estimate of $\delta$ in first differences is too big. Note that in this simple model, differencing turns out to be ok in the unlikely event $\theta = 1$ in (5.4.2), but that is not true in general.

Part III

# Extensions

# Chapter 6

# Getting a Little Jumpy: Regression Discontinuity Designs

But when you start exercising those rules, all sorts of
processes start to happen and you start to find out all sorts
of stuff about people.... It's just a way of thinking about a
problem, which lets the shape of the problem begin to
emerge. The more rules, the tinier the rules, the more
arbitrary they are, the better.

Douglas Adams, *Mostly Harmless*

Regression discontinuity (RD) research designs exploit
precise knowledge of the rules determining treatment.
RD identification is based on the idea that in a highly
rule-based world, some rules are arbitrary and therefore
provide good experiments. RD comes in two styles, fuzzy
and sharp. The sharp design can be seen as a selection-on-
observables story. The fuzzy design leads to an instrumental
variables (IV) type of setup.

## 6.1 Sharp RD

Sharp RD is used when treatment status is a deterministic
and discontinuous function of a covariate, $x_i$. Suppose, for
example, that

$$D_i = \begin{cases} 1 & \text{if } x_i \geq x_0, \\ 0 & \text{if } x_i < x_0, \end{cases} \qquad (6.1.1)$$

where $x_0$ is a known threshold or cutoff. This assignment mechanism is a deterministic function of $x_i$ because once we know $x_i$ we know $D_i$. Treatment is a discontinuous function of $x_i$ because no matter how close $x_i$ gets to $x_0$, treatment is unchanged until $x_i = x_0$.

This may seem a little abstract, so here is an example. American high school students are awarded National Merit Scholarships on the basis of PSAT scores, a test taken by most college-bound high school juniors, especially those who will later take the SAT. The question that motivated one of the first discussions of RD is whether students who win National Merit Scholarships change their career or study plans as a result. For example, National Merit Scholars may be more likely to go to graduate school (Thistlewaithe and Campbell, 1960; Campbell, 1969). Sharp RD compares the graduate school attendance rates of students with PSAT scores just above and just below the National Merit Award thresholds. In general, we might expect students with higher PSAT scores to be more likely to go to graduate school, but this effect can be controlled by fitting a regression to the relationship between graduate school attendance rates and PSAT scores, at least in the neighborhood of the award cutoff. In this example, jumps in the relationship between PSAT scores and graduate school attendance in the neighborhood of the award threshold are taken as evidence of a treatment effect. It is this jump in regression lines that gives RD its name.[1]

An interesting and important feature of RD, highlighted in a recent survey by Imbens and Lemieux (2008), is that there is *no* value of $x_i$ at which we get to observe both treatment and control observations. Unlike full covariate matching strategies, which are based on treatment-control comparisons conditional on covariate values where there is some overlap,

---

[1] The basic structure of RD designs appears to have emerged simultaneously in a number of disciplines but has only recently become important in applied econometrics. Cook (2008) gives an intellectual history. In an analysis using Lalonde (1986)-style within-study comparisons, Cook and Wong (2008) find that RD generally does a good job of reproducing the results from randomized trials.

the validity of RD turns on our willingness to extrapolate across covariate values, at least in a neighborhood of the discontinuity. This is one reason why sharp RD is usually seen as distinct from other control strategies. For this same reason, we typically cannot afford to be as agnostic about regression functional form in the RD world as in the world of chapter 3.

Figure 6.1.1 illustrates a hypothetical RD scenario where those with $x_i \geq 0.5$ are treated. In panel A, the trend relationship between outcomes and $x_i$ is linear, while in panel B it's nonlinear. In both cases there is a discontinuity in the observed CEF, $E[Y_i|x_i]$, around the point $x_0$, while $E[Y_{0i}|x_i]$ is smooth.

A simple model formalizes the RD idea. Suppose that in addition to the assignment mechanism, (6.1.1), potential outcomes can be described by a linear, constant effects model

$$E[Y_{0i}|x_i] = \alpha + \beta x_i$$
$$Y_{1i} = Y_{0i} + \rho.$$

This leads to the regression,

$$Y_i = \alpha + \beta x_i + \rho D_i + \eta_i, \qquad (6.1.2)$$

where $\rho$ is the causal effect of interest. The key difference between this regression and others we've used to estimate treatment effects (e.g., in chapter 3) is that $D_i$, the regressor of interest, not only is correlated with $x_i$, it is a deterministic function of $x_i$. RD captures causal effects by distinguishing the nonlinear and discontinuous function, $1(x_i \geq x_0)$, from the smooth and (in this case) linear function, $x_i$.

But what if the trend relation, $E[Y_{0i}|x_i]$, is nonlinear? To be precise, suppose that $E[Y_{0i}|x_i] = f(x_i)$ for some reasonably smooth function, $f(x_i)$. Panel B in figure 6.1.1 suggests there is still hope even in this more general case. Now we can construct RD estimates by fitting

$$Y_i = f(x_i) + \rho D_i + \eta_i, \qquad (6.1.3)$$

where again, $D_i = 1(x_i \geq x_0)$ is discontinuous in $x_i$ at $x_0$. As long as $f(x_i)$ is continuous in a neighborhood of $x_0$, it should be possible to estimate a model like (6.1.3), even with a flexible

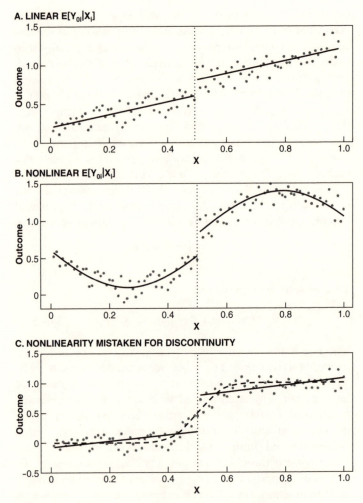

**A. LINEAR $E[Y_{0i}|X_i]$**

**B. NONLINEAR $E[Y_{0i}|X_i]$**

**C. NONLINEARITY MISTAKEN FOR DISCONTINUITY**

**Figure 6.1.1**  The sharp regression discontinuity design.

functional form for $f(x_i)$. For example, modeling $f(x_i)$ with a $p$th-order polynomial, RD estimates can be constructed from the regression

$$Y_i = \alpha + \beta_1 x_i + \beta_2 x_i^2 + \cdots + \beta_p x_i^p + \rho D_i + \eta_i. \qquad (6.1.4)$$

A generalization of RD based on (6.1.4) allows different trend functions for $E[Y_{0i}|x_i]$ and $E[Y_{1i}|x_i]$. Modeling both of these CEFs with $p$th-order polynomials, we have

$$E[Y_{0i}|x_i] = f_0(x_i) = \alpha + \beta_{01}\tilde{x}_i + \beta_{02}\tilde{x}_i^2 + \cdots + \beta_{0p}\tilde{x}_i^p$$
$$E[Y_{1i}|x_i] = f_1(x_i) = \alpha + \rho + \beta_{11}\tilde{x}_i + \beta_{12}\tilde{x}_i^2 + \cdots + \beta_{1p}\tilde{x}_i^p,$$

where $\tilde{x}_i \equiv x_i - x_0$. Centering $x_i$ at $x_0$ is a normalization that ensures that the treatment effect at $x_i = x_0$ is the coefficient on $D_i$ in a regression model with interaction terms.

To derive a regression model that can be used to estimate the causal effect of interest in this case, we use the fact that $D_i$ is a deterministic function of $x_i$ to write

$$E[Y_i|x_i] = E[Y_{0i}|x_i] + (E[Y_{1i}|x_i] - E[Y_{0i}|x_i])D_i. \quad (6.1.5)$$

Substituting polynomials for conditional expectations, we then have

$$Y_i = \alpha + \beta_{01}\tilde{x}_i + \beta_{02}\tilde{x}_i^2 + \cdots + \beta_{0p}\tilde{x}_i^p$$
$$+ \rho D_i + \beta_1^* D_i\tilde{x}_i + \beta_2^* D_i\tilde{x}_i^2 + \cdots + \beta_p^* D_i\tilde{x}_i^p + \eta_i, \quad (6.1.6)$$

where $\beta_1^* = \beta_{11} - \beta_{01}$, $\beta_2^* = \beta_{12} - \beta_{02}$, and $\beta_p^* = \beta_{1p} - \beta_{0p}$ and $\eta_i$ is the residual.

Equation (6.1.4) is a special case of (6.1.6) where $\beta_1^* = \beta_2^* = \beta_p^* = 0$. In the more general model, the treatment effect at $x_i - x_0 = c > 0$ is $\rho + \beta_1^*c + \beta_2^*c^2 + \cdots + \beta_p^*c^p$, while the treatment effect at $x_0$ is $\rho$. The model with interactions has the attraction that it imposes no restrictions on the underlying conditional mean functions. But in our experience, RD estimates of $\rho$ based on the simpler model, (6.1.4), usually turn out to be similar to those based on (6.1.6). This is not surprising, since either way the estimated $\rho$ is mostly driven by variability in $E[Y_i|x_i]$ in the neighborhood of $x_0$.

The validity of RD estimates of causal effects based on (6.1.4) or (6.1.6) turns on whether polynomial models provide an adequate description of $E[Y_{0i}|x_i]$. If not, then what looks like a jump due to treatment might simply be an unaccounted-for nonlinearity in the counterfactual conditional mean function. This possibility is illustrated in panel C of figure 6.1.1, which shows how a sharp turn in $E[Y_{0i}|x_i]$ might be mistaken for a jump from one regression line to another. To reduce the likelihood of such mistakes, we can look only at data in a neighborhood around the discontinuity, say the interval $[x_0 - \Delta, x_0 + \Delta]$ for some small positive number $\Delta$. Then we have

$$E[Y_i|x_0 - \Delta < x_i < x_0] \simeq E[Y_{0i}|x_i = x_0]$$
$$E[Y_i|x_0 \leq x_i < x_0 + \Delta] \simeq E[Y_{1i}|x_i = x_0],$$

so that

$$\lim_{\Delta \to 0} E[Y_i|x_0 \leq x_i < x_0 + \Delta] - E[Y_i|x_0 - \Delta < x_i < x_0]$$
$$= E[Y_{1i} - Y_{0i}|x_i = x_0]. \qquad (6.1.7)$$

In other words, comparisons of average outcomes in a small enough neighborhood to the left and right of $x_0$ estimate the treatment effect in a way that does not depend on the correct specification of a model for $E[Y_{0i}|x_i]$. Moreover, the validity of this nonparametric estimation strategy does not turn on the constant effects assumption, $Y_{1i} - Y_{0i} = \rho$; the estimand in (6.1.7) is the average causal effect, $E[Y_{1i} - Y_{0i}|x_i = x_0]$.

The nonparametric approach to RD requires good estimates of the mean of $Y_i$ in small neighborhoods to the right and left of $x_0$. Obtaining such estimates is tricky. The first problem is that working in a small neighborhood of the cutoff means you don't have much data. Also, the sample average is biased for the CEF in the neighborhood of a boundary (in this case, $x_0$). Solutions to these problems include the use of a nonparametric version of regression called local linear regression (Hahn, Todd, and van der Klaauw, 2001) and the partial linear and local polynomial regression estimators developed by Porter (2003). Local regression amounts to weighted least squares (WLS) estimation of an equation like (6.1.6), with more weight given to points close to the cutoff.

Sophisticated nonparametric RD methods have not yet found wide application in empirical practice; most applied RD work is still parametric. But the idea of focusing on observations near the cutoff value—what Angrist and Lavy (1999) call a "discontinuity sample"—suggests a valuable robustness check: Although RD estimates become less precise as the window used to select a discontinuity sample gets smaller, the number of polynomial terms needed to model $f(x_i)$ should go down. Hopefully, as you zero in on $x_0$ with fewer and fewer controls, the estimated effect of $D_i$ remains stable.[2] A second important check looks at the behavior of pretreatment variables near the discontinuity. Since pretreatment variables are unaffected by treatment, there should be no jump in the CEF of these variables at $x_0$.

Lee's (2008) study of the effect of party incumbency on reelection probabilities illustrates the sharp RD design. Lee is interested in whether the Democratic candidate for a seat in the U.S. House of Representatives has an advantage if his party won the seat last time. The widely noted success of House incumbents raises the question of whether representatives use the privileges and resources of their office to gain advantage for themselves or their parties. This conjecture sounds plausible, but the success of incumbents need not reflect a real electoral advantage. Incumbents—by definition, candidates and parties who have shown they can win—may simply be better at satisfying voters or getting the vote out.

To capture the causal effect of incumbency, Lee looks at the likelihood a Democratic candidate wins as a function of relative vote shares in the previous election. Specifically, he exploits the fact that an election winner is determined by $D_i = 1(x_i \geq 0)$, where $x_i$ is the vote share margin of victory (e.g., the difference between the Democratic and Republican vote shares when these are the two largest parties). Note that, because $D_i$ is a deterministic function of $x_i$, there are no confounding

---

[2]Hoxby (2000) also uses this idea to check RD estimates of class size effects. A fully nonparametric approach requires data-driven rules for selection of the width of the discontinuity-sample window, also known as "bandwidth". The bandwidth must shrink with the sample size at a rate sufficiently slow so as to ensure consistent estimation of the underlying conditional mean functions. See Imbens and Lemieux (2008) for details. We prefer to think of estimation using (6.1.4) or (6.1.6) as essentially parametric: in any given sample, the estimates are only as good as the model that you happen to be using. Promises about how you might change the model if you had more data should be irrelevant.

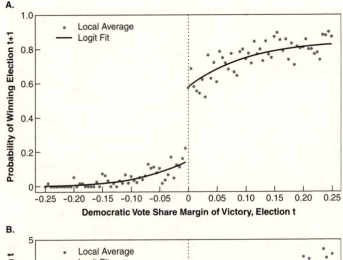

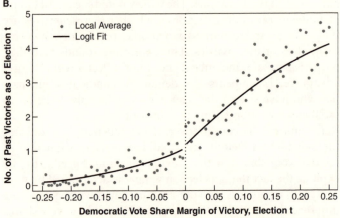

**Figure 6.1.2**   The probability of winning an election by past and future vote share (from Lee, 2008). (A) Candidate's probability of winning election $t+1$, by margin of victory in election $t$: local averages and logit polynomial fit. (B) Candidate's accumulated number of past election victories, by margin of victory in election $t$: local averages and logit polynomial fit.

variables other than $x_i$. This is a signal feature of the RD setup.

Figure 6.1.2A, from Lee (2008), shows the sharp RD design in action. This figure plots the probability that a Democrat wins against the difference between Democratic and Republican vote shares in the previous election. The dots in the figure are local averages (the average win rate in nonoverlapping windows of share margins that are .005 wide); the lines in the figure are fitted values from a parametric model with a discontinuity at zero.[3] The probability of a Democratic win is an increasing function of past vote share. The most important feature of the plot, however, is the dramatic jump in win rates at the 0 percent mark, the point where a Democratic candidate gets more votes. Based on the size of the jump, incumbency appears to raise party reelection probabilities by about 40 percentage points.

Figure 6.1.2B checks the sharp RD identification assumptions by looking at Democratic victories *before* the last election. Democratic win rates in older elections should be unrelated to the margin-of-victory cutoff in the last election, a specification check that works out well and increases our confidence in the RD design in this case. Lee's investigation of pretreatment victories is a version of the idea that covariates should be balanced by treatment status as if in a randomized trial. A related check examines the density of $x_i$ around the discontinuity, looking for bunching in the distribution of $x_i$ near $x_0$. The concern here is that individuals with a stake in $D_i$ might try to manipulate $x_i$ near the cutoff, in which case observations on either side may not be comparable (McCrary, 2008, proposes a formal test for this). Until recently, we would have said this is unlikely in election studies like Lee's. But the recount in Florida after the 2000 presidential election suggests we probably should worry about manipulable vote shares when U.S. elections are close.

## 6.2   Fuzzy RD Is IV

Fuzzy RD exploits discontinuities in the *probability* or *expected value* of treatment conditional on a covariate. The

---

[3]The fitted values in this figure are from a logit model for the probability of winning as a function of the cutoff indicator $D_i = 1(x_i \geq 0)$, a 4th-order polynomial in $x_i$, and interactions between the polynomial terms and $D_i$.

result is a research design where the discontinuity becomes an instrumental variable for treatment status instead of deterministically switching treatment on or off. To see how this works, let $D_i$ denote treatment status as before, though here $D_i$ is no longer deterministically related to the threshold-crossing rule, $x_i \geq x_0$. Rather, there is a jump in the probability of treatment at $x_0$, so that

$$P(D_i = 1|x_i) = \begin{cases} g_1(x_i) & \text{if } x_i \geq x_0 \\ g_0(x_i) & \text{if } x_i < x_0 \end{cases}, \text{ where } g_1(x_0) \neq g_0(x_0).$$

The functions $g_0(x_i)$ and $g_1(x_i)$ can be anything as long as they differ (and the more the better) at $x_0$. We'll assume $g_1(x_0) > g_0(x_0)$, so $x_i \geq x_0$ makes treatment more likely. We can write the relation between the probability of treatment and $x_i$ as

$$E[D_i|x_i] = P(D_i = 1|x_i) = g_0(x_i) + [g_1(x_i) - g_0(x_i)]T_i,$$

where

$$T_i = 1(x_i \geq x_0).$$

The dummy variable $T_i$ indicates the point where $E[D_i|x_i]$ is discontinuous.

Fuzzy RD leads naturally to a simple 2SLS estimation strategy. Assuming that $g_0(x_i)$ and $g_1(x_i)$ can be described by $p$th-order polynomials as we did for $f_0(x_i)$ and $f_1(x_i)$, we have

$$\begin{aligned} E[D_i|x_i] &= \gamma_{00} + \gamma_{01}x_i + \gamma_{02}x_i^2 + \cdots + \gamma_{0p}x_i^p \quad (6.2.1) \\ &\quad + [\pi + \gamma_1^* x_i + \gamma_2^* x_i^2 + \cdots + \gamma_p^* x_i^p]T_i \\ &= \gamma_{00} + \gamma_{01}x_i + \gamma_{02}x_i^2 + \cdots + \gamma_{0p}x_i^p \\ &\quad + \pi T_i + \gamma_1^* x_i T_i + \gamma_2^* x_i^2 T_i + \cdots + \gamma_p^* x_i^p T_i, \end{aligned}$$

where the $\gamma^*$'s are coefficients on the polynomial interactions with $T_i$.

From this we see that $T_i$, as well as the interaction terms $\{x_i T_i, x_i^2 T_i, \ldots x_i^p T_i\}$ can be used as instruments for $D_i$ in (6.1.4).[4]

---

[4]The idea of using jumps in the probability of assignment as a source of identifying information appears to originate with Trochim (1984), although

The simplest fuzzy RD estimator uses only $T_i$ as an instrument, without the interaction terms (with the interaction terms in the instrument list, we might also like to allow for interactions in the second stage as in 6.1.6). The resulting just-identified IV estimator has the virtues of transparency and good finite-sample properties. The first stage in this case is

$$D_i = \gamma_0 + \gamma_1 x_i + \gamma_2 x_i^2 + \cdots + \gamma_p x_i^p + \pi T_i + \xi_{1i}, \qquad (6.2.2)$$

where $\pi$ is the first-stage effect of $T_i$.

The fuzzy RD reduced form is obtained by substituting (6.2.2) into (6.1.4):

$$Y_i = \mu + \kappa_1 x_i + \kappa_2 x_i^2 + \cdots + \kappa_p x_i^p + \rho\pi T_i + \xi_{2i}, \qquad (6.2.3)$$

where $\mu = \alpha + \rho\gamma_0$ and $\kappa_j = \beta_j + \rho\gamma_j$ for $j = 1, \ldots, p$. As with sharp RD, identification in the fuzzy case turns on the ability to distinguish the relation between $Y_i$ and the discontinuous function, $T_i = 1(x_i \geq x_0)$, from the effect of polynomial controls included in the first and second stage. In one of the first RD studies in applied econometrics, van der Klaauw (2002) used a fuzzy design to evaluate the effects of university financial aid awards on college enrollment. In van der Klaauw's study, $D_i$ is the size of the financial aid award offer and $T_i$ is a dummy variable indicating applicants with an ability index above predetermined award threshold cutoffs. His fuzzy RD estimates control for polynomial functions of this index.[5]

Fuzzy RD estimates with treatment effects that change as a function of $x_i$ can be constructed by 2SLS estimation of an equation with treatment-covariate interactions. The second-stage model with interaction terms is the same as (6.1.6),

---

the IV interpretation came later. Not everyone agrees that fuzzy RD is IV, but this view is catching on. In a recent history of the RD idea, Cook (2008) writes about the fuzzy design: "In many contexts, the cutoff value can function as an IV and engender unbiased causal conclusions ... fuzzy assignment does not seem as serious a problem today as earlier."

[5]Van der Klaauw's original working paper circulated in 1997. Note that the fact that the additive model, (6.2.2), is only an approximation of $E[D_i|x_i]$ is not very important; second-stage estimates are still consistent.

while the first stage is similar to (6.2.1), except that to match the second-stage parametrization, we center polynomial terms at $x_0$. In this case, the excluded instruments are $\{T_i, \tilde{x}_i T_i, \tilde{x}_i^2 T_i, \ldots \tilde{x}_i^p T_i\}$ while the variables $\{D_i, \tilde{x}_i D_i, D_i \tilde{x}_i^2, \ldots D_i \tilde{x}_i^p\}$ are treated as endogenous. The first stage for $D_i$ becomes

$$D_i = \gamma_{00} + \gamma_{01}\tilde{x}_i + \gamma_{02}\tilde{x}_i^2 + \cdots + \gamma_{0p}\tilde{x}_i^p$$
$$+ \pi T_i + \gamma_1^* \tilde{x}_i T_i + \gamma_2^* \tilde{x}_i^2 T_i + \cdots + \gamma_p^* \tilde{x}_i^p T_i + \xi_{1i}. \quad (6.2.4)$$

An analogous first stage must be constructed for each of the polynomial interaction terms in the set $\{\tilde{x}_i D_i, D_i \tilde{x}_i^2, \ldots D_i \tilde{x}_i^p\}$.

The nonparametric version of fuzzy RD consists of IV estimation in a small neighborhood around the discontinuity. The reduced-form conditional expectation of $Y_i$ near $x_0$ is

$$E[Y_i|x_0 \le x_i < x_0 + \Delta] - E[Y_i|x_0 - \Delta < x_i < x_0] \simeq \rho\pi.$$

Similarly, for the first stage for $D_i$, we have

$$E[D_i|x_0 \le x_i < x_0 + \Delta] - E[D_i|x_0 - \Delta < x_i < x_0] \simeq \pi.$$

Therefore

$$\lim_{\Delta \to 0} \frac{E[Y_i|x_0 < x_i < x_0 + \Delta] - E[Y_i|x_0 - \Delta < x_i < x_0]}{E[D_i|x_0 < x_i < x_0 + \Delta] - E[D_i|x_0 - \Delta < x_i < x_0]} = \rho.$$
$$(6.2.5)$$

The sample analog of (6.2.5) is a Wald estimator of the sort discussed in section 4.1.2, in this case using $T_i$ as an instrument for $D_i$ in a $\Delta$-neighborhood of $x_0$.[6] As with other dummy variable instruments, the result is a local average treatment effect. In particular, the Wald estimand for fuzzy RD captures the causal effect on compliers, defined as individuals whose treatment status changes as we move the value of $x_i$ from just to the left of $x_0$ to just to the right of $x_0$. This interpretation of fuzzy RD was introduced by Hahn, Todd, and van der Klaauw

---

[6]To allow for changes in slope on either side of the cutoff, Imbens and Lemieux (2008) suggest (6.2.5) be computed by 2SLS using $T_i$ as an instrument for $D_i$ in a small neighborhood of the cutoff, with the interaction terms $\{\tilde{x}_i T_i, \tilde{x}_i^2 T_i, \ldots \tilde{x}_i^p T_i\}$ included as exogenous controls.

(2001). However, there is another sense in which this version of LATE is local: the estimates are for those with $x_i$ near $x_0$, a feature of sharp nonparametric RD estimates as well.

Finally, as with the nonparametric version of sharp RD, the finite-sample behavior of the sample analog of (6.2.5) is not likely to be very good. Hahn, Todd, and van der Klaauw (2001) develop a nonparametric IV procedure using local linear regression to estimate the top and bottom of the Wald estimator with less bias. This takes us back to a 2SLS model with linear or polynomial controls, but the model is fit in a discontinuity sample using a data-driven bandwidth. The idea of using discontinuity samples informally also applies in this context: start with a parametric 2SLS setup in the full sample, say, based on (6.1.4). Then restrict the sample to points near the discontinuity and get rid of most or all of the polynomial controls. Ideally, 2SLS estimates in the discontinuity samples with few controls will be broadly consistent with the more precise estimates constructed using the larger sample.

Angrist and Lavy (1999) use a fuzzy RD research design to estimate the effects of class size on children's test scores, the same question addressed by the STAR experiment discussed in chapter 2. Fuzzy RD is an especially powerful and flexible research design, a fact highlighted by the Angrist and Lavy study, which generalizes fuzzy RD in two ways relative to the discussion above. First, the causal variable of interest, class size, takes on many values (as in the discussion of average causal response an chapter 4). So the first stage exploits jumps in average class size instead of probabilities. Second, the Angrist and Lavy (1999) research design uses multiple discontinuities.

The Angrist and Lavy study begins with the observation that class size in Israeli schools is capped at 40. Students in a grade with up to 40 students can expect to be in classes as large as 40, but grades with 41 students are split into two classes, grades with 81 students are split into three classes, and so on. Angrist and Lavy call this "Maimonides' rule," since a maximum class size of 40 was first proposed by the medieval Talmudic scholar Maimonides. To formalize Maimonides' rule, let $m_{sc}$ denote the predicted class size (in a given grade) assigned to class

$c$ in school $s$, where enrollment in the grade is denoted $e_s$. Assuming grade cohorts are split up into classes of equal size, the predicted class size that results from a strict application of Maimonides' rule is

$$m_{sc} = \frac{e_s}{int\left[\frac{(e_s-1)}{40}\right]+1},$$

where $int(a)$ is the integer part of a real number, $a$. This function, plotted with dotted lines in figure 6.2.1 for fourth and fifth graders, has a sawtooth pattern with discontinuities (in this case, sharp drops in predicted class size) at integer multiples of 40. At the same time, $m_{sc}$ is clearly an increasing function of enrollment, $e_s$, making the enrollment variable an important control.

Angrist and Lavy exploit the discontinuities in Maimonides' rule by constructing 2SLS estimates of an equation like

$$Y_{isc} = \alpha_0 + \alpha_1 d_s + \beta_1 e_s + \beta_2 e_s^2 + \cdots + \beta_p e_s^p + \rho n_{sc} + \eta_{isc},$$
$$(6.2.6)$$

where $Y_{isc}$ is student $i$'s test score in school $s$ and class $c$, $n_{sc}$ is the size of this class, and $e_s$ is enrollment. In this version of fuzzy RD, $m_{sc}$ plays the role of $T_i$, $e_s$ plays the role of $x_i$, and class size, $n_{sc}$, plays the role of $D_i$. Angrist and Lavy also include a nonenrollment covariate, $d_s$, to control for the proportion of students in the school from a disadvantaged background. This is not necessary for RD, since the only source of omitted variables bias in the RD model is $e_s$, but it makes the specification comparable to the model used to construct a corresponding set of OLS estimates.[7]

Figure 6.2.1 plots the average of actual and predicted class sizes against enrollment in fourth and fifth grade. Maimonides' rule does not predict class size perfectly, mostly because some schools split grades at enrollments lower than 40. This is what

---

[7]The Angrist and Lavy (1999) study differs modestly from the description here in that the data used to estimate equation (6.2.6) are class averages. But since the covariates are all defined at the class or school level, the only difference between student-level and class-level estimation is the implicit weighting by number of students in the student-level estimates.

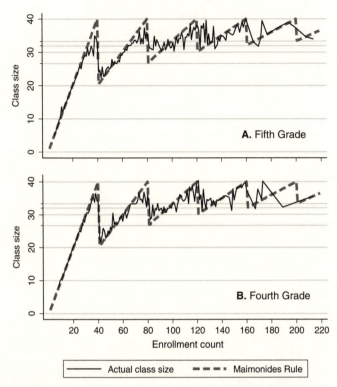

**Figure 6.2.1**   The fuzzy-RD first-stage for regression-discontinuity estimates of the effect of class size on test scores (from Angrist and Lavy, 1999).

makes the RD design fuzzy. Still, there are clear drops in class size at enrollment levels of 40, 80, and 120. Note also that the $m_{sc}$ instrument implicitly combines both discontinuities and slope-discontinuity interactions such as $\tilde{x}_i \text{T}_i$ in (6.2.4) in a single variable ($m_{sc}$ becomes a shallower function of $e_s$ above each kink). This compact parametrization comes from a specific understanding of the institutions and rules that determine Israeli class size.

Estimates of equation (6.2.6) for fifth-grade math scores are reported in table 6.2.1, beginning with OLS. With no controls, there is a strong positive relationship between class size and

TABLE 6.2.1

OLS and fuzzy RD estimates of the effect of class size on
fifth-grade math scores

| | OLS | | | 2SLS | | | | |
| | | | | Full Sample | | Discontinuity Samples | | |
| | | | | | | ±5 | | ±3 |
| | (1) | (2) | (3) | (4) | (5) | (6) | (7) | (8) |
|---|---|---|---|---|---|---|---|---|
| Mean score | | 67.3 | | 67.3 | | 67.0 | | 67.0 |
| (SD) | | (9.6) | | (9.6) | | (10.2) | | (10.6) |
| **Regressors** | | | | | | | | |
| Class size | .322 | .076 | .019 | −.230 | −.261 | −.185 | −.443 | −.270 |
| | (.039) | (.036) | (.044) | (.092) | (.113) | (.151) | (.236) | (.281) |
| Percent | | −.340 | −.332 | −.350 | −.350 | −.459 | −.435 | |
| disadvantaged | | (.018) | (.018) | (.019) | (.019) | (.049) | (.049) | |
| Enrollment | | | .017 | .041 | .062 | | .079 | |
| | | | (.009) | (.012) | (.037) | | (.036) | |
| Enrollment | | | | | −.010 | | | |
| squared/100 | | | | | (.016) | | | |
| Segment 1 | | | | | | | | −12.6 |
| (enrollment 38–43) | | | | | | | | (3.80) |
| Segment 2 | | | | | | | | −2.89 |
| (enrollment 78–83) | | | | | | | | (2.41) |
| $R^2$ | .048 | .249 | .252 | | | | | |
| Number of classes | | 2,018 | | 2,018 | | 471 | | 302 |

*Notes:* Adapted from Angrist and Lavy (1999). The table reports estimates of equation (6.2.6) in the text using class averages. Standard errors, reported in parentheses, are corrected for within-school correlation.

test scores. Most of this vanishes however, when the percent disadvantaged in the school is included as a control. The positive correlation between class size and test scores shrinks to insignificance when enrollment is added as an additional control, as can be seen in column 3. Still, there is no evidence that smaller classes are better, as the results from the Tennessee STAR randomized trial would lead us to expect.

In contrast to the OLS estimates in column 3, 2SLS estimates of similar specifications using $m_{sc}$ as an instrument for $n_{sc}$ strongly suggest that smaller classes increase test scores. These results, reported in column 4 for models that include a linear enrollment control and in column 5 for models that include a quadratic enrollment control, range from −.23 to −.26, with standard error around .1. These results suggest a seven-student reduction in class size (as in Tennessee STAR) raises math scores by about 1.75 points, for an effect size of .18$\sigma$, where $\sigma$ is the standard deviation of class average scores. This is not too far from the Tennessee estimates.

Importantly, the functional form of the enrollment control does not seem to matter very much (though estimates with no controls, not reported in the table, come out much smaller and insignificant). Columns 6 and 7 check the robustness of the main findings further using a ±5 discontinuity sample. Not surprisingly, these results are much less precise than those reported in columns 4 and 5 since they were estimated with only about one-quarter of the data used to construct the full-sample estimates. Still, they bounce around the −.25 mark. Finally, the last column shows the results of estimation using an even narrower discontinuity sample limited to schools with an enrollment of plus or minus three students around the discontinuities at 40, 80, and 120 (with dummy controls for which of these discontinuities is relevant). These are Wald estimates in the spirit of Hahn, Todd, and van der Klaauw (2001) and formula (6.2.5); the instrument used to construct these estimates is a dummy for being in a school with enrollment just to the right of the relevant discontinuity. The result is an imprecise −.270, but still strikingly similar to the other estimates in the table. This set of estimates illustrates the price to be paid in terms of precision when we shrink the sample around the discontinuities. Happily, however, the picture that emerges from table 6.2.1 is fairly clear.

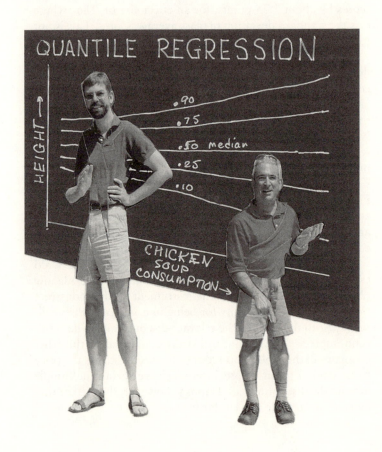

# Chapter 7

# Quantile Regression

Here's a prayer for you. Got a pencil? . . . "Protect me from knowing what I don't need to know. Protect me from even knowing that there are things to know that I don't know. Protect me from knowing that I decided not to know about the things I decided not to know about. Amen." There's another prayer that goes with it. "Lord, lord, lord. Protect me from the consequences of the above prayer."

Douglas Adams, *Mostly Harmless*

Rightly or wrongly, 95 percent of applied econometrics is concerned with averages. If, for example, a training program raises average earnings enough to offset the costs, we are happy. The focus on averages is partly because it's hard enough to produce good estimates of average causal effects. And if the dependent variable is a dummy for something like employment, the mean describes the entire distribution. But many variables, such as earnings and test scores, have continuous distributions. These distributions can change in ways not revealed by an examination of averages; for example, they can spread out or become more compressed. Applied economists increasingly want to know what is happening to an entire distribution, to the relative winners and losers, as well as to averages.

Policy makers and labor economists have been especially concerned with changes in the wage distribution. We know, for example, that flat average real wages are only a small part of what's been going on in the labor market for the past 25 years. Upper earnings quantiles have been increasing, while lower quantiles have been falling. In other words, the rich are getting richer and the poor are getting poorer. Recently, inequality has grown asymmetrically; for example, among college graduates, it's mostly the rich getting richer, with wages at the lower decile unchanging. The complete story of the changing wage distribution is fairly complicated and would seem to be hard to summarize.

Quantile regression is a powerful tool that makes the task of modeling distributions easy, even when the underlying story is complex and multidimensional. We can use this tool to see whether participation in a training program or membership in a labor union affects earnings inequality as well as average earnings. We can also check for interactions, such as whether and how the relation between schooling and inequality has been changing over time. Quantile regression works very much like conventional regression: confounding factors can be held fixed by including covariates; interaction terms work similarly too. And sometimes we can even use instrumental variables methods to estimate causal effects on quantiles when a selection-on-observables story seems implausible.

## 7.1    The Quantile Regression Model

The starting point for quantile regression is the conditional quantile function (CQF). Suppose we are interested in the distribution of a continuously distributed random variable, $Y_i$, with a well-behaved density (no gaps or spikes). Then the CQF at quantile $\tau$ given a vector of regressors, $X_i$, can be defined as:

$$Q_\tau(Y_i|X_i) = F_y^{-1}(\tau|X_i)$$

where $F_y(y|X_i)$ is the distribution function for $Y_i$ at y, conditional on $X_i$. When $\tau = .10$, for example, $Q_\tau(Y_i|X_i)$ describes the lower decile of $Y_i$ given $X_i$, while $\tau = .5$ gives us the conditional median.[1] By looking at the CQF of earnings as a function of education, we can tell whether the dispersion in

---

[1] More generally, we can define the CQF for discrete random variables and random variables with less than well-behaved densities as

$$Q_\tau(Y_i|X_i) = \inf\{y : F_y(y|X_i) \geq \tau\}.$$

earnings goes up or down with schooling. The CQF of earnings as a function of education and time tells us whether the relationship between schooling and inequality is changing over time.

The CQF is the conditional quantile version of the conditional expectation function (CEF). Recall that the CEF can be derived as the solution to a mean-squared error prediction problem,

$$E[Y_i|X_i] = \underset{m(X_i)}{\arg\min} E[(Y_i - m(X_i))^2].$$

In the same spirit, the CQF solves the following minimization problem,

$$Q_\tau(Y_i|X_i) = \underset{q(X)}{\arg\min} E[\rho_\tau(Y_i - q(X_i))], \qquad (7.1.1)$$

where $\rho_\tau(u) = (\tau - 1(u \leq 0))u$ is called the "check function" because it looks like a check-mark when you plot it. If $\tau = .5$, this becomes least absolute deviations because $\rho_{.5}(u) = \frac{1}{2}(\text{sign } u)u = \frac{1}{2}|u|$. In this case, $Q_\tau(Y_i|X_i)$ is the conditional median since the conditional median minimizes absolute deviations. Otherwise, the check function weights positive and negative terms asymmetrically:

$$\rho_\tau(u) = 1(u > 0) \cdot \tau|u| + 1(u \leq 0) \cdot (1 - \tau)|u|.$$

This asymmetric weighting generates a minimand that picks out conditional quantiles (a fact that is not immediately obvious but can be proved with a little work; see Koenker, 2005).

With continuous or high-dimensional $X_i$, the CQF shares the disadvantages of the CEF: it may be hard to estimate and summarize. We'd therefore like to boil this function down to a small set of numbers, one for each element of $X_i$. Quantile regression accomplishes this by substituting a linear model for $q(X_i)$ in (7.1.1), producing

$$\beta_\tau \equiv \underset{b}{\arg\min} E[\rho_\tau(Y_i - X_i'b)]. \qquad (7.1.2)$$

The *quantile regression estimator*, $\hat{\beta}_\tau$, is the sample analog of (7.1.2). It turns out this minimization is a linear programming problem that is fairly easy (for computers) to solve.

Just as OLS fits a linear model to $Y_i$ by minimizing expected squared error, quantile regression fits a linear model to $Y_i$ using the asymmetric loss function, $\rho_\tau(u)$. If $Q_\tau(Y_i|X_i)$ is in fact linear, the quantile regression minimand will find it (just as if the CEF is linear, OLS will find it). The original quantile regression model, introduced by Koenker and Bassett (1978), was motivated by the assumption that the CQF is linear. As it turns out, however, the assumption of a linear CQF is unnecessary: quantile regression is useful whether or not we believe this.

Before turning to a more general theoretical discussion of quantile regression, we illustrate the use of this tool to study the wage distribution. The motivation for the use of quantile regression to look at the wage distribution comes from labor economists' interest in the question of how inequality varies conditional on covariates like education and experience (see, e.g., Buchinsky, 1994). The overall gap in earnings by schooling group (e.g., the college wage premium) grew considerably in the 1980s and 1990s. Less clear, however, is how the wage distribution was changing *within* education and experience groups. Many labor economists believe that increases in within-group inequality provide especially strong evidence of fundamental changes in the labor market, not easily accounted for by changes in institutional features such as the percentage of workers who belong to labor unions.

Table 7.1.1 reports schooling coefficients from quantile regressions estimated using the 1980, 1990, and 2000 censuses. The models used to construct these estimates control for race and a quadratic function of potential labor market experience (defined as $age - education - 6$). The .5 quantile coefficients—for the conditional median—are close to the OLS coefficients in the far right columns. For example, the OLS estimate of .072 in the 1980 census is not very different from the .5 quantile coefficient of about .068 in the same data. If the conditional-on-covariates distribution of log wages is symmetric, so that the conditional median equals the conditional mean, we should expect these two coefficients to be the same. Also noteworthy is that fact that the quantile coefficients are

TABLE 7.1.1
Quantile regression coefficients for schooling in the 1980,
1990, and 2000 censuses

| Census | Obs. | Desc. Stats. | | Quantile Regression Estimates | | | | | OLS Estimates | |
|---|---|---|---|---|---|---|---|---|---|---|
| | | Mean | SD | 0.1 | 0.25 | 0.5 | 0.75 | 0.9 | Coeff. | Root MSE |
| 1980 | 65,023 | 6.4 | .67 | .074 | .074 | .068 | .070 | .079 | .072 | .63 |
| | | | | (.002) | (.001) | (.001) | (.001) | (.001) | (.001) | |
| 1990 | 86,785 | 6.5 | .69 | .112 | .110 | .106 | .111 | .137 | .114 | .64 |
| | | | | (.003) | (.001) | (.001) | (.001) | (.003) | (.001) | |
| 2000 | 97,397 | 6.5 | .75 | .092 | .105 | .111 | .120 | .157 | .114 | .69 |
| | | | | (.002) | (.001) | (.001) | (.001) | (.004) | (.001) | |

Notes: Adapted from Angrist, Chernozhukov, and Fernandez-Val (2006). The table reports quantile regression estimates of the returns to schooling in a model for log wages, with OLS estimates shown at the right for comparison. The sample includes U.S.-born white and black men aged 40–49. The sample size and the mean and standard deviation of log wages in each census extract are shown at the left. Standard errors are reported in parentheses. All models control for race and potential experience. Sampling weights were used for the 2000 census estimates.

similar across quantiles in 1980. An additional year of schooling raises median wages by 6.8 percent, with slightly higher effects on the lower and upper quartiles of the conditional wage distribution equal to .074 and .070. Although the estimated returns to schooling increased sharply between 1980 and 1990 (up to .106 at the median, with an OLS return of .114 percent), there is still a reasonably stable pattern of returns across quantiles in the 1990 census. The largest effect is on the upper decile, a coefficient of .137, while the other quantile coefficients are around .11.

We should expect to see constant coefficients across quantiles if the effect of schooling on wages amounts to what is sometimes called a *location shift*. Here, this means that as higher schooling levels raise average earnings, other parts of the wage distribution move in tandem (i.e., within-group inequality does not change). Suppose, for example, that log wages can be described by a classical linear regression model:

$$Y_i \sim N(X_i'\beta, \sigma_\varepsilon^2), \qquad (7.1.3)$$

where $E[Y_i|X_i] = X_i'\beta$ and $Y_i - X_i'\beta \equiv \varepsilon_i$ is a normally distributed error with constant variance $\sigma_\varepsilon^2$. Homoskedasticity means the conditional distribution of log wages is no more spread out for college graduates than for high school graduates. The implications of the linear homoskedastic model for quantiles are apparent from the fact that

$$P[Y_i - X_i'\beta < \sigma_\varepsilon \Phi^{-1}(\tau)|X_i] = \tau,$$

where $\Phi^{-1}(\tau)$ is the inverse of the standard normal CDF. From this we conclude that $Q_\tau(Y_i|X_i) = X_i'\beta + \sigma_\varepsilon \Phi^{-1}(\tau)$. In other words, apart from the changing intercept, $\sigma_\varepsilon \Phi^{-1}(\tau)$, quantile regression coefficients are the same at each quantile. The results in table 7.1.1 for 1980 and 1990 are not too far from this stylized representation.

In contrast to the simple pattern in 1980 and 1990 census data, quantile regression estimates from the 2000 census differ markedly across quantiles, especially in the right tail. An additional year of schooling raises the lower decile of wages by 9.2 percent, the median by 11.1 percent, and the upper decile by 15.7 percent. Thus, in addition to increases in overall inequality in the 1980s and 1990s (a fact we know from simple descriptive statistics), by 2000, inequality began to increase with education as well (since a pattern of increasing schooling coefficients across quantiles means the wage distribution spreads out as education increases). This development is the subject of considerable discussion among labor economists, who are particularly concerned with whether it points to fundamental or institutional changes in the labor market (see, e.g., Autor, Katz, and Kearney, 2005, and Lemieux, 2008).

A parametric example helps us see the link between quantile regression coefficients and conditional variance. Specifically, we can generate increasing quantile regression coefficients by adding heteroskedasticity to the classic normal regression model, (7.1.3). Suppose that

$$Y_i \sim N(X_i'\beta, \sigma^2(X_i)),$$

where $\sigma^2(X_i) = (\lambda'X_i)^2$ and $\lambda$ is a vector of positive coefficients such that $\lambda'X_i > 0$ (perhaps proportional to $\beta$, so that the conditional variance grows with the conditional mean).[2] Then

$$P[\mathrm{Y}_i - \mathrm{X}_i'\beta < (\lambda'\mathrm{X}_i)\Phi^{-1}(\tau)|\mathrm{X}_i] = \tau,$$

with the implication that

$$Q_\tau(\mathrm{Y}_i|\mathrm{X}_i) = \mathrm{X}_i'\beta + (\lambda'\mathrm{X}_i)\Phi^{-1}(\tau) = \mathrm{X}_i'[\beta + \lambda\Phi^{-1}(\tau)].$$
$$(7.1.4)$$

so that quantile regression coefficients increase across quantiles with $\beta_\tau = \beta + \lambda\Phi^{-1}(\tau)$.

Putting the pieces together, table 7.1.1 neatly summarizes two stories, both related to variation in within-group inequality. First, results from the 2000 census show inequality increasing sharply with education. The increase is asymmetric, however, and appears much more clearly in the upper tail of the wage distribution. Second, this increase is a new development. In 1980 and 1990, schooling affected the wage distribution in a manner roughly consistent with a simple location shift.[3]

### 7.1.1   Censored Quantile Regression

Quantile regression allows us to look at features of the conditional distribution of $\mathrm{Y}_i$ when part of the distribution is hidden. Suppose you have have data of the form

$$\mathrm{Y}_{i,obs} = \mathrm{Y}_i \cdot 1[\mathrm{Y}_i < c] + c \cdot 1[\mathrm{Y}_i \geq c], \qquad (7.1.5)$$

---

[2]See Card and Lemieux (1996) for an empirical example of a regression model with this sort of heteroskedasticity. Koenker and Portnoy (1996) call this a linear location-scale model.

[3]The formula for asymptotic quantile regression standard errors assuming a linear CQF is

$$\tau(1-\tau)\{E[f_{u_\tau}(0|\mathrm{X}_i)\mathrm{X}_i\mathrm{X}_i']^{-1}E[\mathrm{X}_i\mathrm{X}_i']E[f_{u_\tau}(0|\mathrm{X}_i)\mathrm{X}_i\mathrm{X}_i']^{-1},$$

where $f_{u_\tau}(0|\mathrm{X}_i)$ is the conditional density of the quantile regression residual at zero. If the residuals are homoskedastic this simplifies to $\frac{\tau(1-\tau)}{f_{u_\tau}^2(0)}E[\mathrm{X}_i\mathrm{X}_i']^{-1}$, where $f_{u_\tau}^2(0)$ is the square of the unconditional residual density. Angrist, Chernozhukov, and Fernandez-Val (2006) give a more general formula allowing the CQF to be nonlinear.

where $Y_{i,obs}$ is what you get to see and $Y_i$ is the variable you would like to see. The variable $Y_{i,obs}$ is *censored*—information about $Y_i$ in $Y_{i,obs}$ is limited for confidentiality reasons or because it was too difficult or time-consuming to collect more information. In the CPS, for example, high earnings are top-coded to protect respondent confidentiality. This means that data above the topcode are recoded to have the topcode value. Duration data may also be censored: in a study of the effects of unemployment insurance on the duration of employment, we might follow new claimants for up to 40 weeks. Anyone out of work for longer has an unemployment spell length that is censored at 40. Note that limited dependent variables such as hours worked or medical expenditure, discussed in section 3.4.2, are not censored; they take on the value zero by their nature, just as dummy variables such as employment status do.

When dealing with censored dependent variables, quantile regression can be used to estimate the effect of covariates on conditional quantiles that are below the censoring point (assuming censoring is from above). This reflects the fact that censoring earnings above, say, the median has no effect on the median. So if CPS topcoding affects relatively few people (as is often true), censoring has no effect on estimates of the conditional median or even $\beta_\tau$ for $\tau = .75$. Likewise, if less than 10 percent of the sample is censored conditional on all values of $X_i$, then, when estimating $\beta_\tau$ for $\tau$ up to .9, you can simply ignore censoring. Alternatively, you can limit the sample to values of $X_i$ where $Q_\tau(Y_i|X_i)$ is below $c$ (or above, if censoring is from the bottom with $Y_{i,obs} = Y_i \cdot 1[Y_i > c] + c \cdot 1[Y_i \leq c]$).

Powell (1986) formalizes this idea with the censored quantile regression estimator. Because we may not know which conditional quantiles are below the censoring point (continuing to think of top codes for example), Powell proposes we work with

$$Q_\tau(Y_i|X_i) = \min{(c, X_i'\beta_\tau^c)}.$$

The parameter vector $\beta_\tau^c$ solves

$$\beta_\tau^c = \arg\min_b E\{1[X_i'b < c] \cdot \rho_\tau(Y_i - X_i'b)\}. \qquad (7.1.6)$$

In other words, we solve the quantile regression minimization problem for values of $X_i$ such that $X_i'\beta_\tau^c < c$. (In practice, we minimize the sample analog of (7.1.6).) As long is there are enough uncensored data, the resulting estimates give us the quantile regression function we would have gotten had the data not been censored (assuming the conditional quantile function is, in fact, linear). And if it turns out that the conditional quantiles you are estimating are all below the censoring point, then you are back to regular quantile regression.

The sample analog of (7.1.6) is no longer a linear programming problem, but Buchinsky (1994) proposes a simple iterated linear programming algorithm that seems to work. The iterations go like this. First estimate $\beta_\tau^c$ ignoring the censoring. Then find the cells with $X_i'\beta_\tau^c < c$. Then estimate the quantile regression again using these cells only, and so on. This algorithm is not guaranteed to converge, but it appears to do so in practice. Standard errors can be bootstrapped. Buchinsky (1994) used this approach to estimate the returns to schooling for highly experienced workers who may have earnings above the CPS top code. The censoring adjustment tends to increase the returns to schooling for this group.[4]

## 7.1.2  The Quantile Regression Approximation Property★

The CQF of log wages given schooling is unlikely to be exactly linear, so the assumptions of the original quantile regression model fail to hold in this example. Luckily, quantile regression can be understood as giving a MMSE linear approximation to the CQF, though in this case the approximation is a little more complicated and harder to derive than the regression-CEF theorem. For any quantile index $\tau \in (0, 1)$, define the quantile regression specification error as:

$$\Delta_\tau(X_i, \beta_\tau) \equiv X_i'\beta_\tau - Q_\tau(Y_i|X_i).$$

[4]See Buchinsky and Hahn (1998) and Chernozhukov and Hong (2002) for more sophisticated estimators with better theoretical properties.

The population quantile regression vector can be shown to minimize an expected weighted average of the squared specification error, $\Delta_\tau^2(X_i, \beta_\tau)$, as described in the following theorem from Angrist, Chernozhukov, and Fernandez-Val (2006):

**Theorem 7.1.1** *Quantile Regression Approximation.*
*Suppose that (i) the conditional density $f_y(y|X_i)$ exists almost surely, (ii) $E[Y_i]$, $E[Q_\tau(Y_i|X_i)]$, and $E\|X_i\|$ are finite, and (iii) $\beta_\tau$ uniquely solves (7.1.2). Then*

$$\beta_\tau = \arg\min_b E[w_\tau(X_i, b) \cdot \Delta_\tau^2(X_i, b)], \qquad (7.1.7)$$

*where*

$$
\begin{aligned}
w_\tau(X_i, b) &= \int_0^1 (1-u) \cdot f_{\varepsilon(\tau)}(u\Delta_\tau(X_i, b)|X_i)du \\
&= \int_0^1 (1-u) \cdot f_y(u \cdot X_i'b + (1-u) \cdot Q_\tau(Y_i|X_i)|X_i)du \\
&\geq 0
\end{aligned}
$$

*and $\varepsilon_i(\tau)$ is a quantile-specific residual,*

$$\varepsilon_i(\tau) \equiv Y_i - Q_\tau(Y_i|X_i),$$

*with conditional density $f_{\varepsilon(\tau)}(e|X_i)$ at $\varepsilon_i(\tau) = e$. Moreover, when $Y_i$ has a smooth conditional density, we have for $\beta$ in the neighborhood of $\beta_\tau$:*

$$w_\tau(X_i, \beta) \approx 1/2 \cdot f_y(Q_\tau(Y_i|X_i)|X_i). \qquad (7.1.8)$$

The quantile regression approximation theorem looks complicated, but the big picture is simple. We can think of quantile regression as approximating $Q_\tau(Y_i|X_i)$, just as OLS approximates $E[Y_i|X_i]$. The OLS weighting function is the histogram of $X_i$, denoted $P(X_i)$. The quantile regression weighting function, implicitly given by $w_\tau(X_i, \beta_\tau) \cdot P(X_i)$, is more elaborate than $P(X_i)$ alone (the histogram is implicitly part of the quantile regression weighting function because the expectation in (7.1.7) is over the distribution of $X_i$). The term $w_\tau(X_i, \beta_\tau)$ involves the quantile regression vector, $\beta_\tau$, but can be rewritten with $\beta_\tau$ partialed out so that it is a function of $X_i$ only (see Angrist, Chernozhukov, and Fernandez-Val, 2006, for details). In any case, the quantile regression weights are approximately proportional to the density of $Y_i$ in the neighborhood of the CQF.

The quantile regression approximation property is illustrated in figure 7.1.1, which plots the conditional quantile function of log wages given highest grade completed using 1980 census data. Here we take advantage of the discreteness of schooling and large census samples to estimate the CQF nonparametrically by computing the quantile of wages for each schooling level. Panels A–C plot a nonparametric estimate of $Q_\tau(Y_i|X_i)$ along with the linear quantile regression fit for the 0.10, 0.50, and 0.90 quantiles, where $X_i$ includes only the schooling variable and a constant. The nonparametric cell-by-cell estimate of the CQF is plotted with circles in the figure, while the quantile regression line is solid. The figure shows how linear quantile regression approximates the CQF.

It's also interesting to compare quantile regression to a histogram-weighted fit to the CQF, similar to that provided by OLS for the CEF. The histogram-weighted approach to quantile regression was proposed by Chamberlain (1994). The Chamberlain minimum distance (MD) estimator is the sample analog of the vector $\tilde{\beta}_\tau$ obtained by solving

$$\tilde{\beta}_\tau = \arg\min_b E[(Q_\tau(Y_i|X_i) - X_i'b)^2]$$

$$= \arg\min_b E[\Delta_\tau^2(X_i, b)].$$

In other words, $\tilde{\beta}_\tau$ is the slope of the linear regression of $Q_\tau(Y_i|X_i)$ on $X_i$, weighted by the histogram of $X_i$. In contrast to quantile regression, which requires only one pass through the data, MD relies on the ability to estimate $Q_\tau(Y_i|X_i)$ consistently in a nonparametric first step.

Figure 7.1.1 plots MD fitted values with a dashed line. The quantile regression and MD lines are close, but they are not identical because of the implicit weighting by $w_\tau(X_i, \beta_\tau)$ in the quantile regression fit. This weighting accentuates the quality of the fit at values of $X_i$ where $Y_i$ is more densely distributed

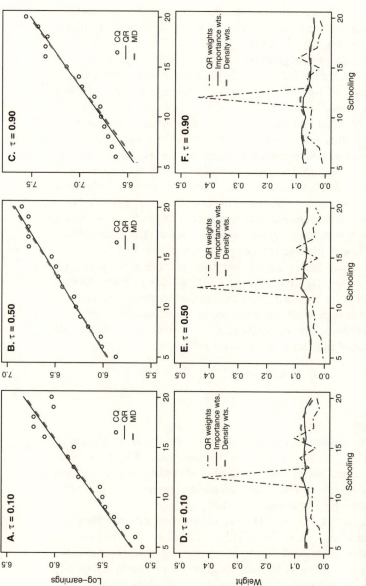

**Figure 7.1.1** The quantile regression approximation property (adapted from Angrist, Chernozhukov, and Fernandez-Val, 2006). The figure shows alternative estimates of the conditional quantile function of log wages given highest grade completed using 1980 Census data, along with the implied weighting function. Panels A-C report nonparametric (CQ), quantile regression (QR) and minimum distance (MD) estimates for $\tau = .1, .5, .9$. Panels D-F

near the CQF. Panels D–F in figure 7.1.1 plot the overall quantile weights, $w_\tau(X_i, \beta_\tau) \cdot P(X_i)$, against $X_i$. The panels also show estimates of $w_\tau(X_i, \beta_\tau)$, labeled "importance weights," and their density approximations, $1/2 \cdot f_y(Q_\tau(Y_i|X_i)|X_i)$. The importance weights and the density weights are similar and fairly flat. The overall weighting function looks a lot like the schooling histogram, and therefore places the highest weight on 12 and 16 years of schooling.

### 7.1.3    Tricky Points

The language of conditional quantiles is tricky. Sometimes we talk about "quantile regression coefficients at the median," or "effects on those at the lower decile." But it's important to remember that quantile coefficients tell us about effects on *distributions*, not on *individuals*. If we discover, for example, that a training program raises the lower decile of the wage distribution, this does not necessarily mean that someone who would have been poor (i.e., at the lower decile without training) is now less poor. It only means that those who are poor in the regime with training are less poor than the poor would be in a regime without training.

The distinction between making a given set of poor people richer and changing what it means to be poor is subtle. This distinction has to do with whether we think an intervention preserves an individual's rank in the wage (or other dependent variable) distribution. If an intervention is rank-preserving, then an increase in the lower decile indeed makes those who would have been poor richer, since rank preservation means relative status is unchanged. Otherwise, we can only say that the poor—defined as the group in the bottom 10 percent of the wage distribution, whoever they may be—are better off. We elaborate on this point briefly in section 7.2.

A second tricky point is the transition from conditional quantiles to marginal quantiles. A link from conditional to marginal quantiles allows us to investigate the impact of changes in quantile regression coefficients on overall inequality. Suppose, for example, that quantile coefficients fan out even further with schooling, beyond what is observed in the 2000 census. What does this imply for the ratio of upper-decile to lower-decile wages? Alternatively, we can ask: How much of the overall increase in inequality (say, as measured by the ratio of upper to lower deciles) is explained by increases in within-group inequality summarized by the fanning out of quantile regression coefficients? These sorts of questions turn out to be surprisingly difficult to answer. The difficulty has to do with the fact that *all* conditional quantiles are needed to pin down a *particular* marginal quantile (Machado and Mata, 2005). In particular, $Q_\tau(Y_i|X_i) = X_i'\beta_\tau$ does *not* imply $Q_\tau(Y_i) = Q_\tau(X_i)'\beta_\tau$. This contrasts with the much more tractable expectations operator, where, if $E(Y_i|X_i) = X_i'\beta$, then by iterating expectations, we have $E(Y_i) = E(X_i)'\beta$.

### Extracting Marginal Quantiles★

To show the link between conditional quantiles and marginal distributions more formally, suppose the CQF is indeed linear, so that $Q_\tau(Y_i|X_i) = X_i'\beta_\tau$. Let $F_y(y|X_i) \equiv P[Y_i < y|X_i]$ be the conditional CDF of $Y_i$ given $X_i$, with marginal distribution $F_y(y) = P[Y_i < y]$. The CDF and its inverse are related by

$$\int_0^1 1[F_y^{-1}(\tau|X_i) < y]d\tau = F_y(y|X_i),  \qquad (7.1.9)$$

where $F_y^{-1}(\tau|X_i)$ is also the CQF, $Q_\tau(Y_i|X_i)$.

In other words, the proportion of the population below y conditional on $X_i$ is the same as the proportion of conditional quantiles that are below y.[5] Substituting for the CQF inside the integral using the linear model, gives

$$F_y(y|X_i) = \int_0^1 1[X_i'\beta_\tau < y]d\tau.$$

Next, we use the law of iterated expectations to get the marginal distribution function, $F_y(y)$:

$$F_y(y) = E\left[\int_0^1 1[X_i'\beta_\tau < y]d\tau\right]  \qquad (7.1.10)$$

---

[5] For example, if y is the conditional median, then $F_y(y|X_i) = .5$, and half of all conditional quantiles are below y. The relation (7.1.9) can be proved formally using the change of variables formula.

Finally, marginal quantiles, say, $Q_\tau(\mathrm{Y}_i)$ for $\tau \in (0,1)$, come from inverting $F_y(y)$:

$$Q_\tau(\mathrm{Y}_i) = \inf\{y : F_y(y) \geq \tau\}.$$

An estimator of the marginal distribution replaces the integral and expectations with sums in (7.1.10), where the sum over quantiles comes from quantile regression estimates at, say, every .01 quantile. In a sample of size $N$, this becomes:

$$\hat{F}_y(y) = N^{-1} \sum_i (1/100) \sum_{\tau=0}^{\tau=1} 1[X_i'\hat{\beta}_\tau < y].$$

The corresponding marginal quantile estimator inverts $\hat{F}_y(y)$.

A number of difficulties arise with this approach in practice. For one thing, you have to estimate lots of quantile regressions. Another is that the asymptotic distribution theory is complicated (though not insurmountable; see, Chernozhukov, Fernandez-Val, and Melly, 2008). Simplifying the conditional to marginal quantile transition is an active research area. Gosling, Machin, and Meghir (2000) and Machado and Mata (2005) are among the first empirical studies to go from conditional to marginal quantiles. When the variable of primary interest in a quantile regression model is a dummy variable such as treatment status and the other regressors are seen as controls, a propensity score type of weighting scheme can be used to estimate effects on marginal distributions. See Firpo (2007) for the exogenous case and Frölich and Melly (2007) for a marginalization scheme that works for endogenous treatment effects models of the sort discussed in the next section.

## 7.2   IV Estimation of Quantile Treatment Effects

The $42,000 question regarding any set of regression estimates is whether they have a causal interpretation. This is no less true for quantile regression than ordinary least squares. Suppose we are interested in estimating the effect of a training program on earnings. OLS regression estimates measure the impact of the program on average earnings while quantile regression estimates can be used to measure the impact of the program on median earnings. In both cases, we must worry about whether the estimated program effects are contaminated by omitted variables bias (OVB).

Here too, omitted variables problems can be solved using instrumental variables, though IV methods for quantile models are a relatively new development and not yet as flexible as conventional 2SLS. We discuss an approach that captures the causal effect of a binary variable on quantiles (i.e., a treatment effect) using a binary instrument. The quantile treatment effects (QTE) estimator for IV, introduced in Abadie, Angrist, and Imbens (2002), relies on essentially the same assumptions as the LATE framework for average causal effects. The result is an Abadie-type weighting estimator of the causal effect of treatment on quantiles for compliers.[6]

Our discussion of the QTE estimator is based on an additive model for conditional quantiles, so that a single treatment effect is estimated in a model with covariates. The resulting estimator simplifies to Koenker and Bassett (1978) linear quantile regression when there is no instrumenting. The relationship between QTE and quantile regression is therefore analogous to that between conventional 2SLS and OLS when the regressor of interest is a dummy.

The parameters of interest are defined as follows. For $\tau \in (0,1)$, we assume there exist $\alpha_\tau$ and $\beta_\tau$ such that

$$Q_\tau(Y_i|X_i, D_i, D_{1i} > D_{0i}) = \alpha_\tau D_i + X_i'\beta_\tau, \qquad (7.2.1)$$

where $Q_\tau(Y_i|X_i, D_i, D_{1i} > D_{0i})$ denotes the $\tau$-quantile of $Y_i$ given $X_i$ and $D_i$ for compliers. Thus, $\alpha_\tau$ and $\beta_\tau$ are quantile regression coefficients for compliers.

Recall that $D_i$ is independent of potential outcomes conditional on $X_i$ and $D_{1i} > D_{0i}$, as we discussed in (4.5.2). The parameter $\alpha_\tau$ in this model therefore gives the difference in

---

[6]For an alternative approach, see Chernozhukov and Hansen (2005), which allows for regressors of any type (i.e., not just dummies) but invokes a rank-similarity assumption that is unnecessary in the QTE framework.

the conditional-on-$X_i$ quantiles of $Y_{1i}$ and $Y_{0i}$ for compliers. In other words,

$$Q_\tau(Y_{1i}|X_i, D_{1i} > D_{0i}) - Q_\tau(Y_{0i}|X_i, D_{1i} > D_{0i}) = \alpha_\tau \quad (7.2.2)$$

This tells us, for example, whether a training program changed the conditional median or lower decile of earnings for compliers. Note that the parameter $\alpha_\tau$ does not tell us whether treatment changed the quantiles of the unconditional distributions of $Y_{1i}$ and $Y_{0i}$. For that, we have to integrate families of quantile regression results using a procedure like the one described in section 7.1.3.

It also bears emphasizing that $\alpha_\tau$ is not the conditional quantile of the individual treatment effects, $(Y_{1i} - Y_{0i})$. You might want to know, for example, whether the median treatment effect is positive. Unfortunately, questions like this are very hard to answer without making strong assumptions such as rank-invariance.[7] Even a randomized trial with perfect compliance fails to reveal the distribution of $(Y_{1i} - Y_{0i})$. Although a difference in averages is the same as an average difference, other features of the distribution of $Y_{1i} - Y_{0i}$ are hidden because we never get to see both $Y_{1i}$ and $Y_{0i}$ for any one person. The good news for applied econometricians is that differences in distributions are usually more important than the distribution of treatment effects because comparisons of social welfare typically require only the distributions of $Y_{1i}$ and $Y_{0i}$, and not the distribution of their difference (see, e.g., Atkinson, 1970). This point can be made without reference to quantiles. When evaluating an employment program, we are inclined to view the program favorably if it increases overall employment rates. In other words, we are happy if the average $Y_{1i}$ is higher than the average $Y_{0i}$. The number of individuals who gain jobs $(Y_{1i} - Y_{0i} = 1)$ or lose jobs $(Y_{1i} - Y_{0i} = -1)$ should be of secondary interest, since a good program will necessarily have more gainers than losers.

---

[7] In this context, rank-invariance means $Y_{1i}$ and $Y_{0i}$ are related by an invertible function. See, for example, Heckman, Smith, and Clements (1997).

## 7.2.1    The QTE Estimator

The QTE estimator is motivated by the observation that quantile regression coefficients for compliers can (theoretically) be estimated by running quantile regressions in the population of compliers. We cannot list the compliers in a given data set, but as in section 4.5.2, we can use the Abadie kappa theorem to find them. Specifically,

$$(\alpha_\tau, \beta_\tau) = \arg \min_{a,b} E\{\rho_\tau(Y_i - aD_i - X_i'b)|D_{1i} > D_{0i}\}$$

$$= \arg \min_{a,b} E\{\kappa_i \rho_\tau(Y_i - aD_i - X_i'b)\}, \qquad (7.2.3)$$

where

$$\kappa_i = 1 - \frac{D_i(1 - Z_i)}{1 - P(Z_i = 1|X_i)} - \frac{(1 - D_i)Z_i}{P(Z_i = 1|X_i)},$$

as before. The QTE estimator is the sample analog of (7.2.3).

A number of practical issues arise when implementing QTE. First, $\kappa_i$ must be estimated, and the sampling variance induced by this first-step estimation should be reflected in the relevant asymptotic distribution theory. Abadie, Angrist, and Imbens (2002) derive the limiting distribution of the sample analog of (7.2.3) when $\kappa_i$ is estimated nonparametrically. In practice, however, it is easier to bootstrap the whole procedure (i.e., beginning with the construction of estimated kappas) than to use the asymptotic formulas.

Second, $\kappa_i$ is negative when $D_i \neq Z_i$. The kappa-weighted quantile regression minimand is therefore nonconvex and, unlike the regular quantile regression estimator, does not have a linear programming representation. This problem can be solved by minimizing

$$E\{E[\kappa_i|Y_i, D_i, X_i]\rho_\tau(Y_i - aD_i - X_i'b)\} \qquad (7.2.4)$$

instead. This minimand is derived by iterating expectations in (7.2.3). The practical difference between (7.2.3) and (7.2.4) is that the term

$$E[\kappa_i|Y_i, D_i, X_i] = P[D_{1i} > D_{0i}|Y_i, D_i, X_i]$$

is a probability and therefore between zero and one.[8] A further simplification comes from the fact that

$$E[\kappa_i|Y_i, D_i, X_i] = 1 - \frac{D_i(1 - E[z_i|Y_i, D_i = 1, X_i])}{1 - P(z_i = 1|X_i)}$$
$$- \frac{(1 - D_i)E[z_i|Y_i, D_i = 0, X_i]}{P(z_i = 1|X_i)}. \quad (7.2.5)$$

Angrist (2001) used this to implement QTE with probit models for $E[z_i|Y_i,D_i,X_i]$ estimated separately in the $D_i = 0$ and $D_i = 1$ subsamples, constructing $E[\kappa_i|Y_i,D_i,X_i]$ using (7.2.5), and then trimming any of the resulting estimates of $E[\kappa_i|Y_i,D_i,X_i]$ that are outside the unit interval. The resulting non-negative first-step estimates of $E[\kappa_i|Y_i,D_i,X_i]$ can be plugged in as weights using Stata's qreg command to construct weighted quantile regression estimates in a second step.[9]

### Estimates of the Effect of Training on the Quantiles of Trainee Earnings

The Job Training Partnership Act was a large federal program that provided subsidized training to disadvantaged American workers in the 1980s. JTPA services were delivered at 649 sites, also called Service Delivery Areas (SDAs), located

---

[8]The expectation of $\kappa_i$ is a probability because $\kappa_i$ "finds compliers." A formal statement of this result appears in Abadie, Angrist, and Imbens (2002; lemma 3.2).

[9]Step-by-step, it goes like this:

1. Probit $z_i$ on $Y_i$ and $X_i$ separately in the $D_i = 0$ and $D_i = 1$ subsamples. Save these fitted values.
2. Probit $z_i$ on $X_i$ in the whole sample. Save these fitted values.
3. Construct $E[\kappa_i|Y_i,D_i,X_i]$ by plugging the two sets of fitted values into (7.2.5). Set anything less than zero to zero and anything greater than one to one.
4. Use these kappas to weight quantile regressions.
5. Bootstrap this whole procedure to construct standard errors.

throughout the country. The original study of the labor-market impact of JTPA services was based on a sample of men and women for whom continuous data on earnings (from either state unemployment insurance records or two follow-up surveys) were available for at least 30 months after random assignment.[10] There are 5,102 adult men with 30-month earnings data in the sample.

In our notation, $y_i$ is 30-month earnings, $D_i$ indicates enrollment for JTPA services, and $z_i$ indicates the randomly assigned *offer* of JTPA services. A key feature of most social experiments, as with many randomized trials of new drugs and therapies, is that some participants decline the intervention being offered. In the JTPA, those offered services were not compelled to participate in training. Consequently, although the offer of subsidized training was randomly assigned, only about 60 percent of those offered training actually received JTPA services. Treatment received is therefore partly self-selected and likely to be correlated with potential outcomes. On the other hand, as discussed in 4.4.3, the randomized offer of training provides a good instrument for training received, since the two are obviously correlated and the offer of treatment is independent of potential outcomes. Moreover, because of the very low percentage of individuals receiving JTPA services in the control group (less than 2 percent), effects for compliers can be interpreted as effects on those who were treated (as discussed in 4.4.3: LATE equals the effect on the treated when there are no always-takers).

Since training offers were randomized in the National JTPA Study, covariates ($X_i$) are not required to consistently estimate effects on compliers. Even in experiments like this, however, it's customary to control for covariates to correct for chance associations between treatment status and applicant characteristics and to increase precision (see chapter 2). The covariates used here are baseline measures from the JTPA intake process. They include dummies for black and Hispanic applicants, a dummy for high school graduates (including GED holders), dummies for married applicants, five age-group

---

[10]See Bloom et al. (1997) and Orr et al. (1996).

dummies, and a dummy for whether the applicant worked at least 13 weeks in the year preceding random assignment. Also included are dummies for the original recommended service strategy (classroom training, on-the-job training, job search assistance, other) and a dummy for whether earnings data are from the second follow-up survey. Since these covariates mostly summarize subjects' demographic and socioeconomic background, we can think of the quantile analysis as telling us how the JTPA experiment affected the earnings distribution within demographic and socioeconomic groups.

As a benchmark, OLS and conventional instrumental variables (2SLS) estimates of the impact of training on adult men are reported in the first column of table 7.2.1. The OLS training coefficient is a precisely estimated $3,754. This is the coefficient on $D_i$ in a regression of $Y_i$ on $D_i$ and $X_i$. These estimates ignore the fact that trainees are self-selected. The 2SLS estimates in table 7.2.1 use the randomized offer of treatment $Z_i$ as an instrument for $D_i$. The 2SLS estimate is $1,593 with a standard error of $895, less than half the size of the corresponding OLS estimate.

Quantile regression estimates show that the gap in quantiles by trainee status is much larger (in proportionate terms) below the median than above it. This can be seen in the top right-hand columns of table 7.2.1, which reports quantile regression estimates for the .15, .25, .5, .75, and .85 quantiles. Specifically, the .85 quantile of trainee earnings is about 13 percent higher than the corresponding quantile for non-trainees, while the .15 quantile is 136 percent higher. Like the OLS estimates in the table, these quantile regression coefficients do not necessarily have a causal interpretation. Rather, they provide a descriptive comparison of the earnings distributions of trainees and nontrainees.

QTE estimates of the effect of training on median earnings are similar in magnitude though less precise than the benchmark 2SLS estimates. On the other hand, the QTE estimates exhibit a pattern very different from the quantile regression estimates. The estimates at low quantiles are substantially smaller than the corresponding quantile regression estimates, and they are small in absolute terms. For

TABLE 7.2.1

Quantile regression estimates and quantile treatment effects from the JTPA experiment

A. OLS and Quantile Regression Estimates

| | | | | Quantile | | |
|---|---|---|---|---|---|---|
| Variable | OLS | .15 | .25 | .50 | .75 | .85 |
| Training effect | 3,754 | 1,187 | 2,510 | 4,420 | 4,678 | 4,806 |
| | (536) | (205) | (356) | (651) | (937) | (1,055) |
| % Impact of training | 21.2 | 135.6 | 75.2 | 34.5 | 17.2 | 13.4 |
| High school or GED | 4,015 | 339 | 1,280 | 3,665 | 6,045 | 6,224 |
| | (571) | (186) | (305) | (618) | (1,029) | (1,170) |
| Black | −2,354 | −134 | −500 | −2,084 | −3,576 | −3,609 |
| | (626) | (194) | (324) | (684) | (1087) | (1,331) |
| Hispanic | 251 | 91 | 278 | 925 | −877 | −85 |
| | (883) | (315) | (512) | (1,066) | (1,769) | (2,047) |
| Married | 6,546 | 587 | 1,964 | 7,113 | 10,073 | 11,062 |
| | (629) | (222) | (427) | (839) | (1,046) | (1,093) |
| Worked < 13 | −6,582 | −1,090 | −3,097 | −7,610 | −9,834 | −9,951 |
| weeks in past year | (566) | (190) | (339) | (665) | (1,000) | (1,099) |
| Constant | 9,811 | −216 | 365 | 6,110 | 14,874 | 21,527 |
| | (1,541) | (468) | (765) | (1,403) | (2,134) | (3,896) |

B. 2SLS and QTE Estimates

| | | | | Quantile | | |
|---|---|---|---|---|---|---|
| Variable | 2SLS | .15 | .25 | .50 | .75 | .85 |
| Training effect | 1,593 | 121 | 702 | 1,544 | 3,131 | 3,378 |
| | (895) | (475) | (670) | (1,073) | (1,376) | (1,811) |
| % Impact of training | 8.55 | 5.19 | 12.0 | 9.64 | 10.7 | 9.02 |
| High school or GED | 4,075 | 714 | 1,752 | 4,024 | 5,392 | 5,954 |
| | (573) | (429) | (644) | (940) | (1,441) | (1,783) |
| Black | −2,349 | −171 | −377 | −2,656 | −4,182 | −3,523 |
| | (625) | (439) | (626) | (1,136) | (1,587) | (1,867) |
| Hispanic | 335 | 328 | 1,476 | 1,499 | 379 | 1,023 |
| | (888) | (757) | (1,128) | (1,390) | (2,294) | (2,427) |
| Married | 6,647 | 1,564 | 3,190 | 7,683 | 9,509 | 10,185 |
| | (627) | (596) | (865) | (1,202) | (1,430) | (1,525) |
| Worked <13 | −6,575 | −1,932 | −4,195 | −7,009 | −9,289 | −9,078 |
| weeks in past year | (567) | (442) | (664) | (1,040) | (1,420) | (1,596) |
| Constant | 10,641 | −134 | 1,049 | 7,689 | 14,901 | 22,412 |
| | (1,569) | (1,116) | (1,655) | (2,361) | (3,292) | (7,655) |

*Notes*: The table reports OLS, quantile regression, 2SLS, and QTE estimates of the effect of training on earnings (adapted from Abadie, Angrist, and Imbens, 2002). The sample includes 5,102 adult men. Assignment status is used as an instrument for training status in Panel B. In addition to the covariates shown in the table, all models include dummies for service strategy recommended and age group, and a dummy indicating data from a second follow-up survey. Robust standard errors are reported in parentheses.

example, the QTE estimate of the effect on the .15 quantile is $121, while the corresponding quantile regression estimate is $1,187. Similarly, the QTE estimate of the effect on the .25 quantile is $702, while the corresponding quantile regression estimate is $2,510. Unlike the results at low quantiles, however, the QTE estimates of effects on earnings above the median are large and statistically significant (though still smaller than the corresponding quantile regression estimates).

The result that JTPA training for adult men did not raise the lower quantiles of their earnings distribution is the most interesting finding arising from this analysis. This suggests that the quantile regression estimates in the top half of table 7.2.1 are contaminated by positive selection bias. One response to this finding might be that few JTPA applicants were very well off, so that distributional effects within applicants are of less concern than the fact that the program appears to have helped many applicants overall. However, the upper quantiles of earnings were reasonably high for adults who participated in the National JTPA Study. Increasing the upper tail of the trainee earnings distribution is therefore unlikely to have been a high priority for policy makers.

# Chapter 8

# Nonstandard Standard Error Issues

||||||||||||||||||||||||||||||||||||||||||||||||||||||||||■||◆||■||||||||||||||||||||||||||||||||||||||||||||||||||||||||||

We have normality. I repeat, we have normality.
Anything you still can't cope with is therefore your own
problem.
    Douglas Adams, *The Hitchhiker's Guide to the Galaxy*

Today, software packages routinely compute asymptotic standard errors derived under weak assumptions about the sampling process or underlying model. For example, you get regression standard errors based on formula (3.1.7) using the Stata option `robust`. Robust standard errors improve on old-fashioned standard errors because the resulting inferences are asymptotically valid when the regression residuals are heteroskedastic, as they almost certainly are when regression approximates a nonlinear conditional expectation function (CEF). In contrast, old-fashioned standard errors are derived assuming homoskedasticity. The hangup here is that estimates of robust standard errors can be misleading when the asymptotic approximation that justifies these estimates is not very good. The first part of this chapter looks at the failure of asymptotic inference with robust standard error estimates and some simple palliatives.

A pillar of traditional cross section inference—and the discussion in section 3.1.3—is the assumption that the data are independent. Each observation is treated as a random draw from the same population, uncorrelated with the observation before or after. We understand today that this sampling model is unrealistic and potentially even foolhardy. Much as in the time series studies common in macroeconomics, cross section analysts must worry about correlation between observations. The most important form of dependence arises in data with a group structure—for example, the test scores of children observed within classes or schools. Children in the same school or class tend to have test scores that are correlated, since they are subject to some of the same environmental and family background influences. We call this correlation the clustering problem, or the Moulton problem, after Moulton (1986), who made it famous. A closely related problem is correlation over time in the data sets commonly used to implement differences-in-differences (DD) estimation strategies. For example, studies of state-level minimum wages must confront the fact that state average employment rates are correlated over time. We call this the serial correlation problem, to distinguish it from the Moulton problem.

Researchers plagued by clustering and serial correlation also have to confront the fact that the simplest fixups for these problems, like Stata's `cluster` option, may not be very good. The asymptotic approximation relevant for clustered or serially correlated data relies on a large number of clusters or time series observations. Alas, we are not always blessed with many clusters or long time series. The resulting inference problems are not always insurmountable, though often the best solution is to get more data. Econometric fixups for clustering and serial correlation are discussed in the second part of this chapter. Some of the material in this chapter is hard to work through without matrix algebra, so we take the plunge and switch to a mostly matrix motif.

## 8.1   The Bias of Robust Standard Error Estimates★

In matrix notation

$$\hat{\beta} = \left[ \sum_i X_i X_i' \right]^{-1} \sum_i X_i Y_i = (X'X)^{-1} X'y,$$

where $X$ is the $N \times K$ matrix with rows $X_i'$ and $y$ is the $N \times 1$ vector of $Y_i$'s. We saw in section 3.1.3 that $\hat{\beta}$ has an asymptotically normal distribution. We can write:

$$\sqrt{N}(\hat{\beta} - \beta) \sim N(0, \Omega)$$

where $\Omega$ is the asymptotic covariance matrix and $\beta = E[X_i X_i']^{-1} E[X_i Y_i]$. Repeating (3.1.7), the formula for $\Omega$ in this case is

$$\Omega_r = E[X_i X_i']^{-1} E[X_i X_i' e_i^2] E[X_i X_i']^{-1}, \qquad (8.1.1)$$

where $e_i = Y_i - X_i'\beta$. When residuals are homoskedastic, the covariance matrix simplifies to $\Omega_c = \sigma^2 E[X_i X_i']^{-1}$, where $\sigma^2 = E[e_i^2]$.

We are concerned here with the bias of robust standard error estimates in independent samples (i.e., no clustering or serial correlation). To simplify the derivation of bias, we assume that the regressor vector can be treated as fixed, as it would be if we sampled stratifying on $X_i$. Nonstochastic regressors gives a benchmark sampling model that is often used to look at finite-sample distributions. It turns out that we miss little of theoretical importance by making this assumption, while simplifying the derivations considerably.

With fixed regressors, we have

$$\Omega_r = \left(\frac{X'X}{N}\right)^{-1} \left(\frac{X'\Psi X}{N}\right) \left(\frac{X'X}{N}\right)^{-1}, \qquad (8.1.2)$$

where

$$\Psi = E[ee'] = diag(\psi_i)$$

is the covariance matrix of residuals. Under homoskedasticity, $\psi_i = \sigma^2$ for all $i$ and we get

$$\Omega_c = \sigma^2 \left(\frac{X'X}{N}\right)^{-1}.$$

Asymptotic standard errors are given by the square root of the diagonal elements of $\Omega_r$ and $\Omega_c$, after removing the asymptotic normalization by dividing by $N$.

In practice, the pieces of the asymptotic covariance matrix are estimated using sample moments. An old-fashioned or conventional covariance matrix estimator is

$$\hat{\Omega}_c = (X'X)^{-1}\hat{\sigma}^2 = (X'X)^{-1}\left(\sum \frac{\hat{e}_i^2}{N}\right),$$

where $\hat{e}_i = Y_i - X_i'\hat{\beta}$ is the estimated regression residual and

$$\hat{\sigma}^2 = \sum \frac{\hat{e}_i^2}{N}$$

estimates the residual variance. The corresponding robust covariance matrix estimator is

$$\hat{\Omega}_r = N(X'X)^{-1}\left(\sum \frac{X_i X_i' \hat{e}_i^2}{N}\right)(X'X)^{-1}. \qquad (8.1.3)$$

We can think of the middle term as an estimator of the form $\sum \frac{X_i X_i' \hat{\psi}_i}{N}$, where $\hat{\psi}_i = \hat{e}_i^2$ estimates $\psi_i$.

By the law of large numbers and Slutsky's theorem, $N\hat{\Omega}_c$ converges in probability to $\Omega_c$, while $N\hat{\Omega}_r$ converges to $\Omega_r$. But in finite samples, both variance estimators are biased. The bias in $\hat{\Omega}_c$ is well-known from classical least squares theory and easy to correct. Less appreciated is the fact that if the residuals are homoskedastic, the robust estimator is more biased than the conventional estimator, perhaps a lot more. From this we conclude that robust standard errors can be more misleading than conventional standard errors in situations where heteroskedasticity is modest. We also propose a rule of thumb that uses the maximum of old-fashioned and robust standard errors to avoid gross misjudgments of precision.

Our analysis begins with the bias of $\hat{\Omega}_c$. With nonstochastic regressors, we have

$$E[\hat{\Omega}_c] = (X'X)^{-1}\hat{\sigma}^2 = (X'X)^{-1}\left(\sum \frac{E(\hat{e}_i^2)}{N}\right).$$

To analyze $E[\hat{e}_i^2]$, start by expanding $\hat{e} = y - X\hat{\beta}$:

$$\hat{e} = y - X(X'X)^{-1}X'y = [I_N - X(X'X)^{-1}X'](X\beta + e) = Me,$$

where $e$ is the vector of population residuals, $M = I_N - X(X'X)^{-1}X'$ is a nonstochastic residual-maker matrix with

$i$th row $m_i'$, and $I_N$ is the $N \times N$ identity matrix. Then $\hat{e}_i = m_i'e$, and

$$E(\hat{e}_i^2) = E(m_i'ee'm_i)$$
$$= m_i'\Psi m_i.$$

To simplify further, write $m_i = \ell_i - h_i$, where $\ell_i$ is the $i$th column of $I_N$ and $h_i = X(X'X)^{-1}X_i$, the $i$th column of the projection matrix $H = X(X'X)^{-1}X'$. Then

$$E(\hat{e}_i^2) = (\ell_i - h_i)'\Psi(\ell_i - h_i)$$
$$= \psi_i - 2\psi_i h_{ii} + h_i'\Psi h_i, \qquad (8.1.4)$$

where $h_{ii}$, the $i$th diagonal element of $H$, satisfies

$$h_{ii} = h_i'h_i = X_i'(X'X)^{-1}X_i. \qquad (8.1.5)$$

Parenthetically, $h_{ii}$ is called the *leverage* of the $i$th observation. Leverage tells us how much pull a particular value of $X_i$ exerts on the regression line. Note that the $i$th fitted value ($i$th element of $Hy$) is

$$\hat{Y}_i = h_i'y = h_{ii}Y_i + \sum_{j \neq i} h_{ij}Y_j. \qquad (8.1.6)$$

A large $h_{ii}$ means that the $i$th observation has a large impact on the $i$th predicted value. In a bivariate regression with a single regressor, $x_i$,

$$h_{ii} = \frac{1}{N} + \frac{(x_i - \overline{x})^2}{\sum(x_j - \overline{x})^2}. \qquad (8.1.7)$$

This shows that leverage increases when $x_i$ is far the mean. In addition to (8.1.6), we know that $h_{ii}$ is a number that lies in the interval $[0, 1]$ and that $\sum_{i=1}^{N} h_{ii} = \kappa$, the number of regressors (see, e.g., Hoaglin and Welsch, 1978).[1]

---

[1] The property $\sum_{i=1}^{N} h_{ii} = \kappa$ comes from the fact that $H$ is idempotent, and so has trace equal to rank. We can also use (8.1.7) to verify that in a bivariate regression, $\sum_{i=1}^{N} h_{ii} = 2$.

Suppose residuals are homoskedastic, so that $\psi_i = \sigma^2$. Then (8.1.4) simplifies to

$$E(\hat{e}_i^2) = \sigma^2[1 - 2h_{ii} + h_i'h_i] = \sigma^2(1 - h_{ii}) < \sigma^2.$$

So $\hat{\Omega}_c$ tends to be too small. Using the properties of $h_{ii}$, we can go one step further:

$$\sum \frac{E(\hat{e}_i^2)}{N} = \sigma^2 \sum \frac{1 - h_{ii}}{N} = \sigma^2 \left( \frac{N - \kappa}{N} \right).$$

Thus, the bias in $\hat{\Omega}_c$ can be fixed by a simple degrees-of-freedom correction: divide by $N - \kappa$ instead of $N$ in the formula for $\hat{\sigma}^2$. This correction is used by default in most regression software.

We now want to show that under homoskedasticity, the bias in $\hat{\Omega}_r$ is likely to be worse than the bias in $\hat{\Omega}_c$. The expected value of the robust covariance matrix estimator is

$$E[\hat{\Omega}_r] = N(X'X)^{-1} \left( \sum \frac{X_i X_i' E(\hat{e}_i^2)}{N} \right) (X'X)^{-1}, \quad (8.1.8)$$

where $E(\hat{e}_i^2)$ is given by (8.1.4). Under homoskedasticity, $\psi_i = \sigma^2$ and we have $E(\hat{e}_i^2) = \sigma^2(1 - h_{ii})$ as in $\hat{\Omega}_c$. It's clear, therefore, that the bias in $\hat{e}_i^2$ tends to pull robust standard errors down. The general expression, (8.1.8), is hard to evaluate, however. Chesher and Jewitt (1987) show that as long as there is not "too much" heteroskedasticity, robust standard errors based on $\hat{\Omega}_r$ are indeed biased downward.[2]

How do we know that $\hat{\Omega}_r$ is likely to be *more* biased than $\hat{\Omega}_c$? Partly this comes from Monte Carlo evidence (e.g., MacKinnon and White, 1985, and our own small study, discussed below). We also prove this here for a bivariate example, where the single regressor, $\tilde{x}_i$, is assumed to be in deviations-from-means form, so there is a single coefficient. In this case, the estimator of interest is $\hat{\beta}_1 = \frac{\sum \tilde{x}_i y_i}{\sum \tilde{x}_i^2}$ and the leverage is

---

[2]In particular, as long as the ratio of the largest $\psi_i$ to the smallest $\psi_i$ is less than 2, robust standard errors are biased downward.

$h_{ii} = \frac{\tilde{x}_i^2}{\sum \tilde{x}_i^2}$ (we lose the $\frac{1}{N}$ term in (8.1.7) by partialing out the constant). Let $s_x^2 = \frac{\sum \tilde{x}_i^2}{N}$. For the conventional covariance estimator, we have

$$E[\hat{\Omega}_c] = \frac{\sigma^2}{N s_x^2} \left[ \frac{\sum (1 - h_{ii})}{N} \right] = \frac{\sigma^2}{N s_x^2} \left[ 1 - \frac{1}{N} \right],$$

so the bias here is small. A simple calculation using (8.1.8) shows that under homoskedasticity, the robust estimator has expectation:

$$E[\hat{\Omega}_r] = \frac{\sigma^2}{N s_x^2} \sum \frac{(1 - h_{ii})}{N} \left( \frac{\tilde{x}_i^2}{s_x^2} \right)$$

$$= \frac{\sigma^2}{N s_x^2} \sum (1 - h_{ii}) h_{ii} = \frac{\sigma^2}{N s_x^2} \left[ 1 - \sum h_{ii}^2 \right].$$

The bias of $\hat{\Omega}_r$ is therefore worse than the bias of $\hat{\Omega}_c$ if $\sum h_{ii}^2 > \frac{1}{N}$, as it is by Jensen's inequality unless the regressor has constant leverage, in which case $h_{ii} = \frac{1}{N}$ for all $i$.[3]

We can reduce the bias in $\hat{\Omega}_r$ by trying to get a better estimator of $\psi_i$, say $\hat{\psi}_i$. The estimator $\hat{\Omega}_r$ sets $\hat{\psi}_i = \hat{e}_i^2$, as proposed by White (1980a) and our starting point in this section. The residual variance estimators discussed in MacKinnon and White (1985) include this and three others:

$$HC_0 : \hat{\psi}_i = \hat{e}_i^2$$

$$HC_1 : \hat{\psi}_i = \frac{N}{N - \kappa} \hat{e}_i^2$$

---

[3]Think of $h_{ii}$ as a random variable with a uniform distribution in the sample. Then

$$E[h_{ii}] = \frac{\sum h_{ii}}{N} = \frac{1}{N},$$

and

$$E[h_{ii}^2] = \frac{\sum h_{ii}^2}{N} > (E[h_{ii}])^2 = \left( \frac{1}{N} \right)^2$$

by Jensen's inequality unless $h_{ii}$ is constant. Therefore $\sum h_{ii}^2 > \frac{1}{N}$. The constant leverage case occurs when $(\tilde{x}_i)^2$ is constant.

$$HC_2 : \hat{\psi}_i = \frac{1}{1 - h_{ii}}\hat{e}_i^2$$

$$HC_3 : \hat{\psi}_i = \frac{1}{(1 - h_{ii})^2}\hat{e}_i^2.$$

$HC_1$ is a simple degrees of freedom correction as is used for $\hat{\Omega}_c$. $HC_2$ uses the leverage to give an unbiased estimate of the variance of the $i$th residual when the residuals are homoskedastic, while $HC_3$ approximates a jackknife estimator.[4] In the applications we've seen, the estimated standard errors tend to get larger as we go down the list from $HC_0$ to $HC_3$, but this is not a theorem.

## Time-Out for the Bootstrap

Bootstrapping is a resampling scheme that offers an alternative to inference based on asymptotic formulas. A bootstrap sample is a sample drawn from our own data. In other words, if we have a sample of size $N$, we treat this sample as if it were the population and draw repeatedly from it (with replacement). The bootstrap sampling distribution is the distribution of an estimator across many draws of this sort. Intuitively, we expect the sampling distribution constructed by sampling from our own data to provide a good approximation to the sampling distribution we are after.

There are many ways to bootstrap regression estimates. The simplest is to draw pairs of $\{Y_i, X_i\}$ values, sometimes called the "pairs bootstrap" or a "nonparametric bootstrap." Alternatively, we can keep the $X_i$ values fixed, draw from the distribution of residuals ($\hat{e}_i$), and create a new estimate of the dependent variable based on the predicted value and the residual draw for each observation. This procedure, which is a type of parametric bootstrap, mimics a sample drawn with non-stochastic regressors and ensures that $X_i$ and the regression

---

[4]A jackknife variance estimator estimates sampling variance from the empirical distribution generated by omitting one observation at a time. Stata computes $HC_1$, $HC_2$, and $HC_3$. You can also use a trick suggested by Messer and White (1984): divide $Y_i$ and $X_i$ by $\sqrt{\hat{\psi}_i}$ and instrument the transformed model by $X_i/\sqrt{\hat{\psi}_i}$ for your preferred choice of $\hat{\psi}_i$.

residuals are independent. On the other hand, we don't want independence if we're interested in standard errors under heteroskedasticity. An alternative residual bootstrap, called the wild bootstrap, draws $X_i'\hat{\beta} + \hat{e}_i$ (which, of course, is just the original $Y_i$) with probability 0.5, and $X_i'\hat{\beta} - \hat{e}_i$ otherwise (see, e.g., Mammen, 1993, and Horowitz, 1997). This preserves the relationship between residual variances and $X_i$ observed in the original sample, while imposing mean-independence of residuals and regressors, a restriction that improves bootstrap inference when true.

Bootstrapping is useful as a computer-intensive but otherwise straightforward calculator for asymptotic standard errors. The bootstrap calculator is especially useful when the asymptotic distribution of an estimator is hard to compute or involves a number of steps (e.g., the asymptotic distributions of the quantile regression and quantile treatment effects estimates discussed in chapter 7 require the estimation of densities). Typically, however, we have no problem deriving or evaluating asymptotic formulas for the standard errors of OLS estimates.

More relevant in this context is the use of the bootstrap to improve inference. Improvements in inference potentially come in two forms: (1) a reduction in finite-sample bias in estimators that are consistent (for example, the bias in estimates of robust standard errors) and (2) inference procedures which make use of the fact that the bootstrap sampling distribution of test statistics may be closer to the finite-sample distribution of interest than the relevant asymptotic approximation. These two properties are called asymptotic refinements (see, e.g., Horowitz, 2001).

Here we are mostly interested in use of the bootstrap for asymptotic refinement. The asymptotic distribution of regression estimates is easy enough to compute, but we worry that the traditional robust covariance estimator ($HC_0$) is biased. The bootstrap can be used to estimate this bias, and then, by a simple transformation, to construct standard error estimates that are less biased. However, for now at least, bootstrap bias correction of regression standard errors is not often used in empirical practice, perhaps because the bias calculation is not automated and perhaps because bootstrap bias corrections introduce extra variability. Also, for simple estimators like regression coefficients, analytic bias corrections such as $HC_2$ and $HC_3$ are readily available (e.g., in Stata).

An asymptotic refinement can also be obtained for hypothesis tests (and confidence intervals) based on statistics that are *asymptotically pivotal*. These are statistics that have asymptotic distributions that do not depend on any unknown parameters. An example is a $t$-statistic: this is asymptotically standard normal. Regression coefficients are not asymptotically pivotal; they have an asymptotic distribution that depends on the unknown residual variance. To refine inference for regression coefficients, you calculate the $t$-statistic in each bootstrap sample and compare the analogous $t$-statistic from your original sample to this bootstrap "$t$-distribution." A hypothesis is rejected if the absolute value of the original $t$-statistic is above, say, the 95th percentile of the absolute values from the bootstrap distribution.

Theoretical appeal notwithstanding, as applied researchers, we don't like the idea of bootstrapping pivotal statics very much. This is partly because we're not only (or even primarily) interested in formal hypothesis testing: we like to see the standard errors in parentheses under our regression coefficients. These provide a summary measure of precision that can be used to construct confidence intervals, compare estimators, and test any hypothesis that strikes us, now or later. In our view, therefore, practitioners worried about the finite-sample behavior of robust standard errors should focus on bias corrections like $HC_2$ and $HC_3$. As we show below, for moderate heteroskedasticity at least, an inference strategy that uses the larger of conventional and bias-corrected standard errors often seems to give us the best of both worlds: reduced bias with a minimal loss of precision.

## An Example

For further insight into the differences between robust covariance estimators, we analyze a simple but important example that has featured in earlier chapters in this book. Suppose you are interested in an estimate of $\beta_1$ in the model

$$Y_i = \beta_0 + \beta_1 D_i + \varepsilon_i, \tag{8.1.9}$$

where $D_i$ is a dummy variable. The OLS estimate of $\beta_1$ is the difference in means between those with $D_i$ switched on and off. Denoting these subsamples by the subscripts 1 and 0, we have

$$\hat{\beta}_1 = \overline{Y}_1 - \overline{Y}_0.$$

For the purposes of this derivation we think of $D_i$ as nonrandom, so that $\sum D_i = N_1$ and $\sum (1 - D_i) = N_0$ are fixed. Let $r = N_1/N$.

We know something about the finite-sample behavior of $\hat{\beta}_1$ from statistical theory. If $Y_i$ is normal with equal but unknown variance in both the $D_i = 1$ and $D_i = 0$ populations, then the conventional $t$-statistic for $\hat{\beta}_1$ has a $t$-distribution. This is the classic two-sample $t$-test. Heteroskedasticity in this context means that the variances in the $D_i = 1$ and $D_i = 0$ populations are different. In this case, the testing problem in small samples becomes surprisingly difficult: the exact small-sample distribution for even this simple problem is unknown.[5] The robust variance estimators $HC_0$–$HC_3$ give asymptotic approximations to the unknown finite-sample distribution for the case of unequal variances.

The differences between $HC_0$, $HC_1$, $HC_2$, and $HC_3$ are differences in how the sample variances in the two groups defined by $D_i$ are processed. Define $S_j^2 = \sum_{D_i = j} ( Y_i - \overline{Y}_j)^2$ for $j = 0, 1$. The leverage in this example is

$$h_{ii} = \begin{cases} \frac{1}{N_0} & \text{if } D_i = 0 \\ \frac{1}{N_1} & \text{if } D_i = 1 \end{cases}.$$

Using this, it's straightforward to show that the five variance estimators we've been discussing are

$$Conventional: \quad \frac{N}{N_0 N_1}\left(\frac{S_0^2 + S_1^2}{N-2}\right) = \frac{1}{Nr(1-r)}\left(\frac{S_0^2 + S_1^2}{N-2}\right)$$

[5] This is called the Behrens-Fisher problem (see, e.g., DeGroot and Schervish, 2001, chap. 8).

$$HC_0: \frac{S_0^2}{N_0^2} + \frac{S_1^2}{N_1^2}$$

$$HC_1: \frac{N}{N-2}\left(\frac{S_0^2}{N_0^2} + \frac{S_1^2}{N_1^2}\right)$$

$$HC_2: \frac{S_0^2}{N_0(N_0-1)} + \frac{S_1^2}{N_1(N_1-1)}$$

$$HC_3: \frac{S_0^2}{(N_0-1)^2} + \frac{S_1^2}{(N_1-1)^2}.$$

The conventional estimator pools subsamples: this is efficient when the two variances are the same. The White (1980a) estimator, $HC_0$, adds separate estimates of the sampling variances of the means, using the consistent (but biased) variance estimators, $\frac{S_j^2}{N_j}$. The $HC_2$ estimator uses unbiased estimators of the sample variance for each group, since it makes the correct degrees-of-freedom correction. $HC_1$ makes a degrees-of-freedom correction outside the sum, which will help but is generally not quite correct. Since we know $HC_2$ to be the unbiased estimate of the sampling variance under homoskedasticity, $HC_3$ must be too big.[6] Note that with $r = 0.5$, a case where the regression design is said to be balanced, the conventional estimator equals $HC_1$ and all five estimators differ little.

A small Monte Carlo study based on (8.1.9) illustrates the pluses and minuses of alternative estimators and the extent to which a simple rule of thumb goes a long way toward ameliorating the bias of the $HC$ class. We choose $N = 30$ to highlight small sample issues, and $r = 0.10$ (10 percent treated), which implies $h_{ii} = \frac{1}{3}$ if $D_i = 1$ and $h_{ii} = \frac{1}{27}$ if $D_i = 0$. This is a highly unbalanced design. We draw residuals from the distributions:

$$\varepsilon_i \sim \begin{cases} N(0, \sigma^2) & \text{if } D_i = 0 \\ N(0, 1) & \text{if } D_i = 1 \end{cases}$$

and report results for three cases. The first has lots of heteroskedasticity, with $\sigma = 0.5$, while the second has relatively

---

[6]In this simple example, $HC_2$ is unbiased whether or not residuals are homoskedastic.

little heteroskedasticity, with $\sigma = 0.85$. No heteroskedasticity is the benchmark case.

Table 8.1.1 displays the results. Columns 1 and 2 report means and standard deviations of the various standard error estimates across 25,000 replications of the sampling experiment. The standard deviation of $\hat{\beta}_1$ is the sampling variance we are trying to measure. With lots of heteroskedasticity, as in the upper panel of the table, conventional standard errors are badly biased and, on average, only about half the size of the Monte Carlo sampling variance that constitutes our target. On the other hand, while the robust standard errors perform better, except for $HC_3$, they are still too small.[7]

The standard errors are themselves estimates and have considerable sampling variability. Especially noteworthy is the fact that the robust standard errors have much higher sampling variability than the conventional standard errors, as can be seen in column 2.[8] The sampling variability of estimated standard errors further increases when we attempt to reduce bias by dividing the residuals by $1 - h_{ii}$ ($HC_2$) or $(1 - h_{ii})^2$ ($HC_3$). The worst case is $HC_3$, with a standard deviation about 50 percent above the standard deviation of the White (1980a) standard error, $HC_0$.

The last two columns in the table show empirical rejection rates in a nominal 5 percent test for the hypothesis $\beta_1 = 0$, the population parameter in this case. The test statistics are compared with a normal distribution and to a $t$-distribution with $N - 2$ degrees of freedom. Rejection rates are far too high for all tests, even with $HC_3$. Using a $t$-distribution rather than a normal distribution helps only marginally.

---

[7]Although $HC_2$ is an unbiased estimator of the sampling variance, the mean of the $HC_2$ standard errors across sampling experiments (0.52) is still below the standard deviation of $\hat{\beta}_1$ (0.59). This comes from the fact that the standard error is the square root of the sampling variance, the sampling variance is itself estimated and hence has sampling variability, and the square root is a concave function.

[8]The large sampling variance of robust standard error estimators is noted by Chesher and Austin (1991). Kauermann and Carroll (2001) propose an adjustment to confidence intervals to correct for this.

TABLE 8.1.1
Monte Carlo results for robust standard error estimates

| Parameter Estimate | Mean (1) | Standard Deviation (2) | Empirical 5% Rejection Rates | |
|---|---|---|---|---|
| | | | Normal (3) | $t$ (4) |
| **A. Lots of heteroskedasticity** | | | | |
| $\hat{\beta}_1$ | −.001 | .586 | | |
| *Standard Errors* | | | | |
| Conventional | .331 | .052 | .278 | .257 |
| $HC_0$ | .417 | .203 | .247 | .231 |
| $HC_1$ | .447 | .218 | .223 | .208 |
| $HC_2$ | .523 | .260 | .177 | .164 |
| $HC_3$ | .636 | .321 | .130 | .120 |
| max($HC_0$, Conventional) | .448 | .172 | .188 | .171 |
| max($HC_1$, Conventional) | .473 | .190 | .173 | .157 |
| max($HC_2$, Conventional) | .542 | .238 | .141 | .128 |
| max($HC_3$, Conventional) | .649 | .305 | .107 | .097 |
| **B. Little heteroskedasticity** | | | | |
| $\hat{\beta}_1$ | .004 | .600 | | |
| *Standard Errors* | | | | |
| Conventional | .520 | .070 | .098 | .084 |
| $HC_0$ | .441 | .193 | .217 | .202 |
| $HC_1$ | .473 | .207 | .194 | .179 |
| $HC_2$ | .546 | .250 | .156 | .143 |
| $HC_3$ | .657 | .312 | .114 | .104 |
| max($HC_0$, Conventional) | .562 | .121 | .083 | .070 |
| max($HC_1$, Conventional) | .578 | .138 | .078 | .067 |
| max($HC_2$, Conventional) | .627 | .186 | .067 | .057 |
| max($HC_3$, Conventional) | .713 | .259 | .053 | .045 |
| **C. No heteroskedasticity** | | | | |
| $\hat{\beta}_1$ | −.003 | .611 | | |
| *Standard Errors* | | | | |
| Conventional | .604 | .081 | .061 | .050 |
| $HC_0$ | .453 | .190 | .209 | .193 |
| $HC_1$ | .486 | .203 | .185 | .171 |
| $HC_2$ | .557 | .247 | .150 | .136 |
| $HC_3$ | .667 | .309 | .110 | .100 |
| max($HC_0$, Conventional) | .629 | .109 | .055 | .045 |
| max($HC_1$, Conventional) | .640 | .122 | .053 | .044 |
| max($HC_2$, Conventional) | .679 | .166 | .047 | .039 |
| max($HC_3$, Conventional) | .754 | .237 | .039 | .031 |

*Notes*: The table reports results from a sampling experiment with 25,000 replications. Columns 1 and 2 shows the mean and standard deviation of estimated *standard errors*, except for the first row in each panel which shows the mean and standard deviation of $\hat{\beta}_1$. The model is as described by (8.1.9), with $\beta_1 = 0$, $r = .1$, $N = 30$, and heteroskedasticity as indicated in the panel headings.

The results with little heteroskedasticity, reported in the second panel, show that conventional standard errors are still too low; this bias is now on the order of 15 precent. $HC_0$ and $HC_1$ are also too small, about as before in absolute terms, though they now look worse relative to the conventional standard errors. The $HC_2$ and $HC_3$ standard errors are still larger than the conventional standard errors, on average, but empirical rejection rates are higher for these two than for conventional standard errors. This means the robust standard errors are sometimes too small "by accident," an event that happens often enough to inflate rejection rates so that they exceed the conventional rejection rates.

One lesson we can take away from this is that robust standard errors are no panacea. They can be smaller than conventional standard errors for two reasons: the small sample bias we have discussed and their higher sampling variance. We therefore take empirical results where the robust standard errors fall below the conventional standard errors as a red flag. This is very likely due to bias or a chance occurrence that is better discounted. In this spirit, the maximum of the conventional standard error and a robust standard error may be the best measure of precision. This rule of thumb helps on two counts: it truncates low values of the robust estimators, reducing bias, and it reduces variability. Table 8.1.1 shows the empirical rejection rates obtained using $\max(HC_j, Conventional)$. Rejection rates using this rule of thumb look pretty good in panel B and are considerably better than the rates using robust estimators alone, even with lots of heteroskedasticity, as shown in panel A.[9]

Since there is no gain without pain, there must be some cost to using $\max(HC_j, Conventional)$. The cost is that the best standard error when there is no heteroskedasticity is the conventional estimate. This is documented in the bottom panel of the table. Use of the maximum inflates standard errors unnecessarily under homoskedasticity, depressing rejection rates. Nevertheless, the table shows that even in this case, rejection

---

[9]Yang, Hsu, and Zhao (2005) formalize the notion of test procedures based on the maximum of a set of test statistics with differing efficiency and robustness properties.

rates don't go down all that much. We also view an underestimate of precision as being less costly than an overestimate. Underestimating precision, we come away thinking the data are not very informative and that we should try to collect more or improve the research design, while in the latter case we may mistakenly draw important substantive conclusions.

A final comment on this Monte Carlo investigation concerns the small sample size. Labor economists like us are used to working with tens of thousands of observations or more. But sometimes we don't. In a study of the effects of busing on public school students, Angrist and Lang (2004) worked with samples of about 3,000 students grouped in 56 schools. The regressor of interest in this study varied within grade only at the school level, so some of the analysis uses 56 school means. Not surprisingly, therefore, Angrist and Lang (2004) obtained $HC_1$ standard errors below conventional OLS standard errors when working with school-level data. As a rule, even if you start with the microdata on individuals, when the regressor of interest varies at a higher level of aggregation—a school, state, or some other group or cluster—effective sample sizes are much closer to the number of clusters than to the number of individuals. Inference procedures for clustered data are discussed in detail in the next section.

## 8.2    Clustering and Serial Correlation in Panels

### 8.2.1    Clustering and the Moulton Factor

Heteroskedasticity rarely leads to dramatic changes in inference. In large samples where bias is not likely to be a problem, we might see standard errors increase by about 25 percent when moving from the conventional to the $HC_1$ estimator. In contrast, clustering can make all the difference.

The clustering problem can be illustrated using a simple bivariate model estimated in data with a group structure. Suppose we're interested in the bivariate regression,

$$Y_{ig} = \beta_0 + \beta_1 x_g + e_{ig}, \qquad (8.2.1)$$

where $Y_{ig}$ is the dependent variable for individual $i$ in cluster or group $g$, with $G$ groups. Importantly, the regressor of interest, $x_g$, varies only at the group level. For example, data from the STAR experiment analyzed by Krueger (1999) come in the form of $Y_{ig}$, the test score of student $i$ in class $g$, and class size, $x_g$.

Although students were randomly assigned to classes in the STAR experiment, the STAR data are unlikely to be independent across observations. The test scores of students in the same class tend to be correlated because students in the same class share background characteristics and are exposed to the same teacher and classroom environment. It's therefore prudent to assume that, for students $i$ and $j$ in the same class, $g$,

$$E[e_{ig}e_{jg}] = \rho_e \sigma_e^2 > 0, \qquad (8.2.2)$$

where $\rho_e$ is the residual intraclass correlation coefficient and $\sigma_e^2$ is the residual variance.

Correlation within groups is often modeled using an additive random effects model. Specifically, we assume that the residual, $e_{ig}$, has a group structure,

$$e_{ig} = v_g + \eta_{ig}, \qquad (8.2.3)$$

where $v_g$ is a random component specific to class $g$ and $\eta_{ig}$ is a mean-zero student-level error component that's left over. We focus here on the correlation problem, so both of these error components are assumed to be homoskedastic. The group-level error component is assumed to capture all within-group correlation, so the $\eta_{ig}$ are uncorrelated.[10]

When the regressor of interest varies only at the group level, an error structure like (8.2.3) can increase standard errors sharply. This unfortunate fact is not news—Kloek (1981) and

---

[10]This sort of residual correlation structure is also a consequence of stratified sampling (see, e.g., Wooldridge, 2003). Most of the samples that we work with are close enough to random that we typically worry more about the dependence due to a group structure than clustering due to stratification. Note that there is no GLS estimator for equation 8.2.1 with error structure 8.2.3 because the regressor is fixed within groups. In any case, here as elsewhere we prefer a "fix-the-standard-errors" approach to GLS.

Moulton (1986) both made the point—but it seems fair to say that clustering didn't really become part of the applied econometrics zeitgeist until about 15 years ago.

Given the error structure, (8.2.3), the intraclass correlation coefficient becomes

$$\rho_e = \frac{\sigma_v^2}{\sigma_v^2 + \sigma_\eta^2},$$

where $\sigma_v^2$ is the variance of $v_g$ and $\sigma_\eta^2$ is the variance of $\eta_{ig}$. A word on terminology: $\rho_e$ is called the *intraclass correlation coefficient* even when the groups of interest are not classrooms.

Let $V_c(\hat{\beta}_1)$ be the conventional OLS variance formula for the regression slope (a diagonal element of $\Omega_c$ in the previous section), while $V(\hat{\beta}_1)$ denotes the correct sampling variance given the error structure, (8.2.3). With nonstochastic regressors fixed at the group level and groups of equal size, $n$, we have

$$\frac{V(\hat{\beta}_1)}{V_c(\hat{\beta}_1)} = 1 + (n-1)\rho_e, \qquad (8.2.4)$$

a formula derived in the appendix to this chapter. We call the square root of this ratio the Moulton factor, after Moulton's (1986) influential study. Equation (8.2.4) tells us how much we overestimate precision by ignoring intraclass correlation. Conventional standard errors become increasingly misleading as $n$ and $\rho_e$ increase. Suppose, for example, that $\rho_e = 1$. In this case, all the errors within a group are the same, so the $Y_{ig}$ values are the same as well. Making a data set larger by copying a smaller one $n$ times generates no new information. The variance $V_c(\hat{\beta}_1)$ should therefore be scaled up from $V_c(\hat{\beta}_1)$ by a factor of $n$. The Moulton factor increases with group size because with a fixed overall sample size, larger groups mean fewer clusters, in which case there is less independent information in the sample (because the data are independent across clusters but not within).[11]

---

[11] With nonstochastic regressors and homoscedastic residuals, the Moulton factor is a finite-sample result. Survey statisticians call the Moulton factor the

Even small intraclass correlation coefficients can generate a big Moulton factor. In Angrist and Lavy (2008), for example, 4,000 students are grouped in 40 schools, so the average $n$ is 100. The regressor of interest is school-level treatment status: all students in treated schools were eligible to receive cash awards for passing their matriculation exams. The intraclass correlation in this study fluctuates around .1. Applying formula (8.2.4), the Moulton factor is over 3, so the standard errors reported by default are only one-third what they should be.

Equation (8.2.4) covers an important special case where the regressors are fixed within groups and group size is constant. The general formula allows the regressor, $x_{ig}$, to vary at the individual level and for different group sizes, $n_g$. In this case, the Moulton factor is the square root of

$$\frac{V(\hat{\beta}_1)}{V_c(\hat{\beta}_1)} = 1 + \left[\frac{V(n_g)}{\bar{n}} + \bar{n} - 1\right]\rho_x\rho_e, \qquad (8.2.5)$$

where $\bar{n}$ is the average group size, and $\rho_x$ is the intraclass correlation of $x_{ig}$:

$$\rho_x = \frac{\displaystyle\sum_g \sum_j \sum_{i \neq j} (x_{ig} - \bar{x})(x_{jg} - \bar{x})}{V(x_{ig}) \displaystyle\sum_g n_g(n_g - 1)}.$$

Note that $\rho_x$ does not impose a variance components structure like (8.2.3); here, $\rho_x$ is a generic measure of the correlation of regressors within groups. The general Moulton formula tells us that clustering has a bigger impact on standard errors with variable group sizes and when $\rho_x$ is large. The impact vanishes when $\rho_x = 0$. In other words, if the $x_{ig}$ values are uncorrelated within groups, the grouped error structure does not matter for standard errors. That's why we worry most about clustering when the regressor of interest is fixed within groups.

---

*design effect* because it tells us how much to adjust standard errors in stratified samples for deviations from simple random sampling (Kish, 1965).

We illustrate formula (8.2.5) using the Tennessee STAR example. A regression of kindergartners' percentile score on class size yields an estimate of $-.62$ with a robust $(HC_1)$ standard error of .09. In this case, $\rho_x = 1$ because class size is fixed within classes, while $V(n_g)$ is positive because classes vary in size (in this case, $V(n_g) = 17.1$). The intraclass correlation coefficient for residuals is .31 and the average class size is 19.4. Plugging these numbers into (8.2.5) gives a value of about 7 for $\frac{V(\hat{\beta}_1)}{V_c(\hat{\beta}_1)}$, so that conventional standard errors should be multiplied by a factor of $2.65 = \sqrt{7}$. The corrected standard error is therefore about 0.24.

The Moulton factor works similarly with 2SLS estimates. In particular, we can use (8.2.5), replacing $\rho_x$ with $\rho_{\hat{x}}$, where $\rho_{\hat{x}}$ is the intraclass correlation coefficient of the first-stage fitted values and $\rho_e$ is the intraclass correlation of the second-stage residuals (Shore-Sheppard, 1996). To understand why this works, recall that conventional standard errors for 2SLS are derived from the residual variance of the second-stage equation divided by the variance of the first-stage fitted values. This is the same asymptotic variance formula as for OLS, with first-stage fitted values playing the role of the regressor.

To conclude, we list and compare solutions to the Moulton problem, starting with the parametric approach described above.

1. Parametric: Fix conventional standard errors using (8.2.5). The intraclass correlations $\rho_e$ and $\rho_x$ are easy to compute and supplied as descriptive statistics in some software packages.[12]

2. Cluster standard errors: Liang and Zeger (1986) generalize the White (1980a) robust covariance matrix to allow for clustering as well as heteroskedasticity. The clustered covariance matrix is

$$\hat{\Omega}_{cl} = \left(X'X\right)^{-1} \left(\sum_g X_g \hat{\Psi}_g X_g\right) \left(X'X\right)^{-1}, \text{ where}$$

$$(8.2.6)$$

---

[12]Use Stata's loneway command, for example.

$$\hat{\Psi}_g = a\hat{e}_g\hat{e}'_g$$

$$= a\begin{bmatrix} \hat{e}_{1g}^2 & \hat{e}_{1g}\hat{e}_{2g} & \cdots & & \hat{e}_{1g}\hat{e}_{n_gg} \\ \hat{e}_{1g}\hat{e}_{2g} & \hat{e}_{2g}^2 & \cdots & & \vdots \\ \vdots & \vdots & & & \hat{e}_{n_g-1,g}\hat{e}_{n_gg} \\ \hat{e}_{1g}\hat{e}_{n_gg} & \cdots & & \hat{e}_{n_g-1,g}\hat{e}_{n_gg} & \hat{e}_{n_gg}^2 \end{bmatrix}.$$

Here, $X_g$ is the matrix of regressors for group $g$ and $a$ is a degrees of freedom adjustment factor similar to that which appears in $HC_1$. The clustered estimator is consistent as the number of groups gets large given any within-group correlation structure and not just the parametric model in (8.2.3). $\hat{\Omega}_{cl}$ is not consistent with a fixed number of groups, however, even when the group size tends to infinity. Consistency is determined by the law of large numbers, which says that we can rely on sample moments to converge to population moments (section 3.1.3). But here the sums are at the group level and not over individuals. Clustered standard errors are therefore unlikely to be reliable with few clusters, a point we return to below.

3. Use group averages instead of microdata: let $\bar{Y}_g$ be the mean of $Y_{ig}$ in group $g$. Estimate

$$\bar{Y}_g = \beta_0 + \beta_1 x_g + \bar{e}_g$$

by WLS using the group size as weights. This is equivalent to OLS using micro data but the grouped-equation standard errors reflect the group structure, (8.2.3).[13] Again, the asymptotics here are based on the number of groups and not the group size. Importantly, however, because the group means are close to normally distributed with modest group sizes, we can expect the good finite-sample properties of regression with normal errors to kick in. The standard errors that come out of grouped estimation are therefore likely to be more reliable than clustered standard errors in samples with few clusters.

[13]The grouped residuals are heteroskedastic unless group sizes are equal but this is less important than the fact that the error has a group structure in the microdata.

Grouped-data estimation can be generalized to models with microcovariates using a two-step procedure. Suppose the equation of interest is

$$Y_{ig} = \beta_0 + \beta_1 x_g + \beta_2 w_{ig} + e_{ig}, \qquad (8.2.7)$$

where $w_{ig}$ is a covariate that varies within groups. In step 1, construct the covariate-adjusted group effects, $\mu_g$, by estimating

$$Y_{ig} = \mu_g + \beta_2 w_{ig} + \eta_{ig}.$$

The $\mu_g$, called group effects, are coefficients on a full set of group dummies. The estimated $\hat{\mu}_g$ are group means adjusted for differences in the individual level variable, $w_{ig}$. Note that, by virtue of (8.2.7) and (8.2.3), $\mu_g = \beta_0 + \beta_1 x_g + v_g$. In step 2, therefore, we regress the estimated group effects on group-level variables:

$$\hat{\mu}_g = \beta_0 + \beta_1 x_g + \{v_g + (\hat{\mu}_g - \mu_g)\}. \qquad (8.2.8)$$

The efficient GLS estimator for (8.2.8) is WLS, using the reciprocal of the estimated variance of the group-level residual, $\{v_g + (\hat{\mu}_g - \mu_g)\}$, as weights. This can be a problem, since the variance of $v_g$ is not estimated very well with few groups. We might therefore weight by the reciprocal of the variance of the estimated group effects, the group size, or use no weights at all.[14] In an effort to better approximate the relevant finite-sample distribution, Donald and Lang (2007) suggest that inference for grouped equations like (8.2.8) be based on a $t$-distribution with $G - K$ degrees of freedom.

Note that the grouping approach does not work when $x_{ig}$ varies within groups. Averaging $x_{ig}$ to $\bar{x}_g$ is a version of IV, as we saw in chapter 4. So with micro-variation in the regressor of interest, grouped estimation identifies parameters that differ from the target parameters in a model like (8.2.7).

---

[14]See Angrist and Lavy (2008) for an example of the latter two weighting schemes.

4. Block bootstrap: In general, bootstrap inference uses the empirical distribution of the data by resampling. But simple random resampling won't do in this case. The trick with clustered data is to preserve the dependence structure in the target population. We can do this by block bootstrapping, that is, drawing blocks of data defined by the groups $g$. In the Tennessee STAR data, for example, we'd block bootstrap by resampling entire classes instead of individual students.

5. In some cases, you may be able to estimate a GLS or maximum likelihood model based on a version of (8.2.1) combined with a model for the error structure like (8.2.3). This fixes the clustering problem but also changes the estimand unless the CEF is linear, as detailed in section 3.4.1 for LDV models. We therefore prefer other approaches.

Table 8.2.1 compares standard-error fixups in the STAR example. The table reports six estimates: conventional robust standard errors (using $HC_1$); two versions of corrected standard errors using the Moulton formula (8.2.5), the first using the formula for the intraclass correlation given by Moulton and the second using Stata's estimator from the loneway command; clustered standard errors; block-bootstrapped standard errors; and standard errors from weighted estimation at the group level. The coefficient estimate is $-.62$. In this case, all cluster adjustments deliver similar results, a standard error of about $.23$. This happy outcome is due in large part to the fact that with 318 classrooms, we have enough clusters for group-level asymptotics to work well. With few clusters, however, things are much dicier, a point we return to at the end of the chapter.

### 8.2.2    Serial Correlation in Panels and Difference-in-Difference Models

Serial correlation—the tendency for one observation to be correlated with those that have gone before—used to be Somebody Else's Problem, specifically, the unfortunate souls who make their living out of time series data (macroeconomists, for

TABLE 8.2.1
Standard errors for class size effects in the STAR
data (318 clusters)

| Variance Estimator | Std. Err. |
|---|---|
| Robust ($HC_1$) | .090 |
| Parametric Moulton correction (using Moulton intraclass correlation) | .222 |
| Parametric Moulton correction (using Stata intraclass correlation) | .230 |
| Clustered | .232 |
| Block bootstrap | .231 |
| Estimation using group means (weighted by class size) | .226 |

Notes: The table reports standard errors for the estimates from a regression of kindergartners' average percentile scores on class size using the public use data set from Project STAR. The coefficient on class size is −.62. The group level for clustering is the classroom. The number of observations is 5,743. The bootstrap estimate uses 1,000 replications.

example). Applied microeconometricians have therefore long ignored it.[15] But our data often have a time dimension, too, especially in DD models. This fact combined with clustering can have a major impact on statistical inference.

Suppose, as in section 5.2, that we are interested in the effects of a state minimum wage. In this context, the regression version of DD includes additive state and time effects. We therefore get an equation like (5.2.2), repeated below:

$$Y_{ist} = \gamma_s + \lambda_t + \delta D_{st} + \varepsilon_{ist}, \qquad (8.2.9)$$

[15] The Somebody Else's Problem (SEP) field, first identified as a natural phenomenon in Adams's *Life, the Universe, and Everything*, is, according to Wikipedia, "a generated energy field that affects perception. . . . Entities within the field will be perceived by an outside observer as 'Somebody Else's Problem,' and will therefore be effectively invisible unless the observer is specifically looking for the entity."

As before, $Y_{ist}$ is the outcome for individual $i$ in state $s$ in year $t$ and $D_{st}$ is a dummy variable that indicates treatment states in posttreatment periods.

The error term in (8.2.9) reflects the idiosyncratic variation in potential outcomes across people, states, and time. Some of this variation is likely to be common to individuals in the same state and year, for example, a regional business cycle. We can model this common component by thinking of $\varepsilon_{ist}$ as the sum of a state-year shock, $\upsilon_{st}$, and an idiosyncratic individual component, $\eta_{ist}$. So we have:

$$Y_{ist} = \gamma_s + \lambda_t + \delta D_{st} + \upsilon_{st} + \eta_{ist}. \qquad (8.2.10)$$

We assume that in repeated draws across states and over time, $E[\upsilon_{st}] = 0$, while $E[\eta_{ist}|s, t] = 0$ by definition.

State-year shocks are bad news for DD models. As with the Moulton problem, state- and time-specific random effects generate a clustering problem that affects statistical inference. But that might be the least of our problems in this case. To see why, suppose we have only two periods and two states, as in the Card and Krueger (1994) New Jersey-Pennsylvania study. The empirical DD estimator is

$$\hat{\delta}_{CK} = (\overline{Y}_{s=NJ,t=Nov} - \overline{Y}_{s=NJ,t=Feb}) - (\overline{Y}_{s=PA,t=Nov} - \overline{Y}_{s=PA,t=Feb}).$$

This estimator is unbiased, since $E[\upsilon_{st}] = E[\eta_{ist}] = 0$. On the other hand, assuming we think of probability limits as increasing group size while keeping the choice of states and periods fixed, state-year shocks render $\hat{\delta}_{CK}$ inconsistent:

$$plim\ \hat{\delta}_{CK}$$
$$= \delta + \{(\upsilon_{s=NJ,t=Nov} - \upsilon_{s=NJ,t=Feb}) - (\upsilon_{s=PA,t=Nov} - \upsilon_{s=PA,t=Feb})\}.$$

Averaging larger and larger samples within New Jersey and Pennsylvania in a pair of periods does nothing to eliminate the regional shocks specific to a given location and period. With only two states and years, we have no way to distinguish the differences-in-differences generated by a policy change from the difference-in-dfferences due to the fact that, say, the New Jersey economy was holding steady in 1992 while Pennsylvania was experiencing a cyclical downturn. The presence of $v_{st}$ amounts to a failure of the common trends assumption discussed in section 5.2.

The solution to the inconsistency induced by random shocks in differences in differences models is to analyze samples including multiple time periods or many states (or both). For example, Card (1992) uses 51 states to study minimum wage changes, while Card and Krueger (2000) take another look at the New Jersey-Pennsylvania experiment with a longer monthly time series of payroll data. With multiple states or periods, we can hope that the $v_{st}$ average out to zero. As in the first part of this chapter on the Moulton problem, the inference framework in this context relies on asymptotic distribution theory with many groups and not on group size (or, at least, not on group size alone). The most important inference issue then becomes the behavior of $v_{st}$. In particular, if we are prepared to assume that shocks are independent across states and over time—that is, that they are serially uncorrelated—we are back to the plain vanilla Moulton problem in section 8.2.1, in which case clustering standard errors by state × year should generate valid inferences. But in most cases, the assumption that $v_{st}$ is serially uncorrelated is hard to defend. Almost certainly, for example, regional shocks are highly serially correlated: if things are bad in Pennsylvania in one month, they are likely to be about as bad in the next.

The consequences of serial correlation for clustered panels are highlighted by Bertrand, Duflo, and Mullainathan (2004) and Kézdi (2004). Any research design with a group structure where the group means are correlated can be said to have the serial correlation problem. The upshot of recent research on serial correlation in data with a group structure is that, just as we must adjust our standard errors for the correlation within groups induced by the presence of $v_{st}$, we must further adjust for serial correlation in the $v_{st}$ themselves. There are a number of ways to do this, not all equally effective in all situations. It seems fair to say that the question of how best to approach the serial correlation problem is currently under study, and a consensus has not yet emerged.

The simplest and most widely applied approach is to pass the clustering buck one level higher. In the state-year example, we can report Liang and Zeger (1986) standard errors clustered by state instead of by state and year (e.g., using Stata `cluster`). This might seem odd at first blush, since the model controls for state effects. The state effect, $\gamma_s$, in (8.2.10) removes the state mean of $\nu_{st}$, which we denote by $\bar{\nu}_s$. Nevertheless, $\nu_{st} - \bar{\nu}_s$ is probably still serially correlated. Clustering standard errors at the state level takes account of this, since the one-level-up clustered covariance estimator allows for unrestricted residual correlation within clusters, including the time series correlation in $\nu_{st} - \bar{\nu}_s$. This is a quick and easy fix.[16] The problem here is that passing the buck up one level reduces the number of clusters. And asymptotic inference supposes we have a large number of clusters because we need many states or periods to estimate the correlation between $\nu_{st} - \bar{\nu}_s$ and $\nu_{st-1} - \bar{\nu}_s$ reasonably well. A paucity of clusters can lead to biased standard errors and misleading inferences.

### 8.2.3    Fewer than 42 Clusters

Bias from few clusters is a risk in both the Moulton and the serial correlation contexts because in both cases, inference is cluster-based. With few clusters, we tend to underestimate either the serial correlation in a random shock like $\nu_{st}$ or the intraclass correlation, $\rho_e$, in the Moulton problem. The relevant dimension for counting clusters in the Moulton problem is the number of groups, G. In a DD scenario where you'd like to cluster on state or some other cross-sectional dimension, the relevant dimension for counting clusters is the number of states or cross-sectional groups. Therefore, following Douglas Adams's dictum that the ultimate answer to life, the universe, and everything is 42, we believe the question is: How many clusters are enough for reliable inference using the standard cluster adjustment derived from (8.2.6)?

If 42 is enough for the standard cluster adjustment to be reliable, and if less is too few, then what should you do when

---

[16]Arellano (1987) appears to have been the first to suggest higher-level clustering for models with a panel structure.

the cluster count is low? First-best is to get more clusters by collecting more data. But sometimes we're too lazy for that, or the number of groups is naturally fixed, so other ideas are detailed below. It's worth noting at the outset that not all of these ideas are equally well-suited for the Moulton and serial correlation problems.

1. Bias correction of clustered standard errors: Clustered standard errors are biased in small samples because $E(\hat{e}_g\hat{e}_g') \neq E(e_ge_g') = \Psi_g$, just as with the residual covariance matrix in section 8.1. Usually, $E(\hat{e}_g\hat{e}_g')$ is too small. One solution is to inflate residuals in the hopes of reducing bias. Bell and McCaffrey (2002) suggest a procedure (called bias-reduced linearization, or BRL) that adjusts residuals by

$$\hat{\Psi}_g = a\tilde{e}_g\tilde{e}_g'$$
$$\tilde{e}_g = A_g\hat{e}_g$$

where $A_g$ solves

$$A_g'A_g = (I - H_g)^{-1},$$
$$H_g = X_g(X'X)^{-1}X_g',$$

and $a$ is a degrees-of-freedom correction.

This is a version of $HC_2$ for the clustered case. BRL works for the straight-up Moulton problem with few clusters but for technical reasons cannot be used for the typical DD serial correlation problem.[17]

---

[17]The matrix $A_g$ is not unique; there are many such decompositions. Bell and McCaffrey (2002) use the symmetric square root of $(I - H_g)^{-1}$, or

$$A_g = R\Lambda^{1/2},$$

where $R$ is the matrix of eigenvectors of $(I - H_g)^{-1}$ and $\Lambda^{1/2}$ is the diagonal matrix of the square roots of the eigenvalues. One problem with the Bell and McCaffrey adjustment is that $(I - H_g)$ may not be of full rank, and hence the inverse may not exist for all designs. This happens, for example, when one of the regressors is a dummy variable that is one for exactly one of the clusters, and zero otherwise. This scenario occurs in the panel DD model discussed by Bertrand et al. (2004), which includes a full set of state dummies and clusters by state.

2. Recognizing that the fundamental unit of observation is a cluster and not an individual unit within clusters, Bell and McCaffrey (2002) and Donald and Lang (2007) suggest that inference be based on a $t$-distribution with $G - K$ degrees of freedom rather than on the standard normal distribution. For small $G$, this makes a difference: confidence intervals will be wider, thereby avoiding some mistakes. Cameron, Gelbach, and Miller (2008) report Monte Carlo examples where the combination of a BRL adjustment and the use of $t$-tables works well.

3. Donald and Lang (2007) argue that estimation using group means works well with small $G$ in the Moulton problem, and even better when inference is based on a $t$-distribution with $G - K$ degrees of freedom. But, as we discussed in section 8.2.1, for grouped estimation the regressor should be fixed within groups. The level of aggregation is the level at which you'd like to cluster, such as schools in Angrist and Lavy (2008). For serial correlation, this is the state, but state averages cannot be used to estimate a model with a full set of state effects. Also, since treatment status varies within states, averaging up to the state level averages the regressor of interest as well, changing the rules of the game in a way we may not like (the estimator becomes IV using group dummies as instruments). The group means approach is therefore out of bounds for the serial correlation problem. Note also that if the grouped residuals are heteroskedastic, and you therefore use robust standard errors, you may have to worry about bias of the form discussed in section 8.1. In some cases, heteroskedasticity in the grouped residuals can be fixed by weighting by the group size. But weighting changes the estimand when the CEF is nonlinear, so the case for weighting is not open and shut (Angrist and Lavy, 1999, chose not to weight school-level averages because the variation in their study comes mostly from small schools). Weighted or not, a conservative approach when working with group-level averages is to use our rule of thumb from section 8.1: take the larger of robust and conventional standard errors as your measure of precision.

4. Cameron, Gelbach, and Miller (2008) report that some forms of a block bootstrap work well with small numbers of groups, and that the block bootstrap typically outperforms Stata-clustered standard errors. This appears to be true both for the Moulton and serial correlation problems. But Cameron, Gelbach, and Miller (2008) focus on rejection rates using (pivotal) test statistics, while we like to see standard errors.

5. Parametric corrections: For the Moulton problem, this amounts to use of the Moulton factor. With serial correlation, this means correcting your standard errors for first-order serial correlation at the group level. Based on our sampling experiments with the Moulton problem and a reading of the literature, parametric approaches may work well, and better than the nonparametric cluster estimator (8.2.6), especially if the parametric model is not too far off (see, e.g., Hansen, 2007a, which also proposes a bias correction for estimates of serial correlation parameters). Unfortunately, however, beyond the greenhouse world of controlled Monte Carlo studies, we're unlikely to know whether parametric assumptions are a good fit.

Alas, the bottom line here is not entirely clear, nor is the more basic question of when few clusters are fatal for inference. The severity of the resulting bias seems to depend on the nature of your problem, in particular whether you confront straight-up Moulton or serial correlation issues. Aggregation to the group level as in Donald and Lang (2007) seems to work well in the Moulton case as long as the regressor of interest is fixed within groups and there is not too much underlying heteroskedasticity. At a minimum, you'd like to show that your conclusions are consistent with the inferences that arise from an analysis of group averages, since this is a conservative and transparent approach. Angrist and Lavy (2008) use BRL standard errors to adjust for clustering at the school level but validate this approach by showing that key results come out the same using covariate-adjusted group averages.

As far as serial correlation goes, most of the evidence suggests that when you are lucky enough to do research on U.S. states, giving 51 clusters, you are on reasonably safe ground with a naive application of Stata's `cluster` command at the state level. But you might have to study Canada, which offers only 10 clusters in the form of provinces, well below 42. Hansen (2007b) finds that Liang and Zeger (1986) (Stata-clustered) standard errors are reasonably good at correcting for serial correlation in panels, even in the Canadian scenario. Hansen also recommends use of a $t$-distribution with $G - K$ degrees of freedom for critical values.

Clustering problems have forced applied microeconometricians to eat a little humble pie. Proud of working with large microdata sets, we like to sneer at macroeconomists toying with small time series samples. But he who laughs last laughs best: if the regressor of interest varies only at a coarse group level, such as over time or across states or countries, then it's the macroeconomists who have had the most realistic mode of inference all along.

## 8.3    Appendix: Derivation of the Simple Moulton Factor

Write

$$
y_g = \begin{bmatrix} Y_{1g} \\ Y_{2g} \\ \vdots \\ Y_{n_g g} \end{bmatrix} \qquad
e_g = \begin{bmatrix} e_{1g} \\ e_{2g} \\ \vdots \\ e_{n_g g} \end{bmatrix}
$$

and

$$
y = \begin{bmatrix} y_1 \\ y_2 \\ \vdots \\ y_G \end{bmatrix} \qquad
x = \begin{bmatrix} \iota_1 x_1 \\ \iota_2 x_2 \\ \vdots \\ \iota_G x_G \end{bmatrix} \qquad
e = \begin{bmatrix} e_1 \\ e_2 \\ \vdots \\ e_G \end{bmatrix},
$$

where $\iota_g$ is a column vector of $n_g$ ones and G is the number of groups. Note that

$$E(ee') = \Psi = \begin{bmatrix} \Psi_1 & 0 & \cdots & 0 \\ 0 & \Psi_2 & & \vdots \\ \vdots & & \ddots & 0 \\ 0 & \cdots & 0 & \Psi_G \end{bmatrix}$$

$$\Psi_g = \sigma_e^2 \begin{bmatrix} 1 & \rho_e & \cdots & \rho_e \\ \rho_e & 1 & & \vdots \\ \vdots & & \ddots & \rho_e \\ \rho & \cdots & \rho_e & 1 \end{bmatrix} = \sigma_e^2 \left[ (1 - \rho_e)I + \rho_e \iota_g \iota_g' \right],$$

where $\rho_e = \frac{\sigma_v^2}{\sigma_v^2 + \sigma_\eta^2}$.

Now

$$X'X = \sum_g n_g x_g x_g'$$

$$X'\Psi X = \sum_g x_g \iota_g' \Psi_g \iota_g x_g'.$$

But

$$x_g \iota_g' \Psi_g \iota_g x_g' = \sigma_e^2 x_g \iota_g' \begin{bmatrix} 1 + (n_g - 1)\rho_e \\ 1 + (n_g - 1)\rho_e \\ \cdots \\ 1 + (n_g - 1)\rho_e \end{bmatrix} x_g'$$

$$= \sigma_e^2 n_g \left[ 1 + (n_g - 1)\rho_e \right] x_g x_g'.$$

Let $\tau_g = 1 + (n_g - 1)\rho_e$, so we get

$$x_g \iota_g' \Psi_g \iota_g x_g' = \sigma_e^2 n_g \tau_g x_g x_g'$$

$$X'\Psi X = \sigma_e^2 \sum_g n_g \tau_g x_g x_g'.$$

With this in hand, we can write

$$V(\hat{\beta}) = (X'X)^{-1}X'\Psi X(X'X)^{-1}$$

$$= \sigma_e^2 \left(\sum_g n_g x_g x_g'\right)^{-1} \sum_g n_g \tau_g x_g x_g' \left(\sum_g n_g x_g x_g'\right)^{-1}.$$

We want to compare this with the standard OLS covariance estimator

$$V_c(\hat{\beta}) = \sigma_e^2 \left(\sum_g n_g x_g x_g'\right)^{-1}.$$

If the group sizes are equal, $n_g = n$ and $\tau_g = \tau = 1 + (n-1)\rho_e$, so that

$$V(\hat{\beta}) = \sigma_e^2 \tau \left(\sum_g n x_g x_g'\right)^{-1} \sum_g n x_g x_g' \left(\sum_g n x_g x_g'\right)^{-1}$$

$$= \sigma_e^2 \tau \left(\sum_g n x_g x_g'\right)^{-1}$$

$$= \tau V_c(\hat{\beta}),$$

which implies (8.2.4).

# LAST WORDS

I f applied econometrics were easy, theorists would do it. But it's not as hard as the dense pages of *Econometrica* might lead you to believe. Carefully applied to coherent causal questions, regression and 2SLS almost always make sense. Your standard errors probably won't be quite right, but they rarely are. Avoid embarrassment by being your own best skeptic, and especially, DON'T PANIC!

# ACRONYMS AND ABBREVIATIONS

TECHNICAL TERMS

**2SLS** Two-stage least squares, an instrumental variables (IV) estimator.

**ACR** Average causal response, the weighted average causal response to an ordered treatment.

**ANOVA** Analysis of variance, a decomposition of total variance into the variance of the conditional expectation function (CEF) and the average conditional variance.

**BRL** Biased reduced linearization estimator, a bias-corrected covariance matrix estimator for clustered data.

**CDF** Cumulative distribution function, the probability that a random variable takes on a value less than or equal to a given number.

**CEF** Conditional expectation function, the population average of $Y_i$ with $X_i$ held fixed.

**CIA** Conditional independence assumption, a core assumption that justifies a causal interpretation of regression and matching estimators.

**COP** Conditional on positive effect, the treatment-control difference in means for a non-negative random variable looking at positive values only.

**CQF** Conditional quantile function, defined for each quantile $\tau$, the $\tau$-quantile of $Y_i$, holding $X_i$ fixed.

**DD** Differences-in-differences estimator. In its simplest form, a comparison of changes over time in treatment and control groups.

**GLS** Generalized least squares estimator, a regression estimator for models with heteroskedasticity and/or serial correlation. GLS provides efficiency gains when the conditional expectation function (CEF) is linear.

**GMM** Generalized method of moments, an econometric estimation framework in which estimates are chosen to minimize a matrix-weighted average of the squared difference between sample and population moments.

*$HC_0$–$HC_3$* Heteroskedasticity consistent covariance matrix estimators discussed by MacKinnon and White (1985).

**ILS** Indirect least squares estimator, the ratio of reduced-form to first-stage coefficients in an instrumental variables (IV) setup.

**ITT** Intention to treat effect, the effect of being offered treatment.

**IV** Instrumental variables estimator or method.

**JIVE** Jackknife instrumental variables (IV) estimator.

**LATE** Local average treatment effect, the causal effect of treatment on compliers.

**LDVs** Limited dependent variables, such as dummies, counts, and non-negative random variables on the left-hand side of regression and related statistical models.

**LIML** Limited information maximum likelihood estimator, an alternative to two-stage least squares (2SLS) with less bias.

**LM** Lagrange multiplier test, a statistical test of the restrictions imposed by an estimator.

**LPM** Linear probability model, a linear regression model for a dummy dependent variable.

**MFX** Marginal effects. In nonlinear models, the derivative of the conditional expectation function (CEF) implied by the model with respect to the regressors.

**MMSE** Minimum mean squared error, the minimum expected squared prediction error, or the minimum of the expected square of the difference between an estimator and a target.

**OLS** Ordinary least squares estimator, the sample analog of the population regression vector.

**OVB**    Omitted variables bias, the relationship between regression estimates in models with different sets of control variables.

**QTE**    Quantile treatment effect, the causal effect of treatment on conditional quantiles of the outcome variable for compliers.

**RD**    Regression discontinuity design, an identification strategy in which treatment, the probability of treatment, or the average treatment intensity is a known, discontinuous function of a covariate.

**SEM**    Simultaneous equations model, an econometric framework in which causal relationships between variables are described by several equations.

**SSIV**    Split-sample instrumental variables estimator, a version of the two-sample instrumental variables (TSIV) estimator.

**TSIV**    Two-sample instrumental variables estimator, an instrumental variables (IV) estimator that can sometimes be constructed from two data sets when either data set alone would be inadequate.

**VIV**    Visual instrumental variables, a plot of reduced form against first-stage fitted values in instrumental variables models with dummy instruments.

**WLS**    Weighted least squares, a GLS estimator with a diagonal weighting matrix.

DATA SETS AND VARIABLE NAMES

**AFDC**    Aid to Families with Dependent Children, an American welfare program no longer in effect.

**AFQT**    Armed Forces Qualification Test, used by the U.S. armed forces to gauge recruits' academic and cognitive ability.

**CPS**    Current Population Survey, a large monthly survey of U.S. households, source of the U.S. unemployment rate.

**GED**   General Educational Development certificate, a substitute for traditional high school credentials, obtained by passing a test.

**IPUMS**   Integrated public use microdata series, consistently coded samples of census records from the United States and other countries.

**NHIS**   National Health Interview Survey, a large American survey with many questions related to health.

**NLSY**   National Longitudinal Survey of Youth, a long-running panel survey that started with a high school-aged cohort in 1979.

**PSAT**   Preliminary SAT, qualifies American high school sophomores for a National Merit Scholarship.

**PSID**   Panel Study of Income Dynamics, a panel survey of American households begun in 1968.

**QOB**   Quarter of birth.

**RSN**   Random sequence numbers, draft lottery numbers randomly assigned to dates of birth in the Vietnam-era draft lotteries held from 1970 to 1973.

**SDA**   Service delivery area, one of the 649 sites where Job Training Partnership Act (JTPA) services were delivered.

**SSA**   Social Security Administration, a U.S. government agency.

## STUDY NAMES

**HIE**   Health Insurance Experiment conducted by the RAND Corporation, a randomized trial in which participants were exposed to health insurance programs with different features.

**JTPA**   Job Training Partnership Act, a large, federally funded training program that included a randomized evaluation.

**MDVE**   Minneapolis Domestic Violence Experiment, a randomized trial in which police response to a domestic disturbance was determined in part by random assignment.

**NSW**   National Supported Work demonstration, an experimental mid-1970s training program that provided work experience to men and women with weak labor force attachment.

**STAR**   The Tennessee Student/Teacher Achievement Ratio experiment, a randomized study of elementary school class size.

**WHI**   Women's Health Initiative, a series of randomized trials that included an evaluation of hormone replacement therapy.

# EMPIRICAL STUDIES INDEX

This index lists studies contributing to tables and figures in the book.

a reanalysis of the Lalonde (1986) NSW sample. Discussed in section 3.3.3. Results appear in table 3.3.2.

**Freeman (1984)**   Uses fixed effects models to construct panel-data estimates of the effect of union status on wages. Discussed in section 5.1. Results appear in table 5.1.1.

**Krueger (1999)**   Uses the Tennessee STAR randomized trial to construct IV estimates of the effect of class size on test scores. Discussed in section 2.2. Results appear in tables 2.2.1, 2.2.2, and 8.2.1.

**Lee (2008)**   Uses a regression discontinuity design to estimate the effect of party incumbency on reelection. Discussed in section 6.1. Results appear in figure 6.1.2.

**Manning et al. (1987)**   Uses randomized assignment to estimate the impact of health insurance plans on health care use, cost, and outcomes. Discussed in section 3.4.2. Results appear in table 3.4.1.

**Pischke (2007)**   Uses a sharp change in the length of the German school year to estimate the effect of school term length on achievement. Discussed in section 5.2. Results appear in figure 5.2.3.

# REFERENCES

ABADIE, ALBERTO (2003): "Semiparametric Instrumental Variable Estimation of Treatment Response Models." *Journal of Econometrics* 113, 231–63.

ABADIE, ALBERTO, JOSHUA D. ANGRIST, AND GUIDO IMBENS (2002): "Instrumental Variables Estimates of the Effect of Subsidized Training on the Quantiles of Trainee Earnings." *Econometrica* 70, 91–117.

ABADIE, ALBERTO, ALEXIS DIAMOND, AND JENS HAINMUELLER (2007): "Synthetic Control Methods for Comparative Case Studies: Estimating the Effect of California's Tobacco Control Program." Working Paper No. 12831. National Bureau of Economic Research, Cambridge, Mass.

ABADIE, ALBERTO, AND GUIDO IMBENS (2006): "Large Sample Properties of Matching Estimators for Average Treatment Effects." *Econometrica* 74, 235–67.

——— (2008): "Bias-Corrected Matching Estimators for Average Treatment Effects." Mimeo. Department of Economics, Harvard University, Cambridge, Mass.

ACEMOGLU, DARON, AND JOSHUA ANGRIST (2000): "How Large Are the Social Returns to Education? Evidence from Compulsory Schooling Laws," in *National Bureau of Economics Macroeconomics Annual 2000*, ed. Ben S. Bernanke and Kenneth S. Rogoff, pp. 9–58. MIT Press, Cambridge, Mass.

ACEMOGLU, DARON, SIMON JOHNSON, AND JAMES A. ROBINSON (2001): "The Colonial Origins of Comparative Development: An Empirical Investigation." *The American Economic Review* 91, 1369–401.

ACKERBERG, DANIEL A. AND PAUL J. DEVEREUX (2008): "Improved JIVE Estimators for Overidentified Linear Models With and Without Heteroskedasticity." *The Review of Economics and Statistics*, forthcoming.

ADAMS, DOUGLAS (1979): *The Hitchhiker's Guide to the Galaxy*. Pocket Books, New York.

———— (1990): *Dirk Gently's Holistic Detective Agency*. Simon & Schuster, New York.

———— (1995): *Mostly Harmless*. Harmony Books, New York.

ALTONJI, JOSEPH G., AND LEWIS M. SEGAL (1996): "Small-Sample Bias in GMM Estimation of Covariance Structures." *Journal of Business and Economic Statistics* 14, 353–66.

AMEMIYA, TAKESHI (1985): *Advanced Econometrics*. Harvard University Press, Cambridge, Mass.

AMMERMUELLER, ANDREAS, AND JÖRN-STEFFEN PISCHKE (2006): "Peer Effects in European Primary Schools: Evidence from PIRLS." Discussion Paper No. 2077. Institute for the Study of Labor (IZA), Bonn, Germany.

ANANAT, ELIZABETH, AND GUY MICHAELS (2008): "The Effect of Marital Breakup on the Income Distribution of Women with Children." *Journal of Human Resources*, forthcoming.

ANDERSON, MICHAEL (2008): "Multiple Inference and Gender Differences in the Effect of Early Intervention: A Reevaluation of the Abecedarian, Perry Preschool, and Early Training Projects." *Journal of the American Statistical Association*, forthcoming.

ANGRIST, JOSHUA D. (1988): "Grouped Data Estimation and Testing in Simple Labor Supply Models." Working Paper No. 234. Princeton University, Industrial Relations Section, Princeton, N.J.

———— (1990): "Lifetime Earnings and the Vietnam Era Draft Lottery: Evidence from Social Security Administrative Records." *American Economic Review* 80, 313–35.

———— (1991): "Grouped Data Estimation and Testing in Simple Labor Supply Models." *Journal of Econometrics* 47, 243–66.

———— (1998): "Estimating the Labor Market Impact on Voluntary Military Service Using Social Security Data on Military Applicants." *Econometrica* 66, 249–88.

———— (2001): "Estimations of Limited Dependent Variable Models with Dummy Endogenous Regressors: Simple Strategies for Empirical Practice." *Journal of Business and Economic Statistics* 19, 2–16.

———— (2004): "American Education Research Changes Track." *Oxford Review of Economic Policy* 20, 198–212.

——— (2006): "Instrumental Variables Methods in Experimental Criminological Research: What, Why and How." *Journal of Experimental Criminology* 2, 22–44.

ANGRIST, JOSHUA, ERIC BETTINGER, ERIK BLOOM, ELIZABETH KING, AND MICHAEL KREMER (2002): "Vouchers for Private Schooling in Colombia: Evidence from a Randomized Natural Experiment." *The American Economic Review* 92, 1535–58.

ANGRIST, JOSHUA D., AND STACEY H. CHEN (2007): "Long-Term Consequences of Vietnam-Era Conscription: Schooling, Experience, and Earnings." Working Paper No. 13411. National Bureau of Economic Research, Cambridge, Mass.

ANGRIST, JOSHUA D., VICTOR CHERNOZHUKOV, AND IVAN FERNANDEZ-VAL (2006): "Quantile Regression Under Misspecification, with an Application to the U.S. Wage Structure." *Econometrica* 74, 539–63.

ANGRIST, JOSHUA D., AND WILLIAM N. EVANS (1998): "Children and Their Parents' Labor Supply: Evidence from Exogenous Variation in Family Size." *American Economic Review* 88, 450–477.

——— (1999): "Schooling and Labor Market Consequences of the 1970 State Abortion Reforms," in *Research in Labor Economics*, ed. Solomon W. Polachek, vol. 18, pp. 75–113. Elsevier Science, Amsterdam.

ANGRIST, JOSHUA D., KATHRYN GRADDY, AND GUIDO W. IMBENS (2000): "The Interpretation of Instrumental Variables Estimators in Simultaneous Equations Models with an Application to the Demand for Fish." *Review of Economic Studies* 67, 499–527.

ANGRIST, JOSHUA D., AND JINYONG HAHN (2004): "When to Control for Covariates? Panel Asymptotics for Estimates of Treatment Effects." *Review of Economics and Statistics* 86, 58–72.

ANGRIST, JOSHUA D., AND GUIDO W. IMBENS (1995): "Two-Stage Least Squares Estimation of Average Causal Effects in Models with Variable Treatment Intensity." *Journal of the American Statistical Association* 90, 430–42.

ANGRIST, JOSHUA D., GUIDO IMBENS, AND ALAN B. KRUEGER (1999): "Jackknife Instrumental Variables Estimation." *Journal of Applied Econometrics* 14, 57–67.

ANGRIST, JOSHUA D., GUIDO IMBENS, AND DONALD B. RUBIN (1996): "Identification of Causal Effects Using Instrumental Variables." *Journal of the American Statistical Association* 91, 444–72.

ANGRIST, JOSHUA D., AND ALAN B. KRUEGER (1991): "Does Compulsory Schooling Attendance Affect Schooling and Earnings?" *The Quarterly Journal of Economics* 106, 976–1014.

——— (1992): "The Effect of Age at School Entry on Educational Attainment: An Application of Instrumental Variables with Moments from Two Samples." *Journal of the American Statistical Association* 418, 328–36.

——— (1994): "Why Do World War II Veterans Earn More than Nonveterans?" *Journal of Labor Economics* 12, 74–97.

——— (1995): "Split-Sample Instrumental Variables Estimates of the Return to Schooling." *Journal of Business and Economic Statistics* 13, 225–35.

——— (1999): "Empirical Strategies in Labor Economics," in *Handbook of Labor Economics*, ed. Orley C. Ashenfelter and David Card, vol. 3. North Holland, Amsterdam.

——— (2001): "Instrumental Variables and the Search for Identification: From Supply and Demand to Natural Experiments." *Journal of Economic Perspectives* 15(4), 69–85.

ANGRIST, JOSHUA D., AND GUIDO KUERSTEINER (2004): "Semiparametric Causality Tests Using the Policy Propensity Score." Working Paper No. 10975. National Bureau of Economic Research, Cambridge, Mass.

ANGRIST, JOSHUA D., AND KEVIN LANG (2004): "Does School Integration Generate Peer Effects? Evidence from Boston's Metco Program." *The American Economic Review* 94, 1613–34.

ANGRIST, JOSHUA D., AND VICTOR LAVY (1999): "Using Maimonides' Rule to Estimate the Effect of Class Size on Scholastic Achievement." *The Quarterly Journal of Economics* 114, 533–75.

——— (2008): "The Effects of High Stakes High School Achievement Awards: Evidence from a Group-Randomized Trial." *The American Economic Review*, forthcoming.

ANGRIST, JOSHUA D., VICTOR LAVY, AND ANALIA SCHLOSSER (2006): "Multiple Experiments for the Causal Link Between the Quantity and Quality of Children." Working Paper No. 06–26. Department of Economics, Massachusetts Institute of Technology, Cambridge, Mass.

ARELLANO, MANUEL (1987): "Computing Robust Standard Errors for Within-groups Estimators." *Oxford Bulletin of Economics and Statistics* 49, 431–34.

ARELLANO, MANUEL, AND STEPHEN BOND (1991): "Some Tests of Specification for Panel Data: Monte Carlo Evidence and an Application to Employment Equations." *The Review of Economic Studies* 58, 277–97.

ASHENFELTER, ORLEY A. (1978): "Estimating the Effect of Training Programs on Earnings." *Review of Economics and Statistics* 60, 47–57.

——— (1991): "How Convincing Is the Evidence Linking Education and Income?" Working Paper No. 292. Princeton University, Industrial Relations Section, Princeton, N.J.

ASHENFELTER, ORLEY A., AND DAVID CARD (1985): "Using the Longitudinal Structure of Earnings to Estimate the Effect of Training Programs." *The Review of Economics and Statistics* 67, 648–60.

ASHENFELTER, ORLEY A., AND ALAN B. KRUEGER (1994): "Estimates of the Economic Return to Schooling from a New Sample of Twins." *American Economic Review* 84, 1157–73.

ASHENFELTER, ORLEY A., AND CECILIA ROUSE (1998): "Income, Schooling, and Ability: Evidence from a New Sample of Identical Twins." *The Quarterly Journal of Economics* 113, 253–84.

ATHEY, SUSAN, AND GUIDO IMBENS (2006): "Identification and Inference in Nonlinear Difference-in-Difference Models." *Econometrica* 74, 431–97.

ATKINSON, ANTHONY B. (1970): "On the Measurement of Inequality." *Journal of Economic Theory* 2, 244–63.

AUTOR, DAVID (2003): "Outsourcing at Will: The Contribution of Unjust Dismissal Doctrine to the Growth of Employment Outsourcing." *Journal of Labor Economics* 21, 1–42.

AUTOR, DAVID, LAWRENCE F. KATZ, AND MELISSA S. KEARNEY (2005): "Rising Wage Inequality: The Role of Composition and Prices." Working Paper No. 11628. National Bureau of Economic Research, Cambridge, Mass.

BARNETT, STEVEN W. (1992): "Benefits of Compensatory Preschool Education." *Journal of Human Resources* 27, 279–312.

BARNOW, BURT S., GLEN G. CAIN, AND ARTHUR GOLDBERGER (1981): "Selection on Observables." *Evaluation Studies Review Annual* 5, 43–59.

BECKER, SASCHA O., AND ANDREA ICHINO (2002): "Estimation of Average Treatment Effects Based on Propensity Scores." *The Stata Journal* 2, 358–77.

BEKKER, PAUL A. (1994): "Alternative Approximations to the Distributions of Instrumental Variable Estimators." *Econometrica* 62, 657–81.

BEKKER, PAUL A. AND J. VAN DER PLOEG (2005): "Instrumental Variable Estimation Based on Grouped Data." *Statistica Neerlandica* 59, 239–267.

BELL, ROBERT M., AND DANIEL F. MCCAFFREY (2002): "Bias Reduction in Standard Errors for Linear Regression with Multistage Samples." *Survey Methodology* 28, 169–81.

BENNEDSEN, MORTEN, KASPER M. NIELSEN, FRANCISCO PÉREZ-GONZÁLEZ, AND DANIEL WOLFENZON (2007): "Inside the Family Firm: The Role of Families in Succession Decisions and Performance." *The Quarterly Journal of Economics* 122, 647–92.

BERTRAND, MARIANNE, ESTHER DUFLO, AND SENDHIL MULLAINATHAN (2004): "How Much Should We Trust Differences-in-Differences Estimates?" *The Quarterly Journal of Economics* 119, 249–75.

BERTRAND, MARIANNE, AND SENDHIL MULLAINATHAN (2004): "Are Emily and Greg More Employable than Lakisha and Jamal? A Field Experiment on Labor Market Discrimination." *The American Economic Review* 94, 991–1013.

BESLEY, TIMOTHY, AND ROBIN BURGESS (2004): "Can Labour Market Regulation Hinder Economic Performance? Evidence from India." *The Quarterly Journal of Economics* 113, 91–134.

BJORKLUND, ANDERS, AND MARKUS JANTTI (1997): "Intergenerational Income Mobility in Sweden Compared to the United States." *The American Economic Review* 87, 1009–18.

BLACK, DAN A., JEFFREY A. SMITH, MARK C. BERGER, AND BRETT J. NOEL (2003): "Is the Threat of Reemployment Services More Effective than the Services Themselves? Evidence from Random Assignment in the UI System." *The American Economic Review* 93, 1313–27.

BLACK, SANDRA E., PAUL J. DEVEREUX, AND KJELL G. SALVANES (2005): "The More the Merrier? The Effect of Family Size and Birth Order on Children's Education." *The Quarterly Journal of Economics* 120, 669–700.

——— (2008): "Too Young to Leave the Nest: The Effect of School Starting Age." Working Paper No. 13969. National Bureau of Economic Research, Cambridge, Mass.

BLOOM, HOWARD S. (1984): "Accounting for No-shows in Experimental Evaluation Designs." *Evaluation Review* 8, 225–246.

BLOOM, HOWARD S., LARRY L. ORR, STEPHEN H. BELL, GEORGE CAVE, FRED DOOLITTLE, WINSTON LIN, AND JOHANNES M. BOS (1997): "The Benefits and Costs of JTPA Title II-A Programs: Key Findings from the National Job Training Partnership Act Study." *The Journal of Human Resources* 32, 549–76.

BLUNDELL, RICHARD, AND STEPHEN BOND (1998): "Initial Conditions and Moment Restrictions in Dynamic Panel Data Models." *Journal of Econometrics* 87, 115–43.

BORJAS, GEORGE (1992): "Ethnic Capital and Intergenerational Mobility." *Quarterly Journal of Economics* 107, 123–50.

———— (2005): *Labor Economics*, 3rd ed. McGraw-Hill/Irwin, New York.

BOUND, JOHN, DAVID JAEGER, AND REGINA BAKER (1995): "Problems with Instrumental Variables Estimation when the Correlation between the Instruments and the Endogenous Variables Is Weak." *Journal of the American Statistical Association* 90, 443–50.

BOUND, JOHN, AND GARY SOLON (1999): "Double Trouble: On the Value of Twins-Based Estimation of the Returns of Schooling." *Economics of Education Review* 18, 169–82.

BRONARS, STEPHEN G., AND JEFF GROGGER (1994): "The Economic Consequences of Unwed Motherhood: Using Twin Births as a Natural Experiment." *The American Economic Review* 84, 1141–56.

BUCHINSKY, MOSHE (1994): "Changes in the U.S. Wage Structure 1963–1987: Application of Quantile Regression." *Econometrica* 62, 405–58.

BUCHINSKY, MOSHE, AND JINYONG HAHN (1998): "An Alternative Estimator for the Censored Quantile Regression Model." *Econometrica* 66, 653–71.

BUSE, A. (1992): "The Bias of Instrumental Variable Estimators." *Econometrica* 60, 173–80.

CAMERON, COLIN, JONAH GELBACH, AND DOUGLAS L. MILLER (2008): "Bootstrap-Based Improvements for Inference with Clustered Errors." *The Review of Economics and Statistics* 90, 414–27.

CAMPBELL, DONALD THOMAS (1969): "Reforms as Experiments." *American Psychologist* 24, 409–29.

CAMPBELL, DONALD THOMAS, AND JULIAN C. STANLEY (1963): *Experimental and Quasi-experimental Designs for Research*. Rand McNally, Chicago.

CARD, DAVID (1992): "Using Regional Variation to Measure the Effect of the Federal Minimum Wage." *Industrial and Labor Relations Review* 46, 22–37.

—— (1995): "Earnings, Schooling and Ability Revisited," in *Research in Labor Economics*, ed. Solomon W. Polachek, vol. 14, pp. 23–48. JAI Press, Greenwich, Conn.

—— (1996): "The Effect of Unions on the Structure of Wages: A Longitudinal Analysis." *Econometrica* 64, 957–79.

—— (1999): "The Causal Effect of Education on Earnings," in *Handbook of Labor Economics*, ed. Orley C. Ashenfelter and David Card, vol. 3. North Holland, Amsterdam.

CARD, DAVID, AND ALAN KRUEGER (1994): "Minimum Wages and Employment: A Case Study of the Fast Food Industry in New Jersey and Pennsylvania." *The American Economic Review* 84, 772–84.

—— (2000): "Minimum Wages and Employment: A Case Study of the Fast-Food Industry in New Jersey and Pennsylvania: Reply." *The American Economic Review* 90, 1397–420.

CARD, DAVID, AND THOMAS LEMIEUX (1996): "Wage Dispersion, Returns to Skill, and Black-White Differentials." *Journal of Econometrics* 74, 316–61.

CARD, DAVID E., AND DANIEL SULLIVAN (1988): "Measuring the Effect of Subsidized Training on Movements in and out of Employment." *Econometrica* 56, 497–530.

CARDELL, NICHOLAS SCOTT, AND MARK MYRON HOPKINS (1977): "Education, Income, and Ability: A Comment." *Journal of Political Economy* 85, 211–15.

CHAMBERLAIN, GARY (1977): "Education, Income, and Ability Revisited." *Journal of Econometrics* 5, 241–57.

—— (1978): "Omitted Variables Bias in Panel Data: Estimating the Returns to Schooling." *Annales De L'INSEE* 30–31, 49–82.

—— (1984): "Panel Data," in *Handbook of Econometrics*, ed. Zvi Griliches, and Michael D. Intriligator, vol. 2, pp. 1247–318. North Holland, Amsterdam.

—— (1994): "Quantile Regression, Censoring and the Structure of Wages," in *Proceedings of the Sixth World Congress of the*

*Econometrics Society, Barcelona, Spain*, ed. Christopher A. Sims, and Jean-Jacques Laffont, pp. 179–209. Cambridge University Press, New York.

CHAMBERLAIN, GARY, AND EDWARD E. LEAMER (1976): "Matrix Weighted Averages and Posterior Bounds." *Journal of the Royal Statistical Society, Series B* 38, 73–84.

CHERNOZHUKOV, VICTOR, AND CHRISTIAN HANSEN (2005): "An IV Model of Quantile Treatment Effects." *Econometrica* 73, 245–61.

——— (2008): "The Reduced Form: A Simple Approach to Inference with Weak Instruments." *Economics Letters* 100, 68–71.

CHERNOZHUKOV, VICTOR, AND H. HONG (2002): "Three-step Censored Quantile Regression and Extramarital Affairs." *Journal of the America Statistical Assoc.* 92, 872–82.

CHERNOZHUKOV, VICTOR, IVAN FERNANDEZ-VAL, AND BLAISE MELLY (2008): "Inference on Counterfactual Distributions." Working Paper No. 08–16. MIT Department of Economics, Cambridge, Mass.

CHESHER, ANDREW, AND GERALD AUSTIN (1991): "The Finite-Sample Distributions of Heteroskedasticity Robust Wald Statistics." *Journal of Econometrics* 47, 153–73.

CHESHER, ANDREW, AND IAN JEWITT (1987): "The Bias of the Heteroskedasticity Consistent Covariance Estimator." *Econometrica* 55, 1217–22.

COCHRAN, WILLIAM G. (1965): "The Planning of Observational Studies of Human Populations." *Journal of the Royal Statistical Society, Series A* 128, 234–65.

COOK, THOMAS D. (2008): "Waiting for Life to Arrive: A History of the Regression-Discontinuity Design in Psychology, Statistics, and Economics." *Journal of Econometrics* 142, 636–54.

COOK, THOMAS D., AND VIVIAN C. WONG (2008): "Empirical Tests of the Validity of the Regression-Discontinuity Design." *Annales d'Economie et de Statistique*, forthcoming.

CRUMP, RICHARD K., V. JOSEPH HOTZ, GUIDO W. IMBENS, AND OSCAR A. MITNIK (2009): "Dealing with Limited Overlap in the Estimation of Average Treatment Effects." *Biometrica*, forthcoming.

CRUZ, LUIZ M., AND MARCELO J. MOREIRA (2005): "On the Validity of Econometric Techniques with Weak Instruments: Inference on Returns to Education Using Compulsory School Attendance Laws." *Journal of Human Resources* 40, 393–410.

CURRIE, JANET, AND AARON YELOWITZ (2000): "Are Public Housing Projects Good for Kids?" *Journal of Public Economics* 75, 99–124.

DAVIDON, RUSSELL, AND JAMES G. MACKINNON (1993): *Estimation and Inference in Econometrics.* Oxford University Press, New York.

DEARDEN, LORRAINE, SUE MIDDLETON, SUE MAGUIRE, KARL ASHWORTH, KATE LEGGE, TRACEY ALLEN, KIM PERRIN, ERICH BATTISTIN, CARL EMMERSON, EMLA FITZSIMONS, AND COSTAS MEGHIR (2003): "The Evaluation of Education Maintenance Allowance Pilots: Three Years' Evidence. A Quantitative Evaluation." Research Report No. 499. Department for Education and Skills, DFES Publications, Nottingham, UK.

DEATON, ANGUS (1985): "Panel Data from a Time Series of Cross-sections." *Journal of Econometrics* 30, 109–126.

—— (1997): *The Analysis of Household Surveys: A Microeconometric Approach to Development Policy.* Johns Hopkins University Press for the World Bank, Baltimore, Md.

DEE, THOMAS S., AND WILLIAM N. EVANS (2003): "Teen Drinking and Educational Attainment: Evidence from Two-Sample Instrumental Variables Estimates." *Journal of Labor Economics* 21, 178–209.

DEGROOT, MORRIS H., AND MARK J. SCHERVISH (2001): *Probability and Statistics,* 3rd ed. Addison-Wesley, Boston.

DEHEJIA, RAJEEV H. (2005): "Practical Propensity Score Matching: A Reply to Smith and Todd." *Journal of Econometrics* 125, 355–364.

DEHEJIA, RAJEEV H., AND SADEK WAHBA (1999): "Causal Effects in Nonexperimental Studies: Reevaluating the Evaluation of Training Programs." *Journal of the American Statistical Association* 94, 1053–62.

DEMING, DAVID, AND SUSAN DYNARSKI (2008): "The Lengthening of Childhood." *The Journal of Economic Perspectives* 22(3), 71–92.

DEVEREUX, PAUL J. (2007): "Improved Errors-in-variables Estimators for Grouped Data." *The Journal of Business and Economic Statistics* 27, 278–287.

DONALD, STEPHEN G., AND KEVIN LANG (2007): "Inference with Difference-in-Differences and Other Panel Data." *Review of Economics and Statistics* 89, 221–33.

DUAN, NAIHUA, WILLARD D. MANNING, JR., CARL N. MORRIS, AND JOSEPH P. NEWHOUSE (1983): "A Comparison of Alternative

Models for the Models for the Demand for Medical Care." *Journal of Business & Economic Statistics* 1, 115–26.

——— (1984): "Choosing Between the Sample-Selection Model and the Multi-Part Model." *Journal of Business & Economic Statistics* 2, 283–289.

DURBIN, JAMES (1954): "Errors in Variables." *Review of the International Statistical Institute* 22, 23–32.

EICKER, FRIEDHELM (1967): "Limit Theorems for Regressions with Unequal and Dependent Errors," in *Proceedings of the Fifth Berkeley Symposium on Mathematical Statistics and Probability*, vol. 1, pp. 59–82. University of California Press, Berkeley and Los Angeles.

FINN, JEREMY D., AND CHARLES M. ACHILLES (1990): "Answers and Questions About Class Size: A Statewide Experiment." *American Educational Research Journal* 28, 557–77.

FIRPO, SERGIO (2007): "Efficient Semiparametric Estimation of Quantile Treatment Effects." *Econometrica* 75, 259–76.

FLORES-LAGUNES, ALFONSO (2007): "Finite Sample Evidence of IV Estimators under Weak Instruments." *Journal of Applied Econometrics* 22, 677–94.

FREEDMAN, DAVID (2005): "Linear Statistical Models for Causation: A Critical Review," in *The Wiley Encyclopedia of Statistics in Behavioral Science*, ed. B. Everitt, and D. Howell. John Wiley, Chichester, UK.

FREEMAN, RICHARD (1984): "Longitudinal Analyses of the Effect of Trade Unions." *Journal of Labor Economics* 3, 1–26.

FRISCH, RAGNAR, AND FREDERICK V. WAUGH (1933): "Partial Time Regression as Compared with Individual Trends." *Econometrica* 1, 387–401.

FRÖLICH, MARKUS, AND BLAISE MELLY (2007): "Unconditional Quantile Treatment Effects Under Endogeneity." Working Paper No. CWP32/07. Centre for Microdata Methods and Practice.

FRYER, ROLAND G., AND STEVEN D. LEVITT (2004): "The Causes and Consequences of Distinctively Black Names." *The Quarterly Journal of Economics* 119, 767–805.

GALTON, FRANCIS (1886): "Regression Towards Mediocrity in Hereditary Stature." *Journal of the Anthropological Institute* 15, 246–63.

GOLDBERGER, ARTHUR S. (1972): "Selection Bias in Evaluating Treatment Effects: Some Formal Illustrations." Working paper. Department of Economics, University of Wisconsin, Madison.

——— (1991): *A Course in Econometrics*. Harvard University Press, Cambridge, Mass.

GOSLING, AMANDA, STEPHEN MACHIN, AND COSTAS MEGHIR (2000): "The Changing Distribution of Male Wages in the U.K." *Review of Economic Studies* 67, 635–66.

GRANGER, CLIVE W. J. (1969): "Investigating Causal Relations by Econometric Models and Cross-spectral Methods." *Econometrica* 37, 424–38.

GRILICHES, ZVI (1977): "Estimating the Returns to Schooling: Some Econometric Problems." *Econometrica* 45, 1–22.

GRILICHES, ZVI, AND JERRY A. HAUSMAN (1986): "Errors in Variables in Panel Data." *Journal of Econometrics* 31, 93–118.

GRILICHES, ZVI, AND WILLIAM M. MASON (1972): "Education, Income, and Ability." *Journal of Political Economy* 80, S74–103.

GRUMBACH, KEVIN, DENNIS KEANE, AND ANDREW BINDMAN (1993): "Primary Care and Public Emergency Department Overcrowding." *American Journal of Public Health* 83, 372–78.

GURYAN, JONATHAN (2004): "Desegregation and Black Dropout Rates." *American Economic Review* 94, 919–43.

HAAVELMO, TRYGVE (1944): "The Probability Approach in Econometrics." *Econometrica* 12, S1–115.

HAHN, JINYONG (1998): "On the Role of the Propensity Score in Efficient Semiparametric Estimation of Average Treatment Effects." *Econometrica* 66, 315–31.

HAHN, JINYONG, PETRA TODD, AND WILBUR VAN DER KLAAUW (2001): "Identification and Estimation of Treatment Effects with a Regression-Discontinuity Design." *Econometrica* 69, 201–9.

HANSEN, CHRISTIAN B. (2007a): "Asymptotic Properties of a Robust Variance Matrix Estimator for Panel Data When T Is Large." *Journal of Econometrics* 141, 597–620.

——— (2007b): "Generalized Least Squares Inference in Panel and Multilevel Models with Serial Correlation and Fixed Effects." *Journal of Econometrics* 140, 670–94.

HANSEN, LARS PETER (1982): "Large Sample Properties of Generalized Method of Moments Estimators." *Econometrica* 50, 1029–54.

HAUSMAN, JERRY (1978): "Specification Tests in Econometrics." *Econometrica* 46, 1251–71.

——— (1983): "Specification and Estimation of Simultaneous Equation Models," in *Handbook of Econometrics*, ed. Zvi Griliches, and Michael Intriligator, vol. 1, pp. 391–448. North Holland, Amsterdam.

——— (2001): "Mismeasured Variables in Econometric Analysis: Problems from the Right and Problems from the Left." *Journal of Econometric Perspectives* 15(4), 57–67.

HAUSMAN, JERRY, WHITNEY NEWEY, TIEMEN WOUTERSEN, JOHN CHAO, AND NORMAN SWANSON (2008): "Instrumental Variable Estimation with Heteroskedasticity and Many Instruments." Unpublished manuscript. Department of Economics, Massachusetts Institute of Technology, Cambridge, Mass.

HAY, JOEL W., AND RANDALL J. OLSEN (1984): "Let Them Eat Cake: A Note on Comparing Alternative Models of the Demand for Medical Care." *Journal of Business & Economic Statistics* 2, 279–82.

HECKMAN, JAMES J. (1978): "Dummy Endogenous Variables in a Simultaneous Equations System." *Econometrica* 46, 695–712.

HECKMAN, JAMES J., HIDEHIKO ICHIMURA, AND PETRA E. TODD (1998): "Matching as as Econometric Evaluation Estimator." *Review of Economic Studies* 62, 261–94.

HECKMAN, JAMES J., JEFFREY SMITH, AND NANCY CLEMENTS (1997): "Making the Most out of Programme Evaluations and Social Experiments: Accounting for Heterogeneity in Programme Impacts." *The Review of Economic Studies* 64, 487–535.

HIRANO, KEISUKE, GUIDO W. IMBENS, AND GEERT RIDDER (2003): "Efficient Estimation of Average Treatment Effects Using the Estimated Propensity Score." *Econometrica* 71, 1161–89.

HOAGLIN, DAVID C., AND ROY E. WELSCH (1978): "The Hat Matrix in Regression and ANOVA." *The American Statistician* 32, 17–22.

HOLLAND, PAUL W. (1986): "Statistics and Causal Inference." *Journal of the American Statistical Association* 81, 945–70.

HOLTZ-EAKIN, DOUGLAS, WHITNEY NEWEY, AND HARVEY S. ROSEN (1988): "Estimating Vector Autoregressions with Panel Data." *Econometrica* 56, 1371–1395.

HOROWITZ, JOEL L. (1997): "Bootstrap Methods in Econometrics: Theory and Numerical Performance," in *Advances in Economics and Econometrics: Theory and Applications*, ed. David M. Kreps and Kenneth F. Wallis, vol. 3, pp. 188–222. Cambridge University Press, Cambridge, UK.

——— (2001): "The Bootstrap," in *Handbook of Econometrics*, ed. James J. Heckman and Edward E. Leamer, vol. 5, pp. 3159–228. Elsevier Science, Amsterdam.

HORVITZ, DANIEL G., AND DONOVAN J. THOMPSON (1952): "A Generalization of Sampling Without Replacement from a Finite Population." *Journal of the American Statistical Association* 47, 663–85.

HOXBY, CAROLINE (2000): "The Effects of Class Size on Student Achievement: New Evidence from Population Variation." *The Quarterly Journal of Economics* 115, 1239–85.

HSIA, JUDITH, ROBERT D. LANGER, JoANN E. MANSON, LEWIS KULLER, KAREN C. JOHNSON, SUSAN L. HENDRIX, MARY PETTINGER, SUSAN R. HECKBERT, NANCY GREEP, SYBIL CRAWFORD, CHARLES B. EATON, JOHN B. KOSTIS, PAT CARALIS, ROSS PRENTICE, FOR THE WOMEN'S HEALTH INITIATIVE INVESTIGATORS (2006): "Conjugated Equine Estrogens and Coronary Heart Disease: The Women's Health Initiative." *Archives of Internal Medicine* 166, 357–65.

IMBENS, GUIDO (2000): "The Role of the Propensity Score in Estimating Dose-Response Functions." *Biometrika* 87, 706–10.

——— (2004): "Nonparametric Estimation of Average Treatment Effects Under Exogeneity: A Review." *The Review of Economics and Statistics* 86, 4–29.

IMBENS, GUIDO, AND JOSHUA ANGRIST (1994): "Identification and Estimation of Local Average Treatment Effects." *Econometrica*, 62, 467–76.

IMBENS, GUIDO, AND THOMAS LEMIEUX (2008): "Regression Discontinuity Designs: A Guide to Practice." *Journal of Econometrics* 142, 615–35.

INOUE, ATSUSHI, AND GARY SOLON (2009): "Two-Sample Instrumental Variables Estimators." *The Review of Economics and Statistics*, forthcoming.

JAPPELLI, TULLIO, JÖRN-STEFFEN PISCHKE, AND NICHOLAS S. SOULELES (1998): "Testing for Liquidity Constraints in Euler Equations with Complementary Data Sources." *The Review of Economics and Statistics* 80, 251–62.

JOHNSON, NORMAN L., AND SAMUEL KOTZ (1970): *Distributions in Statistics: Continuous Distributions*, vol. 2. John Wiley, New York.

KAUERMANN, GORAN, AND RAYMOND J. CARROLL (2001): "A Note on the Efficiency of Sandwich Covariance Estimation." *Journal of the American Statistical Association* 96, 1387–96.

KELEJIAN, HARRY H. (1971): "Two Stage Least Squares and Econometric Systems Linear in Parameters but Nonlinear in the Endogenous Variables." *Journal of the American Statistical Association* 66, 373–74.

KENNAN, JOHN (1995): "The Elusive Effects of Minimum Wages." *Journal of Economic Literature* 33, 1950–65.

KÉZDI, GÁBOR (2004): "Robust Standard Error Estimation in Fixed-Effects Panel Models." *Hungarian Statistical Review (Special English Volume)* 9, 95–116.

KISH, LESLIE (1965): "Sampling Organizations and Groups of Unequal Sizes." *American Sociological Review* 30, 564–72.

KLOEK, TEUN (1981): "OLS Estimation in a Model Where a Microvariable Is Explained by Aggregates and Contemporaneous Disturbances Are Equicorrelated." *Econometrica* 49, 205–7.

KNIGHT, KEITH (2000): *Mathematical Statistics.* Chapman & Hall/CRC, Boca Raton, Fla.

KOENKER, ROGER (2005): *Quantile Regression.* Cambridge University Press, Cambridge, UK.

KOENKER, ROGER, AND GILBERT BASSETT (1978): "Regression Quantiles." *Econometrica* 46, 33–50.

KOENKER, ROGER, AND STEPHEN PORTNOY (1996): "Quantile Regression." Working Paper No. 97-0100. College of Commerce and Business Administration, Office of Research, University of Illinois at Urbana-Champaign.

KRUEGER, ALAN B. (1999): "Experimental Estimates of Education Production Functions." *The Quarterly Journal of Economics* 114, 497–532.

KUGLER, ADRIANA, JUAN F. JIMENO, AND VIRGINIA HERNANZ (2005): "Employment Consequences of Restrictive Permanent Contracts: Evidence from Spanish Labor Market Reforms." FEDEA Working Paper No. 2003-14. FEDEA: Foundation for Applied Economic Research, Madrid, Spain.

LaLonde, Robert J. (1986): "Evaluating the Econometric Evaluations of Training Programs Using Experimental Data." *The American Economic Review* 76, 602–20.

——— (1995): "The Promise of Public Sector-Sponsored Training Programs." *Journal of Economic Perspectives* 93(2), 149–68.

Lee, David S. (2008): "Randomized Experiments from Non-random Selection in U.S. House Elections." *Journal of Econometrics* 142, 675–97.

Lemieux, Thomas (2008): "The Changing Nature of Wage Inequality." *Journal of Population Economics* 21, 21–48.

Liang, Kung-Yee, and Scott L. Zeger (1986): "Longitudinal Data Analysis Using Generalized Linear Models." *Biometrika* 73, 13–22.

Machado, Jose, and Jose Mata (2005): "Counterfactual Decompositions of Changes in Wage Distributions Using Quantile Regression." *Journal of Applied Econometrics* 20, 445–65.

MacKinnon, James G., and Halbert White (1985): "Some Heteroskedasticity Consistent Covariance Matrix Estimators with Improved Finite Sample Properties." *Journal of Econometrics* 29, 305–25.

Maddala, Gangadharrao Soundalyarao (1983): "Methods of Estimation for Models of Markets with Bounded Price Variation." *International Economic Review* 24, 361–78.

Mammen, Enno (1993): "Bootstrap and Wild Bootstrap for High Dimensional Linear Models." *Annals of Statistics* 21, 255–85.

Manning, Willard G., Joseph P. Newhouse, Naihua Duan, Emmett B. Keeler, Arleen Leibowitz, and Susan M. Marquis (1987): "Health Insurance and the Demand for Medical Care: Evidence from a Randomized Experiment." *American Economic Review* 77, 251–77.

Manski, Charles F. (1991): "Regression." *Journal of Economic Literature* 29, 34–50.

Mariano, Roberto S. (2001): "Simultaneous Equation Model Estimators: Statistical Properties," in *A Companion to Theoretical Econometrics*, ed. B. Baltagi. Blackwell, Oxford, UK.

McClellan, Mark B., Barbara J. McNeil, and Joseph P. Newhouse (1994): "Does More Intensive Treatment of Acute Myocardial Infarction Reduce Mortality? Analysis Using Instrumental Variables." *Journal of the American Medical Association* 272, 859–66.

McCRARY, JUSTIN (2008): "Manipulation of the Running Variable in the Regression Discontinuity Design: A Density Test." *Journal of Econometrics* 142, 698–714.

McDONALD, JOHN F., AND ROBERT A. MOFFITT (1980): "The Uses of Tobit Analysis." *The Review of Economics and Statistics* 62, 318–21.

MELTZER, ALLAN H., AND SCOTT F. RICHARD (1983): "Tests of a Rational Theory of the Size of Government." *Public Choice* 41, 403–18.

MESSER, KAREN, AND HALBERT WHITE (1984): "A Note on Computing the Heteroskedasticity Consistent Covariance Matrix Using Instrumental Variables Techniques." *Oxford Bulletin of Economics and Statistics* 46, 181–84.

MEYER, BRUCE D., W. KIP VISCUSI, AND DAVID L. DURBIN (1995): "Workers' Compensation and Injury Duration: Evidence from a Natural Experiment." *The American Economic Review* 85, 322–40.

MEYER, BRUCE D., AND DAN T. ROSENBAUM (2001): "Welfare, the Earned Income Tax Credit, and the Labor Supply of Single Mothers." *The Quarterly Journal of Economics* 116, 1063–114.

MILGRAM, STANLEY (1963): "Behavioral Study of Obedience." *Journal of Abnormal and Social Psychology* 67, 371–78.

MOFFITT, ROBERT (1992): "Incentive Effects of the U.S. Welfare System: A Review." *Journal of Economic Literature* 30, 1–61.

MORGAN, MARY S. (1990): *The History of Econometric Ideas.* Cambridge University Press, Cambridge, UK.

MOULTON, BRENT (1986): "Random Group Effects and the Precision of Regression Estimates." *Journal of Econometrics* 32, 385–97.

NELSON, CHARLES R., AND RICHARD STARTZ (1990a): "The Distribution of the Instrumental Variables Estimator and Its $t$-Ratio when the Instrument Is a Poor One." *Journal of Business* 63, 125–40.

——— (1990b): "Some Further Results on the Exact Small-Sample Properties of the Instrumental Variable Estimator." *Econometrica* 58, 967–76.

NEUMARK, DAVID, AND WILLIAM WASCHER (1992): "Employment Effects of Minimum and Subminimum Wages: Panel Data on State Minimum Wage Laws." *Industrial and Labor Relations Review* 46, 55–81.

NEWEY, WHITNEY K. (1985): "Generalized Method of Moments Specification Testing." *Journal of Econometrics* 29, 299–56.

———— (1990): "Semiparametric Efficiency Bounds." *Journal of Applied Econometrics* 5, 99–135.

NEWEY, WHITNEY K., AND KENNETH D. WEST (1987): "Hypothesis Testing with Efficient Method of Moments Estimation." *International Economic Review* 28, 777–87.

NICKELL, STEPHEN (1981): "Biases in Dynamic Models with Fixed Effects." *Econometrica* 49, 1417–26.

OBENAUER, MARIE, AND BERTHA VON DER NIENBURG (1915): "Effect of Minimum Wage Determinations in Oregon." Bulletin of the U.S. Bureau of Labor Statistics, No. 176. Washington, D.C., U.S. Government Printing Office.

OREOPOULOS, PHILIP (2006): "Estimating Average and Local Average Treatment Effects of Education When Compulsory Schooling Laws Really Matter." *American Economic Review* 96, 152–75.

ORR, LARRY L., HOWARD S. BLOOM, STEPHEN H. BELL, FRED DOOLITTLE, AND WINSTON LIN (1996): *Does Training for the Disadvantaged Work? Evidence from the National JTPA Study.* Urban Institute Press, Washington, D.C.

PFEFFERMAN, DANIEL (1993): "The Role of Sampling Weights When Modeling Survey Data." *International Statistical Review* 61, 317–37.

PISCHKE, JÖRN-STEFFEN (2007): "The Impact of Length of the School Year on Student Performance and Earnings: Evidence from the German Short School Years." *Economic Journal* 117, 1216–42.

PORTER, JACK (2003): "Estimation in the Regression Discontinuity Model." Unpublished manuscript. Department of Economics, University of Wisconsin, Madison, Wis.

POTERBA, JAMES, STEVEN VENTI, AND DAVID WISE (1995): "Do 401K Contributions Crowd Out Other Personal Savings." *Journal of Public Economics* 58, 1–32.

POWELL, JAMES L. (1986): "Censored Regression Quantiles." *Journal of Econometrics* 32, 143–55.

———— (1989): "Semiparametric Estimation of Censored Selection Models." Unpublished manuscript. Department of Economics, University of Wisconsin, Madison.

PRAIS, SIG J., AND JOHN AITCHISON (1954): "The Grouping of Observations in Regression Analysis." *Revue de l'Institut International de Statistique (Review of the International Statistical Institute)* 22, 1–22.

REIERSOL, OLAV (1941): "Confluence Analysis by Means of Lag Moments and Other Methods of Confluence Analysis." *Econometrica* 9, 1–24.

ROBINS, JAMES M., STEVEN D. MARK, AND WHITNEY K. NEWEY (1992): "Estimating Exposure Effects by Modeling the Expectation of Exposure Conditional on Confounders." *Biometrics* 48, 479–95.

ROSENBAUM, PAUL R. (1984): "The Consequences of Adjustment for a Concomitant Variable That Has Been Affected by the Treatment." *Journal of the Royal Statistical Society, Series A* 147, 656–66.

———— (1995): *Observational Studies*. Springer-Verlag, New York.

ROSENBAUM, PAUL R., AND DONALD B. RUBIN (1983): "The Central Role of the Propensity Score in Observational Studies for Causal Effects." *Biometrika* 70, 41–55.

———— (1985): "The Bias Due to Incomplete Matching." *Biometrics* 41, 106–16.

ROSENZWEIG, MARK R., AND KENNETH I. WOLPIN (1980): "Testing the Quantity-Quality Fertility Model: The Use of Twins as a Natural Experiment." *Econometrica* 48, 227–240.

RUBIN, DONALD B. (1973): "Matching to Remove Bias in Observational Studies." *Biometrics* 29, 159–83.

———— (1974): "Estimating the Causal Effects of Treatments in Randomized and Non-Randomized Studies." *Journal of Educational Psychology* 66, 688–701.

———— (1977): "Assignment to a Treatment Group on the Basis of a Covariate." *Journal of Educational Statistics* 2, 1–26.

———— (1991): "Practical Implications of Modes of Statistical Inference for Causal Effects and the Critical Role of the Assignment Mechanism." *Biometrics* 47, 1213–34.

RUUD, PAUL A. (1986): "Consistent Estimation of Limited Dependent Variable Models Despite Misspecification of Distribution." *Journal of Econometrics* 32, 157–87.

SHADISH, WILLIAM R., THOMAS D. COOK, AND DONALD T. CAMPBELL (2002): *Experimental and Quasi-Experimental Designs for Generalized Causal Inference*. Houghton-Mifflin, Boston.

SHERMAN, LAWRENCE W., AND RICHARD A. BERK (1984): "The Specific Deterrent Effects of Arrest for Domestic Assault." *American Sociological Review* 49, 261–72.

SHORE-SHEPPARD, LARA (1996): "The Precision of Instrumental Variables Estimates with Grouped Data." Working Paper No. 374. Princeton University, Industrial Relations Section, Princeton, N.J.

SMITH, JEFFREY A., AND PETRA E. TODD (2001): "Reconciling Conflicting Evidence on the Performance of Propensity-Score Matching Methods." *American Economic Review* 91, 112–18.

——— (2005): "Does Matching Overcome LaLonde's Critique of Nonexperimental Estimators?" *Journal of Econometrics* 125, 305–53.

SNOW, JOHN (1855): *On the Mode of Communication of Cholera*, 2nd ed. John Churchill, London.

STIGLER, STEPHEN M. (1986): *The History of Statistics: The Measurement of Uncertainty Before 1900*. The Belknap Press of Harvard University Press, Cambridge, Mass.

STOCK, JAMES H., AND FRANCESCO TREBBI (2003): "Who Invented Instrumental Variables Regression?" *The Journal of Economic Perspectives* 17(3), 177–94.

STOCK, JAMES H., JONATHAN H. WRIGHT, AND MOTOHIRO YOGO (2002): "A Survey of Weak Instruments and Weak Identification in Generalized Method of Moments." *Journal of Business & Economic Statistics* 20, 518–29.

TAUBMAN, PAUL (1976): "The Determinants of Earnings: Genetics, Family and Other Environments: A Study of White Male Twins." *American Economic Review* 66, 858–70.

THISTLEWAITE, DONALD L., AND DONALD T. CAMPBELL (1960): "Regression-Discontinuity Analysis: An Alternative to the Ex Post Facto Experiment." *Journal of Educational Psychology* 51, 309–17.

TROCHIM, WILLIAM (1984): *Research Designs for Program Evaluation: The Regression Discontinuity Design*. Sage Publications, Beverly Hills, Calif.

VAN DER KLAAUW, WILBERT (2002): "Estimating the Effect of Financial Aid Offers on College Enrollment: A Regression-Discontinuity Approach." *International Economic Review* 43, 1249–1287.

WALD, ABRAHAM (1940): "The Fitting of Straight Lines if Both Variables Are Subject to Error." *Annals of Mathematical Statistics* 11, 284–300.

——— (1943): "Tests of Statistical Hypotheses Concerning Several Parameters When the Number of Observations Is Large." *Transactions of the American Mathematical Society* 54, 426–82.

WHITE, HALBERT (1980a): "A Heteroskedasticity-Consistent Covariance Matric Estimator and a Direct Test for Heteroskedasticity." *Econometrica* 48, 817–38.

——— (1980b): "Using Least Squares to Approximate Unknown Regression Functions." *International Economic Review* 21, 149–70.

——— (1982): "Instrumental Variables Regression with Independent Observations." *Econometrica* 50, 483–99.

——— (1984): *Asymptotic Theory for Econometricians.* Academic Press, Orlando, Fla.

WOOLDRIDGE, JEFFREY (2003): "Cluster-Sample Methods in Applied Econometrics." *American Economic Review* 93, 133.

——— (2005): "Fixed-Effects and Related Estimators for Correlated Random-Coefficient and Treatment-Effect Panel Data Models." *The Review of Economics and Statistics* 87, 385–90.

——— (2006): *Introductory Econometrics: A Modern Approach.* Thomson/South-Western, Mason, Oh.

WRIGHT, PHILLIP G. (1928): *The Tariff on Animal and Vegetable Oils.* Macmillan, New York.

YANG, SONG, LI HSU, AND LUEPING ZHAO (2005): "Combining Asymptotically Normal Tests: Case Studies in Comparison of Two Groups." *Journal of Statistical Planning and Inference* 133, 139–58.

YELOWITZ, AARON (1995): "The Medicaid Notch, Labor Supply and Welfare Participation: Evidence from Eligibility Expansions." *The Quarterly Journal of Economics* 110, 909–39.

YITZHAKI, SHLOMO (1996): "On Using Linear Regression in Welfare Economics." *Journal of Business and Economic Statistics* 14, 478–86.

YULE, GEORGE UDNY (1895): "On the Correlation of Total Pauperism with Proportion of Out-Relief." *The Economic Journal* 5, 603–11.

——— (1897): "On the Theory of Correlation." *Journal of the Royal Statistical Society* 60, 812–54.

——— (1899): "An Investigation into the Causes of Changes in Pauperism in England, Chiefly During the Last Two Intercensal Decades (Part I)." *Journal of the Royal Statistical Society* 62, 249–95.

# INDEX